# CENTURIES' ENDS, NARRATIVE MEANS

**Edited by Robert Newman**

## Contributors

Kathy Acker
Stephen D. Arata
Ali Behdad
Sacvan Bercovitch
Rita Felski
Thomas Foster
Jeffrey Knapp
Jean-François Lyotard
David McWhirter
Susan Mizruchi
Steven Mullaney
Robert Newman
Margot Norris
Susan Stewart
Brook Thomas
Hayden White
Jennifer Wicke

# Centuries' Ends, Narrative Means

Stanford University Press

Stanford, California

1996

Stanford University Press
Stanford, California
© 1996 by the Board of Trustees of the
Leland Stanford Junior University
Printed in the United States of America

CIP data are at the end of the book

Stanford University Press publications
are distributed exclusively by Stanford
University Press within the United States,
Canada, Mexico, and Central America;
they are distributed exclusively by
Cambridge University Press throughout
the rest of the world.

# ACKNOWLEDGMENTS

This volume grew out of the conference "Centuries' Ends, Narrative Means," sponsored by the Interdisciplinary Group for Historical Literary Study at Texas A&M University on March 24–27, 1994. The essays contained within have been substantially developed from the papers originally presented at this stimulating conference. I wish to express my gratitude to Larry Reynolds for organizing the conference and to him and Jeffrey Cox for reading an early draft of my introduction and providing helpful suggestions. The Interdisciplinary Group generously provided funds to assist with production costs. Dalaiah Eiland and Hyon-Jin Kim helped with correspondence and manuscript preparation. I also appreciate the useful comments offered by the outside reviewers solicited by Stanford University Press, the excellent editorial work by Jan Spauschus Johnson and Andrew B. Lewis, and the help with proofing and indexing from Randy Miller.

Steven Mullaney's "Mourning and Misogyny" was originally published in *Shakespeare Quarterly* 45, no. 2 (1994), and is reprinted by permission. Rita Felski's "Fin de Siècle, Fin de Sexe" first appeared in *New Literary History* 27 (Spring 1996). An earlier version of Kathy Acker's "Once Upon a Time, Not Long Ago, O" was published in *Pussy: The King of the Pirates,* © 1995 by Kathy Acker. Used by permission of Grove/Atlantic, Inc.

For Milly—sweet narratives without end.

R.N.

# CONTENTS

**Kathy Acker** is the author of numerous works of fiction, among them *Pussy: King of the Pirates* (Grove, 1995), *My Mother: Demonology* (Pantheon, 1993), *Portrait of an Eye* (Pantheon, 1992), *In Memoriam to Identity* (Pandora, 1990), *Don Quixote, Which Was a Dream* (Grove, 1989), *Empire of the Senseless* (Pantheon, 1988), *Blood and Guts in High School, Plus Two* (Pantheon, 1987), and *The Adult Life of Toulouse Lautrec* (TVRT, 1975).

**Stephen D. Arata** is Assistant Professor of English at the University of Virginia and the author of *Fictions of Loss in the Victorian Fin de Siècle* (Cambridge, 1996).

**Ali Behdad** teaches English and Comparative Literature at the University of California, Los Angeles. He is the author of *Belated Travelers: Orientalism in the Age of Colonial Dissolution* (Duke, 1994).

**Sacvan Bercovitch** is Charles H. Carswell Professor of American Literature and Professor of Comparative Literature at Harvard University. He is the editor of many essay collections, including *Ideology and Classic American Literature* (Cambridge, 1986) and *Reconstructing American Literary History* (Harvard, 1986), and the general editor of the multivolume *Cambridge History of American Literature* (Cambridge, 1994). He is the author of *The Puritan Origins of the American Self* (Yale, 1975), *The American Jeremiad* (Wisconsin, 1978), *The Office of "The Scarlet Letter"* (Johns Hopkins, 1991), and *The Rites of Assent: Transformations in the Symbolic Construction of America* (Routledge, 1993).

**Rita Felski** is Professor of English at the University of Virginia. Her publications include *Beyond Feminist Aesthetics: Feminist Literature and Social Change* (Harvard, 1989) and *The Gender of Modernity* (Harvard, 1995).

**Thomas Foster** is Assistant Professor of Twentieth-Century Literature and Culture at Indiana University. He is a general editor of *Genders*, for which he guest-edited the special issue "Cyberpunk: Technologies of Cultural Identity."

**Jeffrey Knapp** is Associate Professor of English at the University of California, Berkeley. The author of *An Empire Nowhere: England, America, and Literature from "Utopia" to "The Tempest"* (California, 1992), his essay is part of a larger project on religion, nationalism, and theater in the English Renaissance, tentatively titled "Shakespeare's People."

**Jean-François Lyotard** is Professor Emeritus of Philosophy at the University of Paris, Distinguished Professor of Philosophy at the University of California, Irvine, and Professor of French at Emory University. His many books include *The Postmodern Condition: A Report on Knowledge* (Minnesota, 1984), *The Differend: Phrases in Dispute* (Minnesota, 1988), and *Peregrinations: Law, Form, Event* (Columbia, 1988).

**David McWhirter** is Associate Professor of English at Texas A&M University. He is the author of *Desire and Love in Henry James: A Study of the Late Novels* (Cambridge, 1989) and editor of *Henry James's New York Edition: The Construction of Authorship* (Stanford, 1995).

**Susan Mizruchi** is Associate Professor of English at Boston University. She is the author of *The Power of Historical Knowledge: Narrating the Past in Hawthorne, James, and Dreiser* (Princeton, 1988).

**Steven Mullaney** is Associate Professor of English at the University of Michigan. He is the author of *The Place of the Stage: License, Play, and Power in Renaissance England* (Chicago, 1988).

**Robert Newman** is Professor and Chair of the Department of English at the University of South Carolina. His publications include *Transgressions of Reading: Narrative Engagement as Exile and Return* (Duke, 1993), *Understanding Thomas Pynchon* (South Carolina, 1986), *Joyce's "Ulysses": The Larger Perspective* (Delaware, 1987), and *Pedagogy, Praxis, "Ulysses"* (Michigan, 1995).

**Margot Norris** is Professor of English and Comparative Literature at the University of California, Irvine. She is the author of *The Decentered Uni-*

verse of *"Finnegans Wake"* (Johns Hopkins, 1976), *Beasts of the Modern Imagination: Darwin, Nietzsche, Kafka, Ernst, and Lawrence* (Johns Hopkins, 1985), and *Joyce's Web: The Social Unraveling of Modernism* (Texas, 1992).

**Susan Stewart** is Professor of English at Temple University and the author of *Nonsense: Aspects of Intertextuality in Folklore and Literature* (Johns Hopkins, 1979, 1989), *On Longing: Narratives of the Miniature, the Gigantic, the Souvenir, the Collection* (Johns Hopkins, 1984: Duke, 1993), *Crimes of Writing: Problems in the Containment of Representation* (Oxford, 1991; Duke, 1994), and three books of poetry, the most recent of which is *The Forest* (Chicago, 1995).

**Brook Thomas** teaches American Literature and Culture at the University of California, Irvine. He is the author of *American Literary Realism and the Failed Promise of Contract* (forthcoming), *The New Historicism and Other Old-Fashioned Topics* (Princeton, 1991), *Cross-Examinations of Law and Literature: Cooper, Hawthorne, Stowe, and Melville* (Cambridge, 1987), and *James Joyce's "Ulysses": A Book of Many Happy Returns* (Louisiana State, 1982). He also has edited *Plessy v. Ferguson: A Documentary History* (forthcoming).

**Hayden White** is Professor Emeritus of the History of Consciousness at the University of California, Santa Cruz. He is the author of *Metahistory: The Historical Imagination in Nineteenth-Century Europe* (Johns Hopkins, 1973), *Tropics of Discourse: Essays in Cultural Criticism* (Johns Hopkins, 1985), and *The Content of the Form: Narrative Discourse and Historical Representation* (Johns Hopkins, 1987).

**Jennifer Wicke** is Professor and Chair of Comparative Literature at New York University. She is the author of *Advertising Fictions: Literature, Advertisement, and Social Reading* (Columbia, 1988) and *Mistaken Identities: The Politics of Feminist Theory* (Basil Blackwell, 1996).

# Introduction

> An absence of meaning opens a
> rift in time.
> —Michel de Certeau,
> 'The Writing of History'

As Frank Kermode points out in *The Sense of an Ending*, chronological divisions such as "millennium" and "century" affect us profoundly despite their fundamental arbitrariness. They evoke our anxieties and hopes; they offer explanations for both decay and restoration; and because "we cannot break free of them, we must make sense of them." This volume uses the approaching conclusion of the second millennium as a context in which to discuss questions about temporal division and narrative continuity. It investigates assumptions about teleology and eschatology while exploring how temporal markers affect the creation and production of cultural texts and, reciprocally, how narrative techniques, forms, and conventions shape, explain, and justify history. Through this exploration, the volume examines how temporal thresholds tend simultaneously to reinforce and to disrupt conceptual boundaries. The essays within use the significance typically invested in historical junctures marked by centuries' ends to investigate perceived paradigm shifts as well as consequent reactions to these implicit and explicit transitions. By doing so, they also seek to illuminate the relations between narrative and history and to enhance our understanding of the present historical moment.

The significance of this volume resonates with the implications of the time in which it appears and through which it attempts to construe the present and the past. The erosion of belief in the myths of modernism has led to an emphasis on multiplicities and marginalities and a heterogeneity of discourses that question the stability of the subject in response to the rapid shifts

1

inherent in our information age. By self-reflexively investigating the episte-mology of their own construction, postmodern texts challenge the notions of closure and the narratives that promulgate such notions. The denial of caus-ality and objectivity, the rejection of distinctions between high and low art, the realization of the exclusionary nature of language, the view of history as a silencing of the past, these enter the stylistic and hermeneutic framework and underpinnings of the postmodern. Postmodernism exposes the modern quest to compensate for increasing social and material alienation and inse-curity through intellectual mastery as so much authoritarian deception. Be-cause of this, our increased scholarly attention to the construction and recon-struction of culture has dovetailed with a waning of belief in the adequacy of narratives to represent personal, social, and national realities.

Although this waning of belief in narrative pervades the academy, nar-rative seems to be thriving in other aspects of our culture. While many schol-ars question racialist myths, popular books like *The Bell Curve* work to rein-state them. While we play with gender, the media genders all play. Implicit in the need to historicize, which permeates this volume, then, is the recognition that the Christian Broadcasting Network, Rush Limbaugh, *Melrose Place*, and *Beavis and Butthead* are also part of our moment.

The Kermode quotation with which I opened argues that we must im-pose meaning on potentially meaningless breaks in time. The de Certeau epi-graph, however, reverses this to suggest that an absence of meaning might open a rift in time. I use these two quotations to embody the juxtapositions I allude to above. The redemptive concern for endings that Kermode expresses is opposed to de Certeau's postmodern sense of an ending, where an avowed absence of meaning may be seen as opening up a rift in time before the chronological rift of the end of this century arrives. The present range of narratives and attitudes concerning them make it important that we acknowl-edge both of these views as culturally operative and that we acknowledge them as being in perpetual dialogue. We cannot assume that this dialogue proceeds coherently or yields resolution. Despite our posturings of theoreti-cal control, we often find ourselves positioned as precariously as any past moment of which we presume to make sense.

If we conceive of narrative as an effort to reach origins through end-ings, the awareness that origin is recoverable only through mnemonic traces that blend into phantasm produces an attendant melancholia that is fore-grounded in the chronological transitions marked by centuries' ends. The apocalyptic discernment that we are at the threshold of either an abyss or an era of renewal becomes the writing of the history of affective life, of dialogues of loss and (attempts at) recovery. This history, however, is a narrative enterprise that must constantly theorize its own narrating. Perched lopsidedly at a temporal divide, we peer simultaneously into past and future through the flickering lens of the present.

In exploring the cultural implications within diverse and specific narratives of subjectivity, nationalism, technology, and gender, *Centuries' Ends, Narrative Means* offers new knowledge of past configurations and speculations on future possibilities. Although questions concerning representation, the textual contingencies of paradigms, the fictive nature of history, and the cultural coding of bodies have dominated attempts to explain what Lyotard has termed the postmodern condition, these scarcely resolved issues are given new clarity and urgency as we stand on the brink of a new temporal division. While not proposing permanent resolutions to these issues, this volume raises the stakes of critical inquiry by speaking to these questions within the context of the reciprocal relation between temporal closure and narrative continuity.

In selecting and then arranging the works contained in *Centuries' Ends, Narrative Means*, I found myself caught in the endlessly mutating self-consciousness that necessarily accompanies contemporary attempts at ordering. Although the primary chronological emphases of this volume—the 1590s, 1890s, and 1990s—offer an opportunity to map how culture has sought to deal with temporality and to demonstrate parallels between these periods, a strict chronological arrangement of the essays would privilege the very teleology being questioned. In establishing my conceptual groupings, I was guided by Walter Benjamin's view of history not as the unfolding of an unbroken, Hegelian narrative, but rather as a collision between the present and a particular moment in the past, a shock that illuminates and helps to augment both past and present while shifting chronological and conceptual boundaries. I have endeavored to establish an organization that expresses overlapping concerns between historical periods while fostering implicit conversations about the historicizing of narrative and the narratizing of history as highlighted by centuries' ends.

Part I, "Stories of Narrative and History," presents four broadly conceived essays that investigate the diverse implications of how and why we construe particular events and lives into retellings and ordered systems. Each of these essays offers an alternative approach for analyzing and for narrating such histories while remaining attentive to the contingencies of paradigms and the paradigm of contingency.

The first essay, Sacvan Bercovitch's "Games of Chess: A Model of Literary and Cultural Studies," accuses the aesthetics of transcendence and cultural materialism of reductively disconnecting one form of discourse from the rest, thus isolating and privileging it as causal, foundational, or essential. Such practices, he contends, have contributed to the separation of literature and social history. Instead, Bercovitch seeks a nontranscendent social symbology that links text and context and establishes a flexible yet inextricable relation between particular and universal. By historicizing Wittgenstein's chess analogy, he poses a model of literary studies where boundaries are premised on reciprocity rather than dichotomy and where synchronic absolutes and diachronic flow intersect. He invokes Emersonian recommencement to argue that aesthetic play must move from abstract solutions to particular dilemmas to reconnect us to the world we inhabit. In cultural studies, the chess analogy recasts ideology from a vehicle of telos into an agency of process, against endgame strategies. The language game, by refuting endgame gambits, is also analogous to chess in combining the play of context and function in an infinitely variable conflict relationship. For Bercovitch, literature is life's criticism of transcendence.

In "Storytelling: Historical and Ideological," Hayden White offers a penetrating investigation of the relations between history, ideology, and narrative. Locating the problem of the ideological content of historical storytelling at the level of the figurative meaning of the discourse, White asks a question central to this volume: if storytelling can be said to endow historical events with figurative meaning by emplotting them in terms of a generic story type, does this mean that historical stories cannot be held to criteria of truthfulness and consistency that we would use for assessing their factual and explanatory contents? In his consideration of the cognitive status of literary and mythic discourse, White traces and explicates several theories of historical-narrative representation, including the structuralist suspicion that historiography is a kind of storytelling advanced by Braudel and Barthes, Lukacs's contention that narration is both a means of ideological production and a mode of consciousness, and Carr's and Ricoeur's views of refiguration. He concludes by applying Danish linguist Louis Hjelmslev's multiplanar theory of discourse to the problem of distinguishing between historical and ideological storytelling, between what we call "factual" and what we call "interpretive."

In "Being Done with Narrative by Cubism and André Malraux," Jean-François Lyotard presents a poetic consideration of the dialogue between loss and recovery that constitutes the enigma of storytelling. He poses a disjunctive temporal relationship of narrative voice to story and considers the modern to be a disordering of heterogeneity which subjects itself to time, thereby beginning an eschatology. In André Malraux's prose poems, Lyotard sees both the cubist rejection of the rhetoric of modernity, as advocated in Max Jacob's "cubist jewel," and the haunting of modernity's abjection, a mourning over narrative as well as an act of forgetting. In describing a poetics of the fact which excludes itself from the consumption of time, Lyotard continues his provocative scrutiny of the contemporary status of narrative and its intersections with fact, event, and the inhuman.

Susan Stewart finds in Traherne's *Centuries of Meditation* a model for thinking about the genealogy of lyrical subjectivity and its relations to the determinations of narrative history. In suggesting a lyrical model of internal time in tension and accord with social models of time, she offers an alternative to taxonomic narratives and the teleology of emplotment. Arguing for a transition *toward* subjectivity, Stewart finds in Traherne an obviation of history through the use of the concept of the century as a poetic form, a theology of time rather than a heuristic. Through its own form, her essay "Traherne's Centuries" testifies that time is thought and made lyrically. Recalling Augustine's statement "As the past increases, the future is diminished," the essay demonstrates the dynamic of internal time consciousness where the writer "writes himself or herself deeper and deeper into the past, so that the unfolding of the text, the realization of time, is the simultaneous encompassing and uncovering of what has come before."

Whereas the essays in Part I treat the interrelations between narrative and history through intricate and richly textured theoretical models, the four essays in Part II focus on the specific issue of nationalism and how the hegemonic normality within the unifying discourse of "nation" effectively translates questions of race and cultural difference into an ethics of social affiliation. The essays in "Projections of Nationalism" demonstrate the invention of tradition through the reconceptualization of space and the scapegoating or racializing of populations to displace anxiety, justify eradication, or control movement. In doing so, they investigate how national unity and definition is premised on the cultural exclusion of identifiable groups.

Perhaps the most famous essay by an American historian, Frederick Jackson Turner's *Significance of the Frontier in American History* (1894) paradoxically launched a new tradition of interpretation about American exceptionalism. The power of this narrative about an end to generate new beginnings is related to its capacity to reconstruct itself. That capacity, in turn, is related to the role of the frontier in the narrative. In an important way, Brook Thomas argues, the frontier serves as a metaphor; that is, a space of displacement in which something or someone is reconstructed as something or someone else. Thomas's essay "Turner's 'Frontier Thesis' as a Narrative of Reconstruction" explores the tensions between the two ways in which Turner's narrative is one of reconstruction. By focusing on the frontier as the formative space of American history, Turner transforms the frontier from a space of conflict between European and indigenous peoples to a space of reconciliation while displacing historical attention from the past conflicts between North and South in order to focus on a common Western frontier of renewal. He offers a revisionist narrative about the era of Reconstruction as part of a late-nineteenth-century effort to reunite the country, a reconstructive effort that, Thomas shows, had serious consequences for the racial definition of the American constructed in his frontier.

Recently, historians have offered good evidence for doubting whether the rogue underworld described by the Elizabethans ever existed, but no one has attempted to explain why the Elizabethans bothered to invent a separate rogue society in the first place. In "Rogue Nationalism" Jeffrey Knapp argues that this new "nation" of rogues embodied Protestant anxieties about the separate nation created by England's break with Rome. It also helped alleviate those anxieties by turning the vagabonds, not the Protestants, into the secret instigators of England's internal disintegration. To no other group in England did this scapegoating of rogues more appeal than to theater people, who, even after the establishment of permanent theaters, could never shake the stigma of vagrancy themselves. By the turn of the century, playwrights dominated the production of pamphlets on the rogue underworld, and vagabondage became a central theme of their drama. The desire to differentiate an open and serviceable vagrancy from a secret and injurious one was, however, only part of the reason theater people specialized in representations of vagabondage. Increasingly, playwrights recognized that they could turn the defense of their own vagrancy into national service as a defense of wandering England too. Thus the rogue underworld demonized in the pamphlets of the sixteenth century's fin de siècle came in later plays to seem more and more comic, a "free" society whose openness and flexibility the theater could contrast to the growing sectarianism of the Puritans. In opposition to most accounts of the Renaissance theater in the past few decades, Knapp asserts that many English playwrights conceived of the theater as a means of promoting religious toleration, not secularization.

In "The (Lethal) Turn of the Twentieth Century: War and Population Control," Margot Norris constructs a polemical narrative exploring one of the twentieth century's unique phenomena: mass warfare. She begins her essay with what was at the time the most recent example of mass warfare at the end of this century—the Persian Gulf War—and argues that by granting permission for the large-scale, systematic murder of a nation's populace this military action marked a particularly lethal twist in the century's changing attitudes toward wars that destroy populations. The military action at the end of this century is subsequently contextualized as belonging to a tradition of cultural hostility toward populations or large human aggregations that began in the eighteenth century and became transformed in the late nineteenth century into a particular contempt for the proletarianized masses or crowds invoked in Matthew Arnold's *Culture and Anarchy*. The impact of Arnoldian population angst is reflected in World War I artistic avant-garde representations of the battlefield as an industrial slum, and of the war as an exercise in prophylactic eugenics. After World War I indiscriminate mass killing of civilians by conventional and nuclear weapons was made acceptable military strategy by a complex set of rationales that identified civilians as combatants. Norris shows that these rationales reflect a subtle shift from the proletarianization of the masses and the eugenic uses of martial technology to a racialization of populations in order to justify their extermination.

In "Border INSpection: Reflections on Crossing the U.S. Border," Ali Behdad addresses our late-twentieth-century anxiety about violation by a threatening Other in an examination of popular narratives and legal discourses of immigration. Through personal anecdotes and readings of governmental documents, he discusses the micro-mechanisms of immigration procedures and border control and the binary categories on which immigration law relies. The scale of control in border inspection, Behdad contends, is detail, the infinitesimal mechanism that purports to distinguish between different gestures, accents, and attitudes. Immigration examination forces upon both the agent and the "alien" a detailed system of identification, description, and categorization. The eye of immigration power ultimately subjects us all to its field of visibility, and thus makes us the principals of our own subjection.

Part III, "Fin de Siècle Fates, Mournings, and In-Betweens" departs from the volume's general resistance to strict chronological groupings to address the historical period initially referred to by the term "fin de siècle." The essays in this section intersect, echo, and expand concerns analyzed in other parts of this book, particularly the implicit dialogue between cultural myths of progress and expansion and a pervasive sense of decline and decay. In ways that present striking parallels to the 1590s and 1990s, the 1890s attempted to constrain threats to the social order in a context marked by shifting articulations of gender, sexuality, class, and ethnicity. Transformation arises through embrace of the hybrid, the monstrosity, the protean "in-betweenness" of historical process.

In "Strange Cases, Common Fates: Degeneration and the Pleasures of Professional Reading," Stephen Arata examines some of the primary paradigms of degeneration theory, then shows how they inflected both literature and literary criticism in the Victorian fin de siècle. As a critical designation, "degeneration" was one of a small handful of concepts no late-Victorian thinker could do without. Like its better-documented counterpart, "progress," degeneration provided a series of overlapping models for the movements across time of individuals, families, races, nations, and species. It could be used to trace the vicissitudes of single-celled organisms, map the genealogies of exhausted families, and reveal the fate of nations. It could account for deviations in literary form and explain the behavior of crowds. Tying physical maladies, psychological disorders, and social disturbances together in a vast analogical universe, degeneration became, in Daniel Pick's apt phrasing, "the condition of conditions, the ultimate signifier of pathology." The term was thus peculiarly suited to any age that saw itself living at the end of history. Degeneration revealed itself not simply as a state of being but also as a narrative, one that knitted together the stages of a single life as well as the lives of different generations. Indeed, the power of this narrative model lay largely in how it linked the personal with the collective, the individual life with the life of the nation. The linkage is explicit in the work of prominent degeneration theorists throughout the period. Arata gives extended attention to the period's most influential attack on the "degenerative" aspects of modern culture, Nordau's notorious *Degeneration*.

In "Neighbors, Strangers, Corpses: Death and Sympathy in the Early Writings of W. E. B. Du Bois," Susan Mizruchi reconsiders the elegiac centerpiece on the death of W. E. B. Du Bois's son in *The Souls of Black Folk* in terms of a turn-of-the-century "sociology of sympathy" that was bound up with questions about the survival capacities of the Black (and other "lower") races. She argues that the intellectual agenda of Du Bois's early career—his interest, for example, in the problem of dialogue between the races, which is often portrayed as a relationship between the animate and the inanimate, or his juxtaposition, in the chapter on his son in particular, of the conditions and practices of death, grieving, sympathy, and otherness—was part of a "dialogue of death" that at once invented, sustained, and challenged prevailing predictions of the demise of Blacks. Mizruchi reads death as a problem of reception and demonstrates how Du Bois's moment of mourning encom-

passes the increasing commodification of death at the turn of the century and
its racial implications.

If the title of Henry James's 1899 novel *The Awkward Age* refers most
directly to the problematical age of its heroine, it also evokes the troubling
historical moment at which it was written and which it represents. Working
with the novel as well as with the preface James wrote for it in 1907, David
McWhirter argues that *The Awkward Age* refigures the crises, disjunctions,
and discontinuities of the fin de siècle as the potentially productive "awkwardnesses" of an "appealing 'modernity.'" James eschews the urgent exceptionalism of so much fin de siècle rhetoric, and the teleology of origins and
ends that rhetoric implies, instead embracing the inevitable in-betweenness
of historical process. In "What's Awkward About *The Awkward Age?*"
McWhirter examines James's exploration and celebration of various kinds of
awkwardness—the awkward social and conversational circumstances experienced by the novel's characters; the ungainliness and self-proclaimed
"monstrosity" of its form; the in-betweenness that marks James's sense of his
own gender identification and "queer" sexual identity, as well as this transitional moment in his writing career—as spaces in which social and cultural
forms, especially those codes which prescribe sexual and gender identity, are
denaturalized and hence rehistoricized. The experience of awkwardness, for
James, carries with it the potentiality for transforming the social and discursive structures within which we understand and make history.

Part IV, "Narrative Embodiment: Gender and Desire in History," looks
to the past as well as the future to assess the inextricable intertwining of gender with history and how that relation is being refigured in a postmodern and
potentially post-body age. The five pieces of Part IV examine contradictory
discursive practices that use the body as a locus for presumptions regarding
social, sexual, and gender distinctions and attendant formulations regarding
knowledge, power, and desire. They also postulate narrative disruptions and
epistemological upheavals through the undermining of mind/body bifurca-
tion in the transgendered subject, the eroticizing of technology, and the technological sublime.

Rita Felski's "Fin de Siècle, Fin de Sexe: Transsexuality, Postmodernism, and the Death of History" uses the fin de siècle association of gender
crisis with historical exhaustion as a starting point from which to explore
broader questions of the gendering of history and the historicity of gender.
Through a brief discussion of the work of Jean Baudrillard and Donna Haraway, she highlights the central and ambiguous significance of the transgen-

dered subject through recent theories of the postmodern, as well as the paradoxical reinscription of history in the very act of its disavowal. She uses the work of Gianni Vattimo to elucidate the inevitable historicity of postmodern thought, even as she argues that from a feminist perspective Vattimo's own history of history remains problematically schematic and linear. In her essay she seeks a more nuanced assessment of discourses of the end of history and the end of sex as they relate to the intersection of feminist and postmodernist thought.

In the final decade of Elizabeth's reign, her aging body received increasingly pointed and critical commentary while at the same time her image as Gloriana, the youthful Virgin Queen, was being disseminated in new and revitalized forms. The contradiction between these versions of the queen exacerbated rather than resolved the increasingly apparent contradiction between her two bodies, producing a complex admixture of longing and revulsion that was directed toward the queen during the last years of her reign and after her death. As Steven Mullaney argues in "Mourning and Misogyny," mourning for such a figure in such an age—that is to say, for an extraordinarily powerful woman in an age of rigidly hierarchical patriarchy—was inextricably intertwined with misogyny. The main body of his essay traces this unstable dialectic as it was "worked through" on stage, notably in revenge tragedies such as *Hamlet* and *The Revenger's Tragedy*. The revenge tradition in the years immediately prior to and after Elizabeth's death constituted a cultural processing of her "age" and its contradictions and provides us with a glimpse of (male) mourning under the sign of patriarchy.

Kathy Acker's fictional narrative appropriately follows Mullaney's account of patriarchal processing with a clitoral gynocracy. Part surrealist memoir, part anti-phallic polemic, this apocalyptic narrative uses Antonin Artaud and Gerard de Nerval as muses in a search for a feminine space where sexuality can no longer be denied. A ferocious and passionate collage, "Once Upon a Time, Not Long Ago, O" offers Acker's reimagining of the relations between narrative components as products and producers of the postmodern conclusion to this century and whatever new world lies beyond.

In the Cartesian tradition that governs the thinking of philosophical modernity, the body, along with animals and machines, is associated with the quality of extension and therefore with the category of space, whereas the mind is associated with the abstract and purely formal realm of reason and conceptualization. But the emergent technologies that call into question our definitions of the human have challenged this dualistic structure. In particular, the development of the human-computer interface promises to disrupt mind-body dualism by giving the conceptual realm phenomenal form, through the creation of virtual spaces where knowledge and information can be experienced and manipulated in concrete, sensory ways. But when the domain of the mind can be experienced in terms previously reserved for the category of the body, what happens to the experience of embodiment? Thomas Foster's essay " 'The Sex Appeal of the Inorganic': Posthuman Narratives and the Construction of Desire" argues that this question defines what is at stake in the development of these new technologies. When new technologies are popularly represented as having sexual consequences, the contradictions surrounding them and their cultural implications become most clearly visible. To answer the question of the body's fate in a "post-body" age, Foster turns to a variety of popular materials that represent the eroticizing of technology and the technologizing of the sexed body. He argues that popular culture provides a site where the possible outcomes of the disruption of mind-body dualism are already being narrated.

Jennifer Wicke uses David Cronenberg's film *The Fly* as a narrative of a century's end and consequent rebirth epitomized by a technologized apotheosis she names the technological sublime. Although shaped by mass-cultural electronic mediations, such narratives still retain a bodiedness while terrorizing us with the suggestion that our technology is no longer representable. As such, *The Fly* is a fin de siècle text, an apocalyptic narrative that takes theology into cyberspace and whose protagonist's decomposition mimics the degeneration of AIDS. The computer screen close-ups that fill the frame and the lack of close-ups of human faces translate the movie screen into an immense computer monitor while underscoring the uncertainty about the narrative body and disrupting the positions of narrator and narratee. In "Fin de Siècle and the Technological Sublime" Wicke presents *The Fly* as an intertwining of issues about sexual, representational, and social reproduction, a film that uses the metaphor of the body invaded and rearranged on the genetic level to engage issues ranging from abortion, the simulacra of mass identity, corporate appropriation of technology, and the ideologies of love. At this century's end, Wicke tells us, the technologies of narrative have moved even to the submolecular level, where metaphor can also be seen to inhere.

By narrating centuries' ends, the works in this collection show, we inevitably allegorize these temporal junctures, condensing them into emblematic moments where we seek to ascertain historical meaning. Such allegorizing, whether we call it hieroglyph, expressive causality, or a "tiger's leap into the past," inevitably gestures toward memento mori, a sense of loss or deferral where even progress may be translated as the eternal return of catastrophe.

Attempts to arrest time by accounting for it repeatedly resist the impossibility they have always demonstrated.

By ascribing or inscribing fissures in temporal or narrative surfaces, we reenact both a redemptive intervention into the past and an ironic retelling of the failure to read the erosion of meaning. Our struggles to find the narrative means to explain the temporal turn we approach collide with our self-conscious need to reassess those means and the ends they justify and by which they are justified. *Centuries' Ends, Narrative Means* voices this collision and its diverse echoes, which ripple in the ever-shifting dialogue between the passage of time and the search for meaning.

# PART I

# Stories of History and Narrative

# Games of Chess:
# A Model of
# Literary and
# Cultural Studies

## The Chess Analogy

> For some minutes Alice stood without speaking,
> looking out in all directions over the country—and a
> most curious country it was. . . .
>      "I declare it's marked out just like a large chess-
> board!" Alice said at last. . . . "It's a great huge game
> of chess that's being played—all over the world."
>      —Lewis Carroll, *Through the Looking Glass*

The legacy of the New Criticism and the old historicism has been the separation of aesthetic from cognitive analysis. The end-of-the-century challenge
for cultural studies is to overcome the false dichotomy this implies. I refer
not only to the genteel contempt for cultural categories (class, race, gender),
but to the cultural protest against the claims of art. Let me say at once that I
endorse the protest. Reverence for art, like all forms of idolatry, is the road to
mystification. It may be said of some current forms of aesthetic appreciation
what has been said of metaphysics in general: "We think we actually understand things only when we have traced them back to what we do not understand—to causality, to axioms, to God";[1] or in this case, to genius and the
daemonic, to taste, tact, and sensibility. But the current process of demystification, as registered in debates over canon and value, has worked to widen
the gap between the constitutive parts of literary history. It's as though the
cultural critics, in their aversion to the romantic and postromantic iconog-

raphy of the text, had simply left aesthetics to the aesthetes; as though, in their irritation with the pretensions of high culture, they had cut the body of literature in two, as in Solomon's judgment about the disputed baby. You get beauty, we get substance.[2]

Since wise Solomon's judgment was a trap rather than a solution, I want to propose an alternative model. We might call it cultural close reading: a method of explication where textual meaning is located within common cultural materials, as you would locate the meanings of other cultural artifacts, from exotic tribal masks to run-of-the-mill skyscrapers. Those materials include all aspects of culture: traditions, changing ways of life, established patterns of thought, and modes of production. The means by which they are brought together in this case—the materials of verbal expression, the blocks and pillars of language—derive their special powers, their reportedly magical capacities to evoke a diversity of meanings, not from some unique or supernatural agency, but from the dynamics of the culture within which they function. What's extraordinary about them is the way that their language resonates with its multiple ordinary meanings.

So understood, the text is a function of context, and sometimes viceversa, as when a community is built out of interpretations of a text, such as the Constitution of the United States, the Bible, or handbooks on gender. The common term here is textuality, and what I mean by common is at once a link, a difference (as also implying aspects that are not common), and an area of connectedness: the ordinary uses of language that provide the entire gamut of discourse in a given culture, as (say) a town common provides the ground of countless local encounters, most of these habitual or ephemeral, *en passant*; some of them surprising, memorable; a few so striking that they make a lasting impression. In short, although my perspective is broadly historical, my focus is specifically rhetorical. I offer a description not of how history works but of how literary meaning works in history.

The two questions overlap, of course, but the connection is not causal. Nor is it the product of some larger, self-regulating force, spiritual, material, or spiritual-material. The overlap is variable, contingent, and volatile. As historians or as aesthetes, we tend to emphasize either materialist determinants (laws of history, patterns of culture) or else creative agency (the play of the imagination). My concern lies with the semantic meeting-ground between. By "context" I mean a questionable point of convergence for many different kinds of texts—not the timeless kaleidoscopes of canon, as in Northrop Frye's Mythography, F. R. Leavis's Great Tradition, or Harold Bloom's Western Canon—but the common expressive forms that make for public discourse and shared meaning. My perspective is cultural, my object of study is textual, and my purpose, accordingly, is twofold: first, to affirm differences in quality between literary texts, but differences identified through the contexts that constitute their commonality; and second, to affirm the existence of universals, but universals that express our permanent condition of limitation. Like the gods, literary texts work their wonders relationally and through everyday means: a voice in the whirlwind, a shower of gold, an absent Monsieur Godot. That's what makes the wonderful susceptible to commentary. Significance is a context for common functions, where commonness presupposes specificity: *a* language; certain circumstances; certain ways of seeing and being; certain kinds of response. To paraphrase Ludwig Wittgenstein, I would like to lead meaning back home to culture.

I invoke Wittgenstein as the antifoundational philosopher of function and context. The now-traditional disciplines denoted by cultural studies and literary criticism had venerable foundations to build on: in one case, the grand empiricist schemes adopted by the social sciences; in the other case, a hermeneutics of the absolute, grounded in theology and philosophy, from the Cabbalists through Kant. I regard my use of Wittgenstein as a move toward a different kind of focus. We have been trained to appreciate art by seeing the essential in the particular: femininity in a flower, God in a whale-hunt, and pity in a human face. And to be sure these essences are often inscribed in the text. But it does not follow that we must take them to constitute the text's deeper meanings. Indeed, "depth" may be the wrong standard here, implying as it does a hierarchy of meanings. I retain it for emphasis, to argue that the chief value of interpretation lies in reciprocities, not hierarchies. The conceptual distance we travel from the facts before us is directly proportionate to our capacity to see the particular in the essential: the institutional features of femininity; the social structures sanctioned and subverted by the whalegod; the politics of pity which *this* face projects.

I intend my use of Wittgenstein, accordingly, as a polemic against the aesthetics of transcendence. I refer to the later Wittgenstein—the *Philosophical Investigations* as an instance of philosophy focused on the primacy of particulars and the depths of ordinary meaning. And by aesthetic transcendence I mean a conceptual mediation upward, from a time-bound reality (particulars, limitations) to an abstract Reality (noumenal or phenomenal) that reveals the mentalist or materialist designs that overarch or underlie the conditions of time and place. Aristotle's term for aesthetic mediation is the realm of the probable, somewhere between philosophic abstractions and historical facts. Mediation here is a function of the norms of·human action and thought, universally applicable in spite of or beyond differences between particular persons, times, and places. What I envision instead is a descent into the volatile, time-bound materials of history. This model of downward mobility reverses the traditional meanings of universal and particular. What Aristotle means by universals—our norms and ideals—I take to be culture-specific, the time-bound abstractions that we offer as solutions for our recurrent problems: for example, the myth of Eden or the rules of tragedy. What Aristotle means by particulars—specific manifestations of the problems themselves, such as the endlessly variable facts of death—I take to be universals, the common denominators of cultures past and present. Aristotle begins with variable particulars and rises through them to the abstractions they represent: the Great Man, the Tragic Mistake, the Fear and the Pity of it all. I begin with these abstractions and return through them to the cultural specifics they imply: a certain concept of greatness, a variable set of social and psychological conditions, the historically conceived man behind the abstract tragic mask.

In Wittgenstein's terms, these particulars (and the meanings we invest in them) form a global kinship network. They're related as different branches of a family are related across time and place. Significance here emerges from the interplay of specific characteristics within loosely defined kinship structures. Augustine's concept of the Fall unifies the facts of death into a transcendent solution, a vision of the sovereignty of the laws of Justice and Mercy. The facts themselves may be seen (or made) to confirm that solution, but even so, as particulars, they *also* resist, qualify, and destabilize it. They give aesthetic (as distinct from theological) meaning to Death by particularizing the abstraction in diverse, sometimes unexpected ways—negative, skeptical, positive—through traditions that range from surprising contrasts, like the Jewish shiva and the Irish wake, to unaccountable parallels, like Ghanaian "fantasy coffins" and Oregon logger-gravestones.[3] In this multivocal sense, death/Death constitutes both a common boundary and a common differentiator: the changing coastline of a general human condition. As such it cuts across the entire spectrum of conditions that make manifest our limitations of mind, will, imagination, and endurance—the thousand natural shocks that flesh is heir to, such as the shock of discovering that what we thought natural was recently made up; or like Priam confronting Achilles after Hector's death, that what we considered an absolute evil is a variety of personal and historical connections.

The example of Hector will suffice. Theologically, the explanation is Fate. Its literary counterpart is the great reconciliation scene I just referred to.

The "explanation" this conveys involves a discordance of mourning rituals, reiterations of loss present and past (including mythic pasts) that make *a* death the source of generational rememberings. As we gather these together, following the movement of the text—giving structure and meaning to what the poem's first line calls "the anger of Achilles and its devastation"—we find ourselves enmeshed in a long list of similarly discordant universals: for example, the tangled bonds of obligation, in all differing senses of the word "bonds," such as the conflicting bonds of service, self-interest, contract, kinship, friendship, and humanity. Our interpretive resolutions of the scene—emotional, etymological, cultural, conceptual—are held together by the details of a death by violence and the varying responses it evokes from a father, an enemy, and a society; and the more details we gather, the better. Then, having returned to the scene with all pieces in play, we can begin to appreciate its universal, multilayered significance: *universal* because it centers on a question of limitations; *multilayered* because significance here opens into layers, not levels, of meaning. Levels imply solutions; they provide coherence and closure. Layers, as I intend the term, spill over into varieties of questionable configurations.

To simplify, I will call the transcendent solutions *absolutes* and the questionable specifics, *universals*. My counterconventional proposition is that absolutes are never universal and universals are never absolute.[4] *Absolutes are never universal*: they are solutions devised by certain persons and accepted by certain groups. They're culture-specific by definition, unless they're appropriated by, or imposed upon, other cultures. *And universals are never absolute*: by definition they're always there, in one form or another, transculturally, transhistorically, unless we refuse to acknowledge our relatedness to a common humanity, including the relatedness of our ideals to those of others. In theology, philosophy, and social science—as we've come to define these fields—the connection between absolutes and universals is represented logically, through explanations framed in abstractions, such as those which explain (or explain away) God's behavior toward Job. In literature, as we've come to define the field—and by extension in the "literary" as the means (as well as the object) of literary study—the connection between absolutes and universals is represented figuratively: it's made manifest through a series of particulars that stand in a variety of relations to the abstractions they embody or imply. And however we define the relation—dialectic, symbiotic, complementary, oppositional, contingent, arbitrary—the representation itself always ends, as it begins, in social and psychological particulars.

That's why I spoke of reversing the traditional mode of aesthetic mediation: it's an effort to respond to the materials of literary history. What I called transcendence—the method that privileges the objective overview, the abstraction from outside—applies equally to T. S. Eliot's "objective correlative" and to Georg Lukács's "objective possibilities."[5] Each in its very different way ("idealist," "materialist") tells us that the closer the literary particular (emotional, social) gets us to generalities and solutions (psychological, historical) the better. My concept of mediation requires a movement toward specificity in the realm of the possible. The closer we get to particulars and predicaments, the better. The ground and substance of mediation are the social symbologies that link text and context, rather than the higher laws that are said to fuse time and eternity. The goal of mediation is neither a ladder to the Source nor a spiral to the End, but reciprocities in degree.

This is not to rule out the *question* of ends. Rather, the question reformulates the concept of ends as a function in context, where context signals an open rather than a closed system. A closed system ends in a coherent Reality. It's open, of course, at any given time to further investigation, but the basis for investigation is an ultimate answer. An open system works in the opposite way. It begins and ends in a mixed state, which I will call noncoherence: a provisionally (or apparently) unified configuration of concrete realities that's neither coherent nor incoherent because the absolutes that work to unify them also remain subject to question, universally, by the particulars from which they are abstracted. In any given instance, these realities may be seen to confirm the absolutes; they may even be made to constitute alternative absolutes. But the very process of confirming or remaking tends to undo such resolutions. As a rule, the movement downward toward particulars compels us to solve the predicament anew. A closed system implies progress. It remains open on the premise of better (if not final) explanations to come; the last solution invites new questions on the premise that the new solution will render the earlier system inadequate, antiquated. An open system denies progress. It provides closure on the premise that we'll have to explain things all over again. The last effort at closure here is a standing invitation to try again, *as though* we were beginning anew.

As my reference to Lukács implies, this kind of openness differs no less from cultural than from aesthetic systems. I have in mind here the scientistic terms of closure provided by cultural materialism. Methodologically, these derive from a foundation of hard facts—genetic, economic, environmental—but the foundation itself is a platform for transcendence. In this case, you transcend by discerning the ultimately material structures behind the conceptual design. Mediation involves an upside-down dualism between lower and higher, fact and ideal, where the lower (the social base, the sexual body) is anointed as the Real, and the higher (the idea, the spirit) is its particular expression. What I envision instead is a flexible but inextricable relation between universals and absolutes: flexible because multicausal, and inextricable because the absolutes in question, whether moral or economic, spiritual or biological, are *in question*. An open system, in this view, is not antisystemic. What I called noncoherence is premised on reciprocity, not dichotomy; it's open both to systemic explanation and to constant change. To some extent this resembles Thomas Kuhn's concept of paradigms. The difference, of course, is that scientific paradigms are progressive. Physicists no longer study Ptolemy, whereas *The Brothers Karamazov* returns us to *Oedipus Rex* with renewed interest.

The same contrast obtains, in terms of disciplines and paradigms, between Freud's Oedipus and Sophocles'. From the viewpoint of science (which he intended), or of psychoanalysis as a field of study, Freud returns to a peculiar dilemma in order to solve the general question of self-knowledge. In doing so, he explains the cause of something we didn't understand before: why Oedipus *has* to murder, then and always. But the text itself directs us elsewhere. Here, Oedipus's answer to the general question of the Sphinx leads him, *because* it's *the* answer (Man *sub specie aeternitatis*), into a peculiar dilemma (his marriage to the wrong woman); and in doing so, it problematizes the very concepts of causality, explanation, and self-knowledge. *The Interpretation of Dreams* is an explanation; it provides an interpretive framework adaptable to a variety of persons and occasions across time and place. *Oedipus Rex* remains a problem. Semiotically, it invites solutions on the condition that, as a coherent semiotic structure, it remains open to continual re-solving, both prospectively and retrospectively. What some aestheticians call progress in literature—free verse, the novel, stream-of-consciousness—is a locus of dispute, not the ground of consensus, and in either case, "progress" marks a development only in the photographic sense of the word: as an enlargement, variation, innovation, or refinement in techniques of representing particulars.

Wittgenstein's concept of language games is pertinent here because it connects all these forms of textuality. Indeed, language games in the *Investigations* apply to virtually everything human. My concerns are modest by comparison—the relation between literary and cultural studies—and I limit myself, accordingly, to one angle of Wittgenstein's argument. Language games, he writes, are just like chess games. The game of chess is a picture of "the nature of all propositions," "the basic relation between words and the world." It's an analogy well suited for a model of cultural studies whose focus is literature. Chess has long been a favorite analogy of writers. It's a commonplace in the arts for Necessity, as in Ingmar Bergman's chessmaster, Death, in *The Seventh Seal*, or in Jorge Luis Borges's Ultimate Player, Fate:

> In their serious corner, the players
> move the gradual pieces . . .
>              . . .
>
> They do not realize the dominant
> hand of the player rules their destiny.
> They do not know an adamantine fate
> governs their choices and controls their journey.[6]

Chess has also served as a commonplace in the social sciences for the laws of history, the structures of language, the rules of cultural continuity, and the mechanisms of institutional power. For Ferdinand de Saussure, it's the best single image of the science of linguistics.

That's also how Wittgenstein uses the analogy. Chess for him is *the* model of language games, verbal and mathematical. He assumes, of course, that its rules are arbitrary. Like the rules of all games we play, they're made up in, of, and for the world as we conceive it. But, at any given point in time, they form a coherent system: logically explicable, self-consistent. The victory cry in chess, "checkmate" ("death to the king," *shakh mat*), renders the concept of death, along with the image of the king, both arbitrary and systemic, particular and absolute, all at once and all *in extremis*. This is a microcosm of Wittgenstein's chess model. I hope to appropriate it, with a difference, as a model of literary and cultural studies. My purpose is to show that the chess analogy, in its several implications, applies above all to the literary text, to literary study, and to the disciplines through which literature has been associated (as "sublimation," "artifact," "social text," "cultural production," "textuality") with cultural studies.

The advantage here of literary study is that it highlights the paradox of the arbitrary and systemic. What we classify professionally as literature—the course of studies implied by "a degree in literature"—is more transparently *constructed* than any other body of knowledge. As a discipline, if it can be called that, it's barely a century old, and in its brief career it has gone through several startling metamorphoses, from classical philosophy to poststructuralism. It's so clearly a compound of the language games from which it developed—and it continues so blatantly to draw upon still other language games—that it cannot quite obscure (as other disciplines can) the arbitrary nature of its rules. Is there a *literary* body of knowledge? Does it constitute *an* area of specialization? Scientist models of literature, linguistic and socio-logical, have always remained controversial, marginal to the field. Literary study may be called systemic only insofar as its principle is resistance to any unified system of closure, or (what amounts to the same thing) an astonishing vulnerability to appropriation by other systems of closure. "Whereof one cannot speak," runs Wittgenstein's famous conclusion to the *Tractatus Logico-Philosophicus*, "thereof one must be silent." The *Tractatus* itself, and all philosophy, including Wittgenstein's revisionary *Philosophical Investigations*, tells us what we can articulate. Literature is the voice of cognitive silence. It is a great monument to cultural absolutes; but those absolutes are so constructed from *literary* particulars as to keep recalling us to areas (experienced and imagined) where "explanation fails."[7] Literature speaks to the multiple ironies in Wittgenstein's apparent tautology distinguishing speech from knowledge. It directs us, *as literature*—which *as such* may also include works classified as philosophy, history, psychology, and theology—toward unanswered (and, for all we know, unanswerable) questions in the various explanatory systems we've inherited.

## Traps of Transcendence

> The story is told of an automaton constructed in such a way that it could play a winning game of chess, answering every move of an opponent with a countermove. A puppet in Turkish attire and with a hookah in its mouth sat before a chessboard placed on a large table. A system of mirrors created the illusion that this table was transparent from all sides. Actually, a little hunchback who was an expert chess player sat inside and guided the puppet's hand by means of strings. One can imagine a philosophical counterpart to this device. The puppet called "historical materialism" is to win all the time. It can easily be a match for anyone if it enlists the services of theology, which today, as we know, is wizened and has to keep out of sight.
> —Walter Benjamin, "Theses on the Philosophy of History"

With this distinction in view, I confine the chess analogy, to begin with, to two types of problem: the *endgame puzzle*, a problem in closure, and the *middle-game sacrifice*, a problem in continuity. The endgame puzzle is the more familiar: White to win in three moves. You're asked to detect an already existing solution, as in an acrostic or a murder mystery. The answer is there, somewhere, challenging your ingenuity, and your task is to explain what *must* happen. The middle-game sacrifice challenges you in the opposite direction, toward detecting the trap in what seems to be a winning position. Your opponent offers an exchange of pieces that is clearly to your advantage. If you accept this apparent gift, you'll soon find yourself under attack. The game is not necessarily lost—you're still in the midst of things—but meanwhile the "mistake" has turned out to be a snare. In puzzle language: you're presented with what seems a winning position, and your task is to see why it's not.

Now, let me generalize the contrast—endgame puzzle versus middle-game sacrifice—into the language of literary history. The endgame puzzle requires you to demonstrate why art has won over time and place. Keats was, is, and will be a great poet; explain how he managed to transcend his age. I've already pointed to the disciplinary conventions of transcendence, aesthetic and historical. Aesthetic transcendence is formalist and appreciative. You move either from act to ideal, as in Plato (e.g., the Grecian urn signifies Beauty/Truth); or else you move from the form to its fulfillment, as in Aristotle (the lyric form is fulfilled in Keats's ode). Historical transcendence is contextual and cognitive. It works by the logic of teleology (which may take the form either of doomsday or of millennium). The preferred move in modern literary history has been the nationalist telos. Goethe represents German *Kultur*. Show how his precursors foreshadow him and how in turn he shapes the work of those who follow him. In the global version of this puzzle, you are expected to move from the text to the stage of development it represents, as in Hegel: *Antigone* mirrors the transition from kinship to city-state, and, by extension, the dialectic toward the Prussian millennium. Or else you move from the text to the utopia it foreshadows: *Antigone* implies the struggle of individuality against patriarchy and, by extension, toward the classless society.

Two endgames, then, mentalist and materialist: they are mutually exclusive, precisely because they're endgames: two competing systems of transcendence. The conflict between them is the legacy of the New Criticism and the old historicism to literary and cultural studies.

In cultural studies, the dominant form of play derives from Marx's base-superstructure game. Its principle is dialectical materialism, originally conceived as class struggle, but since then extended to struggles of the oppressed of all kinds. By the rules of this game, agency and ideology combine as "praxis" in the literary text. We might call this the praxis endgame. It divides ideology into three parts: "false consciousness," the most common line and the weakest, since it issues in illusions, distortions, or inversions of reality, as in a *camera obscura*; "class consciousness," an ambiguous line, since the class in question may be either reactionary or progressive, and sometimes both; and "utopian consciousness," which the Frankfurt School Marxists called the strongest line, since as utopia it carries in it the dreams of human wholeness that characterize history's overarching telos. The "x" in praxis, we might say, marks the aesthetic point at which agency and ideology combine to make the winning move.

To be precise, we have a choice of three ways to win: exposé and denunciation; progressivist social analysis; and a prophetic mode that resembles the biblical typology game to which Marxism is indebted via Hegel. Typologically, the church fathers absorbed all of human history (past, passing, and to come) as a prophecy of Christ. Dialectically, cultural studies absorbs the idealist dreams of all literature, including both the Hebrew and the Christian Bibles, as prefigurations of the Good Society. In all three choices the laws of analysis cover the work both of literature and of interpretation. Praxis co-opts textuality.

Let me specify the difficulty. My objection is not that co-optation here precludes the prospect of self-generating consciousness or self-determining agency. Just the reverse: it was Marx's great contribution to have insisted that all human products entail a reciprocity between the rules of the different material and conceptual games we play simultaneously (as political animals and language-users, social beings and symbol makers). Rather, the problem is that this endgame, like all others, posits a solution, whereas literature is universally problematic. To move from Sappho to Whitman is to challenge theories of development—say, Marx's analogy between early Greek poetry and the childhood of humanity—precisely *because* of the transparent reciprocities in both cases between art and ideology. By the very nature of their materials, if not by authorial intention, literary texts remain grounded in history. What sustains them as literature are the experiential and emotive specifics they describe. And such descriptions are generically counterteleological, not because they're set against the visionary endgames of their times—they're often designed to illustrate such endgames—but because, as *literary* descriptions, they speak to a universal condition. That is to say, they render up the vision in ways that direct us away from the sorts of absolutes that mark the advent of New Jerusalem or the Whiggish "march of civilization"—absolutes that define the distinctiveness of *our* civilization—away from those exclusive final solutions to the limitations we share, more or less, as *a* civilization, with other civilizations across time and place.

I'm aware that cultural studies has sought to accommodate such objections by constructing a more active agency and a more flexible telos. Not: White to win in three moves (a puzzle now dismissed as "vulgar Marxism"). Instead: White *should* win, sooner or later. However, flexibility here recurrently projects, because it fundamentally assumes, a coherent resolution. Its disciplinary base, social science, directs analysis toward transcendence. Implicitly or explicitly, it points from an embattled present to a theoretical future. And theoretically, even as theoretical eclecticism, as in Stuart Hall, or as theoretical negation, as in Theodor Adorno, the text in cultural criticism becomes the site of closure: an aesthetic shadow, as in a glass, darkly, of some utopia or dystopia to come. "Just because [literature] is historical," writes Raymond Williams, in a representative defense of cultural studies against charges of base determinism, "just because it is . . . a key concept of a major phase of a culture, [therefore] it is decisive evidence of . . . social development."[8]

The sequence here from "historical" to "development," the assumed objectivity of "decisive evidence," and the specification of "development" as "social," and the work of the social throughout Williams's writing, as an a priori dialectic—residual-dominant-emergent—are inherent in the approach, and may be traced through all varieties of the praxis game. In its sophisticated, highly textualized forms no less than in its naive applications, cultural studies claims to recover literary history because it

> offers a philosophically coherent and ideologically compelling resolution to the dilemma of historicism . . . an adequate account of the essential *mystery* of the cultural past, which, like Tiresias drinking the blood, is momentarily returned to life and warmth and allowed once more to speak, and to deliver its long-forgotten message in surroundings utterly alien to it. [The] long-dead issues [of the past] can recover their original urgency for us only if they are retold within the unity of a single great collective story; only if, in however disguised and symbolic a form, they are seen as sharing a single fundamental theme—for Marxism, the collective struggle to wrest a realm of Freedom from a realm of Necessity.[9]

"Compelling" because "coherent," and coherent philosophically no less than ideologically, once we decipher the code behind the symbols, the "single, fundamental theme" of our "collective struggle" toward the Good: Fredric Jameson's formulation is explicitly Marxist, but as neo-Marxism—a Marxism in his case strongly influenced by aesthetic formalism—it summarizes the basic design of the praxis endgame. Literature wins by transforming an "essential *mystery* of the cultural past" into the sort of prophetic insight that like blind Tiresias decoding Fate, wrests "Freedom from a realm of Necessity."

Now, there may be a realm of Freedom awaiting us, but not in the form of literary texts. Indeed, we might say that the insights of literature wrest our local necessities from abstractions of "collective" Freedom—or, in personal terms, from a certain Truth that promises to set us free—back into the realm of nontranscendence. Literature moves forward either by rejecting the abstraction outright, or else, far more frequently and more forcefully, by accepting it only to expose its limitations—and most forcefully of all, I believe, by exposing those limitations textually rather than programmatically, as the insidious, often surprising result of aesthetic process. Literary texts prevail because they do *not* transcend. As literature, they are no more historically prophetic than they are divinely inspired. The details they're made of derive from ordinary experience. The language they build with—tropes and types, affective and argumentative techniques—*is* community and history. The questions they raise—cunningly or innocently, in bewilderment, outrage, empathy, or amusement—come in response to answers already given. And they challenge those answers not because the authors are essentially dissenters (the archetype of the Subversive Artist is a romantic invention, one more time-bound absolute), but because the language game they're playing returns us to gaps between experience and explanation, now as then.

I conceive of that dynamic as a reciprocity between literary and cultural concerns. It brings from cultural studies an emphasis on common context (as against aesthetic privilege); and it brings from literary study an insistence on textual problematics (as against the solutions privileged by cultural studies). So conceived, the implications of reciprocity are profoundly moral, historical, and political. To recognize the principles of provisionality behind the rules we play by is ipso facto to acknowledge our assent to these particular rules, and, by extension, the depth of our involvement in the game, win, lose, or draw. In this sense, the model I propose takes issue with the aesthetics of essentialism, and in particular these days with the endgames of postmodernism. For although most forms of postmodernism present themselves in opposition to essentialism, it's the oppositionalism of counterdependence, the other side of the same belles-lettres coin. I regard it as a late stage of modern formalism, a kind of *elaboratio ad absurdum* of Kant's separation of the aesthetic from the cognitive faculties.[10]

The strategy here is to solve the puzzle by *pretending* to transcend it. Endgame equals con game. This evasion of history is the latest metamorphosis of the romantic religion of art: the unbounded free play of the imagination, once a spiritual imperative, now become the imp of the perverse. Ordinary writing, in this view, subjects us to conventions and stereotypes. High literature liberates us from the ordinary laws of everyday life through the self-reflexive gaming of Supreme Fictions. By the rules of pretense, it has no significance beyond itself. Literature is freed from context because emptied of substance; fortifying, because immune to doctrine. It gathers energy in proportion to its slipperiness, and meaning through its hostility to constraints of any kind. "Writing unfolds like a game that inevitably moves beyond its own rules and finally leaves them behind. . . . [It] is primarily concerned with creating an opening where the writing subject endlessly disappears."[11] In short, literature transcends structures of power because it refuses to join games of culture.

The technical game terms here are "ilinx" and "mimicry," as distinguished from "alea" and "agon."[12] *Alea* is fate, the primal endgame. *Agon* offers the closest approximation to the middle-game sacrifice. It's a conflict in process between two or more players, and as conflict, it presupposes a state of nontranscendence, even when it's Jacob wrestling with the angel, or Christ on the cross. In contradistinction to these life-and-death struggles, *ilinx* and *mimicry* are variant con games. *Ilinx* is the self-induced hallucination of a trance or a mentally altered state; *mimicry* is the acceptance of make-believe for its own sake, as in a masquerade. Both are the sorts of games that poststructuralism plays. In either form, it's the *jeu d'esprit* of the aesthetically elect, canonized for their miracles of linguistic indefiniteness. Roland Barthes prescribes it for us as a Dionysian purgative, the "liberation" provided by an act that "respects nothing (no content, no choice)." Therein, he writes, lies our "only alternative" to the "fascism" of daily language:

> The pleasure of the text is like that untenable, impossible, purely *novelistic* instant so relished by Sade's libertine when he manages to be hanged and then to cut his rope at the very moment of his orgasm, his bliss. . . . Nietzsche has observed that "truth" is only the solidification of old metaphors. So, in this regard, stereotype is the present path of "truth." The distrust of the stereotype (linked to the bliss of the new word or the untenable discourse) is a principle of absolute instability which respects nothing (no content, no choice).[13]

> [After the age of faith] the only remaining alternative is . . . to cheat with speech, to cheat speech. This salutary trickery, this evasion, this grand imposture which allows us to understand speech *outside the bounds of power*, in the splendor of a permanent revolution of language, I for one call *literature*. . . . The forces of freedom which are in literature depend not on the writer's civil person, nor on

his political commitment . . . nor do they even depend on the doctrinal content of his work, but rather on the labor of displacement he brings to bear upon the language.[14]

Barthes may well be right, in a sense. But what a thin, rarified sense that is! What a contempt it shows (beneath its antipathy to "power") for common meaning and ordinary life! The *contemptus mundi* of Christian hermeneutics gave literature entry into an alternative spiritual reality; the romantic imagination opened a set of moral alternatives to the cash values of market economy. Postmodernism is the antinomianism of the abyss. The regeneration it offers is the capacity of language to slip through its connections to history, including the history of language. Saussure pictures this systematically as an omniscient chess automaton:

> Of all comparisons that might be imagined, the most fruitful is the one that might be drawn between the functioning of language and a game of chess. [A long and detailed comparison follows.] . . . At only one point is the comparison weak: the chessplayer *intends* to bring about a shift and thereby to exert an action on the system, whereas language premeditates nothing. . . . In order to make the game of chess seem at every point like the functioning of language, we would have to imagine an unconscious or unintelligent player. . . . [For linguistic] values depend above all else on an unchangeable convention, the set of rules that exists before a game begins and persists after each move. Rules that are agreed upon once and for all exist in language too; they are the constant principles of semiology.[15]

This is the linguistic endgame within and *against* which Barthes pretends to win by flouting its "unchangeable . . . principles," that sinister "set of rules which exists before a game begins and persists after each move." Semiotically, Nothingness is a foregone conclusion. But we can triumph over it, Barthes answers, by displacing all those banal attempts to win. The text soars above so-called solutions into an intertextual realm of beautiful words, where theology's Life Everlasting merges with philosophy's God-Is-Dead. It's as though our pleasure in chess consisted in the sheer variety of forms its pieces could take; as though we admired a chess piece for its capacity to signify any other and claimed it to be a triumph in chess—"the splendor of a permanent revolution"—if we devised a queen so ambiguous in design that she could be interpreted to be a second king; or so subversively colored that she might pass for a player on either side of the board.

This is a classic case of what I referred to earlier as counterdependence; and indeed it has been argued persuasively that postmodernism is an expression of our commodity culture. In this sense, Barthes' model of literature is a hanging-gardens shopping mall for the aristocracy of art. Barthes himself recognizes the connection, even takes a perverse joy in it, a connoisseur's pride in passing off *mimicry* for *ilinx*, and *ilinx* for *mimesis*. But his perversity in this respect is at one with his scorn for the commonplace. It too is an attempt to transcend through the play of words. Barthes on Barthes notwithstanding, the strength of his *ouevre*, considered (as it should be) as literature, lies in its nontranscendence. It's neither a reflection of Western late capitalism nor an escape from it. Nor is it a rebellion against it through forms of "subversive reiteration." Rather, it implies all of the above in its multilayered *engagement* with history and culture. It's through that *agon* with the ordinary that Barthes's writing derives its aesthetic power and critical brilliance. The pleasure of his text is that what's "untenable, impossible, [and] purely *novelistic*" about it *also, more deeply*, testifies that the text has not escaped, *cannot* escape, the network of political, psychological, intellectual, economic, and ethical games embedded in the metaphors which frame our lives. Its very strategies of evasion—like those of all literature—depend by the nature of its discourse on the depth of the stereotypes it plays upon. In our time these include the commonplace of art-for-art's-sake, the relatively recent clichés about aesthetic free play, and the datable romantic dream of the poet as unacknowledged legislator. That dream issues, by its own dynamic, in W. H. Auden's postromantic dictum that "poetry makes nothing happen,"[16] and, in our time, in the postmodern transmutation of nothingness into an aesthetic endgame.

## The Recommencement Game

> The belief in free will is not in the least incompatible with the belief in Providence, provided you . . . allow him [providence, God] to provide possibilities as well as actualities to the universe, and to carry on his own thinking in those two categories. . . .
> An analogy will make the meaning of this clear. Suppose two men before a chessboard—the one a novice, the other an expert player . . . the expert stand[s] for the infinite mind in which the universe lies. Suppose the latter . . . to say, I will lead things to a certain end, but I will not *now* decide . . . ambiguous possibilities shall be left open, *either* of which, at a given instant, may become actual.
> —William James, "The Dilemma of Determinism"

My alternative to this aesthetic deadend endgame, as also to the materialist endtime endgames, is the middle-game sacrifice. Technically, the middle game starts at about move sixteen and lasts until the "culmination," the final win-lose-draw situation. That situation is characterized by the sorts of predetermined relationships that shape the endgame puzzle. The beginning game is characterized by well-defined combinations, termed "openings"; it's epitomized by the gambit, an opening-game sacrifice that trades a chess piece (usually a pawn) for a positional advantage. The middle game ("the crux of chess") concerns positionality, inventiveness, and strategic combinations.[17] It specializes, we might say, in potentiality. It works through indirections, circumventions, and possibilities, and it's epitomized by a subterfuge: an exchange that seems to be a fatal blunder. At some indefinite midpoint in the complications of our game, you offer to trade (say) your queen for my rook. It seems to be the gift of a certain victory, but it's unexpected and I try to make sense of it. What, in *the logic of the game* we've been playing, could have prompted that move? The options might be translated into the terms of essence and telos. Could it be that chess is essentially a game of chance (we blunder our way to victory or defeat)? Or should I take the apparent blunder to be a sure sign that I've lost: why else would you so confidently give up the queen?[18]

The problem with both answers (and others like them) is that they're solutions. Each offers a once-and-for-all resolution to what's really an open situation. The correct move, whatever it is, requires us to remain within the same old complications, to see in the prospect of victory the problems of a game in process. To recall my opening metaphor, we play to not-win, like the true mother in Solomon's judgment. We reject the sacrifice on the grounds that, however matters will be resolved, *that's* not the way to do it. Locate the designs of local history engraved in Cleanth Brooks's well-wrought urn or inscribed in Paul de Man's abyss. Find the particulars in Hegel's *Antigone*: not those which point systematically towards a higher synthesis (and which therefore *blur* the differences between Sophocles and us)—or at any rate, not only those symptoms—but within them, at many, shifting lower layers, the cultural specifics that apply differently to early Athens and modern Prussia, and so constitute a set of questions still to be answered. The problem is: Why is that absolutist answer (Beauty/Truth; the Progress of the World-Spirit) really a set of historical questions? As Thomas Middleton puts it, in the Prologue to his popular play of 1624, *A Game of Chess*: "the fair'st jewell that our hopes can deck, / Is so to play the game, t'avoid your check."[19]

This is not to say that the power of the middle game (or of the text) lies wholly in its particulars. It lies in the relation between particulars and absolutes, a relation that is volatile to the extent that the particulars assume a dynamic of their own. We "avoid the check" because there's a point to possibilities: we're trying to *get somewhere*. Eventually, things may come down to a familiar endgame situation, or there may be some sudden, unforeseen turn of events, or else the play may grind to a stalemate. Endings, too, that is, are potential in the middle game, both in the conflict between players and in the tensions between circumvention and closure. Indeed, the middle-game sacrifice inverts the zero-sum principle into a universal problematic of process. To be silent about finalities in Wittgenstein's sense is not an act of resignation, but a protest against limitations. It's excessive on our part to *want* to speak about what we can't—to hope to win in the next move, or in the next three moves—and that tendency toward excess is inseparable from our capacity to *resist* the queen sacrifice. We refuse the sacrifice of history because we desire to overcome historical constraints. As a rule of culture, if not by instinct, we play to win—there's an end at stake, if not yet in view—and from that source of conflict, we draw the foresight to see the trap in what's presented to us as a winning advantage. It's not just that we defer the endgame; it's that we're inspired to play out this particular situation *as though* we might resolve things *this time*. The result is a make-believe opening to a game-in-process that has all the urgency and depth of the ends for which we play.

That's what Keats meant, I think, by negative capability. The poet rejects the egotistical sublime in order to play out a variety of particular conditions. The move is from autonomy and infinitude to context and relatedness. The strategy assumes nontranscendence; it requires an imaginative capacity to defer closure by entertaining many different kinds of middle-game prospects, each one of them an ending, prospectively, and each a strategy of recommencement, resonant with alternative possibilities. The connection between these possibilities is what I've called social symbology, the common cultural sources of meaning from which all three language games emerge: endgames, middle games, and openings alike. We might picture the connection itself as the play in process between context and function: *context*, a set of dominant symbolic patterns (involving tradition and convention) that provides a framework for constructing meaning; *function*, a finite but flexible set of symbolic strategies, involving agency and transgression, through which self-consistent systems are built up, held together, torn down, and rebuilt.

So considered, ideological criticism is a middle game by definition. Here, as in chess, symbolic strategies are forms of power; but in the literary text (as I conceive it), the relation between form and power is a problematic one. Ideologies build on the iconic transformation of limits into absolutes: individual into Individualism, man into Humanity. Aesthetic forms universalize that process: they test the limits of Humanity (as in *King Lear*); they specify the processes of Individualism (as in *Moby-Dick*). In this sense, they are bivalent in relation to any given ideology; which is to say, they're ideologically multivalent. The antebellum rhetoric of self-reliance is an iconology of bourgeois norms; Whitman's "I" is its aesthetic counterpart. "I contradict myself? Very well, then, I contradict myself / I am large, I contain multitudes":[20] this is epic language, but it's not the self promulgated by Virgil or Milton. Whitman's insular, ubiquitous "I" is a shout of joy from a poet who recognizes the multiple moves available for self-making under the rules of liberal subjectivity. These rules are absolute and binding. They have empowered a broad range of Americans, from Benjamin Franklin through Frederick Douglass. They have also circumscribed a broad range of oppositional American selves—have limited American opposition (as disobedience, defiance, denial) to the precepts of individualism. Radicalism is "personal." Collective issues (class, race, gender) are resolved by endgame strategies of private enterprise: self-reliance, equal opportunity, free choice. Whether the choice is the right to live or the rights of dissent, and whether (as a dissenter) you say "No in thunder" or "I would prefer not to," subjectivity is reified as the "I" of eternity, like the eye of God on the dollar bill.

But the play does not stop there. For these endgame resolutions, once subjected to particular experiences, may direct us in turn toward middle-game dilemmas, old and new, that open different kinds of approach. For example, we may notice that, in particularizing his omnivorous "I," Whitman restricts it to those who can play the game. The problem is not (as D. H. Lawrence put it) that "Walt" is actually *not* the "cunning, greasy little eskimo . . . sitting in his kayak." He *is* that Eskimo potentially, symbolically. But the rhetorical relation is exclusive, not reciprocal. The Eskimo could not then represent the American multitudes—neither he, nor the "red squaw" that Whitman invokes, nor the "runaway black slave."[21] The aesthetic depth of Whitman's "I" lies in its capacity to make the absolute itself, the American Self, highlight that discrepancy. It resists closure by specifying the transcendent "I." On one level, poetic specification here works as a rhetorical question to *mask* discrepancy. "Song of Myself" yokes Walt, squaws, slaves, and Eskimos by poetry together. And yet as poetry that transcendent resolution is situated in history: "America" in 1855, or 1860 (Second Edition) or at the end of the nineteenth century (as in the 1892 Deathbed Edition) or at the end of ours (as in the current Heath Anthology). It lingers, that is, as a question in time—and potentially, therefore, as a radical variation of symbolic identity. Whitman affirms the absolute, aesthetically, by *particularizing* it; and by particularizing it *aesthetically*, he invites us to question and challenge—and so potentially to decline or circumvent—the endgames of representative individualism.

Ideology is a sacrifice of history that promises to free us from the limitations of culture. Literature re-presents the sacrifice as a middle-game trap of culture. That's not, to repeat, because "works of the imagination" are deeper than what we classify as "ideological writings." (What I say here of "literature" also applies to the writings of DeStrutt de Tracy or to July Fourth orations *considered as literary texts*.) It remains a problem because of the historicity of language and the "literary" impulse toward particularization—a form of particularization in which the specifics may "come to life" *as specifics*, in their own terms and hence in a form that's resistant to totalization. The process here of presenting again neither refutes nor endorses the solution (though it may set out to do one or the other). Rather, it makes the solution manifest as a complication that calls for re-solutions. And it does so not by upending the game but, on the contrary, by recasting its apparent ends as volatile continuities and/or discontinuities.

Whitman's editorials are propagandistic; his poems, universal. The difference lies not in his superiority as poet to games of culture but in the depth of his understanding of cultural rules. Systematically speaking, these rules pertain to different kinds of discourse: journalism versus poetry, popular fiction versus the epic. But literary history testifies to continual interconnections and cross-influences. Whitman's poetry tests those common meanings to the limits. It's thus a full display of the power of boundaries. It also happens to be a clue to transgression, a text that hints by indirections at a different kind of game. But even *as* transgression, his poetry gains power *through* ideology by reaching down to accumulated layers of cultural meaning. It may be said of all writing that the language of cohesion (ritual, hegemony) is also the language of agency (mind, imagination). We work with ideology even if (and, in many cases, especially when) we work against it. Of literary texts, it may further be said that they unsettle forms of culture even if (and, in many cases, especially when) they work through ideology to particularize the norms and beliefs that make for social cohesion.

Characteristically, these tendencies are mutually sustaining. An example is the ideological tableau that ends the story of Joe Christmas in Faulkner's *Light in August*. Joe embodies the racist endgame puzzle (is he black or white?); in reaction against it he murders his benefactor and sets fire to her house. His opponent, a self-declared "agent of American justice," is Percy Grimm, leader of the lynch mob, driven by the endgame "belief that the white race is superior to any and all other races and that the American uniform is superior to all men." The spectators are the people of Jefferson, gathered in a kind of outraged festivity, virtually a July Fourth mood:

> [Grimm] was moving again almost before he had stopped, with that lean, swift, blind obedience to whatever Player moved him on the Board. . . . He seemed indefatigable, not flesh and blood, as if the Player who moved him for pawn likewise found him breath. . . .
>
> But the Player was not done yet. When the others reached the kitchen they saw . . . Grimm stooping over the body . . . and when they saw what Grimm was doing one of the men gave a choked cry and stumbled back into the wall and began to vomit. Then Grimm too sprang back. . . . "Now you'll let white women alone, even in hell," he said. But the man on the floor had not moved. He just lay there, with his eyes empty of everything save consciousness . . . [looking] up at them with peaceful and unfathomable and unbearable eyes. Then his face, body, all, seemed to collapse . . . and from the slashed garments about his hips and loins the pent black blood seemed to rush like a released breath. It seemed to rush out of his pale body like the rush of sparks from a rising rocket; upon that black blast the man seemed to rise soaring into their memories forever and ever.[22]

The mixed metaphor—chess and resurrection—frames a configuration of ideological abstractions. It might be titled "The Racism Endgame" and construed as a model of praxis: the culturally fated act of violence is transformed into a politically engaged process of interpretation. In "their memory," possibly, and in ours, Christian and American ideals are enlisted in humanity's "common struggle" for Freedom.[23] This is not false to the passage, except insofar as it resolves its meaning, whereas the action of "memory" in the passage is to open the meaning of those ideals in a way that problematizes our (and their) engagement with *all* categorical beliefs. The white pawn captures the black, but the capture itself turns into a surprising reversal. Aesthetically, it's the black pawn that wins, or seems to, by emerging (through the rocket's red glare) as the crucified Jesus, a triumphant black king. In the process of emergence, an ahistorical emblem (player and pawn) changes into a violently specific scene, memorable for its details (the "choked cry," the vomit, the "slashed garments," the festive "rush of sparks"); and the terms of description change accordingly: first, from absolute to make-believe (a game of fate to a *seeming* Passion Play); second, from set rules to unaccountable change (pawn becomes king); and third, from an I-win-you-lose situation (pawn takes pawn, checkmate) to a game newly under way, as in a recommencement: the possibility that the black piece—the killer, arsonist, and victim, Joe Christmas—will prevail in memory *as dead king* (*shakh mat*).

What sustains that possibility may be summarized in two ideological *problems*. The first is secular, political, and specific to the scene: a castration of American justice, marked by "black blood." The second is religious, spiritual, and, in conjunction with the political, equally American: the crucifixion of Joe Christmas and Jesus Christ. This civic-religious archetype involves a double relation: (1) between individual consciousness and moral conscience (in the Protestant sense of "king conscience"); and (2) between that spiritual kingship and the tenets of American justice (the "kingly common," "every man a king"). At issue is an ideological critique of American civic religion that requires the whole novel to elaborate, but it entails a familiar aesthetic strategy. The religious archetype, J.C. (Joe Christmas equals Jesus Christ) is the sacrifice, a cultural pretext. To accept it as archetype promises a victory against racism by transcending history (including Joe's own racist and criminal past). But to seize that promise is to miss the point of Faulkner's move from pawn to king. Stylistically and substantively, the substance, texture, and contents of the archetype are historical: certain communal rituals (lynching, holiday fireworks), a certain concept of manhood (black male sexuality), and a certain form of religion (Calvinist fundamentalism), in an unforgettably specified region of the country. It's these mundane *conundrums* which universalize the Christ connection.

Ideology works, aesthetically, because Faulkner particularizes issues of Justice and Individualism as a black-and/or-white fugitive named Joe Christmas and so transforms ideological answers into a series of concrete questions. Such questions do not liberate us from absolutes, including those of Christianity, Justice, Individualism, and American Independence. But they invite us to consider other lines of play that may be available, culturally, under the rules. *Under*, as in subject to the rules, but also within and through them, at once undergirding the rules and undermining them; *under*, as in underlie, involving possibilities that *these* absolutes speak the truth—possibilities, too, of an unsettling kind, prospects that have been declared out of bounds, or that have not yet been explored—variations, transformations, or innovations that may affect the rules themselves, and so alter the nature of the game. *Under* as in depth.

I would like to think that this concept of middle-game depth extends to include the problem of relativism. I take this to be a variation of the ideology endgame—one to which both literary and cultural studies have proved particularly vulnerable. Can we say that one chess strategy is *more beautiful* than another? The middle-game response is: that's a question of function and context. What we're appreciating is neither a move-in-itself (e.g., the beauty of the knight's leap) nor a hierarchy of absolutes (e.g., a queen is more beautiful than a rook), but combinations of possibilities. A beginner in chess is taught its rules as abstract, context-free absolutes. Example: each bishop moves on squares of its own color; white on white squares, black on black (or technically: queen's bishop on one color, king's bishop on another). Translation: as a rule, symbols have multiple meanings; consider Dante's "dark wood" and the forest in *The Scarlet Letter*. The experienced chess player sees context-dependent situations, where the rules apply situationally, hence malleably, according to the specifics of a particular game, and more deeply (in my model) according to an open-ended family network of similar but significantly incongruent situations. Example: consider the vast differences between medieval and modern chess. Translation: multiplicity functions differently in Dante and in Hawthorne—differently to the point of incompatibility. We need not deny the polysemous qualities of all symbols (indeed, we might elicit them as evidence) in explaining that it's simply wrong—historically anachronistic; politically, intellectually, and aesthetically incorrect—to play one game by the rules of the other.

This is a perspectivist view of "beauty" that insists on cognitive as well as appreciative evaluation. The "winning" move in the interpretation of Dante's epic—a ladder of meanings leading upward (as in the medieval theory of correspondences) from *littera-historia* to anagogical Truth—will mislead you in Hawthorne's novel, where meaning depends on intersubjectivity, as in liberal democracy. This does not mean that Hawthorne's ambiguities are more beautiful than (because they can liberally incorporate) Dante's multileveled Beauty. Nor does it mean that they're more beautiful *to us* because (unlike Dante's) they work in ways to which we liberals respond. It means that each method is related in some way to the other *and* that each must be understood in its own right, as an ordering principle. Questions of value thus entail distinctions between different sets of limitations. Through our demonstrable capacity to play such different games as Dante's and Hawthorne's, we have a way to negotiate the competing claims of relativism and value judgment. And negotiation in this sense has an important implication: we are always-already more than our culture says we are, as a language is more than a disciplinary vocabulary and a chess game, at any point in time, is more than the particular system it represents. We are not limited by culture in at least one sense, that we can come to see that we know less than *our* cultural absolutes (including those to which we submit) pretend to know. Or, in a positive sense: we are more than the endgames we play because we can re-cognize them as middle games.

This has consequences, however qualified, for the claims of evaluation. We can say, in any given context, that one text is better than another through a functional analysis of particular variations within certain universally applicable limitations. Abstract answers to problems of value—ambiguity is good, dogmatism is bad—tell us more about the interpreter than about the text, and more about what we believe than about the game at stake. The lesson of the New Criticism was that the same formal qualities which attest to the affinities of all Great Texts also constitute a powerful means for providing thick descriptions of particular social constructions of reality. The lesson of cultural studies is that the same relativism which opens our view to the value of different standards and traditions, and the inadequacies of our own, also allows us to ask rigorous questions about the text-in-itself: What is that essence good for in this situation? How does it function within this set of rules? How do these conditions apply to different situations in ways that connect changing sets of rules? Considered together, these disciplinary lessons support recent arguments that a re-cognition of absolutes *through* the acknowledgment of limitations enables us to move, in time, in degree—through "intersubjectively recognized norms"—"from prejudice to dialogue." [24]

### The Queen with Frightening Eyes

> Fancy what a game of chess would be . . .
> if you were not only uncertain about your
> adversary's men, but a little uncertain also
> about your own.   —George Eliot, *Felix Holt*

As a gesture toward dialogue of this kind, I proceed now to apply my middle-game analogy to chess at large, the polyanalogous game of games. Imagine a perennial middle game, one that requires you, at each decisive juncture, to reconfigure your strategy—in effect to start anew—within a complex situation-in-process, and which (as it were to foster renewal) subjects the rules themselves to agencies of change. What would that game look like? First answer: it would look like the world we inhabit. Second answer: it would look a lot like literary history. Third answer: it would look exactly like chess, the ancient, multilingual, transcultural game—that endless sea (as an Indian proverb has it) "in which a gnat may drink and an elephant may bathe." Experts often describe chess as the history of a hundred great games, but really it's the zigzag histories of cultures, a mishmash of the most unlikely reciprocities between rules governing different areas of life. Wittgenstein speaks in this regard of "a complicated network of similarities overlapping and crisscrossing"—tennis and other ball games, children's ball games and ring-around-a-rosey, hence tennis and ring-around-a-rosey.[25] Chess invites us to extend the analogy from sports to real-life games: chess and war, war and politics, politics and class, class and gender, gender and religion, religion and superstition; hence chess and superstition.

The transposition is not at all fanciful. We know that in Malaya the rules of chess changed with successive religious influences (Hindu, Shinto, Islamic); that in India, Persia, and the Middle East chess moves were directly linked to large-scale war games; and that the original Near Eastern and Arabic names for chess (*chatrang, shantranj*) reflect variations in political hierarchy, as do early Korean forms of the game. We know further that in medieval and Renaissance Europe chess was played as tournaments, carnival-style, with human "pieces" on enormous fields; that the meanings of chess pieces have fluctuated with the fate of empires, from Japanese emperor-god to Soviet worker-king; and that fluctuation has brought with it constant crossings of institutional, conceptual, and even technological structures—in our day, for instance, the radical changes introduced by the Fischer time clock—so that a contemporary match could be contextualized through the overlappings of feudal knight and caste-bound pawn with our space-age timer at a courtly Renaissance tournament.[26]

Consider what it would mean to describe a chess match in this context! We would have to account for an indefinite number of unlikely transcultural correspondences—why does White always have the advantage of the first move? Why is the king virtually impotent? (In both cases, the answers happen to be surprisingly culture-specific.) And at the same time we would have to account for an indefinite series of unexpected cultural transpositions and developments: how was the Indian elephant converted into a Catholic bishop? What was the game like before the advent of the queen? (In both cases, the answers happen to be surprisingly cross-cultural.) The point of analysis—for example, an analysis linking the shiva, the wake, Ghanaian coffins, and Oregon gravestones—would be to explain why the game did not end. How did chess, with its antique castles and knights, survive into our modern world? What explains its abiding fascination for writers of all nations, from Ibn Al-Mutazz to Balzac, Cervantes, Dante, Omar Khayyám, Rabelais, and Rousseau to Stephan Zweig; and in English literature alone from Chaucer through Spenser, Shakespeare, Pope, Scott, Browning, Carlyle, Tennyson, Hardy to

George and T. S. Eliot, and in our time, from Vladimir Nabakov and Thomas Pynchon to Toni Morrison? The "system" of chess at any given time posits a volatile interchange between rules, contexts, and agency: textual rules that govern a particular form of the game (e.g., the bishop's move); contexts of change that link different forms of the game (the Arabic trade routes that brought chess to Christendom); and particular players who effect alterations in the rules (as happened in the bishop's case circa 1460 in the city of Kraków).

This last point, you'll have noticed, is a sleight of hand. I am condensing the history of chess into a model for any particular game. I mean by this to foreground the inadequacy of the analogy in its systemic form, as it's usually represented—the disciplinary view of the game—in order to adapt chess to the volatile conditions of textuality. My model is not a game between two players; it's *the* game(s) of chess across time, a kinship of chess opponents (and spectator-interpreters), within a bewildering disparity of rules and regulations.

One alternative does not exclude the other, of course. It's a question of perspective—a contrast between the short and the long view. In the short view, you will not play a better game if you know about the shift from elephant to bishop, because in any particular match the rules are self-consistent. The game gains meaning as a ludic system by its symbolic autonomy from the various realities the symbols transparently reflect. Kingship stands for a certain kind of political system; but at any given time, under any given conditions (democratic, socialist, dictatorial), the terms of kingship in chess are absolute, independent of institutional vicissitudes. As Sir Philip Sidney points out in his *Defense of Poetry*, it would probably hamper play to mistake a bishop in chess for a figure of Christianity: "We see we cannot play at chess but we must give names to our chessmen; and yet methinks he were a very partial champion of truth that would say we lied for giving a piece of wood the reverend title of bishop. The poet nameth Cyrus or Aeneas no other way." [27] In this sense, chess stands for the extremes both of necessity and of free play: its own necessary rules, its absolute freedom from the rules of culture. This short view I will call totalistic. It's totalistic because it's presentist, applicable to all things because applicable only to things as they are, here and now.

In the long view, historically considered, chess reverses that relation between freedom and necessity. Its rules of necessity are evidently mutable, and its mutability is evidently inseparable from the rules of culture. This long view I will call processual, with the understanding that *processual* in this case implies noncoherence (i.e., variably organic, systemic, revolutionary, fortu-itous). What stands in here for the principle of necessity does not lie in the rules of the game at any given time. Nor does it lie in intertextual rules con-necting those hundred great games. Rather, it's the principle of intercon-textuality: the connections between the common rules and regulations that distinguish different forms of the games as these are ordinarily and extraor-dinarily played. In any one game we win, lose, or draw, absolutely. In the processual view, however, any one game is a configuration of win, lose, and draw that occupies a midway position in *the* game of chess. To contextualize closure in a particular game would lead us through a range of different situ-ations, a variety of discourses, and a procession of contexts.

In textuality as in chess we are asked to suspend disbelief. This entails disconnection in the short view, our entry into what most game theorists, following Johan Huizinga, separate off as ludic space. But this sort of textual appreciation—a hermeneutics of separate spheres—is itself, like *a* religion, the expression of culture-specific rules. In the long view, every endgame that the rules once reflected (the armies of the Ching dynasty, the European feudal system) was eventually a middle-game trap circumvented or declined. The *game* wins, if I may put it so, by its inherent capacity to represent closure as a middle of the journey disguised as a new beginning, as in Dante's *Divine Comedy*, or in Judaic monotheism, or in Christian trinitarianism, or in the democratic, antiroyalist reversal of kingship to mean the divine right of the individual.

The act of appreciation, then, like that of analysis, is a middle game that invites us (sometimes through an unwilling suspension of belief) to enter a variety of contingent histories, including our own. Here, it's crucial to know about different sets of rules (religious, political, etc.), just as it's crucial to the meaning of Sidney's image in his *Defense of Poetry*—his *caustic* analogy, as it happens, of the "wooden" bishop and "the very reverend principle" it stands for—to know about the Elizabethan identification of the bishop in chess with Continental Catholicism. To take the short view of chess—to compare a lit-erary text with *a* chess game—is not wrong but reductive, precisely as tradi-tional aesthetic and cognitive approaches tend to be reductive. Each in its own way disconnects one form of discourse from the rest, isolates and privi-leges it as being causal, foundational. And the corollary is equally true: the chess analogy is illuminating insofar as we contextualize the game, globally as well as temporally.

The result is a model of chess that stands in itself, as a self-sufficient composite, for the variant histories of the game, like the fractal map of a moving cloud. Alice's Wonderland chess-adventures would be one example of such metamorphoses of closure into midgame intercontextuality; another example is the rhythm and structure of Beckett's *End-Game*, or of his end-game novel, *Watt*:

> "Finished, it's finished, nearly finished, it must be nearly finished. . . . All life long the same questions, the same answers."

> "I can't go on."
> "That's what you think." [28]

In this middle game the queen is and is not there. She is simultaneously absolute and made up, timeless and dated, like Goethe's Eternal Feminine. Here as in literature, the rules of coherence at any given time are specific to that time. What makes them transhistorical, transcultural, is the principle of process they convey: a principle of limitation, noncoherence, and recommencement that allows us to participate in the game, critically, vicariously, in spite of broad differences in rules.

That's what I called the depth of Faulkner's *Light in August*. It's not the sort of depth that's associated with disciplinary knowledge, and the difference—a difference in kind (not deeper but differently deep)—is worth remarking. By the very nature of professionalism, disciplines are totalistic. They are games in process, like literature, but their explanation of process at any given point is expressed as an endgame. A discipline is a system of understanding: it demands a certain kind of rigor, certain modes of persuasion, certain standards of validation and invalidation. And, while "certain" here often means processual, nonetheless as a discipline, systematically, it represents process as certainty. We know "x" because it corresponds to a *certain* Q.E.D. In the case of history, the terms of certainty are empirical truth, and empirical truth is systemic. It depends on a *certain* kind of evidence, or more accurately, on a kind of evidence that's declared to be certain by the discipline of history. *Light in August* tells a great deal about the burden of history, but it doesn't tell us what verifiably happened and so cannot stand as a history of the South, not even for historians who endorse the "linguistic turn" of narrativity. And so, too, in the case of religion: it speaks of the Unknowable, but as a discipline it's responsible to one or more systemic totalities: it's expressed through doctrines and dogma that by definition constitute *the* endgame. That's why the church fathers typologized not only the (therefore called) Old Testament, but Homer, Virgil, and Ovid as well. Homer tells us a great deal about religion, but *The Iliad* is a guide into the perplexities of faith, not a guide to the perplexed.

Disciplines are systems that proceed through language games of closure as endgames. Philosophy is responsible to the logic of its propositions, and logic is an endgame. That's why so many philosophers have made it their project, as Hegel and Wittgenstein did, to bring philosophy to an end, and why contemporary antifoundational philosophers, from Rorty to Derrida, find literature so congenial to their purposes. And that's why, like Nietzsche, they so often find themselves in opposition to philosophy as a discipline. Philosophy systemizes experience and so tends toward closure and generality, even when the generality is doubt, even when closure is a proof of skepticism. John Rawls's concept of what's reasonable is meant to distinguish the truths of political liberalism from the Truth, but his *Theory of Justice* issues as a set of absolutes (some have argued, the absolutes of Kantian metaphysics). Robert Nozick's *Philosophical Explanations* affirms the primacy of openness, but the affirmation itself is a testament to the power of systemic logic.

Disciplines, like the materials they deal with, aspire to provide (in Beckett's words) our "same old answers." That's why literary scholars and critics have so often turned to them for interpretative frameworks. They offer the contexts of closure within which to answer the questions generated by literature. And that's why, conversely, a literary approach to cultural studies seems so promising. Perhaps a better way to phrase this is: an approach to literary and cultural studies derived from the materials of literary history. Here the weaknesses of traditional literary studies become a distinctive asset. For, as a so-called discipline, literature has no cognitive foundation (logical, empirical, metaphysical), no clear standards of evidence, no substantive grounds for accepting one approach over another, not even a *certain* body of knowledge. What literature does offer, I think, as no other discipline does, is a series of texts that are transparently mutable: revisable, culture-specific, founded on questionable rules and regulations. And by extension, as a "systemic" approach, it offers a processual view of other disciplines as well. Literature reminds us that, in the long run, they're also middle games. Theologically, God *may* be dead; philosophically, the universe *may* be a chess automaton; but (as Hilary Putnam points out) it requires enormous ignorance or arrogance on our part to draw these conclusions from "what science has taught us."[29] Historically and economically, we really may be progressing toward some end-time utopia, but the evidence so far is far from conclusive. We *don't know* how it will end—win, lose, or draw—or even if it *will* end, in the limited, culture- and biology-bound idea of the endgame. And it's precisely in that (infinite) space of not-knowing—a space, to repeat, in which we can both acknowledge our limits and appreciate our urge to exceed them—that the analogy holds between chess, the literary text, and cultural studies.

Wittgenstein's analogy is a challenging case in point. The philosopher, he tells us, talks about language (and through language) "as we talk about the chess pieces when we are stating the rules of the game." "The question 'What is a word really?' is analogous to 'What is a piece in chess?'" "If you follow other rules than those of chess, you are playing another game."[30] These are practical directives, intended to open up the meaning of language games; but they re-present practicality itself as an abstraction—a certain perennial truth (or falsehood):

> Formalism contains both truth and falsehood. The truth in formalism is that every syntax can be regarded as a system of rules for a game. I have been reflecting on what . . . [it] can mean [to say] . . . that a formalist regards the axioms of mathematics as similar to the rules of chess. I would like to say: not only the axioms of mathematics, but the whole of syntax is arbitrary.
>
> I was asked in Cambridge whether I think that mathematics concerns ink marks on paper [as does literature]. I reply: in just the same sense in which chess concerns wooden figures. Chess, I mean, does not consist in my pushing wooden figures around a board. If I say, 'Now I will make myself a queen with very frightening eyes, she will drive everyone off the board' you will laugh. It does not matter what a pawn looks like. What is much rather the case is that the totality of rules of the game determines the logical place of a pawn. A pawn is a variable, like the 'x' in logic. . . .
>
> If you ask me: where lies the difference between chess and the syntax of a language I reply: solely in their application. . . . If there were men on Mars who made war like the chess pieces, then the generals would use the rules of chess for prediction. It would then be a scientific question whether the king could be mated by a certain deployment of pieces in three moves, and so on.[31]

I've quoted this passage at length to show the stunning combination of inclusiveness and absolutism that marks this most militantly open-ended of philosophies. "A *certain* deployment of pieces in three moves": in Wittgenstein's "formalist" endgame, the random word "certain" assumes the authority of finality; the concept of "variable" becomes a "scientific question" of "every syntax"; the process of "making" is an image of closure, "like the 'x' in logic"; and the sheer indefiniteness of "and so on" bespeaks the relentlessness of disciplinary "rules." These rules, by Wittgensteinian definition, are enclosed within the realm of nontranscendence; but they are also closed off, by their philosophic status as rules, from the noncoherent process of systemic-revolutionary-contingent change—for example, the process through which, circa A.D. 800, the queen was instated in place of the timid, sluggish counselor or vizir, known as *senex*, "the old man." In this sense, Wittgenstein's formulation of the game's "logic" distorts the actual course of chess history. His rules are synchronics in disguise, provisional arrangements that are presented to us under the aspect of eternity (appropriately figured as Mars, planet of rules and regulations, where generals use chess strategies "for prediction").

Wittgenstein does not *mean* this. The Plato of the late Dialogues might call it a defect in human language. I see it as a problem in disciplinary logic; it's intended by the discipline of philosophy. We might call it Wittgenstein's syntactic *donée*. It makes "the whole of [*his*] syntax" seem not just coherent, but totalizing.

"Totality," he declares, the "game determines": the picture at which (by contrast) we are asked to laugh—a player suddenly, willfully, reconceiving the function of the queen—implies the impotence of radical innovation, the absurdity of "my pushing" against the object's "logical place." Of course, Wittgenstein is not talking about willfulness; he means to distinguish convention from mimesis. But, in doing so, he grounds function in the rules of the game and abstracts what's then given, the chessboard as we find it, into a fixed, prescriptive meaning, as though its eight-square shape were not derived from another game, "ashtapada," but an emblem of fate. "You can't just change the size of the board." Common sense, Clifford Geertz remarks, is "an all-purpose idea which acts to reassure [us] that [our] fund of commonplaces is . . . adequate." [32] Like common sense, the essence and teleology games repress the agencies of process: essentialism by positing a metahistorical ideal, teleology by investing history with an origin and telos. Wittgenstein's abstraction, processual though it is, retains the weaknesses of these perspectives in its logic of necessity: its disciplinary common sense represses the agencies of the past, and hence the game's possible futures.

In fact, Wittgenstein has been criticized in these or similar terms for conservatism. But that's not my complaint. Quite the opposite: I invoked him to begin with because his antifoundational outlook is our best alternative to the static totalities of other game theories. For John von Neumann, the theoretician of scientific models of play, games are self-enclosed and self-legitimating, as in a symbolic system which regulates itself through the controlled representation of reality, and which controls representation because its symbols, as in mathematics, are themselves at once systemic and constitutive of reality. Wittgenstein refuses that offer of finality. In his chess analogy, mathematics is just one more made-up game, "ink marks on paper" that we agree to call "axioms" of reality. Here as elsewhere for him, the rules of the game do not carry their own legitimation; they are constantly subject to mitigation, emendation, and negotiation, and they bring with them as they proceed in time a labyrinthine array of meanings.

Perhaps a more direct contrast is the generative or structuralist endgame: Noam Chomsky's foundational model of language. Here syntactic knowledge inheres in human cognition, so that the rules of the game are unalterable, independent of semantic complexity and contextual pressures (history, philology, institutions), "free from the control of detectable stimuli, either external or internal." For Wittgenstein, on the contrary, language is contingent at its core; his chess game represents our makeshift Apollonian solutions: customs, contracts, traditions, and pronouncements ex cathedra to tell us how the world works. His remarks about aesthetics renounce causation altogether, but even in normative, rule-bound matters, what we call necessity, he writes, is "an arbitrary law" of language: "the whole of syntax is arbitrary":

> Where is the connection effected between the sense of the expression "Let's play a game of chess" and all the rules of the game? —Well, in the list of rules of the game, in the teaching of it, in the day-to-day practice of playing. . . .
>
> To understand a sentence means to understand a language. To understand a language means to be the master of a technique. . . .
>
> But isn't chess defined by its rules? . . .
>
> Following a rule is analogous to obeying an order. We are trained to do it so. . . .
>
> [And if someone were to object that *this*] game has no beginning! . . . [the answer is:] Of course it has; otherwise, it would not be a game of chess.[33]

This is the disciplinary logic of nontranscendence. If literary study as I conceive it were to have an aesthetic philosophy, it would begin with Wittgenstein. More than any other philosopher, Arnold Davidson tells us, Wittgenstein authorizes the ordinary language warnings sounded by contemporary thinkers against "misleading analogies and inferences that derive from a historically inappropriate and conceptually untenable perspective." Thus his very conservatism, his insistence on things as they are, not only permits but, as Stanley Cavell argues, may be said to point to the dynamics of change. Arthur Kenny invokes the kinship analogy in this regard: "[For Wittgenstein,] 'rule,' like 'game,' is a family likeness term covering many different but related things: what we call a rule in a game, or language-game, may have very different roles in the game. . . . It is a mistake, when reading what Wittgenstein has to say about rules, to think of the canonical form of a rule as being a conditional imperative."[34]

And yet Wittgenstein's model of chess is ahistorical. All philosophers, he tells us, "talk about it [language] just as we would about the pieces in a game of chess when we are stating the rules of the game." It's a way of talking that leads of its own rational accord to "totality."[35]

Again, I refer not to the analogy as Wittgenstein thinks of it, but as the thinking process is represented as philosophy, through propositions, abstractions, and coherent argumentation (coherent to the point where the numerical sequence of its proposition is integral to its intellectual persuasiveness). Wittgenstein conceptualizes chess as a point in time; but he formulates it as the endgame of the arbitrary. He reminds us that in Cavell's phrase, Plato's sun was made in the cave, but the picture he conveys of the cave, like Plato's (Cavell's, Davidson's), is itself an absolute. I just suggested that that perspective inheres in the discipline. I should perhaps add that it constitutes a universal condition (in my sense of the term)—a problematic necessary to philosophical investigations. Ahistoricism may be a limitation prerequisite to the pursuit of abstract truths, just as, conversely, literary works may require the repression of those abstractions as the necessary cost of their insights. It may be that to declare "cogito ergo sum" requires me to erase the differences separating places and times, whereas to understand Descartes in context— the "cogito" as seventeenth-century artifact—requires me to banish the archetypal "I" that would validate his generalization. When Heraclitus observes that we never step into the same river twice, he may be said to dismiss precisely the sort of questions that cultural analysis begins with: "Which river?" "At what season?" "Who is 'we'?" Philosophy says: "I think therefore I am." Literature says: "That's what *you* think," and then again, with another universal qualification in mind, "That's what you *think*."

I've tried to suggest this distinction through the contrast between, on the one hand, disciplinary *re-presentation*, the systemization of particulars that tends toward the absolute, and, on the other hand, literary *representation*, a particularization of absolutes that tends toward the universal. Disciplines *represent* the "common behavior of mankind" through systems that close off systems of the past. This does not mean that they themselves are closed: they may pride themselves, as neo-Marxists, neo-Freudians, pragmatists, and Wittgensteinians do, on their openness to new directions and the sensitivity to difference. But insofar as they claim to explain things logically, insofar as they constitute frameworks of understanding—a philosophy, a method, a system—they tend to consider earlier frameworks to be invalid and competing systems to be wrongheaded. Literary representation tends the other way. As a discipline, it's concerned with works that specify "totality" in ways that open up connections to configurations of the past as well as the future. Those ways lead through historical layers of language, not the conceptual trajectories of reason. This applies even when literary texts seek to ground the particulars they describe in absolutes, like the exemplary family situation that begins Jane Austin's *Pride and Prejudice*; or like protagonists named Everyman and Ishmael. For, as literature, they represent *a* family, *a* journey, *an* Ishmael; and, in thus moving toward specificity, they tend to provide inter-contextual challenges to abstractions about the "common behavior of mankind." The particular example in economics, ethnography, or philoso-phy is a means to an end. In the literary text, the particular example is the end in question; the cultural norms it embodies are the means to convey its exemplary qualities.

Can that reversal of ends and means be disciplined into a method of literary and cultural studies? Georg Simmel's analogy between chess and the dynamics of cognition provides the traditional disciplinary response:

> Although the boundary as such is necessary, every single determinate boundary can be stepped over, every enclosure can be blasted, and every such act, of course, finds or creates a new boundary. This pair of statements—that the boundary is unconditional, in that its existence is constitutive of our given po-sition in the world, but that no boundary is unconditional, since every one can in principle be altered, reached over, gotten around—this pair of statements appears as the replication of the inner unity of vital action. . . . We are all like the chess player in this regard. If he did not know, to a certain extent, what the consequences of a certain move would be, the game would be impossible; but it would also be impossible if this foresight extended indefinitely. Plato's defi-nition of the philosopher as he who stands between knowing and not-knowing holds for man in general.[36]

My concept of the middle game comes to the same conclusion: foresight is a function of persisting limitations. But Simmel's picture is progressivist; its hero of analysis looks forward, from the "determinate boundaries" around him toward the limits of the horizon. He mediates between knowing and not-knowing from the perspective of knowing. Literature speaks to us from the other side of the divide. It recalls us to "our given position" especially when it overreaches; it mediates through the perspective of not-knowing, even when ignorance is the vehicle to transcendence, as in *The Death of Ivan Ilych*. Tolstoy's story ends with the conquest of death, *in imitatio Christi*; but *as literature* that triumph of the absolute is a pretext for what amounts to a picture of common limitations: a life which was "most terrible" because it was "most ordinary." Could we read that picture philosophically and still see it as literature? And the other way around: Can "philosophy become litera-ture and still know itself"?[37]

These are not intended as rhetorical questions. A prime value for me of the middle-game model is its insistence on reciprocity. To refuse or cir-cumvent the sacrifice of history is to resist the choice between coherence and

noncoherence—between totalizing and processual perspectives—as constituting one more trap of transcendence. Culturally considered, chess requires
*both* perspectives. It's neither systemic, as Wittgenstein represents it in his
*Tractatus*, nor is it arbitrary, as Wittgenstein re-presents it in his *Investigations*. Chess is a configuration of diachronic flow *and* synchronic structure
that unsettles disciplinary endgames. We must see it concretely, "in itself" (*a*
text, *a* game) as a set of absolute but arbitrary rules. And in the same glance,
we must comprehend it universally, processually—again, "in itself" (textuality, *the* game)—as a systemic but open-ended configuration of cultural
variables. For "variables" here are not arbitrary in an absolute sense. The
chess analogy includes (as part of its open-endedness) the possibly substantive value of the conceptual and belief structures within which we play "the
game of life." *That* "chess game" is neither a sport nor divinely ordained
("the sport of the gods"). It's a middle-game strategy designed to mediate
between ludic categories and categorical imperatives.

So understood, the analogy between chess and language game points
to the *historicity* of language. The question "What is a piece in chess really?"
is analogous to "What is the (volatile) function and (malleable) context of
that word?" The concept of the "totality of the game" applies simultaneously
to a binding set of regulations and to a combination of cultural pieces in
process. Particulars (e.g., the pawn's move) point to the universality of "the
rules of the game." But in this case as in others universality is the product of
shifting forces in time. Like the Statue of Liberty or the Black Virgin of Gua-
deloupe, the rule called pawn promotion, whereby the pawn may become a
queen when it reaches the eighth rank, is demonstrably the unforeseen result
of open-ended process: variation, innovation, public receptivity, geographical
transfer, and linguistic transformation.

A classic instance of this process came with the surprising instatement
of the queen in place of the vizir. A long, sharp controversy followed concerning the legitimacy of sex change, with respect both to the displaced old
counselor and the queened pawn. As we might expect, disciplinarily, these
debates turned on logical points of analysis in theology, philosophy, and science. And as we might expect, culturally and rhetorically, the contending
logics of gender were so heavily coded with sexist objectives that (in retrospect) they overwhelm or undermine the arguments. The moral of the story
is that to resolve the question of gender (or class, or race) logically is to miss
its semantic complexity, a complexity that's inextricable from its systemic
meaning (philosophical, legal, theological, even biological). And the converse
holds true for the aesthetic endgame. To immerse oneself only in the semantic

complexities of "gender" ("race," "class")—to claim that these complexities constitute worlds of their own, each with its own essentially aesthetic logic— say, the inherent ambiguity of the symbol, or the laws of linguistic transfor- mation—is to miss the *cultural* work of language, which is crucial to its aes- thetic meaning. And since the systemic move toward closure seems endemic to disciplines, it's the job of literary studies to keep the game going. The proper interdisciplinary context is one that imitates the literary text (cultur- ally understood) by defining all types of closure as middle-game problems of reciprocities.

The method of "solving" these problems constitutes something like a literary-cultural aesthetics of nontranscendence. Its rules are as follows:

**One:** Literature is not a criticism of life. It is life's criticism of abso- lutes, language's skepticism about the consolation of endgames. Generally, literature aspires to archetypes, origins, and cosmic revelations. It deals in laws that seem as binding as those in chess. But in doing so it testifies, as chess does, to the powers of mutability and the commonplace.

**Two:** Insofar as literary study is faithful to its materials, it seeks to understand the very process of mystification, the verbal alchemy by which ordinary language is refined into the extraordinary, as a function in context, like a chemical combination of common elements that yields unexpected results.

**Three:** To see the trap in the sacrifice of history does not release us from endgame difficulties of play (moral, political, spiritual). Rather, it requires us to see why the question is how best to continue within the constraints of recommencement. The creative metaphor is a miracle of intercontextuality.

**Four:** Literature is noble or complex or subversive insofar as it reaches beneath culture-specific ideals to common matters. It broadens our horizon by illuminating the variables through which, in a particular case, the possible becomes probable, then normative, then self-evident, then the rules of the game, and finally, for better and worse, the unstable boundaries of a game in process.

**Five:** The drive to create absolutes is inseparable from the drive to make those absolutes amenable to change. The mixed result is what we call context.

**Six:** All absolutes are the same: culturally constructed. Every universal takes on the substantive significance of the limitations it entails—the abiding moral, philosophical, biological, and spiritual dimensions of the distinctive problems it enacts.

## The America Game

*. . . there were some new positions on the
chessboard, but the game would go on.*
—Toni Morrison, *Song of Solomon*

Having set out these rules of my game, I should acknowledge their limitations. All six of them are predicated on the model of modern chess, the game as we now play it, and those rules represent neither the game's essence nor its telos. Indeed, we can virtually identify the point at which the then-called New Chess became official. Evidently, half a millennium ago, in the last quarter of the fifteenth century, somewhere in Spain, Portugal, or Italy, the game of chess changed qualitatively. The main developments centered on speed of contact and scope of personal initiative. The pivotal change came with the expanded powers of the queen, which, from being the weakest player, suddenly emerged as the strongest single unit on the board, combining in one piece the moves of rook and bishop. By 1492, when Columbus recommenced the quest for Eden, chess had begun anew. A coherent new system had developed, replete with a "theory of its own," sometimes known as the theory of the mad queen, "eschés de la dame enragée," "ala rabiosa." [38]

Chess historians have made the predictable Renaissance correspondences: expanded mobility, the new individualism, the invention of the printing press, and the great queens of empire, from Isabella of Spain to Elizabeth of England. And Isabella herself is indeed implicated: when the first published treatise on the New Chess appeared in 1496, dedicated to Isabella's infant son, its author, the courtier-scholar-poet Luis de Lucena, had it bound together with a Petrarchan sonnet [39] and titled it *Repetición de amores: El arte de axadrez*. According to authorities, the new art of the game centered on "the emancipation of the individual chess piece, which began to undermine the hierarchical [i.e., closed and static] concept of the game." This innovation, they explain, reflected "the development [during this time] of man's power, which stood in causal relationship to his increased urge towards individual independence" [40]—and eventually, I would add, the redefinition of "woman's sphere" in a developing symbology of economic free enterprise.

Something of all this may be read into Lucena's play on words. Chess, he implies, is an art of *repetición* (translated as "game," but implying repeated beginnings) of *amores*, plural: not love, but a succession of acts of love, embodied in a procession of particular lovers, playing at particular games (win, lose, *and* draw). *Arte de axandrez*, then, the art of chess, is the continual *Play of Love*, a series of *Lovers Games—Game(s) of Love(s)*. It's entirely appropriate to the open-ended quality of this pun that, in fact, the complexities instated by the New Chess led to a reversal in the kinds of problems that had typified the game. With the Renaissance, the endgame puzzle ceased to be the dominant chess problem, and gradually receded into a diversion, like solitaire in cards. By now, it's something of an anachronism for serious players. Chess historians tell us that the endgame puzzle survives "almost [only as] an antagonistic reaction to the development of the modern game. Increasingly, players have opted for pragmatism and organized competition. An increasing number of 20th Century [theorists] . . . have not scrupled to vary the rules of the game, inventing new chess pieces and new tasks in order to achieve original . . . effects." [41]

This picture of commodification and speculation opens a new case of text and context. What we now call chess is the game of modernity, of which the United States is the example par excellence. "America" is to the modern world as the middle-game sacrifice is to the game of chess. Metaphorically, it's the gift of history to the United States (an apparent "blunder" that includes, among other advantages, the sacrifice of the "New World" histories of modern French, Spanish, Dutch, and Portugese imperialisms; for, as the Lucena connection reminds us, "America" was *their* recommencement long before the United States "began").

This particular turn of the analogy points to my own involvement in the game, and I want to take a moment to describe the position on the board. I imagine the language game of modern nationhood as a massively entrenched but constantly shifting and increasingly embattled field of expression. Anthropologists now speak of a "global culture" with colliding "cosmopolitanisms," accelerating "deterritorialization," and "ethnoscapes" of bewildering complexity. Ever since the era of Renaissance colonization, writes Arjun Appadurai, the "forces of cultural gravity" have moved steadily away from forms of containment toward "the formation of large-scale ecumenes." Consequently:

> there are some brute facts about the world of the twentieth century that any ethnography must confront. Central among these facts is the changing social, territorial, and cultural reproduction of group identity. As groups migrate, regroup in new locations, reconstruct their histories, and reconfigure their ethnic "projects," the *ethno* in ethnography takes on a slippery, nonlocalized quality. . . . The warp of [traditional] stabilities is everywhere shot through with the woof of human motion, as more persons and groups deal with the realities of having to move or the fantasies of wanting to move. What is more, both these

realities and these fantasies now function on large scales, as [for example] men and women from villages in India think not just of moving to Poona or Madras, but of moving to Dubai and Houston. . . . Especially in regard to the many alternative cosmopolitanisms that characterize the world today, and the complex transnational cultural flows that link them, there is no easy way to "begin at the beginning." . . . Of course, this dialogue of histories and genealogies itself has a history, but for this later history, we . . . do not yet possess a master narrative.[42]

Perhaps not; but meanwhile we have a master narrative called America. In fact, what Appadurai describes as an interparadigmatic moment recalls Benjamin Franklin's description of the new republic:

> We must not expect that a new government may be formed, as a game of chess may be played by a skillful hand, without a fault. The players of our game are so many, their ideas so different, their prejudices so strong and various, and their particular interests, independent of the general, seeming so opposite, that not a move can be made that is not contested; the numerous objections confound the understanding; the wisest must agree to some unreasonable things, that reasonable ones of more consequence may be obtained; and thus chance has its share in many of the determinations, so that the play is more like *tric-trac* with a box of dice.[43]

Franklin's analogy is not entirely satisfactory. The game of liberal democracy has its own severe regulations, as chess has its ineffable elements of chance; and besides, chess skills demand not just faultless play but precisely the sort of flexibility that Franklin calls for: ingenuity, opportunism, a talent for conflict, and a cunning sense of multiple possibilities. It may be that Franklin's recourse to dice indicates a limitation inherent in his own middle-game position. He may have been too closely engaged in the creation of the republic to realize that what seemed like chance was just part of a certain, quite coherent set of rules and regulations.

But there's another possibility. The sly references to chess may indicate that Franklin intended to outmaneuver what was then a commonplace analogy (politics and chess), rather than simply to reject it. He was an extraordinary player in his own right, after all, and he had earlier pointed out (in a bagatelle called "Life is a kind of Chess") how "full of Events" the game is, what "a variety of turns [there is] in it," and how often "the Fortune of [its players is] . . . subject to sudden vicissitudes." In the passage I cited, his emphasis on conceding pieces in return for positions "of more consequence" may be a direct reference to the middle-game sacrifice. Franklin, that is, may have *wanted* to conflate chess and dice in a kind of wild, instinctive middle-game speculation. If so, it was a shrewd move on his part. Chess in its early forms was played by the roll of dice, like monopoly; "tric-trac" is a synonym for backgammon, a game closely connected to chess in its formative stages; and "chessmen" in Sanskrit is a variant of "gambling pieces."[44] Deliberate or not, Franklin's application of the *tric-trac* of chess to the Sturm und Drang of new nationhood is especially appropriate for my purpose. America is the major instance of our current "global cultural economy," as well as of the volatile mixture of conservative and destabilizing forces we call modernity.

I have in mind the multisectarian, multiracial, multilingual culture called the United States, and, in particular, its literary correlative: the language of America, that astonishing complex of sacred-secular meanings developed in the modern era as a symbology of the new. Nationality in the "Old World" (Africa, Asia, Europe) remains an endgame puzzle: identity to be resolved in three or four moves (language, territory, cultural past, religion). "America" is a language game of malleable beginnings and possible futures, especially because the beginnings are textual by definition and the future is apocalyptic by textual authority. German chauvinists believed in racial origins, Panslavists in ethnic destiny. For the American believer, destiny means opportunity, the covenant made new as contract. "Manifest destiny" is process and provisionality: a manifest *potential*, a destiny *on the way*, a dream *becoming* reality (perhaps a nightmare reality). An African-Chinese is a marginal figure caught between two endgames; an African-American or a Chinese-American or an African-Chinese-American is a hybrid emblem of recommencement.[45]

Indeed, I've deliberately taken the term "recommencement" from Emerson to acknowledge my cultural debt. "The American Scholar" celebrates "the recommencement of our literary year." To that end, Emerson, speaking from the Pisgah-top of prophecy—the star-spangled heights of "the constellation Harp, which now flames in our zenith"—unveils the vistas opened by this new culture: its mission to "fill the postponed expectation of the world." Most vividly, Emerson figures recommencement in his essay "Circles," where that immemorial image of closure explodes into the oxymoron of recurrent newness—oxymoron, that is, in the Old World; in the New, an opportunity for open-ended fulfillment:

> Every action admits of being outdone. Our life is an apprenticeship to the truth, that around every circle another can be drawn [as the eye draws the circle of the horizon]; that there is no end in nature, but every end is a beginning. . . . Generalization is always a new influx of the divinity into the mind. . . . Everything looks permanent until its secret is known. . . . Every ultimate fact is only

the first of a new series. . . . There is no virtue which is final; all are initial. . . . The man finishes his story, —how good! how final! how it puts a new face on all things! He fills the sky. Lo! on the other side rises also a man, and draws a circle around the circle we had just pronounced the outline of the sphere. Then already is our first speaker not man, but only a first speaker.[46]

It amounts to a pluralist fantasia. Newness is a continual movement toward endings that issues in an endless affirmation of beginnings. To re-cognize is to see *as though* for the first time. In *this* circle, to trace a point back to origins or forward to finality is to initiate a new circle. "Man" prevails, even (Emerson claims) "ascends"—"Mounts through all the spires of form"—by splitting into an interminable procession of "first speakers."[47] It's a symbol of process that equates progress with newness, newness with starting again, starting again with natural divine origins, and origins with telos.[48] This strategy is characteristic of all of Emerson's great essays. It's not too much to say that it describes the form of the Emersonian essay, starting with "The American Scholar," whose rhythm and logic require us to reconceive the meaning of each of its parts—section, paragraph, sentence—as a recommencement in its own right. The same strategy may be traced through the cultural procession of images of the United States as the New World: land of promise (without guarantees); "country of tomorrow" (if we meet our obligations today); futurity almost made real (but never quite); "self-made" as a synonym for "opportunity" (but "it's up to you"); "frontier" *potentially* reversed from stop sign to starting point; "self-interest" *provisionally* magnified into boundlessness; "position" defined by mobility: upward, outward, and downward too—the *last* best hope of earth.

To add the obvious: this is *not* the only language game in the United States. There are competing symbologies and a diversity of rhetorics as well as separate cultural spheres. But surely one reason that these disparities have not yielded to the violence they generate, one reason that consensus has been more pronounced in this "nation of nations" than elsewhere, whether in "traditional" or in "new" nations, is that the strategies of recommencement have managed on some deep level to enclose the language games of a changing and expanding culture. It's through those strategies, demonstrably, that such risky catchwords as "independence" and "revolution" (and most recently "multiculturalism" and "identity politics") have been made a summons to market-rules conformity. Demonstrably, in spite of Appadurai's claims for global identity, the "ethno" in ethnography tends here, as nowhere else, to take on a decidedly local quality: the marketably hyphenated ("hybrid," "marginal," "borderline") *American*. "As more persons and groups deal with the realities of having to move or of wanting to move," those re-constructed ethnic "projects" slip more and more smoothly into the project of a multicultural United States, connecting Wall Street, the White House, and the groves of Academe; connecting also the suburbs, the radical under-ground, the celebrity enclaves, and the inner cities. Demonstrably, in short, the America game has proved more adaptable to the conditions of modern-ism than any other symbology, regional or global, from the romantic origins game of *Volksgeist* to the communist endgame of world revolution.[49]

We in academia are part of the game plan, like it or not. I include myself in the "we." I'm aware that the model I've just expounded looks sus-piciously like an American fantasy of new beginnings—an effort to adapt the America game to a literary-and-cultural studies errand into a new millen-nium. After all, what's most "American" about "The American Scholar" is that Emersonian recommencement invests newness—the game of discovery and fresh starts—with the potential of apocalypse, an identity-by-promise that has made this culture a model both for imagining communities and for reconstituting selfhood in a postnational world. Isn't *that* model—the sacri-fice of history for the prospects of transcendence (self-transcendence, ethnic transcendence, national transcendence)—the trap to be avoided?

We might picture the question as a confrontation between Lucena's Mad Queen of modernity and Wittgenstein's Queen with Very Frightening Eyes. *First, the philosophic move*: Since, as this essay demonstrates, our terms of analysis are themselves language games reproducing the forms of culture they describe, we have no foundation for objectivity, no Archimedean ful-crum outside culture for disinterested inquiry. How can you decline the sac-rifice if you're part of the plan, an *x* in its logic? *Then, the literary-cultural response*: We may have to accept that particular trap, as Wittgenstein counsels us to come to terms with the trap of language in general; but we can play, as he does, to circumvent the trap. The proper response is to reinstate history, the long view, and the problems of process.

Hence my model of recommencement. The chess analogy, as I conceive it, reminds us that "America" is neither new nor final, but, from start to finish, a fiercely contested middle game. On July 4, 1776, the thirteen states declared themselves independent, united, and free because they were *not*; and that knot of dependencies, discord, and responsibilities remains the United States, rhetoric and all. From then to now, from one recommencement to another—from Great Migration to Revolution to Civil War to F.D.R.'s New Deal to the Reagan-Bush-Clinton endtime City on a Hill—it has been a game of particulars, agency, predicaments, and limitations. This applies to all the various endgames encoded in "America"—centuries' ends, narrative ends (the course of empire), continental ends (the California Dream), and the ends of culture (individualism, progress). All of them are games in process. And whatever ends we think we see in the unfolding, it would be well to have a clear view of the rules we play by. For one thing, this would allow us more fully to appreciate our options within the game. For another thing, it would help us understand the unresolved predicaments that may issue (who knows?) in alternative, post-American forms of the game.

# Storytelling: Historical and Ideological

The question currently being posed by theorists of historical discourse is whether storytelling—or what we can call, more technically, the narrative mode of discourse—is not in some way ideological in its very nature. This question has important implications for historical theory, inasmuch as historical discourse has traditionally featured narration or storytelling as a preferred mode of representation and even of explanation. To be sure, our representations of history do not have to be cast in a story form; they can also be cast in non-narrative discursive modes, descriptive, analytical, even lyrical, as the case may be. And indeed, in modern, "scientific" historiography, the tendency has been to suppress storytelling in favor of synchronic representations of historical phenomena, structural-functional analyses of long-term and for the most part "impersonal" historical processes, and model building as a means of explicating complex forces and long-term trends discernible in the historical record. Storytelling or narration has been reduced to the function of providing specific examples, instances, or illustrations of classes of events, structures, and processes derived by non-narrative representational and analytical procedures. In other words, storytelling in historiography has for quite a while been deprived of its traditional function of explaining historical events and consigned to the more modest roles of explication and illustration.

It is because of the subordinant function of narrativity in contemporary historiography that the recent call for a "return to narrative" in historical writing invites attention from theorists of the social and human sciences. To be sure, the proponents of a "return to narrative" in historical writing explicitly grant to "storytelling" only a rhetorical function. They recommend it only as a means of reviving an interest in history among a laity disaffected by the abstractive methods of structuralist and social scientific historiography and the dryness or impersonality of scientific prose. The suggestion is that it is merely a matter of dressing up their findings, produced by the application of social scientific methods to their objects of interest, in the garb of a story, in order to make the results of their research more palatable to their lay audience.

However, such a recommendation presumes that narration is a neutral discursive form, an ornamental device that carries no message in its own right and does not therefore affect in any important way the representation either of the events spoken about or the historian's thought about the events produced by the application of scientific principles of analysis. It would appear that narrative is a *form* of discourse that can be adapted to the presentation of a wide variety of cognitive *contents*, whether commonsensical in nature or produced by the application of "scientific" procedures—such as econometrics, statistical demography, dialectics, ethnography, psychoanalysis, and so on. It is as if one could simply present the *results* of a structural-functionalist, synchronic, or algorithmic analysis of historical phenomena in a *narrative form* without thereby adding any significant conceptual or cognitive content to the account.

But this notion of narration is at odds with the results of some four decades of research into the nature of rhetoric in general and of narrative discourse or storytelling in particular. This research suggests that far from being a neutral medium in which events, whether imaginary or real, can be represented with perfect transparency, narrative is an expression in discourse of a distinct mode of experiencing and thinking about the world, its structures, and its processes. Indeed, the millennial association of the narrative mode of discourse with mythic and religious thought, on the one side, and with literary fiction, on the other, was what led to the condemnation of narrative history as a manifestation of mythical thinking in historical reflection in the first place.

## Braudel and Barthes on Narrative in Historiography

Thus, for example, as early as 1950, Fernand Braudel, the leader of the *Annales* group of structuralist historians and social scientists, attacked the use of narration in historical representation, not so much as a *container* of one or another ideological messages, as rather the very ideological *content* of any historical account cast in this form. In an essay on the then current situation in historical studies Braudel wrote:

> The narrative history so dear to the heart of Ranke offer[s] . . . a gleam but no illumination; facts but no humanity. Note that this narrative history . . . always claims to relate "things just as they really happened." In fact, though, in its own *covert* way, narrative history consists of an interpretation, an authentic *philosophy of history*. To the narrative historians, the life of men is dominated by *dramatic* accidents, by the actions of those *exceptional beings* who occasionally emerge, and who often are the masters of their own *fate* and even more of ours. And when they speak of "general history," what they are really speaking of is the intercrossing of such exceptional *destinies*, for obviously each *hero* must be matched against another. A delusive fallacy, as we all know. (My emphases)[1]

Note here that Braudel calls narrative *as such* a "philosophy of history" and goes on to characterize it as informed by a specifically *dramatistic* perspective on historical events. The "ideological" effect of this perspective consists in its transformation of history into a spectacle, unfolding before the mind's eye of the reader with all of the color, intensity, and fascination of a theatrical production. The events of a narrative representation must be charged with all the mythic resonances attending the notions of "fate" and "destiny": the characters must be larger than life ("heroic") and more complex, more noble and more interesting ("exceptional") than ordinary people. Everything has to be focused on those grand "conflicts" and "climaxes" of which only "heroes" can be agents.

A similar attack on the use of narrative for the representation of history was mounted from the quarter of literary theory a few years later by Roland Barthes. He put the matter this way:

> As we can see, simply from looking at its structure and without having to invoke the substance of its content, [narrative] *historical discourse is in its essence a form of ideological elaboration* [my emphasis], or to put it more precisely, an *imaginary* elaboration, if we can take the imaginary to be the language through which the utterer of a discourse (a purely linguistic entity) "fills out" the place of the subject of the utterance (a psychological or ideological entity).[2]

On the basis of his own structural analysis of narratives, Barthes concluded that "claims concerning the 'realism' of narrative" must be "discounted. . . . The function of narrative is not to 'represent,' it is to constitute a spectacle."[3] We do not, Barthes argued, "experience" reality more vividly and immediately in narrative than in descriptive discourse; what we experience is the effect of being disengaged and effectively mesmerized "observers" of "spectacular" events.

The indictments of narrative by Braudel and Barthes reflected a general structuralist suspicion of a kind of historiography that because it took the form of storytelling, retained too many formal similarities to mythic thought and fictional discourse. "Does the narration of past events," Barthes asked, ". . . really differ, in some specific trait, in some indubitably distinctive feature, from imaginary narration, as we find it in the epic, the novel, and the drama?"[4] The question was rhetorical, of course, because Barthes supposed that the *form* of a narrative discourse marked it as "imaginary" rather than as "realistic," quite apart from whatever political position or class interest it could be shown on analysis to be implicitly promoting. And this was because narrative discourse inevitably cultivated such mythological notions as the transcendental observer of historical processes, the sovereign subject (whether an individual or a collectivity) as the principal agent of historical events, the episodic event as the basic unit of historical reality, dependence on the anecdote to explain what in reality it only posited, and post hoc ergo propter hoc reasoning as the principal means of linking events in chains of causes and effects.

Barthes's analysis of narrative discourse was part of a wider inquiry into the history and potential fate of the ideology of realism inherited from the period of bourgeois hegemony in the nineteenth century. In Barthes's view, nineteenth-century "realism," in historical no less than fictional writing, was intimately linked to the narrative mode of discourse. Since, for him, "realistic representation" itself was nothing but an effect produced by nineteenth-century bourgeois discursive practices, it followed that as long as narrative remained a dominant mode of historical representation, historical inquiry must remain a merely pseudoscientific and therefore ideological enterprise. A structuralist approach to historical analysis, Barthes maintained, would gain in scientificity precisely in the degree to which it abandoned the idea that "reality" could be "realistically" represented in the form of a story and substituted, not only non- but explicitly anti-narrative representational and explanatory procedures. Historical reality could be rendered more "intelligible" by being detheatricalized, its "drama" played down, and the impersonality of its processes highlighted. History could be made into an object for analysis rather than an object of "specular" fascination only by being "defamiliarized"—in the manner proposed by Brecht for the reformation of the classical theater.

According to Braudel and Barthes, then, historical storytelling was ideological in the extent to which it transformed historical events into the stuff of "theater." This transformation conditioned readers to occupy the imaginary position of "spectators" of a scene on which superhuman "actors" played out "roles" as representatives of "forces" more mythical than natural in kind. Ordinary mortals could only marvel at what transpired on this scene; they could never hope to inhabit it effectively themselves or change the "forces" appearing thereon by their own actions. The general ideological effect of such theatricalization of history by storytelling was to produce "subjects" who were content to be the "patients" of historical "forces" because they had been deprived of any hope of becoming "agents" in their own right, whether as individuals or as members of social collectivities. As thus envisaged, the task of progressive criticism and theory was to destroy the authority of narration, not only in historical writing but also and perhaps preeminently in fictional writing as well.

## Lukács on Narrative in Realistic Representation

The Braudel-Barthes critique of storytelling *as* ideology differs from the view of the function of narration in "realistic" writing that Georg Lukács had developed in his work of the interwar years. The problem of the relation between ideology and narrative was raised by Lukács, in terms relevant to our interests, in his studies on literary realism in the 1930s, and it may be helpful to review one of his considerations of it before proceeding to our own.

According to Lukács, narration is linked to ideology in a complex means-end relationship. On the one hand, ideology alone makes effective narration possible. "Without an ideology," he wrote in 1936, "a writer can neither narrate nor construct a comprehensive, well-organized and multifaceted epic composition." The alternatives to narration, "observation and description," were at best "mere substitutes for a conception of order in life."[5] They were not so much a manifestation of another ideology as rather indices of the effort to repress ideologically inflected consciousness altogether.

On the one hand, then, for Lukács, narration is a manifestation of "ideology" in discourse; narrative discourse is a *means* of ideological production. This view was consonant with that later developed by Braudel and Barthes. But Lukács differed from them in the generally positive value that he assigned to ideology itself in the representation of historical reality. Indeed, Lukács held that it is only by a narrativistic apprehension of reality that the "infinite variety," depth, and epic sweep of human life in history can be grasped in consciousness (144). Thus, it would seem, narrative is not only a *means* of ideological production but also a *mode* of consciousness, a way of viewing the world that conduces to the construction of an ideology. Consequently, narrative discourse does not serve ideology. It produces ideology, and it is ideology that serves a narrativistic apprehension of reality.

Unlike Braudel and Barthes, Lukács did not regard the use of a narrativistic mode of discourse in "realistic" representation, whether in historical or in fictional writing, as an expression of a specific political or even general class perspective. The choice of the narrative mode for the representation of reality indicated, rather, the impulse to engage reality in ideological rather than in nonideological terms. Thus for example, in the case of such conservative writers as Scott, Balzac, and Tolstoy, the predominance of a narrative over a descriptive mode of representation stemmed from the immediacy with which narrative, as against description, would represent historical events: "In Scott, Balzac or Tolstoy we experience events which are inherently significant because of the direct involvement of the characters in the events and because of the general social significance emerging in the unfolding of the characters' lives. We are the audience to events in which the characters take active part. We ourselves experience these events" (116). By contrast, such seemingly progressive writers as Flaubert and Zola undermined their own consciously held ideological convictions in the degree to which they featured "descriptive" over "narrative" representations of events, characters, and situations: "In Flaubert and Zola the characters are merely spectators, more or less interested in the events. As a result, the events themselves become only a tableau for the reader, or, at best, a series of tableaux. We are merely observers" (116). The distinction indicated here, between narration and description, hinges upon the difference between the effect of "experiencing" the events represented in the discourse and that of merely "observing" them. In narrative representation, both the characters in and the readers of the story experience the events from the "inside," whereas in descriptive representation, the events are not "experienced" at all. They are simply "observed" from the "outside" of their occurrence.

It should be noted that in this case, Lukács was not analyzing the difference between "realistic" and "imaginary" (or "historical" and "mythical") discourse, but rather the differences between two kinds of "realistic" fiction. Flaubert and Zola, no less than Scott, Balzac, and Tolstoy, claimed to be representing the world "realistically," though by "fictional" means. The principal difference between the two styles of realism hinged upon the absence of "ideology" in the one and the presence of it in the other. The presence of ideology in the novels of Scott, Balzac, and Tolstoy was signaled by their use of a narrative mode for the representation of reality, while the absence of ideology in Flaubert and Zola was indicated by their tendency to allow "description" to triumph over "narration" in their work.

Now, this view of the matter has interesting implications for any consideration of the relation between storytelling and ideology in historical discourse. In our own cultural moment, the term "ideology" does not carry the same, generally positive connotation that it did for Lukács. For him, it was better to have a "bad" or reactionary ideology than to have no ideology at all. It was not a matter of feigning to have no ideology, since every putatively "objective" or "scientific" worldview feigned the capacity to rise above ideology and to represent reality as it truly was. The principal danger to creative social and political action lay in the impulse to de-ideologize one's experience of the world, which was to say, to adopt the attitude of a purely neutral observer and describer of reality rather than that of an active participant in it. Indeed, this is what "modernism" in general consisted of, in Lukács's view.

Nor was it a matter of "seeing" reality right side up and in true perspective. In literary (and, by extension, historical) representation, Lukács said,

> the opposition between experiencing and observing is not accidental. It arises out of divergent *basic positions about life and about the major problems of society* and not just out of divergent artistic methods of handling content or one specific aspect of content. . . . There are no writers who renounce description absolutely. Nor, on the other hand, can one claim that the outstanding representatives of realism after 1848, Flaubert and Zola, renounced narration absolutely. What is important here are *philosophies of composition*, not any illusory "pure" phenomenon of narration or description. (116; my emphases)

But what does it mean to experience life from the "inside" of "events" and how does a narrative representation of reality produce the effect of experiencing events in a way that is more "realistic" ("truthful," "genuine," "authentic," "verisimilar"—the reader can provide the adjective) than other modes of representation? Evidently, what Lukács meant by narrative representation in literary fiction was nothing other than the representation of the "dramatic" nature of historical reality, the very feature of narration taken by Braudel and Barthes as an index of its ideological (in the bad sense) nature. Thus, for example, Lukács took issue with Flaubert's own critique of his "historical novel," *L'education sentimentale*, for being so "true" to life that it could have neither a "perspective" nor a "climax" (121). "Do 'climaxes' exist in art alone?" Lukács asked. "Of course not," he answered; Flaubert's "belief that 'climaxes' exist only in art and that they are therefore created by artists at will is simply subjective prejudice" (121–22).

Here Lukács raised, only to sweep aside, the crucial question for any consideration of the problem of the relation between historical and ideological storytelling: does life, reality, or history display the same kind of formal attributes as those met with in stories? Do historical agents behave like characters in novels? Do historical processes describe the kinds of trajectories met with in tragedies and comedies? Do historical events or at least some of them have "climactic" significance, turning the general course of history, in the way that certain events function in novels to reveal the "plot" or the "point" of what has happened prior to their occurrence? Or has Lukács fallen victim to a kind of Bovaryism, confusing historical reality with the world represented in a certain kind of literary genre, for example, the epic and possibly even the romance? To raise these questions is to inquire into the kind of coherence that stories in general possess. More specifically, it is to direct attention to the relation between stories and the plots that inform them and give them generic coherence.

## Story and Plot in Historical Narrative

What kind of coherence do stories and especially historical stories typically present? This is a question having to do more with *representation* than with *explanation*. For it is obvious that narrative accounts of real events, whether of individual lives or of complex social processes, do provide a kind of explanation of such events. They explain the events of which they treat by endowing them with the kind of coherence—the structures, tonalities, auras, and meanings—typically met with in "stories." But to put the matter this way is tautologous: it is to suggest that historical storytelling produces a general "story effect" that is grasped by readers as a general "story meaning" as against some other kind of meaning. But I would suggest that there is no such thing as narration-in-general, that there are only different kinds of stories or story types, and that the explanation effect of historical storytelling derives from the kind of coherence with which it endows events by its imposition upon them of a specific plot structure. This is to say that narrative accounts can be said to explain real events by representing them as possessing the coherence of generic plot types—epic, comic, tragic, farcical, and so on. But is this kind of coherence found in reality, or is it imposed upon reality by what we have come to call the technique of *emplotment*?

That the endowment of real events with the kind of coherence that we associate with plots or plot structures is creditable was suggested by Lukács himself when he identified the narrative point of view with that informing the specific literary genre of the epic. While the emplotment of a sequence of real events as an epic, tragedy, or farce is hardly to be considered a scientific explanation thereof, it is nonetheless a kind of explanation. A narrative explanation implicitly invokes principles of classification, characterization, causation, and meaning that are at least analogous to those used in the physical sciences to explain natural events and processes. That such principles are culturally determinate does not deprive them of their authority as explanations.

The problem—as Barthes later insisted—is that the same can be said of both manifestly "fictional" and identifiably "mythical" narrativizations of real events. These too provide explanations of a kind of the events whereof they treat. But this means that one is forced to consider the possibility that any narrative account of historical events remains contaminated by representational practices of a distinctively fictionalizing and mythicalizing kind. And it follows that if accounts of historical reality are to become truly scientific, then such accounts must be purged of any impulse to represent this reality in a generally narrative form. But this conclusion can be said to follow necessarily only if the kind of coherence provided by the imposition of a plot structure—of the sort met with in mythical and fictional discourse—on a given set of historical events has no counterpart in reality.

To pose this last problem is to raise the question of the cognitive status of literary or fictional and, by extension, mythic discourse. If we presume that literature is a purely *imaginary* mode of expression and representation, then of course the issue of the "realism" and veracity of any historical account cast in an identifiably literary form is resolved in advance. Thus, for example, the "epic" plot type, which Lukács took to be the structuring principle (the "philosophy of composition") of all genuinely realistic narration, would have to be taken as an index of the fictionality of any historical account in which it was used to endow historical events with this kind of "generic" coherence. But can we be certain that the apprehension of historical events as possessing the form and manifesting the structures of meaning typically conveyed in such literary genres as the epic, romance, tragedy, comedy, and farce, is mistaken or, as Braudel called it, "a delusive fallacy"? Is it possible, as Lukács might have asked, that not only "climaxes," but also the kinds of *plots* that utilize the "climax" in different ways, *occur* in "reality" or at least in "historical reality," as well as in "fiction" and "myth"?

## Emplotment as Figuration

The plausibility or lifelikeness of fictional representations of imaginary events, their resemblance to the kinds of experiences met with in "real life," is not limited to their depiction of recognizable character types and "possible" situations. It extends as well to their depiction of events as possessing generic plot structures. David Carr has recently argued that narrative representations of historical reality can be considered realistic and veracious to the extent that human agents inhabit a sociocultural world that is structured narrativistically and intend their actions in such a way as effectively to make of them the kinds of actions about which "true" stories can be told. In Carr's view, it is not a matter of historians' *imposing* a narrative form on specific sets of historical events as, rather, of *discovering* the real, lived story of which these events are component elements. In line with Paul Ricoeur's recent work on narrative, Carr argues that human agents *prefigure* their actions as narrative trajectories, such that the outcome of a given action is at least *intended* to be linked to its inauguration in the way that the ending of a story is linked to its beginning.[6] Thus, one meaning of a given sequence of specifically "historical" (as against, say, a sequence of "natural") events, can be said to derive from the "configurative" relations obtaining between the intention motivating an action and its outcome, effects, or consequences. In this view, historical reality differs from natural reality by virtue of the kind of narrative meaning with which the former is endowed by human agents' capacity to structure their actions narrativistically.

A historical-narrative representation of a set of such actions is not, then, to be considered as a product of an arbitrary imposition by the historian of a narrative *form* on what would otherwise be a non-narrative *content*. Carr accepts Ricoeur's view that every historical representation cast in the mode of a narrative discourse constitutes a "refiguration" of action sequences. But he concludes that historiographical "refigurations" should not be accounted as "fictional" insofar as the narrative forms they ascribe to sequences of events are inherent in the structures of the events themselves. In other words, historical narratives should not be considered as "allegorizations" of the events of which they speak—as Braudel and Barthes (and others, including myself) have suggested—but rather should be viewed as *literal* accounts thereof. As thus envisaged, historical narrative is a peculiar kind of discourse, the product of a process of verbal *figuration* that insofar as the story told conforms to the outline of the story lived in real life, is to be taken as *literally* true.

If we accepted this line of analysis, we could then conclude that historical storytelling is neither inherently ideological nor exactly scientific in nature, nor even a mixture of the two, but rather some third kind of discourse especially suited to the representation of that one animal which not only *tells* stories but *lives* them as well. If that were the case, the task of the historian would be what it has always been thought to be, namely, to discover the "real" story or stories that lie embedded within the welter of "facts" and to retell them as truthfully and completely as the documentary record permits.

I am inclined to credit Carr's account of the cognitive authority of narrative representations of historical reality and even the view, which Carr shares with Lukács (and also with Mink, Danto, Ricoeur, Jameson, and others), that narrative is a distinct cognitive mode rather than *only* a form of discourse. But the notion that narrative explains events by "configuring" them as stories is still too general to aid us in our effort to distinguish between historical and ideological storytelling. One can think and speak "narratologically" while telling many different kinds of "stories" about the same set of events. And this suggests that we might profitably distinguish between a narratological *mode* of thought and speech, on the one side, and the various *techniques* of narration, such as characterization, thematization, and emplotment, on the other.

## Generic Plot Types in Historical Narration

Narrators typically (though not always) *emplot* the events of which they speak. This means that they do not tell a story-in-general, but always a story of a specific kind (or a mixture of different kinds of stories). In other words, historical narrators often claim to find in the events of which they speak the forms of one or another of the *plot structures* typically met with in the different genres of artistic fiction, myth, fable, and legend. In historiography, this activity of emplotment can generate alternative and even mutually exclusive interpretations of the same set of phenomena—as when, for example, what one historian has emplotted as an epic or tragedy is emplotted by another as a farce. And it is here, in what appears to be the projection of a given generic plot type onto a given set of historical events, rather than in the choice of a narrative as against a non-narrative discursive mode, that the question of the ideological nature of historical storytelling can be said to arise. In sum, the question of the ideological content of narrative representations of reality hinges on the cognitive authority of the various generic story types available within a given cultural endowment for the provision of real events with a distinctive kind of story meaning, not on the cognitive authority of the narrative mode of speaking about the world.

Thus we might conclude that the ideological content of a specific historical account can be said to consist not so much in the discursive mode in which it is cast as in the dominant plot structure chosen to endow the events spoken of with the form of a recognizable story type. Theorists of historiography have long recognized the ideological nature of certain "master narratives" (what Lyotard calls "grands recits"), which purport to disclose the "Weltplan" or overarching "meaning of history." The classical concept of Fate, the Christian doctrine of Providence, the bourgeois notion of Progress, and the Marxist vision of the world-historical destiny of the Proletariat are cases in point. But within the main line of historical thought in the West, there has always been a tradition of "critical" historical writing, both narrative and analytical, that has laid claim to a certain scientificity or at least to a certain kind of realism in virtue of its resistance to such totalizing conceptions of historical reality. Indeed, critical historiography purports to gain its status as a kind of science precisely by its repudiation of the neat schemata of such "philosophies of history" at the level of concrete historical detail. Traditionally, evidence of professional historians' capacity to resist the seduction of all "master narratives" is provided by their reluctance to deal with "history in general" and to confine themselves to the production of "small narratives" of local and, as it were, regional domains of the historical totality.

However, whether the historian limits herself to the investigation of a finite domain of historical occurrence and to the production of a "small" rather than of a "grand" account thereof, if she decides to cast her account in the form of a story, she must still tell a story of a specific kind (or mixture of specific kinds of stories). This means that she must emplot the events according to the principles informing the structures of distinctive story types or genres. Otherwise the account will not be recognizable as a story and will not provide the kind of understanding or explanation of the events that storytelling, among the various narrational techniques available to the culture of which she is a member, can alone provide. What are we to do with two or more narrative accounts of what, *grosso modo*, appear to be the same set or sequence of historical events, when the stories told about them are manifestly different, contradictory, or even mutually exclusive?

This formulation of the question concerning the nature of narrative explanations of historical phenomena permits us to address the problem of the relation between historical and ideological storytelling in terms of the relative adequacy of different generic plot types to the representation of real events. Thus, for example, instead of locating the problem of the ideological content of historical accounts at the level of their factual accuracy, we are now licensed to ask such questions as the following: Is the emplotment of a set of historical events as an epic inherently more "realistic" and "truthful" (as Lukács thought) than an emplotment of the same set of events as a romance or comedy? Are comic representations of historical events ethically more responsible than tragic representations (as Hegel thought)? Or is it a matter of the common "fictional" nature of all such modes of emplotment? Does the use in a historical narrative of techniques of emplotment, typically met with in myth, fiction, fable, and legend for the representation of "imaginary" events, indicate that the account is more "ideological" than "historical" in nature? Or is it a matter of choosing a specific plot type for the representation of a discrete set of historical events because those events display the form and therefore can be said to possess a meaning of the sort that this particular plot type and no other can adequately represent? Questions such as these permit us to locate the question of the ideological content of historical storytelling at the level of the figurative meaning of the discourse, rather than at the level of its literal factuality.

## Ideology and Plot Type in Historical Narrative

The relevance of this notion of the ideological content of historical storytelling to current discussions of the relation between historical narration and ideology can be suggested by cursory reference to a recent review by C. Vann Woodward of Eli Evans's life of Judah P. Benjamin, a Jewish member of Jefferson Davis's Confederate cabinet during the American Civil War. After summarizing the gripping story of Benjamin's life as told by Evans, Woodward suddenly interrupts his paraphrase of the story told, in order to register the following, seemingly cautionary remarks regarding the appeal of the tale: "But this is an outrageously romantic and improbable tale that few properly scientific and up-to-date historians would likely deem worthy of serious attention. It is very largely concerned with doings of the elite and advances no good cause being currently promoted. Moreover, it is a story told by means of old-fashioned traditional narrative, tests no hypotheses, and employs no approved analytical techniques."[7] Note that Woodward's characterization of the reasons for which Evans's story might not appeal to "scientific and up-to-date historians" has to do, first, with what it contains ("it is concerned with the doings of the elite") and what it does not contain (it "advances no good cause being currently promoted . . . tests no hypotheses . . . employs no approved analytical techniques"). This suggests that the book's contents consist of "facts" ("doings of the elite") rather than of facts plus a certain kind of scientific demonstration or argument and/or ideology (it "advances no good cause being currently promoted"). Yet Woodward astutely discriminates between these two orders of possible content (facts and arguments) and two orders of the form of Evans's account: generic ("an outrageously romantic . . . tale") and modal ("it is a story told by old-fashioned traditional narrative"). Unless we attended to these distinctions, we might find it difficult to credit Woodward's judgment on the truthfulness of Evans's representation of Benjamin's life. For he at once grants it the status of a literary fiction ("an outrageously romantic tale") and absolves it from the kind of distortion we normally associate with ideological special pleading seeking to pass for a simple relating of events "as they really happened." Thus Woodward writes: "Granting all this, I am persuaded that what is told us actually happened and that it happened pretty much, as far as I can see, as the author tells it."

Woodward seems to be suggesting that certain kinds of events, in this case "the doings of the elite" recounted in Evans's history, are appropriately emplotted as a romantic tale—that, in a word, the structure of the romance plot type can be used to represent truthfully and to explain adequately "what really happened" for at least *certain* domains of historical reality. Thus the events are conceived to be narratable because they comprise a story actually lived, and the story is justifiably emplotted as a romance because the *story actually lived* was a romantic kind of story. Indeed, Woodward suggests that, had Evans used another plot type, he might very well have been unable to tell a story fully adequate to the specific set of events he wished to represent. To be sure, Woodward does not go this far; he merely indicates that the romance plot type was a suitable vehicle for a veracious representation of the life of Judah Benjamin and of the "doings of the elite" whose story he wished to tell. But in so indicating, Woodward directs our attention to the problem of the veracity of generic plot types in general and to the question of the status of figurations of historical events as instantiations of generic plot structures effected by the technique of emplotment in historical representation.

Arguably, the ideological element in historical storytelling could be viewed as the misrepresentation of the plot type a given set of historical events *actually* possessed. Thus, for example, in a late preface to his *Eighteenth Brumaire of Louis Bonaparte*, Marx criticizes Hugo and Proudhon for their misrepresentation of the plot informing the cycle of events that comprised the Revolution(s) of 1848–51 in France. In his view, they erred by making Louis Napoléon, the protagonist of the events, in the one case "great" and in the other "heroic." The error was a product of a certain kind of historical "objectivity" that takes events at their face value as facts. Thus Marx writes that Proudhon "falls into the error of our so-called *objective* historians," whereas "I, on the contrary, demonstrate how . . . circumstances and relationships . . . make it possible for a grotesque mediocrity to play a hero's part."[8] It is not Bonaparte's triumph, but its absurdity that has to be accounted for. And it is accounted for in at least two ways: a demonstration of how "the *class struggle*" produced these "circumstances and relationships" and the emplotment of the concatenation of events as a farce. This emplotment of the events as a *farce* should not be viewed as merely a rhetorical ornament of the argument, but as a figurative representation of the events in such a way that poses the problem of historical analysis for which the formal argument will provide a solution.

Were the events leading up to the coup d'etat of 1851 truthfully characterized as a "farce"? Is the characterization of these events as a farce to be taken literally or is it only a matter of a figure of speech? Does the emplotment of these events as a farce add to our understanding of "what really happened" in France between February 1948 and December 1851? Is it only a matter of Marx's genius as a rhetorician and polemicist, a question of his "literary" style? Or is it, rather, that Marx has himself "ideologically" distorted the events in the way that he accused Hugo and Proudhon of doing, though in a different, more "ironic" manner?

## Literal and Figurative Meanings in Historical Narrative

Consideration of these kinds of questions returns us to the problem of the relation between the literal and the figurative dimensions of historical discourse in general and of historical narrative in particular. If storytelling can be said to endow historical events with a figurative meaning by emplotting them in terms of a generic story type, does this mean that historical stories cannot be held to criteria of truthfulness and consistency that we would use for assessing their factual and explanatory contents? If such were the case, we might be able to conclude that the ideological element in historical representations consists, first, in the substitution of figurative for literalist representations of events and, second, in the specific figurations used to endow events with meanings that they do not *in fact* possess.

As we have noted above, such indeed was the argument advanced by semiotic-structuralist analysts of historical ideologization such as Barthes.

Ideology or, as Barthes preferred to call it, "mythical thought," worked in historical representation by surreptitiously substituting a Signified (a specific conceptual content treated as an essence, such as "Frenchness" or "Woman" or "Italianicity") for the Referent (such as "the citizens of France," "a specific group of women," "Italian cuisines or clothing styles," etc.) it pretended merely to describe. This covert substitution of a putative "essence" for a concrete historical reality *was* ideology, in this semiotic view of the nature of ideological production. Thus it would follow that the ideological element in Marx's representation of Louis Bonaparte consists in his attribution to Louis Bonaparte's coup d'etat of a kind of essential "farcicality." And the same would go for Evans's life of Judah Benjamin: it would have to be considered an ideological representation insofar as it endowed the "doings of the elite" with a kind of essential "romanticality."

But it seems evident that Marx at least intended his "farce" to be taken both figuratively and literally. In other words, the characterization of these events as a farce was intended to be taken as "substantially" true. It is a matter less of metaphysical "essences" than of what the Danish linguist Louis Hjelmslev has called "the Substance of the Content" of all discourses more extensive than the single predicative sentence.[9]

## Levels of Analysis of the Historical Story

The significance of Hjelmslev's work for the problem of distinguishing between historical and ideological storytelling consists of his multiplanar theory of discourse. In place of the simple opposition between the literal and the figurative levels of a discourse, Hjelmslev constructs a dual-binary model. First, he distinguishes between the "Expression" level and the "Content" level of a discourse. Then he proceeds to distinguish further between the "Form" and the "Substance" of both. This model has the advantage, for any analysis of the cognitive content of "historical stories," of allowing us to specify the differences between the *two kinds of referentiality*, literal and figurative, which will be present within such stories. Put most briefly, Hjelmslev's model allows us to say that the "story" told about a given set of historical events unfolds at the level of the "Form of Content" of the discourse, whereas what we have called emplotment can be seen to operate at the level of its "Substance of Expression."

On this view, a historical story can be adjudged literally true in the extent to which the "Form of [its] Content" (the story told) "corresponds" to the form of the historical referent (the *facts* of the matter diachronically

73

organized). At the same time, however, the story told can be said to endow historical events with a figurative meaning by endowing them with the structure of a generic plot type, such as farce, romance, tragedy, and so on, at the level of its "Substance of Expression." At the latter level, the criterion to be employed in assessing the truth-value of the historical story is not so much that of literal correspondence as, rather, that of verisimilitude or plausibility. At the level of the "Substance of Expression," historical events are endowed with plot meaning by complex operations of figuration. We can say that at this level historical events are endowed with figurative meaning by being encoded as elements of a generic story type. At this level of narrativization, it is not a question of the outline of a generic plot type corresponding to the form of the events that constitute the referent of the discourse. It is a question, rather, of the plausibility of the plot type chosen to endow events with a specific kind of figurative meaning (epic, tragic, comic, farcical, romantic, as the case might be).

This may appear to be a needlessly complicated way of speaking about such a seemingly "natural" activity as "storytelling." But there is nothing natural about storytelling; it is a highly complex art—or craft, depending on how you look at it. And its use is especially complex when it is a matter of representing real, rather than imaginary, events. This is because, whereas the writer of fictions can "invent" events to conform to the exigencies of storytelling, the writer of a history enjoys no such inventive freedom. Since the events of a historical story are given by research into the historical record, the inventive freedom of the writer of a narrative history consists of the choices that can be made among culturally provided plot types by which to endow the events with different kinds of figurative meaning. In fact, historians can tell many different kinds of stories about the same set of real events without in any way violating criteria of truthfulness at the level of the representation of the facts of the matter.

Hjelmslev's complex multiplanar model of discursivity thus permits us to identify the relationship between the "factual" content of a historical story, on one hand, and what is usually called its "interpretive" (and more derogatorily, its "ideological") content, on the other. The "factual" content is encountered at the level of the "Form of the Content" (in the "facts" registered), whereas the latter appears at the level of the "Substance of Expression" (in the plot type used to endow the events of the story with a specific symbolic meaning). The story told is appropriately assessed according to its "factuality," while the plot type used to generate an interpretation of the events can only be properly assessed in terms of its plausibility.

Consider, for example, what happened in the 1988 primary elections for the Democratic Party's nominee for president of the United States. Senator Joseph Biden was forced to withdraw from the contest when it was shown that he (or his aides) had stolen the "story" of British Labour leader Neal Kennock's life and passed it off as Biden's own life story. It would have been quite another matter had Biden merely adopted the "plot" of Kennock's life and used it to endow his own life story with a general symbolic significance. American politicians regularly use the "plot" of Abraham Lincoln's life (simple man of the people rises from obscurity by hard work and self-education to attain the highest office in the land and to lead the country in a time of crisis) for the representation of the "meaning" of their own lives. It would be quite improper for them to use Lincoln's "story" to tell their own life history. Biden's media advisers failed to distinguish between the Form of the Content of the senator's life and the Substance of Expression that they wished to use in its representation.

It might be objected that Hjelmslev's terminology does little more than translate what we are accustomed to call "story" and "plot" into the jargon of linguistics. But that is not the case at all. I have said nothing about the two levels of discursivity Hjelmslev designated as "Form of Expression" and "Substance of Content." By the term "Form of Expression" Hjelmslev designates the specifically linguistic features of a verbal discourse such as the historical narrative: lexical, grammatical, and syntactical. At the level of analysis thus indicated, we would have to ask whether "historical" and "ideological" discourse are discriminable by their linguistic features alone. And of course they are not thus discriminable. It is because the two kinds of discourse have the same or similar linguistic features that we are forced to confront the problem of the relationship between "ideological" and "historical" stories in the first place. Ideological storytelling *looks like* historical storytelling in its manifest form. Ideological discourse *refers* to historical events, *tells stories* about these events, purports to tell the *true story* of these events, tries to *explain* why they happened as they did, and, finally, claims to reveal the *real historical significance* of these events. In a word, at the level of formal exposition, the Form of Expression, an ideological story is *exactly like* the historical story.

And so too at the level of Substance of Expression. Here the ideological story works exactly like the historical story, which is to say, it transforms "facts" into the elements of a specific story type by complex operations of figuration, poetic and rhetorical in nature. Historical events, agents, and agencies are "characterized" in dramatistic terms and presented as if they were the kinds of things met with in manifestly "fictional" genres: fables, legends, myths, novels, plays, and the like. At this level of analysis, the *identity* of historical with ideological stories, argued for by Braudel and Barthes, can be affirmed. And it is possible to argue that there is no difference at all between the two kinds of discourse.

For example, at this level, that of Substance of Expression, it is impossible to distinguish between Proudhon's and Marx's representations of the coup d'état of Louis Bonaparte and, at the same time, specify the ideological elements in both accounts. Both Marx and Proudhon have emplotted the event as a story of a specific kind. The difference consists only in the *kind* of plot structure, epical and farcical respectively, chosen by each to represent the event. In both cases, we witness the deposition of a meaning at the level of the Form of Content, which consists of the plot structure used to represent events as figurations of a story of a specific kind. What one sees as an epic, the other sees as farce. Both interpretations are plausible, given the difference of political perspective informing them. We cannot, then, conclude that the story told by Marx is more historical than ideological, whereas the story told by Proudhon is more ideological than historical. If there is a difference between the degrees of historicality informing the two accounts of the same event, this must be said to arise at the fourth level of analysis stipulated by Hjelmslev's model: that of the Substance of Content.

## Substance of Content and Ideology

It is only at the level of the Substance of the Content of the discourse that the difference between historical and ideological storytelling can be established. At this level the representation of real events, emplotted as a story of a specific kind (as epic, romance, tragedy, comedy, or farce) can be identified as a special case of a general notion of the nature of historical reality. It is on this level of his narrative that Marx, for example, invokes the "class struggle" as the historical reality that at once justifies his emplotment of the *Eighteenth Brumaire of Louis Bonaparte* as a *farce* and explains why this farce could have taken place when, where, and how it did. On Marx's view, the farcical nature of the event derived from the failure of *all* parties in the conflict to discern that they were engaged in a *class* conflict and their resultant incapacity to act in a manner consistent with their respective class interests. Proudhon's failure to apprehend that class struggle was the key to the understanding of this event is what drove him, in Marx's estimation, to fall back upon the mythical notion of the "hero" to explain Louis Bonaparte's triumph. For Marx, the notion of "heroic" action could "explain" nothing, and the invocation of this notion by Proudhon to explain Louis Bonaparte's triumph is what marks Proudhon's "story" as "ideological" rather than "historical."

In what sense might we confidently affirm that the notion of the "hero" or that of "heroic action" is more "ideological" (and therefore less "historical") than the notion of "class struggle"? The usual response to this question, especially by Marxists, is that the notion of "class struggle" is more realistic, less "imaginary" (less "mythical") than the notion of "heroism." But wherein does the "realism" of the notion of "class struggle" consist? It is not as if the notion of "heroism" is alien to Marx's notion of history. Indeed, it must be said that Marx's characterization of the role of the proletariat in world history effectively endows this social class with all of the attributes of a "hero" (albeit a collective one).

But, and this is crucial to the distinction between a historical and an ideological account of historical events, Marx indicates that a class can be "heroic" in one phase of its development, become, as it were, "villainous" in another, and simply be swept from the scene in yet another. Whence the acuity of his observation that the bourgeoisie played a heroic role in the "tragic" events of 1789 only to become the protagonist of a "farce" in its attempt to re-play the events of 1789 under the changed conditions of 1848. Unlike the notion of "heroism" used by Proudhon to explain the triumph of Louis Bonaparte, Marx's notion of "class struggle" is susceptible to being endowed with different specific contents at different times and places in history. This is one reason for considering the former as a mythical and the latter a historical concept.

Thus, although Marx's "farce" is not less "ideological" than Proudhon's "epic"—or for that matter, Marx's own suggestion that the events of 1789 were "tragic" in nature—the "Substance of the Content" of Marx's account is more historical than that of Proudhon's account. This is not because the historical record contains no accounts of heroic actions by individuals and groups. It is, rather, because a view of history centered upon actions, individuals, and groups considered to be more or less heroic provides no basis for discriminating between heroes and those individuals and groups which, as Marx put it with respect to Louis Bonaparte and his followers, only played the "parts" of heroes.

Considered as the "Substance of the Content" of Marx's conception of history, the notion of "class struggle" is of an entirely different order from Proudhon's notion of "heroism." Whatever the merits of this notion when considered as an explanatory principle of a determinate set of historical events, there is nothing ideological about it at all. This is indicated by the fact that the reality of class struggle is presumed by all historians of every conceivable kind of political persuasion or ideological orientation. Beyond that, this notion provides for the stipulation of a principle by which to admit the reality of heroic actions on the part of individuals and groups and at the same time to discriminate between genuinely heroic achievements and those that only appear to be so. For unlike a notion of heroism that identifies it with a kind of spiritual superiority of one person over all others, the notion of class struggle links heroism, not with an ideal of individual success in a particular line of endeavor, but rather with the global effort of humanity to achieve the conditions of freedom from both natural necessity and social division.

## Being Done with Narrative by Cubism and André Malraux

There is no end without a beginning. How does one know whether the end is an end, if one is not narrating it? The account of the end of a time is told in a new time that conserves this ending and, even in that way, presents itself as a beginning. The relationship of our thought to succession forbids it to immobilize movement at *an instant without continuation*. The end naively presents itself as a limit, but thought immediately crosses this limit to assure itself that the far side is indeed not of the same nature as this side.

Thought itself is carried in succession, but it enjoys the faculty of representing to itself at every moment what is no longer there and what is not yet there. The hand of the clock approaches the end of the century; thought continues to remember and imagine. The turn of the millennium will surely not put an end to this capacity to bring into the present, the past, and the future.

The relationship between the power to dialecticize duration and the mechanical succession of temporal units on the clock is analogous to the relationship of the narrative voice to a narrated story. It's a disjunctive relationship: the voice and the story do not belong to the same temporality. However, this disjunction is inclusive, since the diegesis needs the voice in order to be constituted into the story, and since the story, that which is recounted by one voice, will not fail to count this voice and its account in the number

Translated by Leonard Hinds.

of episodes and at the hour of its clock. Yet, this inclusion keeps intact the heterogeneity of the two planes, the one where things take place, and the other where they are recounted.

I shall call *modern* (from the Latin *modo*, exactly just now) the decision in one bound, which disorders the heterogeneity I just referred to. The voice leaps into the course of events and decides that they begin with this leap. The voice thus marks the moment zero from which the succession from now on will be counted. But, more important, the voice itself subjects itself to the time of the clock, thus sacrificing, so it seems, its representative privilege (transtemporal) to the arbitrariness of raw succession, in which every moment erases the preceding one and erases itself before the following one. The voice exposes itself to the risk of this oblivion; it accepts death. But also, it insufflates its narrative power into the course of ordinary time; it transmutes the blind cycle of hours, of seasons and generations into the narration of its own odyssey. An eschatology begins: the voice, which has been dropped into the story and which withstands its test, will reveal its truth at the end. The final word here assumes the meaning of an accomplishment, the completion of a work. One thing will begin, another reign, from which the time of the story and its suffering will be absent.

The modern leap invents a temporality unknown in antiquity. The voice is incarnated, and it promises the final accomplishment by evil's redemption. Such is the christic mystery elaborated by Paul of Tarsus and Augustine and extending through two millennia of thought and practice in the Occident. The various modernities coming after this first period repeat the unbelievable gesture: "Here's my body," the voice says, "here and now." "To possess the truth in one soul and in one body," restates Rimbaud. The same ostentation in the American and French Declarations: we, the free people; and in the Bolshevik Revolution: the power to the Councils of Workers (Soviets), right here and right now.

In each case, the voice announcing its birth to history also invites a new patience and other sacrifices: torment, more work, waiting. But this time, as they say again, it will not be in vain. However, the word has hardly made itself flesh when the latter becomes a symbol in the Eucharist. The testimonies of the apparition remain like legends. One interprets the slowness taken by the actualization of the promise. One discusses the interpretations. One imputes to them the responsibility of the *deferred*. The war of all against all takes place again, and with it the chaotic and desperately cyclic course of history. One wrangles the authority from a voice extinct from then on; one speaks in its name, in absentia. Stalin embalms Lenin and has Trotsky assassinated.

The body of history, once pardoned, at the moment of the epiphany, remains without a voice, handed over to the insignificance of its natural course, to the indifferent imbecility of deaths and regenerations, to the eternal return of noons and midnights. That is why the Occident must repeat the gesture of its modernity. But it cannot see to it that in the long term the new does not become old and that the presence of the voice does not become inaudible. At every turn, the beginning is forgotten and, with it, the promise of completion. A century has already passed since Nietzsche pronounced the funerary oration of modernity: God, that is to say the Voice incarnated in history, is dead; it's been more than half a century since Valéry diagnosed the Western "crisis of the mind": our civilization is mortal like the others; and since Spengler, in *The Decline of the West*, reimmersed the modern gesture, like a moment from then on obsolete, in the indifferent cycle to which human cultures are subject like every organism and every animal species is.

This reiterated invitation to bury the voice is perhaps premature, not to say precipitated. A Hasidic story says that even if one has forgotten prayer, even if one has forgotten what is asked for, even if one has forgotten the circumstances in which it was to be done, one can still recount this series of acts of forgetting and "that suffices." This narration scans every oversight with an "it suffices" so that the oversight be told. To honor the presence of the voice is still to narrate that it is lost. It suffices that Kafka's Josephine faintly whistles what the multitude of mice once learned to sing and what they no longer remember, for her to obtain a precarious renown. Counter to all modernity, the Jewish narrative relates that the voice has never been heard *in vivo*; that one only has its written *statement*, mute, consisting solely of consonants, to be deciphered; that the Aleph itself is barely a breath, an opening of the throat when it *prepares to voice*. The Western modernities persecuted, as they should have, this melancholic and funny prudence. They sought even to forget it absolutely. That is called the Final Solution, *Endlösung*, and it attempted to make itself forgotten.

Long before our century, modernity saw narratives appear in which the status of the narrative voice is put into question. Cervantes's *Don Quixote* recounts an epic whose ending is missing from the very beginning, and in that very way it deprives the voice telling this epic of its authority over the meaning of the story. If this voice does not lead to the glory of its completion, to the *fama*, then the voice relating this misprision must confess its own *infama*. Borges deployed, in virtue of this infamy, the paradoxical implications that result from it for various instances of modern narration. The distinct determination of the narrator, of the author, and of the reader is a matter of suspicion. The diegetic reality is not very discernible from the "reality effect" produced by narration. So is the modern axiom: that the flesh is not the word, and that the latter must be mysteriously incarnated in the former for the story to begin; it's this axiom of "pre-historic" separation that Borges neutralizes by his dialectic, when he thus forbids any relief in the eschatological promise.

The last great modern novel is *Remembrance of Things Past*. The voice immanent in the story, in the whole course of the narration, reveals itself at the end in the glory of its recovered authority. The book already written in the immanence of worldly vanities, but written only by *impressions*, must be written, that is to say, translated into the language that *knows itself*. *Time Regained* is the fulfillment of the promise to conquer the suffering of time that the voice, incarnated in the story since the beginning, made.

However, at the same time, Joyce's *Ulysses* shows how much memory's means, I mean *language* itself, are missing from then on in the assemblage, in the *remembering*, of even a vulgar Odyssey. The mourning over narration becomes even worse in *Finnegans Wake*, or in Beckett. The voice, which Proust supposed to be immanent in the story, is extinguished. Interior life, quite far from composing the secret book that narration has the duty to publish, is an effect of this narration. Autobiography is a kind of fictional genre. Such will be the anti-Proustian axiom, that of the *Anti-memoirs* of Malraux.

A brief detour is necessary before coming to him. A recurrent motif in the work of Malraux, that of Evil, namely, that of Satan, does not proceed from the sole suspicion that the modern voice, whether Christian or humanist, never again makes itself heard. Malraux himself loves in Bernanos the violence with which a Christian today can suspect the worst: that Satan's voice can come to substitute itself for that of Jesus, even in prayer and in grace. Thomas Mann's *Doktor Faustus*, written at the end of the Second World War, is perhaps even closer to the evil that obsesses Malraux. The narrative voice, having lost all authority (the authority it still had in *Buddenbrooks*), has not only fallen into infamy, but it can no longer be anything but "whispered" by the Devil. Being infamous, it is not only without glory, but being *abject*, it is also rejected by divine glory. To tell a story when there is no longer any narration possible is to lie, to pose as the creator, to obey pride alone in wanting the power nevertheless. The voice speaking in Leverkuhn's music or in the politics of the Third Reich creates a fiction of itself by making a fiction of the work or of history. The end of modernity consists in persuading us that modern eschatology is not finished, while the Occident despairs of its endings and its beginnings. A demoniac cynicism offers this despair recourse to a *myth*, in the postmodern sense, to a narration in which the origin and the beginning are given as fictions, but which suffices for the will to continue to *will itself*. Falseness thus comes to offer itself as the veritable value when the truth promised by the narration of redemption or emancipation has shown itself to be powerless. In *Literature and Evil* or in *Interior Experience*, Georges Bataille makes explicit the motif of a literary or spiritual, *sovereign* act that only takes its authority from its insubordination to all other voices but its own. But what is the Self which speaks in this voice? Bataille, at any rate, does not elude that question. Neither does Malraux.

In 1920, Malraux publishes his first article: "Concerning the Origins of Cubist Poetry." He names his masters: Apollinaire, Max Jacob, Reverdy, and Cendrars. He makes cubist poetics his own, such as Max Jacob decided it to be in the preface of *The Dice Box*. As Mallarmé taught it, the work is a casting of the dice thrown into the haphazard of the night. The work does not abolish the nothingness of the story; it thereby ventures an improbable *deal*, which blind chance has not made up yet.

The work "does not mean anything"; it is a singular, unexpected arrangement of elements that constitute it: the words in literature, the colors and forms in painting. It does not correspond to any reference, history, event, or perceptible reality that would be previous to it. It does not express in any way the subjectivity of its "author." No representation at all, no expression at all. And nothing symbolic either: it does not signify preexisting "ideas." No signification at all, no celebration either. Max Jacob baptizes it a "prose poem," what Baudelaire was perhaps seeking and did not find. The work is prosaic because it takes its elements from ordinary language, just as cubist painting borrows its own from the prose of the visible. It's poetic or poematic because its words, perfectly unset, outside of any context, of any use, and grouped in a tiny, dense, hard mass—like a "jewel," says Max Jacob—have the value of "*facts*."

This art is directly opposed to the surrealist belief that the unconscious is the master of the work and that automatic writing of or the haphazardness of collages must let the unconscious create it. "The unconscious," Malraux will say forty years later, "is confusion itself." A psychoanalysis, he will repeat, is more violent than any confession, but it is not a work of art. The prose poem is without a doubt a throw of the dice; however, each face of each little cube the dice or the word possesses must be deprived of its "numerical," that is semantic or referential, value. Such is the work of style, according to Max Jacob: "The style or will creates, that is to say separates." The style is not man, as Buffon used to say; it's his elimination. "Artists today," wrote Apollinaire in *The Cubist Painters*, "have to make themselves inhuman." Max Jacob adds to the demand of style that of *situation*: "The situation distances, that is to say incites one to artistic emotion." And he thus comments on the twofold demand: "One recognizes that a work has style in that it gives the sensation of closure; one recognizes that it is situated by the small shock one receives, or better yet by the margin surrounding it, by the special atmosphere in which it stirs." The style or will is the "use of material and the composition of the whole." The situation of the work is what removes it from the avid reader's impatience to appropriate it for himself: it puts in his way a "spiritual margin," and this delay, necessary for artistic emotion, does not in any way arise from an aesthetic of surprise (or from shock, in the Baudelairian sense), nor from a seductive maneuver. It results from the autonomy, let us not say the transcendence, of the prose poem in relation to all motivation. Let us say: to its autography.

We see the cubist proceed in the opposite direction of the modern gesture. If there is any voice, it's that which inscribes itself in the work and emanates from it, and the stylistic will has delineated it from its incarceration in life. It is necessary to silence the cacophony of infamous voices that intrigue, that recount their miserable stories, in the world and even in the soul. There was undoubtedly in Max Jacob himself the secret hope that this poetic would reach an *epiphany*. Didn't he have the vision of Jesus appearing one day on the wall of his bedroom?

Pierre Reverdy, whom Malraux prefers in comparison, refuses to accept this soteriology: it's far too final. At the same time that Braque notes in his *Carnets* that painting has no other objective than to allow the "pictorial *fact*," Reverdy writes that the only value of the poem consists in being "*a poetic fact*." No revelation, no less any consolation, it is *there* in the absoluteness of its impenetrable presence. This "*there*" is neither a location in space, nor a moment in historical time. The "poetic fact" is not a human, social, psychical, or historical fact; it is not natural and it is not supernatural. It has the violence of an event: the pure occurrence of a group of words, previous to its capture in explanatory or interpretive discourses; the simple enigma that *there are* words.

We are tempted to add: "and that suffices." But that would be alleging a finality, judging a work fit for testifying that the voice is not lost. Yet the prose poem is a *fact*, it is not evidence. It ignores the rhetorics of modernity. Malraux immediately tries his hand at it. He writes and publishes *Paper Moons*, dedicated to Max Jacob, then still other texts, even after *The Temptation of the West*. Those are failures, or rather, as he says it himself, errors. Instead of the sober density of the prose poem, they're a display of fantastic situations meant to surprise, and they're the narration of a kind of negative epic: their heros are the Sins; under the command of Pride, they plot to kill Death, which is what they do; but at the end, they have forgotten why they did it. One only sees too well what this "bizarre" story owes to the anguish of the declining moderns, and how little it obeys the style and situation demanded by cubist poetics.

I shall therefore not maintain, contrary to all evidence, that Malraux is a cubist writer. He was, from the beginning until his death, much too haunted by the infamy and abjection of the modernity that was contemporary with him. But I do maintain that both his novels and his essays on art, and even the funerary orations, do nothing but confront the nihilist desperation of the century with the poetics of style and situation elaborated by Max Jacob, or better still with the enigma of the poetic or artistic *fact* discerned by Reverdy and Braque. This is the way Malraux reads the *Confession of Staroguine*: even in the worst abjection, the *fact* of this confession and the *style* that is his are still possible. And I will add that this cubist affiliation, which is apparent in Malraux's novelistic essayist themes, also fashions the way he writes.

One may object that a novelist, who tells stories, cannot be a cubist. Indeed, the narration escapes the reality effect with difficulty; it subjects words to their referential use; and, more important, it organizes their content following a development which progresses from its beginning to its end and thus gives the sense of an eschatology. In short, narration is eloquent, whereas the cubist "jewel" is mute like a *fact*. However, it is important to note that Malraux's corpus that is narrative in the proper sense only includes five novels; the first book, *The Temptation of the West*, is an essay in letters; after 1939, from *The Walnut Trees of Altenberg* to *The Mirror of Limbo* and *Precarious Man and Literature*, published at the time of his death, not to mention the funerary orations, the reading notes and the prefaces, Malraux does not write a novel. He does nothing but obstinately meditate, to the point of scrutiny, on the poetic *fact*, which is artistic as well as political (I shall come back to this point in a moment).

But it is especially the novels themselves that fail to satisfy the dual norm of the incarnated voice and the teleological story. It's not that they relate negative adventures (*Hope* alone is perhaps an exception, but I have my doubts); first, it's because they relate very little, rather they *show*. Jean Carduner has demonstrated, and Malraux has repeated, that the novels' characters have little intrinsic consistency, that they are above all the protagonists of critical *scenes*, and that the narration makes way for the staging of dramatic moments. These moments can be dialogues or actions; the drama they show is always the battle of *poetic* power (in the broad sense of the power of the work) against the indifferent and undifferentiated repetition of the course of things: death, life, the same, which in Malraux's work is called destiny.

The novels are montages of "shots" (in the cinematographic sense), carefully edited (that is to say, "styled" and "situated" in the terms of Max Jacob), taken from certain angles and in precise lighting, filling a determined duration (which is generally brief). They are always centered, may I repeat, on a *crisis*. The theme of this crisis can vary: a battle, a murder, sex, incarceration, torture, art, the crisis can take place as a described action or in a reported discussion; it always consists of a convulsion of a *will* grappling with the threat of being engulfed in abject repetition, of a will looking for its *means*. *Will* and *means*, I remind you, are the major terms in Max Jacob's poetics.

In relation with the critical scene, the characters are only actors, who are limitlessly interchangeable (Malraux makes a point of it several times on the subject of murder in Dostoyevsky's *The Idiot*), otherwise they are figures, even mere "factors." They are only there to show that the poetic *fact* is always possible, even when the context makes it more than improbable. And the montage of scenes does not so much obey historical succession as it obeys the demonstration that the precarious metamorphosis of reality into the work has been attempted. This will be the motif of his essays on art and of the *Mirror of Limbo*, which will be likewise staged according to the principle of ordering critical shots. One understands to what degree the objections made to these books, for neglecting historical reality, have left the cubist indifferent. His objective is never to represent givens faithfully; it consists in questioning the enigma of their metamorphosis into a work, and this metamorphosis *already* operates in the presentation, by Malraux's work, of this questioning.

One must however concede that Malraux extends the poetics of the *fact* far beyond literature and art, as far as the political domain. As soon as 1926, after his return from Indochina, he convinced himself that the only value of anticolonial action, soon to become antifascist, resides in the metamorphosis of a destiny of submission into a *poem*. The will can always do it, if it assures itself of its means. Malraux is as far from being a humanist as Reverdy and Apollinaire. It's the inhuman capacity of the *fact* that interests him, what he often calls *grandeur*. It can be the *fact* of little people. There are political facts just as there are poetic or pictorial facts: a deliberate throw of the dice that slices the prose of history.

Malraux is in no way a political man, and even less of a politician. He never thought, even in Spain, that the voice incarnated in history *would finish* by overcoming miseries and humiliations. People reproved him for his complacency with Stalinism and his transitionless "conversion" to Gaullism. I will not discuss here in detail his supposed adherence to one cause or another: it is easy to show that he was never anything but a companion, always the companion of a figure (and not of some party) capable here and now of resisting abject submission in the course of things and of creating an unexpected *historical fact*. The enemy is always the same; it's what breaks or lulls to sleep the force of insubordination: colonial administration, fascism, Nazism, Stalinism, Petainist collaboration. People ask him why he is not a fascist, like his friend Drieu la Rochelle. Because, he answers, I have a *faithfulness*. People are astonished: didn't he change political parties several times? But, unlike Drieu, a purely desperate person, Malraux is faithful to the possibility of the *poem*. The fascist (or Stalinist) mythology is its opposite.

It's not the transformation of the world that occupies him, but the enigma of a *political fact* is to history what the Max Jacob's "jewel" is to ordinary language. Alexander the Great's passionate and even delirious will, albeit systematic, rips from the course of history the *fact* of a limitless empire. History has no need for it, no more than the visible world needs the watercolors of Cézanne or the engravings of Goya, nor any more than the life of the South asked Faulkner to write *Sanctuary*. Why did the men of the Paleolithic era cover the walls of their caves with paintings of animals? And why do they still compel our admiration, many millennia later? Alexander's empire is dispersed a few weeks after his death. But the *fact* is there and remains there, in its opacity that cannot be reduced to any explanation, to any finality.

As for the world, inside us and outside us, it pursues its larval existence. In this respect, Malraux is more than a nihilist. Not only is God dead, but so is Man, like a figure of the voice incarnated in history. But what they leave after them is not a void; it's a vitality swarming with larvae, spiders, octopi, and soft crabs; a nightmare in which the cycle of putrefaction and regeneration endlessly repeats itself. Without end and without purpose. The stars in the sky form a spider's web, indifferent and threatening; and "more interior in one-self than the self," man does not discover the voice of God, as Augustine thought, but horrifying beasts vegetating in the bottoms of pits. The nihilism here is not philosophical; it's the body that experiences it like a filthy Repetition. People have said that Malraux's writing was that of a tragedian. That is an error. Tragedy recounts the completion of a Fatum, of a Pronouncement, through a human life that knows nothing about it and that discovers it in the end. This end has been pronounced (said to be fatal) at the beginning by a divine power. Yet destiny in Malraux's work is not this sort of predestination; it's the blind repetition of the same, the abject life that says nothing. There will be no revelation in the end, a lack of an end. In the kitchens and stables of Shakespeare, the little people laugh endlessly over the supposed tragedy of princes, as in the Khmer jungle, the Moïs laugh about the "tragic destiny" of the heroes in the *Royal Path*.

The *drama* of the work does not reside so much in the novelistic themes as it does in the *fact* of the book, just as Goya's drama does not consist so much in what the *Capricios* and the *The Disasters of War* show as in the "presence" of the etchings. Malraux calls metamorphosis what Max Jacob called "transplantation." The poetic fact excludes itself from consumption by bestial time. And we, contemporaries who know that no voice, the Pieta of Avignon or the David of Michelangelo, no more an ex-voto to the glory of Jesus or of Man, but artistic *facts*. The nihilist disaster turns back into a privilege: the first civilization that cannot name its ending can marvel at the bust of an Egyptian scribe, a Dogon mask, or a Malevitch in the same way. All are indeed marvels sprung from oblivion thanks to the "style" and the "situation" demanded by Max Jacob.

Our disenchantment thus composes an imaginary museum, and an imaginary library as well, and it can be enchanted by the event of metamorphosis. This museum is not historical. It's rather an album of photographic images, a montage, once again, in which the shooting angles, the distances, the lighting, the editing, and the framing can vary infinitely. The works collected in the imaginary museum undergo in turn a series of metamorphoses. A new work, when it enters this protean memory, requires a change in the settings of the images in the album. A Giacometti sheds new light on an Etruscan statuette, a Picasso arouses or displaces our gaze on a Cycladic figurine, and so on. What seems important ceases to be so; what was unknown reveals itself. This museum is not a Pantheon; glory is never acquired there. It would be futile to see in it the ultimate end of the history of art, also futile to denounce in the institution of the museum an object offered up to the consumption of the masses. The imaginary museum is not an institution; it is itself a work; and it cannot be a temple, since we no longer have a priesthood to consecrate it. It's an album of enigmatic *facts* endlessly composed and recomposed by a child taken by marvels.

# Traherne's
# Centuries

Symmetry and proportion are the
very Beauty of Beauty itself.
—Thomas Traherne,
*Select Meditations*

### 1

For some time I have been interested in pursuing two dimensions of lyric—
first, lyric as a site for the emergence of subjectivity in the intersection of the
somatic and the social, and second, how lyric—like all aesthetic forms—
expresses a finality in tension with teleological thought. Specifically, lyric
presents a model of what might be called internal time in tension and accord
with social models of time. In contrast to narrative and the ends of emplotment, lyric in this sense is the form under which the person spoken by sound
becomes the person speaking, moving from reception to production of language and from sense experience to articulation.

### 2

The organization of memory, the determination of feeling, the articulation of
point of view in space and time—these qualities of lyric are not the eruption
of the somatic in an already-determined framework of perception; rather,
these qualities characterize, in lyric practice, a transition *toward* subjectivity.

### 3

As a model of time, lyric expresses the dynamic of internal time consciousness
perhaps most succinctly outlined—at least for my purposes—by Augustine.
In the *Confessions*, Augustine establishes the being of time in the flux of a three-

fold present: the present of past things, or the memory; the present of present things, or direct perception; and the present of future things, or expectation.

### 4

Through the extension of the subjective mind in the present, measurement extends outward. But the basis for the quantification of time is not the movement of things in the world.

### 5

Rather, both movement and rest, or interval, are determined by the projection or extension of time from the mind. In his well-known example, Augustine links a sound that starts, continues, and stops resonating to the past—the "not yet" under which we speak of the stopping of resonance exemplifies the future spoken of as the past and the present under which we are able to say of a sound that it is "resonating."

### 6

This presence is already disjunctive, however, to the presence of resonance. Thus we speak of the very passing of the present already in the past tense. Augustine asks, "Is there a way to measure time passing both when it has ceased and while it continues?"

### 7

He considers how, in memorizing a hymn by Saint Ambrose, his mind forms impressions of the relative terms of duration. Long and short syllables are quantified in relation to the whole.

### 8

And, in recitation, this expectation regarding the whole poem turns then toward what remains of the poem, enacting the process by which the present relegates the future to the past. "The past increases as the future diminishes" until the future is wholly absorbed in the past.[1]

### 9

Augustine's example of the hymn by Saint Ambrose, which bears an internal system of duration and yet is also actively engaged in both continuing and ceasing, does more than merely illustrate the experience and knowledge of duration. It demonstrates as well the simultaneously passive and active subject—that subject who is passive in relation to sense experience, memory, and expectation and active in relation to a present alteration of those terms.

### 10

My point is that time is *thought* and is therefore *made* in lyric form and that the study of lyric form might therefore be a way of exploring the meaning of such issues as seriality and chroniclism beyond the teleology of narrative's ends. The antecedent to this argument lies not just in Augustine on internal time consciousness, but in Sidney's and—later—Vico's claims that metaphor is prior both to history and to philosophy as ideology, in Rousseau's, Coleridge's, and Nietzsche's arguments on the relations between pain and a mastering will to form, and in Croce's explanation of the aesthetic impulses underlying chroniclism.[2]

### 11

I propose to examine the concept of century, or composition by units of one hundred, as a poetic form. This concept in fact structures what is often considered to be the first sonnet sequence in English, Thomas Watson's *Hekatompathia, or Passionate Centurie of Love*, registered in 1582.

### 12

Watson's collection of 100 poems was divided into two parts: "the first expresseth the Authors sufferance in Love; the latter, his long farewell to Love and all his tyrannie" and thus yokes its individual lyrics, which Watson called "passions" (each composed of eighteen lines in iambic pentameter) into the overall unit of 100 and gives ample evidence of a will to form shaping emotion, in fact taking emotion far over into the sphere of convention.

### 13

But Watson's volume, being a scrapbook of experiments in dialogue poems, echo poems, acrostics, aphorisms, quasi-sestinas, Latin hexameters, and a pillar verse stretching beyond the eighteen-line limit, connects not so much to the idea of 100 as a perfect number as it does to the Italian *cento*—a composition made from pieces—coming from the Greek, Sanskrit, and

Latin terms for a ragged or patched garment.[3] And the form appears to be relatively simple, given the complexity of number symbolism in other medieval and Renaissance texts.[4] In *The Hekatompathia* the number of poems (100) serves more as a description of the volume than as a principle of composition.

## 14

As a mode of lyric composition, the century is relatively rare and generally limited in English to the seventeenth century—or what we call the seventeenth century in our habit of counting from the birth of Christ. It is this paradox—the rarity of the century form in the history of poetry and the prevalence of it in our organization of historical thought—that interests me.

## 15

Calculation by units of 100 has become so commonplace that it seems to be given by nature. Beyond the centennial, centurion, or Roman century as a count of eligible voters, or our measurements for test scores and the honeymoon period of the presidency, we can think as well of the Greek *hekaton* in "hectare," "hectograph," and "hectometer."

## 16

Yet the practice of making centuries has lost its aesthetic or made dimension—perhaps more accurately, the lyric practice has dispersed like a dead metaphor into the culture and becomes the basis of certainty about the past and the ground for comparison and prognostication. This process of dispersal in itself is not so remarkable—as Croce wrote regarding the parallel between temporal and metrical form: "Just as in metrical treatises the internal rhythm of a poem is resolved into external rhythm and divided into syllables and feet, into long and short vowels, tonic and rhythmic accents, into strophes and series of strophes, and so on, so the internal time of historical thought (that time which is thought itself) is derived from chroniclism converted into external time or temporal series, of which the elements are spatially separated from one another."[5]

## 17

What seems natural in fact has its origin in thought.

### 18

The century form can be linked to other forms that appear in the intersection of linguistic and arithmetical systems. In any culture a principal of order governs the use and understanding of time, coordinating aspects of social life and integrating internal time consciousness into a social system.[6]

### 19

Bertrand Russell emphasized in his (1920) *Introduction to Mathematical Philosophy* that order will be a property of the members of any set in which there is a recognized relation of precedence and succession. In the measurement of time linguistic and arithmetical concepts are both employed. The conjoined systems of ordinal and cardinal numbers provide the link between them.

### 20

The linguistic system is used to name different, and possibly recurrent, points in time, whereas the arithmetical system measures the lapse of time according to an end in view. The former is consistent with "traditional" time, that is, time as calculated by cultures tied to the cyclic aspects of nature such as slaughter, harvest, and planting. Arithmetical time or abstracted time begins with modernism and the use of measuring instruments tied to distance, money, and other noncyclical features of culture.

### 21

Traditional time is Pythagorean, part of a numerical cosmology based on nonmathematical associations of numbers. Pythagoras said all things are numbers, but by this meant as well that all numbers are things. Numbers are significant for meanings that have been established extrinsically.

### 22

The history of the computation of time therefore tends in both its particular and larger aspects toward abstraction and the eventual severing of any intrinsic relation between numbers and things.

**23**

In other words, just as the use of natural numbers in the West depends upon categorizing in a perfectly abstract way, in order that the system of numbers can operate in relation only to itself, so in the history of the use of numbers does calculation according to increasingly large units of time result in an abstraction of the order of time from the experiencing of events on the level of the individual body—even if the body is nevertheless the basis for such calculation.

**24**

Perhaps the most vivid study of this aspect of thought is the 1977 film *Powers of Ten* by the office of the architects and designers Charles and Ray Eames. In this nine and one-half minute film, the time frame shows the 42 powers of ten by which we currently measure our knowledge—from celestial to human scale to the remotest spaces of particle physics—all structured by the modular taxonomy of the 100 chemical elements.[7]

**25**

Numbers, arising from the bodily experience of time, provide in systems of divination and mysticism an extension out of experiential time. And in the case of numbers beyond ten, written notation and means of calculation such as an abacus can admit of increasing abstraction and complexity in their use or application. In the West the scriptural basis for the relation of numbers to divine order is provided in the *Wisdom of Solomon* 11:20—"Thou hast ordered all things in measure, number, and weight."

**26**

In the Middle Ages, this order is divine. Augustine argues, for example, that the inherent beauty of music results from measure and number as successive repetitions of unity.[8]

**27**

In Renaissance aesthetics, the concept of *ratio* is linked to *concinnitas*—the concordance between nature and reason. Alberti calculates the ideal proportion of the human body to an architectural column as a mean of eight and links this to the role of the octave in musical harmony.[9]

### 28

But, given the intrinsic relation of ten to the body, not all numerical composition is tied to bodily proportion or theories of cosmology. When a number results from squaring or cubing, going one beyond the number will have significance as a transgression of the bounds of a system.

### 29

For example, Scheherazade survives one night longer than the cube of ten—that is, when she steps beyond the system of counting she escapes mortality.[10] The same is true of 33, the number of Christ's years on Earth, as one beyond the fifth power of two. As one more than the number of the Trinity times the number of Christ's years on Earth, one hundred is a particularly rich instance of the merging of linguistic and arithmetical meanings.

### 30

But the boundary between the logic of number and cultural symbolism is itself the source of cognitive pleasure as static contemplation of order is juxtaposed to the movement of experienced time.[11] Lyric and music as the enunciation of this tension between rhythm (or the somatic apprehension of interval) and meter (the abstract system of numerical order governing a given composition) are the aesthetic forms most deeply engaged with this integration.

### 31

Curtius notes that by the twelfth century the concept of *saeculum* or lifetime found in Tacitus and Amobius was combined with the modern reckoning by centuries, *centennium*.[12] But even in antiquity the numbers 10 and 100 and their multiples were considered to be aesthetically satisfying.

### 32

In Plato's *Timaeus* the Great Year, or cycle in which the heavenly bodies go through all their possible courses and return to their original positions, was 3,600 squared or 360 squared times one hundred, if one wanted to express in days the Great Year's duration. For Plato there were ideally 360 days to the year and since the ideal duration of human life was 100 years, or 36,000 days, so a day in the life of a human being corresponds to a year in the progress of the macrocosm.[13] Agrippa had suggested "simple numbers signify Divine things; numbers of ten, Celestiall; numbers of one hundred terrestiall; numbers of a thousand, those things of a future age." [14]

### 33

Under the number symbolism and number mysticism taken from Pythagoras and joined to Christian number symbols, ten is "plenitudo sapientiae," since seven means the creation and three the Trinity.[15] In the cabalistic hierarchy, as it was adapted by the Florentine Neoplatonists, the soul and inner life of the hidden God were expressed in the *sefirot* or ten primordial numbers. There are three spheres: the angelic, the celestial, and the corruptable. The angelic world is the root of unity, or ten; the celestial sphere is "unity squared," or one hundred; and the corruptable sphere is unity cubed, or one thousand.[16]

### 34

Marsilio Ficino links the square of ten to the life of man and the cube of ten to the number of the firmament of fixed stars.[17] From the enneads of the *Vita Nuova* Dante proceeded to the structure of the *Commedia*—$1 + 33 + 33 + 33 = 100$ cantos designed to conduct the reader through three realms, the last of which contains ten heavens.

### 35

It is not so much that we might pursue a genealogy of our current use of the term "century" by looking at these practices. But rather, by following a particular practice, we might pursue the imagining of another's time consciousness and hence arrive at a materialist historiography beyond the contextualist assumptions of chroniclism's century-bound procedures.

### 36

A great deal of research has been conducted on the spiritual exercises of the baroque and their relation to the period's art, literature, and architecture. The general pattern of the Christian progress of the soul (innocence to fall to redemption); the conventional stages of medieval Christian mysticism (preparation, purification, illumination, and perfection); the five-stage Ignatian model, which leads to quickened experience via composition of place, premeditation, memory, understanding, and will; Bonaventure's adaptation of Augustine's precepts in three stages—looking for traces of God in the external world, the self, and God's attributes: these four methods are often noted as influences upon baroque practices of devotional and meditative writing.[18]

### 37

In his treatise *The Art of Divine Meditation* of 1606, Joseph Hall (1574–1656) recommended writing devotional paragraphs of various lengths in units of 100.[19] Hall's earlier *Centuries of Meditations and Vows: Divine and Moral* (1605–6) explicitly links his practice to that of David in the Psalms—the extemporal meditation produced by the free play of the mind over what it sees.

### 38

Hall's *Centuries* thus have a seemingly spontaneous lyricism that distinguishes them from catechisms such as Martin Zeiler's collections, *Centuria Variarum Quaestionum, Oder Ein Hundert Fragen* (1658) and *Centuria III* (1659), and Alexander Ross's 1646 work, *A Centurie of Divine Meditations Upon Predestination and its Adjuncts*. Ross's work consists of prose paragraphs of about 150 words, each divided into two parts, a general observation and a prayer.[20]

### 39

Of course the best-known use of the century form appears in the writings of Thomas Traherne.[21]

### 40

Traherne's writings are now read in light of the dramatic and moving story of the discovery of his manuscripts. In 1895 two manuscripts were found in a London bookstall by W. T. Brooke—a folio volume containing 37 poems and a commonplace book made of extracts from other texts; the second volume containing prose works now titled "Centuries of Meditation," for the works were organized into units of one hundred and labeled "first century," "second century" up to an incomplete fifth century, which stopped at its tenth paragraph or strophe.

### 41

Neither volume was signed or attributed. The works were purchased by the editor and bibliophile Alexander Grosart, who thought, like Brooke, that the poems might belong to Henry Vaughan.

### 42

After Grosart's death in 1899, Bertram Dobell bought the manuscripts. Dobell traced the authorship definitively to Thomas Traherne, a shoemaker's son from Hereford who had received a B.A. and M.A. from Oxford, had been rector of the small Anglican parish of Credenhill just outside Hereford, and had served as chaplain at the end of his life to Sir Orlando Bridgeman, Lord Keeper of the Great Seal. Traherne died at the age of 37 in 1674.

### 43

Dobell published the poems in 1903 and the centuries in 1908. In 1910 another manuscript of Thomas Traherne's poems was found in the British Library. It was titled *Divine Reflections on the Native Objects of an Infant's Ey*; this work had been copied and edited by Traherne's brother Philip.

### 44

In 1964 an additional manuscript of meditations, titled *Select Meditations*, was discovered by James Osborn. The manuscript is also organized into centuries, although it is incomplete, for the first 43 leaves are missing and other pages are damaged or missing as well—there are 376 of 468 meditations remaining, grouped into four centuries. In 1967 Traherne's massive draft of the beginning of an encyclopedia, his *Commentaries of Heaven*, a work of nearly 400 pages of minute double-columned writing, was pulled from a burning rubbish heap in Lancashire.[22]

### 45

This story raises obvious problems of authenticity and textual authority for anyone working in these manuscripts and printed volumes. Traherne readily belongs to the professionalization of literary scholarship and the revival of metaphysical poetry under modernism, just as he belongs to the world of seventeenth-century devotional writers.

### 46

The only work of his published during his lifetime was his *Roman Forgeries* of 1673, a polemical work of scholarship, dedicated to his patron and designed as an attack on the papacy. His *Christian Ethics*, another work composed under Bridgeman's patronage, was designed as a handbook of practical morality for educated laymen and was published in 1675, a year after his death.

### 47

In 1699 his *Thanksgivings* was published anonymously under a different title (*A Serious and Pathetical Contemplation of the Mercies of God*) and in 1717 his *Meditation on the Six Days of Creation* was published as part of a collection of meditations and devotions under the name of his friend and spiritual associate, Susanna Hopton.[23]

### 48

In addition to these works, Traherne kept a book of devotions on the principal days of the Church calendar from Easter to All Saint's Day. A notebook of 396 pages, now in the Bodleian Library, contains undergraduate notes on ethics, geometry, and history, and later notes on the writings of Francis Bacon.[24]

### 49

Yet another notebook is now in the British Library: it is made up of the comments of Ficino affixed to Ficino's translations of Plato and Hermes Trismegistus, notes made by an amanuensis from Theophilus Gale's *Court of the Gentiles*, and notes from a work called "Stoicismus Christianus."[25]

### 50

When we consider these extant texts, Traherne can be seen to be taking up a conversation influenced by the concepts of continuous creation found in

Plato's *Timaeus* and in the writings of Hermes Trismegistus, Agrippa, Augustine, Ficino, Pico della Mirandola, and the Cambridge Platonists. Traherne's writing practices, ranging from public tracts to writings by an amanuensis, to lyrics and notes constructed in solitude, encompass a variety of possible audiences. He at times has dictated the terms of writing to his amanuensis and at other times has left pages blank—a practice tied to the invitation he offers in his inscription on the first leaf of the Dobell manuscript of the *Centuries*: "This book unto the friend of my best friend / As of the wisest Love a mark I send, / That she may write my Makr's prais therin / And make her self therby a Cherubin." Traherne's writing practices in fact fulfill the mandate of the enormously popular anonymous work of 1658—*The Whole Duty of Man*, a mandate commanding that one serve one's self, one's neighbor, and one's God.

### 51

In the entry under "Author" in his *Commentaries of Heaven*, Traherne writes that "an author is a living person, or a free and intelligent Agent that works to voluntarily produce his work of himself and design an End for which he produceth it. He is distinct from his Work and from the Instrument by which he worketh; . . . God alone is the author of all good. . . . Rational persons are God's instrument." The writer is thus the instrument of God's creation, miming that creation by his free activity.

### 52

The two texts that will be my focus here—the *Centuries of Meditation* and *The Commentaries of Heaven*—continue this emphasis upon the microcosmic and macrocosmic orders of creation. Here the influence of the Augustinian theme of mirroring the creation of God is combined with the numerical and taxonomic basis of creativity found in the *Timaeus* and in the temporal plan of Genesis, in cabala, and in devotional exercises.[26]

### 53

The five centuries of the manuscript found by Brooke by now have often been reprinted, whereas the *Select Meditations* and *Commentaries of Heaven* exist only in manuscript—the *Select Meditations* at Yale and the *Commentaries* at the British Library.

**54**

Much has been made of the plan of the five centuries in the Dobell manuscript. The text is composed in heavily stressed prose paragraphs, usually made up of seven sentences or more and characterized by an aphoristic style making frequent use of incremental repetition, exclamation, and shifting modes of direct address. The first century attends to the importance of what Traherne calls "enjoyment," a term he uses to intersect concepts of pleasure and apprehension. "Enjoyment" is rooted in desire yet achieves its positive effects only in the communion of all souls in God. The century discusses Christ and the cross as mediating the relation between the wants of men and the wants of God.

**55**

The second century continues with the theme of the union of souls—man as the image and son of God, the enjoyment of Christ as the son of God, and love as the expression of the Trinity.

**56**

The third century shows the soul's movement toward the attainment of enjoyment; this century has a stronger narrative direction than the other four centuries, for it moves from "infant vision," to the fading of early vision, to the discovery of the Bible as a compensation for such loss, to a discussion of the value of formal education, solitude, and contemplation, to a concluding meditation on the Psalms of David. The third century also is distinguished by having seven poems serve as units of the whole and function as lyric eruptions on themes introduced in the preceding prose paragraphs: these poems appear at 4, 19, 21, 26, 47, 49, and 69.

**57**

The fourth century presents an outline of the principles of enjoyment and their practice, a discussion of the relation between contemplative and active happiness, of the necessities of poverty, free will, and self-love, and a proclamation of God's love of man's creaturely nature.

## 58

The fifth century, which breaks off after the tenth paragraph, emphasizes infinity, eternity, and God's omnipresence.

## 59

We now know that there were probably more centuries written by Traherne and that these were most likely completed before the writing of the Dobell manuscript. The *Select Meditations* contain references to King and Parliament that seem to date them as being later than the Restoration.[27] Further, the fragmented state of the fifth century only emphasizes Traherne's habit of beginning his numbering again after each unit of 100.

## 60

Traherne gives several significant clues to how we are to read the incomplete condition of his manuscript. In paragraph 5 he says, "Infinity of space is like a painter's table, prepared for the ground and field of those colours that are to be laid thereon. Look how great he [God] intends the picture, so great doth he make the table—It would be an absurdity to leave it unfinished or not to fill it. To have any part of it naked and bare, and void of beauty, would render the whole ungrateful to the eye, and argue a defect of time or materials, or wit in the limner."

## 61

In paragraph 6 he continues with an idea from Augustine and Plotinus regarding the split between earthly and heavenly duration: "This moment exhibits infinite space, but there is a space also wherein all moments are infinitely exhibited, and the everlasting duration of infinite space is another region and room of joys. Wherein all ages appear together, all occurrences stand up at once, and the innumerable and endless myriads of years that were before the creation and will be after the world is ended, are objected as a clear and stable object, whose several parts extended out at length, given an inward infinity to this moment and compose an eternity that is seen by all comprehensors and enjoyers."

## 62

He concludes in paragraph 10 that God is busied in all parts and places of his dominion, perfecting and completing humankind's bliss and happiness.

## 63

There cannot be any fragmentation or stray unit for Traherne because all human activity is embraced and completed by God's work in the nexus of infinity and eternity.[28]

## 64

If we look closely at such passages in the centuries and turn as well to the *Commentaries of Heaven*, it becomes evident that the century is not so much a heuristic as a theology of time.

## 65

The full title of the *Commentaries* is *Commentaries of Heaven wherein the Mysteries of Felicitie are Opened and ALL THINGS Discovered to be Objects of Happiness Every Being Created and Increated being Alphabetically Represented (as it will appear) in the Light of Glory Wherein also for the Satisfaction of atheists and the Consolation of Christians, as well as the assistance and Encouragement of Divines; the Transcendent Verities of the Holy Scriptures and the Highest Objects of the Christian faith are in a clear mirror Exhibited to the Ey of Reason in their Realities and Glory.*

## 66

Designed as an encyclopedia, the *Commentaries* are organized by alphabetical entries, extending from "Abhorrence" to "Bastard." There are 90 completed articles, 82 under the letter "A" and 8 under "B."

## 67

Each entry discusses a concept and concludes with a poem, usually in couplets and summarizing the points that have been made. Unlike the poems functioning as units of the third century, which seem to erupt out of the restrictions of the prose form, these works, following the carefully stressed and orchestrated prose passages, are characterized by simple rhymes and a didactic focus.

### 68

The incremental repetitions of the prose work by halting turns and digressions. They show a mind struggling toward definition. But the lyric sections flow with neat precision as if the meaning of the concept now suffused or overwhelmed the speaker.

### 69

Because of the frequent cross-references at the end of entries (for example, under Baseness, Traherne writes "vid. Redemption, Incarnation, Passion, Christ," etc.), it is generally thought that his writing of the manuscript, begun in the 1670s, was cut short by his death.

### 70

The longest entry, extending to 38 columns, addresses the topic of "Ages," and provides an understanding of the meaning of the century form.

### 71

Traherne had mentioned the notion of ages several times in the five centuries. In the first century, paragraph 78, in a passage of direct address to God, he says "since the World is sprinkled with Thy blood, and adorned with all Kingdoms and Ages for me: which are Heavenly Treasure and vastly greater than Heaven and Earth, let me see Thy glory in the preparation of them, and Thy goodness in their government."

### 72

Further, in the third century there is much discussion of the boundaries or limits of the world and its temporal ends. In paragraph 24 Traherne says that "when the Bible was read, my spirit was present in other ages. I saw the light and splendour of them: the land of Canaan, the Israelites entering into it, the ancient glory of the Amorites, their peace and riches, their cities, houses, vines, and fig-trees, the long prosperity of their kings, their milk and honey, their slaughter and destruction, with the joys and triumphs of God's people. . . . I saw and felt all in such a lively manner, as if there had been no other way to those places, but in spirit only. This showed me the liveliness of interior presence, and that all ages were for most glorious ends, accessible to my understanding, yea with it, yea within it. . . . Anything when it was proposed, though it was ten thousand ages ago, being always before me."

### 73

As Traherne begins his description of the "nature" of ages in the *Commentaries of Heaven*, he emphasizes the ratio between human life and the concept of an age: "An age is a part of Time measured by the Life of Man who being the best and most Noble of the Creatures, as he is the Lord of the World, is a Lord of Ages, which is said concerning one and is said concerning all. A Crow may live 300 years and a Raven 900, an Oake perhaps 1000 yet are not Ages adopted to their Lives but accommodated to ours as Empires are measured and distinguished by the Lives and Periods of their Emperors, not of meaner Vassals and inferior Subjects. The Duration of Mans Life being Various and uncertain it is something difficult to find the standard by which an Age is computed but general Custom and Authority has prevailed to define an Age within the Limit and Measure of an Hundred years. Duration is their Matter, to which such a Relation and Quantity gives the forme" (f.57r).

### 74

Traherne goes on to explain that at first, because there was no sin, there were no ages: "No Man's Death had distinguished one Generation and another. Since therefore the Form of one Generation was counted an Age, in Eden certainly there had been no Ages. . . . From the Creation to the Deluge man generally lived 8 or 900 years and sometimes they wanted but little of 1000. During that time, because any round number is perfect and no broken number [respondeth or agreeth as] a whole with the Soul of Man, an Age was reckoned 1000 years. In after times the Life of man was shortened to 120 years and he that lived more upon Earth was esteemed a very Aged person as by man Sin came into the World, and Death by Sin, so by the Multiplication of Sin, Death were multiplied and by the Continuance of Increase in Sin Life was shortened. Much to the Benefit of the World, and man, that Labor and vanity might be a little lessened and Eternity filled perhaps with more persons and Greater Wonders" (f.57r).

## 75

Hence Traherne moves toward his explanation of the discrepancy between the length of life he finds in his contemporary world and the Platonic contention that 100 years is the life of man: "Since threescore years and ten is the Life of Man in these days and of by reason and strength it be fourscore years, it is full of Labor and Sorrow, an Age would be accounted 70 years and the other ten but unprofitable vanitie did not some men yet live to an hundred and Twenty, which gives occasion to Nature always ambitious of Perfection to lay hold on the full Time of an hundred years. Otherwise because the Life of some men even now exceedeth it, an Age would be more were it ever measured by the Longest Life . . . it is tacitly agreed upon by Mankind [that their] years should be reduced to a certain Number since therefore Space of an Hundred Years is the neerest round and perfect Number to the Length of Life, in these days and for many Generations past. Time by the learned is measured by *Centuries* and he that liveth 300 years, as Nestor of Old and Joannos Temporibus of late did, is said to have exceeded his own age and to have continued three" (f.57r).

## 76

Traherne separated the formal device of measurement by century from the content or matter of ages, claiming the latter for God alone (f.57r). In this choice we find him following the Neoplatonic use of number and cosmology to reach beyond experiential time. And his emphasis upon the duration of the life of the individual person adapts Augustine's philosophy of history from *The City of God* to such a numerical scheme. Augustine had argued against the cyclical theories of time in Platonism by making an absolute division between the finite dimensions of human time and the infinity of God's creation. By encompassing ages in eternity, Traherne maintains such a separation, but does not resolve the issues of whether the world was created in time, whether it would end in a specific time known to God (as Augustine contended), or whether time was synonymous with eternity and infinity. Augustine had refused to link the "progress" of Christianity to the progress of the Roman state or any other secular institution; he continually framed history in terms of the individual's relation to revelation: "Like the correct knowledge of an individual man, the correct knowledge of that part of mankind which belongs to the people of God, had advanced by approaches through certain epochs of time, or, as it were ages, so that it might be lifted from the temporal to the perception of the eternal and from the visible to that of the invisible." [29] By measuring ages according to an ideal span of human life, Traherne as well ties ages to individual salvation and the perspective of individual agents.

### 77

Within Traherne's ecstatic reasoning, ages become the vehicle of the apprehension of eternity: "The duration before the Beginning of the World and after its End are measured by Ages, Eternity itself wherein there is no succession of part, being represented and conceived under the Notion of a space including innumerable Ages, ever continuing, neither beginning nor ending. . . . Hence it appeareth that man gave the Denomination and Measure to an Age, tho God to Duration. The Matter of an Age being purely his, but the Form or Manor of its Being ours for its Limits are derived from our Human Conception, without which as there had been no zones and thoughts in the Heavens, so neither had there been any set Periods or Distinctions of Time which are like to Lines in the Zodiack, imaginary all, but fit and serviceable for our calculation. In every Thousand years there are ten ages, as in every Age there are an Hundred Years. The World therefore having lasted 5600 years, hath contained 56 Ages. But where they are is a material and doubtfull question" (f.57r).

### 78

This calculation is most likely borrowed from the *Chronographia* of Julius Africanus. Julius took from Hebrew tradition the idea of the Millennium, or thousand-year-long kingdom of the Messiah; the end of that kingdom would be the end of the world. The whole of history would equal a cosmic week, with each day constituting a thousand years. As Psalm 90, verse 4, had declared, "A thousand years in thy sight are but as yesterday." The first six days cover a period beginning with Creation and ending at the Millennium, or final day, with the second coming of Christ. Julius claimed that five and one-half cosmic days had lapsed between the Creation and the birth of Christ, or 5,500 years. By this reasoning in the year 500 the Second Coming could be expected. Even though that year came and went, a time scheme of 6,000 years more or less lasted well into the period of the Reformation.[30]

## 79

Traherne explains that it is up to the learned men of every period to define and measure the limits of ages, and he presents a sample of etymological reasoning: "Ages are limited and defined by the Sages. Wise and venerable men being therefore called Sages because they see into Ages" (f.57v.). The next section of the entry on ages poses ten questions regarding "ages" and then "another question." The questions and their answers are as follows:

## 80

"Whether ages are creatures?" (f.57v) "Since a creature is a being existent by itself and subject to accidents, age is no creature: eternity alone is the Ground of Ages, as Infinitie is that Ground of Regions or Spaces. . . . If all Ages and Creatures and Rooms were annihilated, the matter of an Age underneath would remain and something in Eternitie answerable to your imagination would stay behind as an invisible and intelligible Space immutable and eternal, this being Materia Substrata of a Existence" (f.58r). "Whether ages be substances or accidents?" "Eternity is a spiritual substance and an age is a spiritual substance" (f.58r).

## 81

"Whether ages are quantities?" "Numbers and motions have a peculiar Consideration among these many Beings. Numbers are in many Subjects, perhaps in all together but in none divided. As for example, Ten is a number it happeneth to so many pears and apples that they be ten. Ten is in them all together because one is in every one, and ten times one makes ten. But ten is not in one alone, tis not in nine of them for without the Last the Accident of Ten is not there, nor is the last that makes ten for that contributes to number no more than the residue. . . . So that Number is founded in Existence, Differation, and Relation. . . . Motion is in Things by Degrees. . . . An age hath something of Number as it is the Result of many Days united. And of motion as it is a continuance which appears in the mind" (f.58r).

## 82

"Whether an Age be a permanent or transient thing?" "It is in its unfolding a transient quantity, yet in fact it is permanent. Even as a line in making recovers its part one after another" (f.58v).

### 83

"Whether an Age be a Real thing or a Notion?" (f.58v) "It is a real effect of Things, but conceived in the mind" (f.59r).

### 84

"Whether an Age be finite or infinite?" "An age is infinite in parts, but finite in extension. If Time be a Duration having *partos extra partos* and every Part of Time is Time, the Parts of Time are infinitely small and the Smallest is infinite for the smallest part of Time is Time and hath *partos extra partos*. . . . There is no Miracle more transcendent nor Mysterious than this" (f.59r).

### 85

"Whether an Age be a Discreet or continued Quantitie?" "[An] Age is [there-fore] a continuous Quantitie because it is in Time perpetually running on without Division or Disturbance" (f.59r).

### 86

In the eighth question, Traherne explicitly links the construction of ages to a practice of writing, asking "whether Ages are abolished or made by passing by?" His answer: "An Age is not abolished certainly, but made by passing for the first moment of an Age is its Inchoation and till the last is in being, the Age is not finished, all that part of Time therefore which is seen between the first and last moment of 100 years is an Age. If an Age be made by passing by, it abideth forever. It endeth when it is finished, but vanisheth to none, but imperfect Creatures Trees and Stones are insensible of Ages past. . . . The Labor passeth away, but the work abideth. . . . A Book is in making, but not made, till it is ended. The Letters, Lines and Leavs are minutes, Hours, and Days, the Paragraphs and chapters are Months and Years. And so many years to make an Age must first go past before an Age can exist. . . . For an Age is a part of Time consisting of so many lesser parts of time united. All which in one appear to the understanding" (f.59v).

### 87

The last three questions are "whether ages now exist or not?" (they do, since in their perfection they are eternal [f.59v–f.60r]); "whether ages are within us or without us?" (here Traherne cites Plato on Ideas being present in the Soul and compares ideas to Light that comes from the Sun through the eye to the retina and brain and is created by the Soul as much as the Sun [f.60r]); and, finally, "whether ages are objects remote or near?" In his answer to this question he creates a picture very much like that of Charles and Ray Eames in *Powers of Ten*: "It seemeth distance and yet present, too, . . . [like] An Atom being fully seen in all its appearances many thousands of Leagues beyond to Heavens many millions of Ages removed from hence . . . the utmost Bounds of the Everlasting Hills being the same as it is in a Mirror, so it is here. The Highest in the Hemisphere is the lowest in the Glass. The Skies above are the pavement beneath, and East is the West, the Remotest thing without, the deepest within" (f.61r).

### 88

Obviously, the concept of the century as an age here reaches a maximal point of mystical imagination. The initial determination of an age as a hundred years on the basis of the span of a human life becomes, through the transformations of God's grace manifested through eternity and infinity, a purely formal determination. Simply put, the triumph over death promised by Christian teleology obviates the necessity of history.

### 89

In Traherne's lyric practice Neoplatonism becomes a formal operation—reference to the world is constantly altered and extended into reference to the ideal. When Traherne turns to the issue of the contents of the ages he turns to the Bible, giving a list of events that, because they occur after the Fall from Eden, enter into the rubric of ages: early rites of offering sacrifice, Abel and Cain, the translation of Enoch, the righteousness of Noah, the renewal of the Covenant, the rebellion and dispersion at Babel, the confusion of languages and genealogies of nations, the calling of Abraham, and so on through the Old Testament until he reaches "the Incarnation of God and Miracles of his Nativity, his Life Doctrine, Parables, Miracles and Virtues, His Cross and Passion his / Love the extent of it and of his merits. Like the Rays of the Sun they reaching all Ages" (f.64v, f.65r, f.65v).

### 90

Traherne goes on to list elements of the New Testament and extends his history to include the conversion of Constantine, councils, church fathers, martyrs, universities, temples created throughout the world; governments, kingdoms, the long-suffering of God and the continuance of the Gospel until our days. "Therefore, are the Joys of Ages in a direct line from the beginning to our Time" (f.65v).[31]

### 91

Just as the birth of Christ reverses time, turning back death and carrying forward the vatic promises of the Old Testament at once, so does a textual history become its own fulfillment.[32] The history that comes from the Bible is the Bible as the manifestation of history. One can look near or far, forward or backward, upside down or right side up, and in every difference will find the glory of the world displayed for the enjoyment of the individual soul.

### 92

In Traherne we find the triumph of a textual practice at odds with death.

### 93

Now all of this might be, as Traherne himself would say, interesting because it is enjoyable. It is obvious that Traherne's lyric practice grows out of and develops a model of time attempting to rewrite the world in celestial terms.

### 94

And it does not take any fineness of discrimination to conclude that the impulse toward mysticism and an encompassing synthesis of positions here comes out of the most painful personal and social circumstances of religious strife.[33] Further, one might conclude with the clear lesson that our sense of periodization by centuries has much to do with the mystical operations of alphabetical and numerical symbolism[34] stretching from Plato, to Cabala, to Florentine Neoplatonism, to the Cambridge Platonists, to Traherne, and beyond. But I am interested here in the genealogy of lyric subjectivity and its relation to the determinations of narrative history.

### 95

Traherne wrote under his entry on "Ancestor": "So many true and real Worlds salute mine Ey as there are generations some one or other of My

Ancestors lived in them all. The Sun gave him Light and Moon refreshment and Earth nourishment the Sea moisture, the Air Breath, the Fire warmth and all those assisted him that he might live and beget me. The influences of all the Stars and of all other things in that Age descend upon me, extend to me and rest in me and that perhaps 10,000 ways exciting my praise."

### 96

In this passage, I believe, is the explanation for the third, autobiographical, century's conclusion in the merging of Traherne's language with that of the Psalms of David.[35] The progress of the writer is to write himself or herself deeper and deeper into the past, so that the unfolding of the text, the realization of time, is the simultaneous encompassing and uncovering of what has come before—a writing practice virtually synonymous with Augustine's terms: "As the past increases, the future is diminished."

### 97

The techniques used in the Psalms—the interchangeability of alphabet and number and their use as modes of composition, the use of semantic parallelism to generate phrase and temporal sequence, the shifts from subject to object within epideictic form, and the orchestration of shifts of pronouns[36]— are taken up by Traherne as a spiritual practice enabling him to articulate the self and revert it, in Platonic terms, to the One. Arbitrariness in alphabetical, numerical, and metrical systems is thereby a way of mastering contingency of reference and extending the freedom of thought.

### 98

But the movement of reversion and reincorporation in Traherne is a narrative turn, a turn of reinscription back into the Christian plot. Here Traherne shows us the synonymity of aspects of seventeenth-century lyric with aspects of the medieval—the particularity of the subject is emergent, but ultimately collapsed back into the generalizations of Christian redemption. In this regard, there can be no Christian tragedy, and it is therefore exemplary that Traherne uses in the third century the first person when he speaks of universal experience and the third person when he turns to spiritual autobiography.[37]

### 99

Yet if we look at lyric history in formal terms, the particularity continued by Aristotelianism, the revival of classical lyric via archaeology, and modernism's diremption of seventeenth-century lyric from its religious context all push us toward a necessary misreading of such work—a reading that would emphasize the extension of mind in lyric as the subject's struggle toward articulation, individuation, and agency.

### 100

This misreading, to my mind, enables both the threshold of historical recognition and the jubilation of the necessarily mistaken historical imagination. Eternity and infinity are for Traherne terms for a universe replete with temporal experiences—experiences without boundary or limit. To think such a universe is to invite ecstasy. It is, I believe, the residue of that theology which confers the aesthetic pleasure in our use of the century form and which as well reminds us that we might proceed from practices rather than taxonomy in thinking about history.

Here endeth the hundredth part of my discourse.

# PART II

# Projections
# of Nationalism

# Turner's "Frontier Thesis" as a Narrative of Reconstruction

In 1893 Frederick Jackson Turner delivered a paper to the American Historical Association that arguably remains the most influential piece ever presented to that organization. In it he describes simultaneously the significance of the frontier in the history of the United States and the closing—forever—of the western frontier. Seventy-two years later, in what deservedly remains an insignificant moment in the country's history, my senior year high school yearbook appeared with "New Frontiers" as its theme. I risk moving from the sublime to the ridiculous with this juxtaposition in order to illustrate one of the most often-noted paradoxes about Turner's "frontier thesis": whereas it seems to announce the end to the exceptional conditions of the United States, it in fact launched a new tradition of interpretations of American exceptionalism.

Turner so powerfully generated a new beginning in understanding American history that considerable energy during the twentieth century has been spent debating whether we have finally reached the end of his influential narrative about an end. That debate itself suggests, as William Cronon puts it, that "we have not yet figured out a way to escape him."[1] In this essay I argue that the durability of the frontier thesis is linked to its structure as a narrative of reconstruction. In the first part I contend that its reconstructive capacity distinguishes it from alternative narratives at the time. In the second I examine reasons for recent attacks on Turner's narrative and how they are linked to his definition of the word "frontier." I conclude by offering two conflicted, yet related, ways of reading Turner that suggest an alternative narrative structure for us at the end of the twentieth century, one that, nonetheless, cannot do without the reconstructive capacity of Turner's narrative.

## I

A good place to begin an analysis of that reconstructive capacity is with Turner's famous ending. "The frontier," he concludes, "has gone, and its going has closed the first period of American history."[2] This ending does not, as Tiziano Bonazzi has recently argued, mean that the "formula for social regeneration" that the frontier allowed is also at an end.[3] It does not because, as Michael P. Malone puts it, the frontier was "defined both as a place—a zone of free land beyond the western edge of settlement—and as process—where social atomization shattered mores. Turner's frontier was a sociocultural furnace that forged a new Americanism embodying democracy, individualism, pragmatism, and a healthy nationalism."[4] The process described by Turner may be threatened by the closing of the frontier, but it is not necessarily at an end because the social organism that it formed has acquired characteristics that can help it adapt to ever-changing conditions. As Turner wrote Carl Becker, "The end of the free lands doesn't mean the end of creative activity in the West."[5] For Turner that creative activity meant, according to Bonazzi, "a gateway to a consciousness of historical continuity through change" (163). If in announcing the end of the frontier Turner warns his countrymen that their basic political ideals of individualism and democracy are not secured once and forever but must be continually renewed while being tested by new conditions, his narrative of progressive emergence implies that such an end is not a moment of tragic closure but the opportunity for a new beginning. As Bonazzi puts it, "There is nothing inherently tragic in the passing of the frontier: the real tragedy would be to keep fast to the old customs and ideas" (163).

One reason that the passing of the frontier is not tragic is that the frontier functions in Turner's narrative as a metaphor; that is, as a space of displacement in which something or someone is reconstructed as something or someone else. The actual space that Turner designates the "frontier" may be at an end, but the end that that space serves can be maintained by various metaphoric substitutions. In subsequent accounts of American history we have seen numerous designations for what became the new frontier. For instance, analyzing transformations at the turn of the century, Martin Sklar claims, "For many Americans, the corporation became the new frontier of opportunity that the western lands had once symbolized."[6] Indeed, Turner suggests that his own narrative can serve as an imaginative substitute for the frontier whose end it proclaims. Noting that the aim or end of his paper "is simply to call attention to the frontier as a *fertile field* for investigation" (3, my emphasis), Turner offers his narrative as a metaphoric space to initiate the regeneration necessary to face changing conditions. The frontier's role as a metaphor of displacement highlights the need to study documents of American cultural history in terms of metaphorology as opposed to symbology. If symbols suggest organic unity and seamless continuity, metaphors call attention to the displacements necessary to maintain continuities and the appearance of unity.

To understand Turner's narrative in terms of its specific metaphoric displacements is to distinguish it from competing narratives at the end of the nineteenth century that were faced with a bizarre phenomenon. The new political entity called the United States now had an existing constitution older than any in the "old" world. In 1890 James Harvey Robinson, later to become famous as a founder of the New History, begins his first major publication with the following:

> Not many months ago the hundredth anniversary of the inauguration of our present constitutional form of government was celebrated in the city of New York. To realize fully the significance of this event, one should consider not only how many years must still elapse before it will be permitted to any one of the states of Europe to solemnize the corresponding event in its national history, but also that this government, established in 1789, has outlived a century of change in social life and political institutions without precedent in the history of the world.[7]

Like the young Robinson, most contemplating the state of the United States in the 1890s were less self-conscious about the end of a century than the coincidence that that end corresponded with a series of anniversaries that granted a history to a land that supposedly lacked one.

Centennial celebrations of the Declaration of Independence, the Constitution, and the Bill of Rights were followed by the 400th anniversary of Columbus's arrival in the Americas, an anniversary that provided the occasion for the meeting that Turner addressed in conjunction with the Chicago World Exposition. In "The Figure of Columbus" in 1892 a writer for the *Atlantic Monthly* notes:

> Nearly a score of years ago the study of American history received a singular impetus through the series of centennial celebrations which began. There can

be no question that not only were popular conceptions of the men and events connected with the War for Independence readjusted and greatly enriched, but the scientific pursuit of American history, especially the history of institutions, received an emphatic impulse.[8]

"Especially the history of institutions." For many trying to explain how the United States had survived a century of unprecedented change the answer lay in the stability of its political institutions. Of course fascination with American political institutions did not suddenly spring up at the end of the century. The most famous European chronicler of the American way of life, Alexis de Tocqueville, emphasized the influence that the country's political institutions had in shaping its national character. But de Tocqueville stressed the novelty of those institutions. Less than fifty years after *Democracy in America* the same institutions were the subject of numerous histories. Institutional histories require that institutions have histories, and by the end of the nineteenth century institutions in the United States clearly did—often longer ones than comparable institutions in Europe.

To be sure, an end-of-the-century series of centennial celebrations was not the only cause for the rise of institutional histories. Another reason was the popularity of institutional histories with German historians, who were the model for the "scientific pursuit" of history. Germans influenced American historians through training those who studied at German universities and through the establishment of a German-style seminar system at Johns Hopkins University. The history seminars of Herbert Baxter Adams institutionalized institutional histories in the United States.

Designed in part to account for stability in a time of change, most institutional histories were politically conservative. Indeed, the focus of Adams's seminars was neither to stress the novelty of American institutions nor to seek their potential for stability in the special circumstances of the New World. Instead, relying on a biological metaphor, they sought the "seed" of those institutions in the distant past. Disputing the "theory of spontaneous generation," Adams insisted, "Whenever organic life occurs there must have been some seed for that life. . . . It is just as improbable that free local institutions should spring up without a germ along American shores as that English wheat should have grown here without planting."[9] For Adams's students those seeds were to be found in the forests of Germany during the fifth and sixth centuries. Tracing the transportation of that seed from Germanic forests to Britain and then to the New World, the so-called Teutonic germ theory has narrative similarities with that of *translatio imperi* or the transfer of empire westward. In a time of heavy immigration from Southern and Eastern Europe, it also served the convenient function of denying a Mediterranean and Roman origin to the democratic institutions of the United States. As a result, it stressed not only the Anglo-Saxon nature of the country, but also the difference between the Protestant institutions of North America and the Catholic ones of Latin America.

Linking national character to institutions whose germ could be found over 1,000 years in the past, institutional histories were an early attempt at what Robert Wiebe has called the "search for order" in a period of rapid social and economic change.[10] They were, however, a failed attempt, a victim of the very forces of change that they tried to combat. Some of the most important challenges to them were mounted by students from Adams's seminars. A particularly significant one came from Woodrow Wilson.

In 1889 Wilson received James Bryce's *The American Commonwealth*. Published the year before, Bryce's book was the most important European account of the United States since de Tocqueville's. On the one hand, Wilson's review reveals his indebtedness to Adams's training. Denying de Tocqueville's argument about the novelty of political institutions in the United States, Wilson praised Bryce for realizing that "there is really, when American institutions are compared with English, nothing essentially novel in our political arrangements: they are simply the normal institutions of the Englishman in America."[11] But if Wilson agreed with institutional historians that American institutions are not novel, he questioned the importance that they granted to institutions. More attention, he argued, should be paid to "material, economic, and social conditions" (181). Furthermore, he disputed the assumption that institutions shape national character. Bryce, according to Wilson, deserves credit for "perceiving that democracy is not a cause but an effect." More important, he sees "that our politics are no explanation of our character, but that our character, rather, is the explanation of our politics" (182–83). The "only stable foundation" of democracy, Wilson argues, is "character." "America has democracy because she is free; she is not free because she has democracy" (187).

The liberation of national character from political institutions was a crucial part of one of Wilson's major contributions to the nature of American political institutions: the development of a bureaucratic, administrative state. Many Americans resisted the institutionalization of what they felt was a continental European bureaucracy, fearing that it would destroy the special quality of American republicanism. For instance, a traditional Republican like Albion W. Tourgée, the lawyer-novelist who pleaded the case of Homer Plessy, opposed civil service reform because it would create a permanent class of governmental bureaucrats and thus take government out of the hands of the people.[12] In contrast, Wilson, believing that American democracy was founded on its people's character rather than vice versa, felt that borrowing efficient administrative structures from continental Europe would pose no threat to the country.[13]

Like his friend Wilson, whom he met while studying at Johns Hopkins, Turner challenged institutional histories by stressing the importance of material, economic, and social forces. But despite similarities, his challenge has a significant difference from Wilson's. Wilson may have separated the question of national character from national institutions, but he did not challenge the notion that those institutions were basically the same as English ones. In contrast, Turner continues to link the question of character and institutions, but insists on the differences between American and English, as well as all European, institutions. "Our early history," he writes, "is the study of European germs developing in an American environment. Too exclusive attention has been paid by institutional students to the Germanic origins, too little to the American factors" (3). "Behind institutions, behind constitutional forms and modifications, lie the vital forces that call these organs into life and shape them to meet changing conditions" (2). The most important forces for Turner are, of course, those connected with the frontier. Those forces shape, not only institutions, but also character. "The outcome is not the old Europe, not simply the development of Germanic germs" (4).

This difference between Wilson and Turner has important implications for the question of race. As we have seen, advocates of the Teutonic germ theory posited a narrative that stressed the Anglo-Saxon character of American democracy. Relying on a particular interpretation of the period's predominant neo-Lamarckianism, they connected institutions and race. Anglo-Saxon institutions were shaped by the Anglo-Saxon character, which was in turn reinforced by its institutions.

As racist as this interpretation of the interrelation between institutions and race seems, it was not inevitable. For instance, Tourgée also linked the democratic character of the Anglo-Saxon race with its institutions. For him, however, that link required a redefinition of what it means to be Anglo-Saxon. "The seventy-odd millions of people who constitute the population of the American Republic, whether white or black, Celt or Slav, or from whatever European stock they may be descended, in political ideals are purely American and derivatively Anglican."[14] At a time when a crucial question was whether African-Americans would achieve responsible political maturity if allowed to vote, Wilson's separation of character and institutions implicitly undercut an argument like Tourgée's that made American blacks as well as whites Anglo-Saxon.

For Wilson, as for advocates of the Teutonic germ theory *and* Tourgée, the United States is an Anglo-Saxon country. But, like the former and unlike the latter, Anglo-Saxon for Wilson meant English. American "character is the result of the operation of forces permanent in the history of the English race, modified in our case by peculiar influences, subtle or obvious" (183), influences that do not include political institutions. By separating racial character from the influence of political institutions Wilson, like another friend of his days at Johns Hopkins, Thomas Dixon Jr., the author of *The Clansman*, mystified the determination of race. That mystification warned against "experiments," such as those granting newly freed blacks the right to vote. Indeed, Wilson chided Bryce for describing the American system as "'an experiment' in government. . . . We are in fact but living an old life under new conditions. Where there is conservative continuity there can hardly be said to be experiment" (184).

Wilson's stress on "conservative continuity" raises the question of how he, like his friend Turner, became associated with progressive thought. A partial answer to that question is that progressivism had many strains and that Wilson's is different from Turner's. Nonetheless, Turner and Wilson do have much in common. In a passage that almost anticipates Turner's "frontier thesis," Wilson warned, "America is now sauntering through her resources and through the mazes of her politics with easy nonchalance; but presently there will come a time when she will be surprised to find herself grown old, —a country crowded, strained, perplexed" (182). "That," he argues, "will be the time of change" (182). If Wilson's emphasis on a moment of closure as a time of important change signaled his similarity with Turner, his difference came in his narrative of how that change would occur. According to Wilson change will come because the country "will be obliged to fall back upon her conservatism, obliged to pull herself together, adopt a new regime of life, husband her resources, concentrate her strength, steady her methods, sober her views, restrict her vagaries, trust her best, not her average, members" (182). An example of what David Noble has called the "paradox of progressive thought," [15] Wilson's narrative imagines change, but change based on the "conservative continuity" of a basically unchanging national character. In contrast, Turner's narrative responds to a moment of crisis by imagining change that is founded, not on an essential character, but on the nation's ability perpetually to reconstruct itself.

For Turner up until 1890 the frontier had served as the space in which such reconstruction occurred. The challenge for the future was to find a way for it to continue. If that challenge was difficult because of the closing of the frontier, it was in part possible to meet because there is a connection between institutions and character. Having shaped flexible and democratic institutions, the character forged from the experience of the frontier might in turn be further influenced by those institutions as it faced the material, social, and economic conditions of the country's next stage of development, provided that those institutions were reformed in the proper manner. Such reform depended, not on the inherent conservatism of Englishness, but the innovative spirit of an American people shaped by the frontier spirit. "In the crucible of the frontier," Turner writes in one of his most memorable passages, "the immigrants were Americanized, liberated, and fused into a mixed race. English in neither nationality nor characteristics" (23). The incomplete grammar in the second phase of the passage helps to dramatize that in the space created by Turner's narrative the process of Americanization is not necessarily over, that in responding to new conditions the American people can—and must, if they are to retain the special characteristics of being American—reconstruct themselves.

It's not hard to see why the implications of Turner's narrative, rather than those of the Teutonic germ theorists, Wilson, or even Tourgée, caught the imagination of the generation to which my high school classmates belonged. In the midst of the civil rights movement, with the nation attempting to reconstruct itself as "the great society," we found the idea of a new frontier compelling. Nonetheless, one hundred years after it was delivered, Turner's thesis finds itself under fundamental attack. We need to look both at the justifiable reasons for those attacks and how Turner continues, nonetheless, to pose a challenge to his critics.

## II

Criticism of Turner is nothing new. But, to indulge in a dangerous generalization, I would argue that for the most part earlier attacks focused on Turner's definition of the frontier as the *place* of American renewal. For instance, Arthur M. Schlesinger Sr. argued that it was in cities, not the frontier, that Americanization took place.[16] David M. Potter claimed that the frontier was only one factor, even if an important one, in the primary shaping force of American character: material abundance.[17] Turner's critics, like Schlesinger and Potter, might have challenged his emphasis on the frontier, but they continued to share his belief in a unique process of Americanization.

Recently, however, there has been a full-fledged attack on narratives of

American exceptionalism. For instance, in his important book *The End of American History* David Noble announces the end of a historical project that located the United States as the *telos* of history.[18] Today Turner's narrative is challenged not only because of its emphasis on the *place* of the frontier but also because of the way in which it links that *place* to a particular *process*. To understand the terms of this challenge, we need briefly to return to and expand upon how Turner constructs a narrative of continuity through change.

As Bonazzi points out, Turner's narrative is punctuated by a series of conflicts that would seem to threaten the continuity of national progress. How these conflicts transform into progressive change rather than revolution, repetition, or decline is at the heart of Turner's progressive vision for America and helps to account for the most important conflict that his narrative constructs, that between America and Europe. For instance, just a few years earlier Henry Adams had described the early United States as a place with "no arts, a provincial literature, a cancerous disease of negro slavery, and differences of political theory fortified within geographic lines." "What," Adams asked, "could be hoped for such a country except to repeat the story of violence and brutality which the world already knew by heart, until repetition for thousands of years had wearied and sickened mankind?" (722–23).[19]

Turner's answer to why that story was not repeated is the frontier. As such, the story he tells gives narrative form to a comment made by Hegel that the existence of free western land in the United States served as a safety valve to potential conflicts.[20] Providing a space of what we might call supplementation, the frontier made possible a narrative of American history in which conflicts could be endlessly deferred rather than dialectically resolved. Even if American history did not produce a classless society, it did, according to Turner, produce one in which class interests were complementary rather than oppositional. For instance, he quotes a description of how three classes—pioneers, settlers, and men of capital and enterprise—lived off and profited from one another by arriving in succession. "Like the waves of the ocean," these three "have rolled one after the other" (19), one after the other in diachronic sequence, not synchronic conflict. By providing a space in which synchronic conflicts could be avoided by transferring them into diachronic sequence, the frontier allowed for an organic synthesis of a diverse population without the need of a dialectical resolution. But it could do so only if Turner's notion of an ever-expanding frontier could displace Adams's description of political differences "fortified within geographic lines." That displacement required a redefinition of "frontier."

"The American frontier," Turner asserts, "is sharply distinguished from

125

the European frontier" (3). The European frontier is "a fortified boundary line running through dense populations. The most significant thing about the American frontier is, that it lies at the hither edge of free land" (3). This distinction between American and European definitions of "frontier" is one of the most significant aspects of Turner's essay.

As John T. Juricek has pointed out, Turner is right to note that "frontier" took on a new meaning in the United States. That meaning did not develop, however, until the late nineteenth century; that is, about the time that Turner announced its closure. This philological detail is highly significant, for it means that, although Turner claimed to be using a peculiarly American notion of the frontier to account for the peculiar nature of American history, he was in fact, as Juricek argues, "reading a late nineteenth-century world view back into the past." [21] Turner's use of the new definition of frontier suggests, in other words, that his compelling narrative of the nation's ability perpetually to reconstruct itself is itself an act of historical reconstruction. What, we might ask, is at stake in that act of reconstruction? As we shall see, quite a lot.

First of all, defining the frontier "to mean the edge of settlement, rather than, as in Europe, the political boundary" [22] allows Turner to shift the focus of previous interpretations of the frontier. Much has been written, Turner acknowledges, "about the frontier from the point of view of border warfare and the chase" (3). Turner, however, as we have seen, is interested in how the United States avoids conflict, not how it perpetuates it. Nonetheless, so long as the frontier is defined as a political boundary, any expansion of it immediately raises the possibility of "border warfare." Indeed, "frontier" derives from the later medieval Latin term "fronteria," which means "line of battle," and an earlier meaning of the term in English is "a barrier against attack." [23] But if a frontier is no longer seen as between two political entities, its function can dramatically change. Rather than a site of conflict, it becomes, for Turner, a site in which conflicts and differences are overcome. It becomes, in other words, what a later Turner, Victor, would call a space of "liminality."

Liminality involves release from normal constraints. "In liminality what is mundanely bound in sociostructural form may be unbound and re-bound." Thus it is in the frontier that the immigrants cast off their old cultures. But they cast them off in order to participate in the construction of a new, composite one. Allowing for a "rite of passage" in which the culture renews itself, the frontier shapes what Victor Turner calls *communitas*, which "breaks in through the interstices of structure, in liminality; at the edges of structure, in marginality." [24]

To see the frontier as a liminal space is to understand its function as a space of cultural regeneration. It regenerates by transforming cultural difference into commonality and community. Whereas many of Frederick Jackson Turner's contemporaries linked race and culture as a way of stressing irreconcilable differences, Turner imagines a space in which people of different cultural backgrounds become one. Strangely enough, then, what is probably the most famous narrative of American exceptionalism is simultaneously a narrative about the universality of human nature. We can get a better feel for the progressive nature of that narrative by comparing it to a powerful European narrative constructed in the late 1890s: Joseph Conrad's *Heart of Darkness*.

Conrad's story is in part a response to conditions that produced a study like Charles Pearson's *National Life and Character*, which appeared in 1893.[25] Noting that there were no new lands to explore and conquer, the Englishman Pearson predicted the inevitable and gradual decline of the influence of European and especially Anglo-Saxon people, whose exemplary individualistic character also happened to be incompatible with life in tropical lands where future economic growth would occur. Conrad too recognizes that there are no new lands for Europeans to explore and conquer when he has Marlow recall his youthful fascination with the remaining "blank spaces on the earth" as designated by Western maps and then remark that the Congo, "the biggest, the most blank," by the time of his trip "was not a blank space anymore."[26] Indeed, Marlow's journey in part confirms Pearson's view that Europeans have experienced their twilight, for the heart of Africa turns out to conquer the would-be conquerors. But Conrad's reason for the European's defeat is quite different from Pearson's. If Pearson argues that Europeans are constitutionally incapable of living in a tropical climate, Conrad constructs a narrative exposing what Pearson values as an inherent European character to be nothing more than the cloak of civilization. It is in Africa that Marlow discovers his "remote kinship" (51) with "savages" that other Europeans dismiss as "inhuman" (51).

But if Conrad's narrative, like Turner's, posits the commonality of all human beings, it does so through a temporal movement backward, not forward. In Conrad's imagination the former blank space of Africa enables a narrative that journeys against the course of history, so that as a wanderer "on a prehistoric earth" (50) Marlow can encounter a terrible "truth stripped of its cloak of time" (51). In contrast, in Turner's imagination the liminal space of the frontier enables a narrative in which a common human community overcoming cultural differences can be constructed through the progressive march of history. Ironically, however, this common history can progress only through a ritual process in which human beings forget their pasts. If it was the German Nietzsche who at the end of the century most loudly called for regeneration through an active forgetting, for Turner it was in America, not Europe with its burden of the past, that such a ritual could occur.

Thus, as much as Turner's narrative celebrates the potential commonality of all human beings, it, nonetheless, locates the United States as the place where universal history can unfold. Indeed, Turner favorably quotes the Italian economist Achille Loria: "America . . . has the key to the historical enigma which Europe has sought for centuries in vain, and the land which has no history reveals luminously the course of universal history" (11). Although Conrad's universal narrative moves backward in time and Turner's forward, both, it turns out, reveal a European perspective by denying non-European lands a history. That denial helps to explain why in Turner's narrative universal history culminates in the United States. If the liminal qualities of Turner's new definition of the frontier open up universal possibilities, its location in the American West limits those possibilities to the United States.

As I have already argued, Turner's notion of the frontier creates a space in which the United States can avoid the conflicts that have plagued European history. This opposition *between* the United States and Europe is possible, however, only because the United States is *between* Europe and the frontier. If Turner's image of the frontier lay in the east of Europe rather than in the west of the United States the narrative would move in the other direction. For instance, later historians, recognizing the universal potential to Turner's thesis, tried to apply it to German and Russian history.[27] But to do so they had to posit an Eastern frontier. Turner's narrative remains a document of American exceptionalism because it maintains a westward movement in which the United States, not Europe, becomes the site where history unfolds.

Paradoxically, however, if the United States's location between Europe and the frontier makes possible an opposition between Europe and America, it also establishes a link between them. This link occurs because the American frontier also serves as Europe's. Even though the frontier does not affect Europe directly, it does affect it. Its effect generates a countermovement to the predominantly westward movement of Turner's narrative. "Steadily the frontier of settlement advanced and carried with it individualism, democracy, and nationalism, and powerfully affected the East and the Old World" (35).

Less noticeable than the opposition between the United States and Europe, this link between the two is important. If the presence of a frontier in the European sense of a political boundary inevitably raises the possibility of conflict, Americans had traditionally felt protected from a conflict with Europe because they were separated by the vast expanse of the Atlantic Ocean. By locating a new sort of frontier in the American West, Turner provides a somewhat different explanation of why the United States faced no threat from Europe. If, on the one hand, the frontier created an opposition between Europe and the United States by exempting the latter from the former's problems, on the other, it transformed what seemed a clearcut opposition into an interconnection. Although the presence of the ocean is important, even without it the boundary between Europe and the United States would be special because of the westward movement of Turner's narrative of progressive history. The major threat to the internal security of the United States in Turner's narrative had not been Europe but barriers to westward movement. As a result, the "common danger" to the country, according to Turner, was the "Indian frontier" (15). By 1893, of course, Indians no longer posed a threat. Appropriately, Turner's new definition of the frontier transforms the "Indian frontier" into simply "the frontier," a transformation that allows a former site of conflict to become a site of *communitas*.

Turner's transformation of a place of historical conflict into a narrative of progress opens him to criticism by those intent on escaping a tradition of American exceptionalism that his narrative so powerfully renewed and reconstructed. If, as Warren I. Susman argues, "The escape from history leads us to the world of myth," [28] Turner seems to offer us more a myth about the frontier than an accurate historical account. Indeed, by emphasizing the frontier as a site of national renewal rather than a site of "border warfare," Turner would seem to dramatize Richard Slotkin's well-known thesis about the mythical quality of the United States's "regeneration through violence." [29] For critics concerned about historical accuracy the mythical quality of Turner's narrative demands that they reverse the process by which he constructs his narrative and reveal the historical actuality disguised by the mythologization.

Such readings of Turner are, of course, part of a larger project of demystification that has captivated the energy of a generation of U.S. critics at the end of the twentieth century. As important as this project of demystification is, however, it meets with resistance when confronted with the reconstructive powers of Turner's narrative. A sign of that resistance is Slotkin's treatment of Turner. Although he is critical of Turner for indulging in the myth of the frontier, Slotkin indirectly acknowledges his debt to him by titling the introduction of his latest book "The Significance of the Frontier

Myth in American History." Despite that debt, Slotkin in fact downplays Turner's significance. Comparing Turner's account of the frontier with Teddy Roosevelt's, Slotkin argues, "Although Turner's work has had the greater influence on academic historiography and has received the greater acknowledgment from historically minded policy-makers, Roosevelt's version of the Myth is closer in style, emphasis, and content to the productions of industrial popular culture and (as the body of the study will show) has had a greater (though unacknowledged) impact on the ideological underpinnings and policy-practice of twentieth-century administrations." [30]

Slotkin's choice of Roosevelt as the more ideologically corrupt of the two fits into his myth of the Myth for a number of reasons. First, as he points out, Roosevelt is much more embedded in turn-of-the-century racialism than Turner. Second, whereas in Roosevelt "the history of the Indian wars *is* the history of the West," Turner's work "is remarkable for the degree to which it marginalizes the role of violence." [31] Roosevelt's overt racism and celebration of violence make him much easier to demystify.

The relative ease by which we can draw on present assumptions to demystify Roosevelt rather than Turner points to the continuing influence that Turner has upon us. That influence is signaled once again by a title in Slotkin's latest book. Slotkin calls the first section in a chapter on the early 1960s "Modernizing Turner: The Ideology of the New Frontier." One reason that Turner rather than Roosevelt could be modernized in the 1960s was because his narrative helps to construct the utopian image of a racial melting pot. Another is that as much as it might seem to dramatize Slotkin's thesis about violence in the country's imagination, it in fact, as Slotkin himself recognizes, has a subtle, but crucial, difference from that myth. Rather than identify the frontier as a space in which the nation regenerates itself *through* violence, Turner imagines it as a space in which the nation regenerates itself by *displacing* violence. As important a part of the national imagination as the attitude toward violence that Slotkin has spent his career identifying, Turner's utopian vision does not invite immediate demystification.

Turner's resistance to complete demystification suggests two conflicted—yet complementary—readings of his thesis for us today. On the one hand, because it minimizes the role of conflict in the nation's history, it invites its own demystification. On the other, by trying to imagine a space in which regeneration can occur without a repetition of the violent conflicts that have plagued human history, it evokes a utopian possibility that would seem to lend itself to those trying to break with a past of violent exploitation. Seemingly opposed, these two ways of reading are structurally related to the reconstructive capacity of Turner's narrative. That reconstructive capacity is, in turn, related to the position that the frontier occupies in Turner's narrative as a space of displacement.

Turner's narrative invites demystification because it constructs a history of national renewal out of a history of internal conflict. In order to do so, however, it represses the involuntary displacement that westward expansion caused to Native Americans and others already occupying land in the West. At the same time, cultural renewal, according to Turner, is possible on the frontier because it allows settlers to undergo a voluntary displacement that allows them to take on a new identity. Similarly, Turner's narrative is potentially renewable because it allows for a perpetual displacement of the actual frontier by metaphoric "new frontiers," new frontiers that take on the function of national renewal.[32] By bringing a demystified and utopian reading together it should be possible to reconstruct the narrative of reconstruction that Turner constructed a hundred years ago.

### III

Because it is almost always easier to do, I'll start with demystification. The most obvious way to proceed is to follow the path laid down by Slotkin and insist on the history of "border warfare" that Turner's narrative displaces. To do so is to recognize, as I have already suggested, that such a displacement can occur in the 1890s precisely because the Indians had virtually been eliminated as a threat. But there is a less obvious way to demystify Turner's celebration of the West, one that sees him producing a narrative of reconstruction in a sense quite different from how I have used that phrase so far.

If, on the one hand, Turner's frontier thesis is an important precursor to progressive narratives of the twentieth century, on the other, it is part of a general project at the end of the nineteenth century by which American historians dramatically revised accounts of the era of Reconstruction.[33] As we have seen, Turner constructs an opposition *between* Europe and America based on the latter's ability to avoid the former's history of dialectical confrontation. But that opposition helps to minimize a conflict *within* the United States that a generation earlier had threatened to tear the country apart: the Civil War and its Reconstruction aftermath. Rather than construct a narrative of American history that focuses on the Mason-Dixon line separating North and South, Turner focuses on a frontier common to both. Not a fixed boundary like the one that created an absolute division between free and slave states, the frontier, as defined by Turner, allowed for expansion rather than

internal conflict. Indeed, "the economic and social characteristics of the frontier worked against sectionalism." A space of consensus, it produced people
who "had closer resemblances to the Middle region than to either of the other
sections" (27).

To be sure, by 1893 the frontier was closed. But by evoking a history in
which a "common danger" along it demanded "united action," Turner
hopes once again to use it "as a consolidating agent in our history" (15). Thus
twice he feels compelled to challenge Hermann Edward von Holst, the German institutional historian of the United States Constitution, who insisted
that the dispute over slavery was the formative event in shaping national character.[34] "When American history comes to be rightly viewed," Turner asserts,
"it will be seen that the slavery question is an incident" (24). As if to signal
his consolatory message, Turner in his second paragraph uses the southerner
John C. Calhoun to define the "distinguishing feature of American life": "We
are great, and rapidly—I was about to say fearfully—growing" (2).

Turner, of course, is a westerner, not a southerner, and later in the essay
he makes clear that he does not condone Calhoun's states' rights philosophy.
Evoking the dedication of the Calhoun monument, he quotes a Mr. Lamar
who declared that "in 1789 the States were the creators of the Federal Government: in 1861 the Federal Government was the creator of a large majority of
the States" (25). More important, Turner cites "the greatest of frontiersmen,"
Lincoln, "who declared: 'I believe this Government can not endure permanently half slave and half free. It will become all of one thing or all of the
other'" (29–30).

Turner's appeal to Lincoln might seem to indicate a clear Northern
sympathy. But by 1893 advocates of the New South were also willing to condemn slavery and stress the need for national reconciliation, so long as the
North admitted the folly of Reconstruction and gave the South control over
the "Negro problem." Thus, in his address entitled "The New South," delivered to the New England Club of New York in 1886, Henry W. Grady drew
on Lincoln's western birth to anoint him the "first typical American," one
who united "Puritans and Cavaliers" by "straightening" their purposes and
"crossing" their blood.[35] Eleven years after Turner's own address, Dixon ap-
pealed to Lincoln in *The Clansman* as someone whose love of his country
would have kept him from imposing Reconstruction on the South. "I love
the South!" declares Dixon's Lincoln. "It is part of the Union. I love every
foot of its soil, every hill and valley, mountain, lake, and sea, and every man,
woman, and child that breathes beneath its skies. I am an American." That
love does not, however, extend to African-Americans, as Dixon plays on Lin-

coln's house-divided rhetoric to have him proclaim, "The Nation cannot exist half white and half black, anymore than it could exist half slave and half free." [36] Dixon's Lincoln advocates the return of blacks to Africa to help with the birth of a nation in the aftermath of the Civil War.

As I have already made clear, Turner's image of the frontier as the crucible in which "immigrants were Americanized, liberated, and fused into a mixed race" (23) is not only different from but potentially at odds with the racism of people like Grady and Dixon. Nonetheless, by deflecting attention from the nation's failed reconstruction in the South, Turner's account of national reconstruction in the West leaves an important part of the country's history and people unaccounted for. Paradoxically, that lack of accountability grows out of Turner's efforts to provide a reconstructed account of American history that pays attention to aspects ignored by existing histories.

While at Johns Hopkins, Turner and Wilson agreed that American history had too often been written from a Northeastern perspective. Their combined effort to remedy that situation saw fruition in 1893. The same year that Turner's "frontier thesis" emphasized the role of the West in overcoming sectional conflict, Wilson's *Division and Reunion, 1829–1889* provided an "unbiased" Southern perspective on the long conflict between North and South. [37] Turner and Wilson share a number of assumptions. But if in his essay Turner acknowledges Wilson for recognizing "the West as a factor in American history" (1n.), the way in which Turner's narrative complements Wilson's perspective has not been properly acknowledged, perhaps because its relationship is so complex.

Looking at American history from the perspective of the West, not that of either North or South, Turner stresses reconciliation, not conflict. One result, as we have seen, is that his narrative is not generated by dialectical confrontation. Instead, for Turner, in the West the American people achieved an organic synthesis through perpetually deferring conflict rather than through dialectical confrontation. But precisely because Turner's image of national synthesis depends on deferring conflict, it opens itself to charges that it represses it. Indeed, an image of immigrants in the West fusing into a mixed race is possible only because Turner fails to take into account the country's inability to achieve the racial inclusion promised by radical Reconstruction. As a result, Turner's effort to reconstruct American history by providing a neglected perspective from the West needs itself to be reconstructed by supplementing it with another end-of-the-century account of the formative conditions of American character, that of W. E. B. Du Bois.

In an 1897 essay written in the wake of the *Plessy* decision and later to appear in revised form in *The Souls of Black Folk* (1903), Du Bois, sounding almost like Turner, looks back on the period since emancipation as "thirty years of renewal and development." Nonetheless, for Du Bois the failure of Reconstruction means that despite such renewal:

> The swarthy ghost of Banquo sits in its old place at the national feast. In vain does the nation cry to its vastest problem, —
> "Take any shape but that, and my firm nerves shall never tremble!"[38]
> The freedman has not yet found in his freedom his promised land.

Pondering what it means for the Negro to be considered by the nation a "problem," Du Bois offers his justly famous description of "double-consciousness, this sense of always looking at one's self through the eyes of others, of measuring one's soul by the tape of a world that looks on in amused contempt and pity. One ever feels his twoness, —an American, a Negro; two souls, two thoughts, two unreconciled strivings; two warring ideals in one dark body, whose dogged strength alone keeps it from being torn asunder" (194). Rather than achieve an identity of organic synthesis, the African-American, left out of Turner's narrative of progressive emergence, has an unresolved, double identity.

Indeed, in his narrative that celebrates the regenerative powers of open space, Turner allows no space for not only African-Americans, but other hyphenated Americans, such as Mexican-Americans and Asian-Americans. If Native Americans are present as a common enemy, other non-European groups remain invisible in his account, even though the march westward that he describes brought American settlers in contact with what today is described as the "Spanish Frontier" and even though Chinese played such an important role in building the transcontinental railroad that helped spell an end to the frontier.[39]

Of course, at this moment in the late twentieth century to point out the invisibility of non-Europeans in our national narratives is a commonplace, if not an obligation. Their invisibility in Turner's narrative is certainly not surprising. A more interesting question is whether the structure of his progressive narrative inevitably excludes them. As I have already suggested, the renewal power of Turner's narrative complicates any exclusions that it seems to perpetuate. Although at the moment of its production it does not account for non-Europeans, its definition of Americanization as fusion into a "mixed race" implies that those previously excluded are welcome to join in a newly reconstructed mixture. Nonetheless, the dependence of Turner's narrative on the existence of some liminal space for that fusion to occur demands closer scrutiny.

Neither Frederick Jackson Turner's notion of the frontier nor Victor Turner's notion of the liminal can accommodate what the later Turner calls "marginals." Marginals are "simultaneously (by ascription, optation, self-definition, or achievement) of two or more groups whose social definitions and cultural norms are distinct from, and often even opposed to, one another. . . . Marginals like liminars are also betwixt and between, but unlike ritual liminars they have no cultural assurance of a final stable resolution of their ambiguity."[40] Rather than achieve the synthetic, unified identity implied by Frederick Turner's metaphor of immigrants fusing into a "mixed race," the marginal, like Du Bois's description of the African-American, is in a state of internal "border warfare."

As inclusive and regenerative as it promises to be, the liminal seems to have no place for the marginal. Its inability to accommodate or find a home for the marginal has opened it to attack by "border" anthropologists like Renato Rosaldo.[41] In this regard it is important to remember that in redefining "frontier" Frederick Jackson Turner effaced the existence of borderlands in American history. A liminal space on the "edge of settlement" rather than a political boundary around which a border can develop, Turner's frontier creates a community of inclusiveness only through a subtle process of repression.

Nonetheless, if the liminal marginalizes the marginal, it also holds out the promise that even marginals can be included. For instance, according to Du Bois, the Negro strives to overcome his twoness. He longs "to attain self-conscious manhood, to merge his double self into a better and truer self" (195). Liminality, it seems, can provide the "cultural assurance" and "final stable resolution of . . . ambiguity" that so troubles the marginal. But it does so at a price. For, if Du Bois's Negro longs to overcome twoness, he also hopes that in his "better and truer self . . . neither of the older selves" will be lost. Americanization, according to Turner, requires precisely this loss of a past self.

For years the positive aspects of the process of Americanization described by Turner have been emphasized. But today more and more critics question the process of forgetting necessary for it to occur. One reason for their resistance is the growing awareness that the only way to understand the marginalized position of many in today's society is to remember an oppressive past that created the conditions of double-consciousness as described by Du Bois. Because part of the power of Turner's narrative grows out of its tendency to displace such oppressions caused by literal and metaphoric "border warfare," it is justly viewed with suspicion.

Nonetheless, as we have seen, the nature of that displacement creates a

moment of resistance of its own for those operating solely within a hermeneutics of suspicion. As important as it is to reconstruct a past of oppression,
we need to ask if such a reconstructive project is possible without some space
of displacement, like that provided in Turner's narrative. We also need to ask
whether we want to privilege as normative the double consciousness that
such a past created. Indeed, is it possible that various celebrations of border
identities growing out of the physical displacement of people result from
various cultural critics imposing their self-image as free-floating (dare I say,
Enlightenment?) intellectuals whose permanent mental displacement grants
them a space of independence?[42] Are we guilty of conflating that metaphoric
space of displacement with actual spaces of displacement and thus perpetu-
ating the sense of homelessness felt by so many of today's marginalized? In
other words, do we want to perpetuate a permanent feeling of displacement
for marginalized people, or should we strive to create conditions in which
those on the border can feel at home?

Of course, our choice need not be one of either/or, nor need we embrace a logic of both/and.[43] If the reconstructive powers of Turner's narrative
depend on the space of displacement that he designates "the frontier," we
need to ask ourselves if there is a way of reimagining that space. One way to
do so is to return to the notion of "frontier" as a boundary around which a
border space emerges. To understand the significance of the frontier in terms
of borders is to construct narratives that dramatically alter Turner's structure.

Such narratives, I need to point out, are becoming commonplace in the
growing field of cultural studies. I will note just a few of their differences from
Turner's. First of all, they do not posit Europe as the origin of civilization.
Instead, they assume the simultaneous existence of various civilizations with
none at the center. Furthermore, they replace the linear movement of Turner's narrative with a reciprocal one. Rather than a narrative about the westward march of civilization, they are about exchanges and conflicts—often
uneven—among cultures. As we have seen, even Turner's narrative implies
some such reciprocity. But he confines it to an exchange between Europe and
America. The new narratives try to describe exchanges occurring in various
directions across various borders around the globe.[44]

As such, these narratives imply a different interpretation of the final
image that Turner evokes to describe the role of the frontier. "What the
Mediterranean Sea was to the Greeks breaking the bond of custom, offering
new experiences, calling out new institutions and activities, that, and more,
the ever retreating frontier has been to the United States directly, and to the
nations of Europe more remotely" (38). Instead of seeing the Mediterranean

as the edge of civilization, we need to see it, as present historians tell us it was, in the middle of various civilizations, a space allowing for trade and the exchange of ideas among cultures of three different continents. Spaces of cultural regeneration, it seems, are border spaces, not "frontier" spaces as defined by Turner.

Nonetheless, as we imagine new narratives in which the frontier is reconstructed as a place of borders—spaces between, not spaces on the edge—we should not forget the military roots of the word "frontier." Borderlands are the sites of war as well as exchange. Indeed, as much as we feel the need to reconstruct Turner's use of the frontier to displace a past history of violence, his narrative remains extremely attractive if we view it, not as a narrative about the past, but as a vision for the future. For instance, given the horrendous problem of violence in American society today and its clear link to issues of race and battles over turf, the vision of a nation regenerating itself by displacing violence is as relevant to the end of the twentieth century as it was to the end of the nineteenth.

Of course, one reason that it retains its relevance is that narratives like Turner's helped to divert attention away from Du Bois's prophetic insight that "the problem of the Twentieth Century is the problem of the color-line." [45] Our challenge today seems to be to come up with narratives that will construct regenerative spaces where, historically, not only lines of color, but also lines of nationality, ethnicity, gender, and class have created boundaries.

Such narratives require an important reconstruction of Turner's notion of the frontier, but they haven't, it seems to me, completely escaped his narrative structure. After all, to announce the end of the usefulness of Turner's notion of the frontier is in one sense merely to repeat—with a difference—what he announced one hundred years ago when he proclaimed the end of one stage of American history and the need to move on to a new one. As much as our new narratives show—as to an extent mine does—that the frontier, as defined by Turner, was always at an end in American history, and as much as we call for the need to confront the conditions of a new age, whether we call it "postmodernity," "postindustrial capitalism," or "postcolonialism," it is hard to imagine coming up with new narratives and new meanings of culture without relying on some space of displacement that Turner in his narrative calls a no-longer-existing frontier.

# Rogue
# Nationalism

> Two Religions cannot be suffered in one
> kingdom: for diversities cause factions, gar-
> boils, and civil wars, which never end but
> with the subversion of the commonwealth.
> The tranquility of all estates consisteth in the
> union and consent of the inhabitants. Take
> away this union, and it is but a den for rovers
> and thieves.
> —William Vaughan, *The Golden-grove*
> (1608)

Once Henry VIII had officially supplanted the pope as the head of the English church, praise of England required a special ingenuity. Propagandists used to the criticism that England was physically and culturally isolated from the rest of Christendom now had to explain why it was good for England to be spiritually isolated as well. This ideological dilemma had, moreover, two distinct yet confusable parts. The first concerned English power, and to judge from a swiftly established conventionality of response, it proved the easier part to handle. Drawing upon a biblical discourse of paradoxes in which the lowly, weak, and foolish subdue the proud, strong, and wise, English Protestants generally did not bother to deny England's smallness in comparison to its Catholic enemies, but rather exalted the material deficiencies of their nation into signs of England's spiritual greatness. Just as David had prevailed against Goliath, so, Protestant writers maintained, England would prevail against Rome: as Joseph Hall (1613) put it, "If any nation under heaven could either parallel or second Israel in the favors of God, this poor little island of ours is it."[1]

When the issue thought to be raised by Henry's schism was not strength but community, however, a Protestant England proved much harder to defend. How, Catholics demanded, could the English possibly justify deserting the rest of Christendom? Not only had they "wander[ed] from the way of truth"; they had also "departed from the company of all nations," withdrawn themselves "from the unity of the whole world."[2] Years before the break with Rome, English writers had already begun to insist that England possessed the same right to self-rule as any other "empire"; yet this nationalist-sounding doctrine remained (as the recourse to an imperial model suggests) embryonic and vague.[3] Modern historians who exaggerate its clarity or authority at the time render us incapable of appreciating how seriously English Protestants regarded the Catholic indictment of their religious "singularity."[4] Apologists for England regularly denied the charge: England, they argued, only *appeared* to have separated itself from Christendom, when in fact it had successfully rejoined the "invisible" church from which the English had long been "wanderers, walking astray" while "under the tuition of romish pastors."[5] The truth was, however, that English Protestants remained more detached from even the Protestant Continent than their professed devotion to a supernatural church allowed them to justify; as the historian Franklin Baumer points out, "English interest in confessional agreement rarely got beyond the writing and talking stage."[6] Surveying the state of European religion at the end of the century, the Elizabethan Protestant Sir Edwin Sandys (1599) devoted most of his time to denouncing Catholic corruption, but he also confessed that Europe's Protestants were "as severed or rather scattered troops, each drawing a diverse way, . . . without any bond to knit them, their forces or courses in one."[7]

Faced with the massive international fellowship of the papists on the one hand and their own "small scattered company" on the other, a number of English Protestants decided the best way to clear their nation from the charge of wandering was first to admit it, and they were aided in this task, once again, by a biblical emphasis on the disparity between worldly appearances and otherworldly reality. Anthony Gilby (1547) defended the English by insisting that God had always given light "only to a few whom he had chosen and long afore appointed, even to the weak abjects and castaways in the sight of the world." Bishop Hooper (1547) likened the true church to "Daniel sitting among the lions": "Deliver it out of the cave yet shall it wander upon the earth as a contemptible thing of no estimation, not knowing where to rest her head." The most famous formulation of this Protestant self-defense appeared at the end of the century in the first half of Spenser's *Faerie Queene* (1590), which depicted the one true church as an "*Errant* damozell" reduced to "wandring in woods and forrests," wherever "wilde fortune" would lead her.[8]

When the castaways under consideration were English Protestants and the settled multitude foreign Catholics, such championing of vagrancy blended nicely with the national interest; even England's detachment from foreign Protestants could appear less troubling. But what happened when the relevant multitude were Protestant and English, and the castaways were an internal matter? The problem was not simply the unsettling presence within England of a large number of alienated papists. From the start of the Reformation, Catholic writers had warned the English that, by breaking "the unity of Christ's Church," they would soon be "cumbered with infinity of sects and opinions pernicious to the state"; having "neither head, order, obedience, neither yet certain rules or grounds whereon to stay," the English were doomed "to run headlong yet wot no more than your guides whither."[9] As early as the Admonition Controversy in the 1570s, English Protestants could not easily deny that such gloomy prognostications were coming true; and by 1589, the future archbishop of Canterbury, Richard Bancroft, had to concede that "so many sectaries and schismatics" were now plaguing England "as that in very deed diverse do revolt daily to Papistry, many are become merely Atheists, and the best do stand in some sort at a gaze."[10]

With the church in such frightening disarray, the very fabric of English society seemed to many Elizabethans in danger of unraveling too. Protestant preachers may have denounced those malcontents who blamed a felt increase in social disorder on "the new learning and preaching of the gospel," but they rarely denied that such an increase had occurred.[11] Catholic polemicists only swelled the ranks of Protestants inveighing against the most visible sign of trouble: "the Infinite numbers of the Idle wandering people and robbers of the land." Never, complained writers of every persuasion, were the highways "so replenished with thieves & robbers," nor were there ever "such numbers of beggars in all parts of the realm."[12] Although modern research has tended to confirm that the number of "masterless men" in England did indeed rise throughout the sixteenth century, recent historians of nationalism have continued to gloss over the fears of national disintegration expressed in Elizabethan social criticism just as they continue to ignore the strong investment of many Elizabethans in the old ideal of a supernatural Christian church.[13] Yet even so fervently Protestant and chauvinist an Elizabethan as John Norden (1591) called the final decade of the sixteenth century "the time of trial" for England, while in Norden's view an ever-growing number of idle drifters were roaming the countryside ("to the great detriment of our quiet abiding in this standing house of our common-weal"), "swarms of false prophets" were at the same time flying "everywhere" throughout England, inciting the English people to join them as "vagabonds from the church of God."[14]

Our anachronistic assumptions about English nationalism have blinded us not only to such trials of nationalism in the sixteenth century but also to the search for answers these trials produced. In their struggle to resist the temptation of believing that the Reformation was a wandering from Christendom that had promoted wandering within England, English Protestants began around the end of the century to receive ideological support from what Norden would have considered the unlikeliest quarter—that breeding ground of "idleness and loitering," the theater.[15] As advocates for a nation accused of vagrancy, players had this advantage over most of their compatriots: they were accustomed to the charge. And now that some players had settled down, for at least part of the year, in permanent theaters, they had new arguments available to them for distinguishing themselves from vagabonds. By the end of the century, the plays of dramatists such as Marlowe and Shakespeare had elevated vagrancy from a merely professional concern to an issue of national significance. And, in the decades to follow, subsequent playwrights—among them Dekker, Jonson, Fletcher, Middleton, and Brome—came to envision the theater as a means not only of defending England against the charge of spiritual wandering but, more surprisingly, of turning England's actual vagabonds into the sponsors of a reformed yet also antisectarian nation.

*

Perhaps the clearest indication that English Protestants feared the Reformation had too radically disrupted traditional notions of community in England was the growing belief among Elizabethans—unprecedented in England before the Reformation—that England's vagrants had not only risen in number but, paradoxically, assembled a society of their own.[16] In 1565 John Awdeley published an exposé of this secret "fraternity of vagabonds," which he also termed a "brotherhood" or "company" or "profession." The next year, Thomas Harman's *Caveat for Common Cursitors* described the structure of the vagabonds' "fleeting Fellowship" in more detail, even supplying a brief vocabulary of the cryptic language they were said to have developed, their "cant." Around the turn of the century, pamphlets on the vagabonds had become a staple of the English book market, and claims about their social organization had grown still more extravagant: soon the playwright Thomas Dekker (1608) could speak of vagabonds—or, in the "cant" terminology, "rogues"—as a separate "people." Another playwright, John Webster (1615), shared Dekker's stronger view: in his account, the rogue seemed part of a "commonwealth" not only separate from England's but more stable and uniform: "His Language is a constant tongue; [our] Northern speech differs from the South, Welsh from the Cornish: but Canting is general, nor ever could be altered by Conquest of the *Saxon, Dane,* or *Norman*." [17]

Despite the vividness and popularity of this belief in a rogue underworld, however, even those scholars who accept that vagrancy increased throughout the sixteenth century insist that "the literary image of the Elizabethan vagrant evaporates as soon as court records are examined." According to J. A. Sharpe, for instance, the only associations formed by the homeless in Elizabethan England appear to have been "loose" and "informal." [18] Yet Sharpe and his fellow historians never ask why the Elizabethans bothered to invent a rogue underworld, nor why they granted a greater cohesiveness to these most desperately poor castoffs of English society than to English society itself. Again, the oversight seems attributable, at least in part, to our anachronistic treatment of nationalism as a fundamental, rather than sketchy and disputable, Elizabethan ideological position. If many Elizabethans interpreted the growing vagabondage in England as an effect of the Reformation, then why should we not also consider whether the Reformation was a source of the Elizabethan scare about organized roguery? For the notion of a vagabond underworld embodied the worst of English fears about the Protestant schism. Not only, it seemed, had the national integrity and solidarity that the break with Rome was supposed to provide the English nightmarishly arisen among England's thriving vagabonds instead, but it had taken a thoroughly profane form: like his fellow rogue critics, the playwright Robert Greene (1591) declared that the vagabonds were "in religion mere atheists." [19] If England's weak abjects and castaways had achieved an invisible community, they had done so at the cost of the only thing that Gilby, Hooper, and Spenser believed could justify vagrancy—their faith.

The literature on English's new rogue nation did more, however, than expose Protestant anxiety about the Reformation's effects on England; it also enabled a productive response to such self-doubt, in stigmatizing vagabonds as culprits, not casualties, as the active promoters of national disintegration rather than as passive victims. Along with shifting the blame for English vagrancy to the vagrants themselves, the demonization of rogues provided a splintered England with a valuable common enemy. In the preface to his *Caveat,* Harman represented his pamphlet as the first salvo in a more comprehensive battle against the rogues: "Faithfully for the profit and benefit of my country I have done it," Harman declared, "that the whole body of the realm may see and understand their lewd life and pernicious practices, that all may speedily help to amend that is amiss" (114). "The whole body of the realm": rogues were so organized, hidden, and pervasive a threat that only

the entire kingdom combined could root them out. This national appeal became the standard by which the production and consumption of rogue literature was to be judged: "Nascimur pro patria," Greene (1591) and his followers proclaimed, while Dekker (1608) dedicated a rogue pamphlet "to my
own Nation."[20]

This utility of rogues in establishing one's devotion to the common
good made them an especially attractive subject for one group of Englishmen
in particular—the personnel of England's theaters. Touring had always rendered players vulnerable to the charge of vagrancy and the penalty of the
whipping post.[21] Yet distinctions had also always been made between licensed
and unlicensed players: between some amateur or else well-placed actors, that
is, and their poor professional counterparts. In fact, theater historians agree
that by tightening the requirements for licenses and thus subjecting more
players to the charge of vagrancy, the 1572 *Acte for the Punishement of Vacabondes* actually provided certain acting companies with the status and security they needed to found London's permanent theaters.[22] Famously, however,
these more privileged players quickly discovered that the assurances of settled
venues and official protection had failed to silence their critics.[23] On the contrary: for many Elizabethans, the new high profile of such "roguing stagers"
constituted a national scandal.[24] What better evidence of organized roguery
could there be, after all, than an acting company—a fraternity of vagabonds
indeed? And where better could one behold the makings of rogue society
than in the permanent theaters, "the ordinary places of meeting," a Lord
Mayor protested in 1594, "for all vagrant persons & masterless men that hang
about the City, . . . where they consort and make their matches to the great
displeasure of Almighty God & the hurt and annoyance of her Majesty's
people."[25] According to the theater's enemies, even those playgoers not originally vagrant were liable to become so, because the theaters inspired "more
truants, and ill husbands, then if open Schools of unthrifts & Vagabonds were
kept."[26] Unable to shake the stigma of vagrancy, the new professional players
thus had a vested interest in persuading the English people to fear another
form of organized vagabondage more harmful and also more clandestine
than their own.[27]

So it was that around the turn of the century the production of rogue
literature came to be dominated by two playmakers, Greene and Dekker, who
claimed to have devoted their lives to England's safety. The novelty of their
pamphlets had little to do with their detective work, however, most of which
they pilfered from earlier writers. What *was* new about the rogue literature of
Greene and Dekker was the way each playmaker represented himself within

it; their literary self-portraits show how well the notion of a rogue under-world helped theater people not only excuse their seeming vagrancy but capitalize on it. Harman had described his campaign against rogues as neces-sitating a very rogue-like ranging "about and through all parts of England" (*Caveat*, 110), yet he made clear that his *book* was the rover; the reason Har-man himself possessed a potentially compromising familiarity with rogue so-ciety, he explained, was that an illness had forced him to stay home, where he spent his time interrogating the vagabonds who came begging to his door. A quarter century later, Greene recast the inherited lore on vagabondage as a racy personal confession: he himself, he announced, had once led a rogue's life, which he now extenuated as both a youthful excess and a special access to knowledge about roguery. Greene's admission of vagrancy thus amounted to a repudiation as well; in his posthumous *Repentance* (1592), he went so far as to renounce all of his writings—including his plays—except his rogue pamphlets, which he hoped would prove "very beneficial to the Common-wealth of England." [28] Fifteen years later, Dekker took a further step in the defense of knowledge about roguery. In *The Belman of London* (1608), Dekker claimed to have been wandering in a mood of *contemptus mundi* through the English countryside when he stumbled upon evidence of a vagabond under-world; the discovery gave him a new sense of purpose, which was to roam London's streets like a bellman, warning its more sheltered citizens of the danger they could otherwise neither see nor know.[29] Unlike the detectors of rogues before him, then, Dekker managed to represent vagrancy as a voca-tion—and, not coincidentally, instead of renouncing the theater as Greene had, he retained his theatrical connections for another two decades.

The overt fancifulness of Dekker's *Belman* marks a further departure from Harman and Greene, both of whom had taken pains to present their works as true stories: Greene (1592), for instance, claimed that his pamphlets had so angered the rogues that "some fourteen or fifteen of them" had tried to kill him at "the Saint John's head within Ludgate." [30] Rogues were cheats and liars, "counterfeit" beggars addicted to every sort of "cozenage"; the rogue writer insisted on a veracity that distinguished him from his faithless opponents. This stake in truth-telling encouraged Greene to disown the the-ater along with vagabondage; yet Dekker's rogue literature manifests as little shame about his fiction-making as it does about his wandering. The pam-phlet to follow the *Belman*, Dekker's *Lanthorne and Candle-light* (1608), re-peatedly goes out of its way, in fact, to comment on the likeness between rogues and players. For Dekker it is a likeness that clarifies differences: even if players are indeed vagrant and counterfeit, the *Lanthorne* intimates, they still serve the cause of stability and truth, insofar as they help display the truth about lying rogues.[31] A version of this argument that plays are *openly* false had long figured in defenses of the theater; even Dekker's implicit distinction between roguish and theatrical cozenage seems anticipated by the earlier practice in the theaters of binding cutpurses "to a post on our stage for all people to wonder at, when at a play they are taken pilfering."[32] But no one before Dekker had subjected the counterfeit rogue to the stage so elaborately. The protheatrical consequences of such rogue work come clearer in a play Dekker cowrote a few years later: *The Roaring Girl* (1610), which turned a well-known denizen of London's streets and theaters, Mary Frith, into both a stage character, Moll Cutpurse, and a devastating informant against the "commonwealth of rogues."[33]

Thanks to the notion of a vagabond underworld, then, Dekker proved remarkably fluent at rationalizing the theater's vagrancy from social and epistemological stability; but Dekker's stake in professional self-justification hardly explains the great popularity of his rogue works, nor does it exhaust his motives in producing them. Around the same time as the *The Belman* and *The Roaring Girl*, Dekker also authored a militantly Protestant play that explicitly addressed the larger vagrancy problem in England with which I began—England's estrangement, as one Catholic character in *The Whore of Babylon* (c. 1606) puts it, from "all the world."[34] The rogue underworld may have appeared a crisis in itself, but it was also capable of seeming to reflect a deeper crisis about English religion; and this ideological commerce between England's rogues and its religious troubles meant that, for Dekker and his readers, the vagrancy of the theater could seem serviceably related to two national scandals at once. I have elsewhere argued that the traditional reputation of poets as marginal triflers specially inclined England's poets to defend the sublimity and power of England *as* a marginal little island;[35] once England's players had established permanent theaters, their traditional reputation as degenerate vagabonds specially inclined *them* not only to detect a criminal organization of vagabonds within England but to treat England's seeming vagrancy from Christendom as the means to a higher civility and community.[36]

Although the full development of this "rogue" nationalism was to come later, a faith in the broader resonance of theatrical vagrancy made its unmistakable appearance on the English stage near the end of the sixteenth century, in the play that, arguably, commenced the golden age of English drama. Marlowe's *Tamburlaine* (c. 1587) concerned a "troop of thieves and vagabonds" who surprise the world not only with their cohesiveness but with their all-conquering power.[37] A few years later, during the time Greene was publishing his rogue pamphlets, the anonymous *Lamentable Tragedy of Locrine* (c. 1592) brought the nomads of *Tamburlaine* closer to home by dramatizing a supposedly historical Scythian invasion of England.[38] Representations of vagrancy and of English history were still more fully blended in Shakespeare's history plays, which associated the rise of two princely English figures—Hal in the *Henriad* (c. 1596–99) and Edgar in *King Lear* (c. 1605)—with roguish companions, disguises, or behavior.[39] And the history plays of other writers as well, among them *I Sir John Oldcastle* (1599) and *When You See Me, You Know Me* (1604), joined Shakespeare in dressing past English kings as roguish "nightwalkers."[40]

While these turn-of-the-century plays thus granted vagabonds an extraordinary significance first in foreign and then in English history, they also manifested a great deal of skepticism about the societies in which rogues come to possess such significance. In *Tamburlaine*, for instance, the Scythian vagabonds had power but little civility; in *Locrine* and *Lear*, they were part of a pre-Christian world; in *Locrine*, *Henry IV*, *Oldcastle*, and *Lear*, roguery became important to the nation only during a time of national division, which the authorities in each play had only a limited success in repairing.[41] A more patently satirical impulse often surfaced in the rogue pamphlets, defending rogues by treating them as types of a general English depravity: as one writer (1592) put it, "there is no estate, trade, occupation, nor mystery, but lives by [cozenage]."[42] Yet, just as Dekker in his pamphlets seemed less troubled by his association with vagrancy and thus better able to exploit it than Greene had been, so later Jacobean playwrights appeared more stimulated than discouraged by uncovering vagrancy at the heart of a nation's affairs. Around 1620, both Fletcher's *Beggars' Bush* (c. 1613–22) and Middleton's *Spanish Gypsy* (1623) tell the story of exiled aristocrats who manage to return to their society and right its wrongs only by first impersonating rogues.[43] Gone is the pretense to historicity in these plays; like the face-saving commitment to factuality in the rogue pamphlets, it fades as the act of consorting with vagabonds grows more restorative. So little trepidation does the closeness of theatricality to roguery excite in Fletcher and Middleton, in fact, that they embrace it as a plot device: at the end of both *The Beggars' Bush* and *The Spanish Gypsy*, the exiled nobility regain their place and power by means of a play they stage while in their roguish disguises.

Perhaps the most striking development in rogue plays after the turn of the century is also the best evidence that they were intended to address concerns about the legitimacy and integrity of the nation. In play after play as the seventeenth century progresses, a group of rogues exhibit a comic rather than a demonic solidarity that makes their society seem not only sturdier than the more conventional or licensed communities from which they have wandered but even, for a time, preferable to them. A song in *The Beggars' Bush* strikes the keynote of these comedies: "Where the Nation live so free, and so merry as do we?" (2.1.145). So lighthearted have rogues become that they happily accept strangers—such as exiled aristocrats—into their company; and it is this charitable openness or flexibility that most distinguishes the rogues from their inevitable foils in these plays, the "precise" puritans.

An early, hence more skeptical representation of such a comic underworld figures in Jonson's *Bartholomew Fair* (c. 1613). As Anne Barton has noted, the rogues in *Bartholomew Fair* "display a remarkable and touching loyalty to one another," while the more socially respectable "visitors to the Fair have a vastly inferior record" on the same score.[44] For all his talk about "the *Brethren*" to whom he is allied, none of these visitors is so profoundly antisocial as the puritan Busy, who continually spurns other characters in the play on the grounds of their supposed devotion to "rags of *Rome*."[45] Such factiousness, Jonson insists, is true roguery: like other Jonson plays, *Bartholomew Fair* depicts puritans as "the second part of the Society of *Canters*," "fitter for woods, and the society of beasts, than houses, and the congregation of men" (5.2.42–44). But Jonson never allies Busy with the play's more ordinary rogues; rather, it is one of the ordinary rogues who finally succeeds in quelling Busy, exposing Busy's love of contention for contention's sake by tempting him into a debate with a puppet. Significantly, this debate begins with Busy's claim that the puppet, like his fellow rogue the player, has no "calling"; while the ensuing squabble further stigmatizes puritans as the promoters of schism in England, it also implicitly elevates players along with the ordinary rogues into the defenders of community.

According to Jonson, however, it takes more than solidarity among rogues to win the war against puritan sectarianism. Although farcical, the terms of the debate between Busy and the puppet are also openly doctrinal; Busy's comeuppance amounts to a defeat for his style of religious polemic as well (Jonson's friend John Selden later praised the scene as a witty commentary on the "vain disputes of Divines").[46] Insofar as the ordinary rogues of *Bartholomew Fair* confute the puritans, they do so, it would seem, not simply by sticking together but also by evacuating doctrinal controversy. This does not mean that Jonson was irreligious, or that he hoped his plays would encourage the formation of an English commonwealth based on other than religious ties. To a puritan such as Busy, it is true, only "a halting *Neutral*"

(4.6.112), a temporizer "without any certain religion," would shrink from religious controversy.[47] Yet Jonson seems to have a more positive conception of religious neutrality in mind. The lower-class rogues cannot fully exemplify it: even at their comic best they remain rogues, and thus never represent more than a limited, negative image of some better society. But they come closest when unmasking puritan cant. At the climax of his battle with Busy, for instance, the puppet disarms Busy of his Old Testament scruples about cross-dressing on the stage by lifting his skirt and citing the New Testament text that "we have neither *Male* nor *Female* amongst us" (5.5.104–5). To the puppetmaster, this exposure of his puppet's literal neutrality may signify nothing more than a parody of Busy's pseudoscripturalism; yet the joke ironically discloses a scriptural countervision to Busy's that allies neutrality not with atheism or indifference but with spiritual inclusiveness: "There is neither Jew nor Greek, there is neither bond nor free, there is neither male nor female: for ye are all one in Christ Jesus."[48]

Whatever the intensity of Jonson's religion at the time he wrote *Bartholomew Fair*, the same investment in rogues as distractions from religious controversy can be seen animating the literature of avowedly zealous Protestants. All of John Awdeley's other extant publications besides *The Fraternity of Vagabonds*, for instance, express the most militant Protestant patriotism: they characterize England as "God's Fort," under assault from papists who have falsely labeled the English "heretics."[49] It would not be hard to treat the *Fraternity*, or for that matter any other rogue pamphlet, as an extension of this overtly sectarian work. "Vagabond" was, as we have seen, a standard term of abuse for one's religious enemies, and in Awdeley's case the connection between Catholic and vagabond seems particularly easy to trace.[50] Like his rogues, Awdeley's papists employ "vicious pranks" against the English, while a cant name for one "order" of rogues in the *Fraternity*, the "Fraters," is also of course a name for one branch of the Catholic clergy, friars.[51] Building on a centuries-old contempt for friars, Protestants had from the start of the Reformation routinely labeled all Catholic churchmen a pack of "idle beggars and vagabonds";[52] toward the end of the century, as a new "order" of "wandering *Romanists*" began to infiltrate England—the "roguing *Jesuits*"—this anticlericalism bled into nearly hysterical fears of an underground English Catholic conspiracy.[53] Yet astonishingly, neither Awdeley nor any of the rogue writers to follow him directly claimed some hidden commerce between the rogue and papist underworlds, because to do so, it seems, would have been to undermine much of their purpose in establishing that a rogue society existed: what one might call the *introversion* of England's spiritual nonconformity with the rest of Christendom. Rather than depict England in oppositional terms that would open the door to charges of English vagrancy and schism, rogue writers turned from their Roman Catholic adversaries to an internal, vagabond, and irreligious enemy who were just as divided from the Continent as the English were—"*Savages*," Dekker calls them, "yet living in an Island very temperate, fruitful, full of a Noble Nation, and rarely governed."[54]

After the turn of the century, the theater's increasingly comic representations of rogue societies seem to manifest a growing confidence among English Protestants that factiousness and fellowship could be more affirmatively reconciled. What made the difference were two historical developments after Awdeley: first, the rising though still lowly status of players stationed in permanent theaters, who were professionally inclined to dramatize a positive vagrant brotherhood; and second, the growth of a nonconformist (as well as antitheatrical) faction of "brethren," who could take the rogues' place as an internal source of national disintegration while also taking society's place as the broader target of rogue satire. Owing especially to the puritans, the supposed atheism of vagabonds became a more flexible ideological vehicle: it could now contrastingly highlight the unitive spirituality of the English not merely as Protestants but as antisectarians too. English audiences were increasingly urged to view the commonwealth of rogues as the crude mirror of a "free" society committed to religious moderation, organized on the simplest, most uncontroversial principles of Christian faith—communion and charity. As Jonson frames it, the very enactment of *Bartholomew Fair*, for instance, associates the theater with the formation of such a community: although the play begins by representing the audience as rigidly stratified along economic lines, in the end this decidedly unspiritual and divisive notion of fellowship has been replaced by an invitation to festive communion.[55] A still greater openness characterizes the blithest society of vagabonds after the rogue plays of Jonson, Fletcher, and Middleton: Richard Brome's *Jovial Crew* (c. 1641). Telling a tale of English gentry who must learn to embrace a moderate form of the charities and liberties encouraged by the vagabonds begging among them, Brome even abandons the limited body politic of the English that Dekker and Jonson patrolled—London—in order to disperse his rogue-reformed community among the English countryside.[56]

The very recurrence of plays that pit vagabonds against puritans suggests that the players found popular support for their roguish alternative to a sectarian England. Even King James was in some sort a fan: his favorite masque appears to have been *The Gypsies Metamorphosed* (1621), in which some of the most powerful men in England dressed as rogues.[57] Retrospectively, however, the problem with the players' attempts to render their vagabondage invaluable to the English commonwealth seems all too clear. Unlike the homeless, the puritans were no easy scapegoats: they had money available to them, as well as social position, learned defenders, able leadership—and above all, religious solidarity. Rather than acquiesce to the players' satirical exposés of their fellowship, they soon rose to power and pulled the stages down. (Ironically, a production of *The Jovial Crew* appears to have been the last performance at the theater for which Brome wrote.)[58] It is largely the success of the puritans, in fact, that has led historians to overvalue the strongly nationalist view of the English Reformation against which I have been arguing.[59] To the personnel of the English theaters, the puritan victory meant more than a defeat for their positive conceptions of English vagrancy, however, more even than the closure of the theaters where those conceptions had been enacted. After ordering that the theaters be shut down, the puritan-led Parliament decreed that "*all* Stage-Players" were now to be considered "Rogues, and punishable, within the statutes" against rogues, "whether they be wanderers or no."[60]

# The (Lethal) Turn of the Twentieth Century: War and Population Control

Because I regularly teach the "trench poets" of World War I, the headline of the September 12, 1991, *Los Angeles Times* article produced an uncanny resonance for me: "U.S. Tank-Plows Said to Bury Thousands of Iraqis." Roughly speaking, warfare at the end of the twentieth century recapitulated images from its beginning, of soldiers dying in huge numbers in trenches. But there were and are differences between mass warfare at the beginning of this century and mass warfare at its end, and it is the most significant of these that I will elaborate as the "lethal turn" of my title. "Using plows mounted on tanks and combat earthmovers, the U.S. Army division that broke through Saddam Hussein's defensive front line buried thousands of Iraqi soldiers—some still alive and firing their weapons—in more than 70 miles of trenches, according to U.S. officials. . . . No Iraqi body count was possible after the assault."[1] No Iraqi body count was ever conducted during the Persian Gulf War as a matter of Pentagon policy. General Schwarzkopf said early in the air war, "I have absolutely no idea what the Iraqi casualties are, and I tell you, if I have anything to say about it, we're never going to get into the body-count business."[2] This gesture of refusing to count was, of course, not impartial, and just as in the Vietnam War, where accounting for the American dead became a national obsession for decades while the 300,000 missing Vietnamese received little thought, a striking incommensurability governed the counting of U.S. and Iraqi casualties. The refusal to count was given both pragmatic and theoretical justifications: the exaggerated "body counts" supposed to betoken military success in Vietnam had proven variously fraudulent and misleading, and the Pentagon had, in any event, made a strategic theoretical shift from the Henri Jomini school of quantifying military activity, which had governed the McNamara mentality during Vietnam, to the more psychological calculations of Clausewitz, which placed increasing stress on information and knowledge control in the post-Vietnam era. Perhaps without knowing it, the Pentagon was replicating postmodern methodological moves by shifting from positivism toward semiotics in its analysis and production of warfare. In this new military metaphysics the dead body becomes a superfluity except as a sign, a present absence whose lack of representation is as useful as its representation. But the consequence of "absenting" the body from the Persian Gulf War was to produce the "lethal turn," namely, the transformation of technologically produced mass death into the acceptable and legitimate object of conventional and limited war.

In reverting to the Persian Gulf War, I recognize that its six week duration and abrupt end transformed it into an all but forgotten historical blip, hardly remembered by the public. But its placement in the last decade of the century requires that its implications be factored into what Elaine Scarry calls "century pride" [3]—the tendency to aggregate time and its contents progressively, particularly insofar as a century's contents become its populations. Warfare's effects on population have been recognized since the eighteenth century, when David Hume in his 1751 essay "Of the Populousness of Ancient Nations" argued "that slavery and warfare were related ways of reducing ancient populations." [4] Indeed, twentieth-century attitudes toward mass warfare have been uniquely conditioned by nineteenth-century theories and discourses of population control. But the Persian Gulf War has radically altered this modern Western attitude toward war and its relation to population. The shock and horror that had clung to the Holocaust and to Hiroshima as extreme examples of the deployments of technologies of mass depopulation abated in the Persian Gulf War. Susan Jeffords sees this as part of a reconfiguration of the very nature of modern warfare, which operates now "to grant permission for the large-scale, *systematic* murder of a nation's populace." [5] Jeffords, who uses Edith Wyschogrod's concept of "the death world" to refer to scientifically engineered and culturally sanctioned systems of man-made mass death, goes on to write of the Persian Gulf War,

> What distinguished the Persian Gulf War from earlier instances though is that the strategies of terror that are part of the death-world were used, not at the end of an already long and brutal war (as in the use of the atom bomb, the fire-bombing of Tokyo, the conflagration of Dresden, the carpet-bombing of Hanoi,

or the massacre at Wounded Knee), but as its initial strategy. In this way, the U.S. engagement in the Persian Gulf War moved warfare in the post–Cold War era into a distinctively different and more terrifying phase: the combination of the death-world and the technological world as a philosophy of war.[6]

The Persian Gulf War reversed the narrative sense of the beginnings and endings of war by making the depopulation that should mark the drama of its end—the last resort and final outcome—its opening gambit.

In order to situate the significance of the Persian Gulf War as the century's end to modern warfare, I need to historicize it by recapitulating the intellectual history of the discourses of population since the Enlightenment, because their course of articulating increasing hostility toward population or human aggregation is implicated in twentieth-century philosophies of modern warfare. In a brilliant 1988 essay, "Malthus, Godwin, Wordsworth, and the Spirit of Solitude," Frances Ferguson makes the argument that until the eighteenth century the ancient view of populousness prevailed that great populations were signs of national prosperity and political success and declining populations indicated national debility and decadence. She goes on to argue that "the actuarial terror" that Thomas Malthus's model of geometrically progressive reproduction inspired signified less a concern for the physical overpopulation of the earth than a fear of psychic or cultural density and crowding. As Ferguson describes Malthus's 1798 essay *On the Principle of Population*, "instead of being a response to the pressure of too many bodies, [it] registers the felt pressure of too many consciousnesses, and his specter of overpopulation represents what might be called a Romantic political economy."[7] This articulation of the hidden politics of the subject and subjectivity within discourses that appear to treat human populations in the manner of biological aggregations is an important clue to the negative import of the cultural extrapolations that were drawn from Darwinian theory in the nineteenth century. To be sure, Darwin's model of natural selection (based on the survival of the most adaptable organisms amid conditions of scarcity) introduced the principle of what we now call "structural violence" into the economics of competing and aggregated organisms. But even the progressive philosophical and political responses to these theories, the utilitarian ethic of providing the greatest happiness for the greatest number and the democratic structural assumptions of classic liberalism, were plagued by anxieties that their premise of the "rational man" as the model moral and political agent could not be extended to mass populations. The resulting dismay with mass culture and fear of mass movements imprints itself clearly on modernistic thinking at the turn of the twentieth century, particularly through Matthew

Arnold's *Culture and Anarchy*. In spite of its polemical focus on the preservation of high culture amid the progress of universal education, Arnold betrays a hostility to human mass formations, continuous with Enlightenment population treatises, when he speaks of "these festering masses" whose "multitude is perpetually swelling" and "swarming the East End of London with paupers" (194–95). Arnold's fear of an irrationally roused populace and his advocacy of sternness in dealing with it appear to have been legacies from the postromantic recoil from the French Revolution, which particularly infected his father, whose sentiments he quotes in the 1869 first edition of *Culture and Anarchy* published two years before the uprising of the Paris Commune. The elder Arnold is said to have written, "As for rioting, the old Roman way of dealing with *that* is always the right one; flog the rank and file, and fling the ring-leaders from the Tarpeian Rock."[8]

In the next century, the high modernists inherited Arnold's population angst along with his elitist aesthetics—a complex set of related ideologies buttressed even in advance of the Red Scare of the Bolshevist Revolution by Continental philosophy—for example, Nietzsche's critiques of crowd and herd mentalities. What Fredric Jameson called "that heroic fascism of the 1920s for which the so-called 'masses' and their standardised city life had become the very symbol of everything degraded about modern life"[9] had its prolepsis in the avant-garde movements at the onset of World War I that merged complex feelings about technology and crowds into an initial militarism that abated only when its threat to art and artists became palpably felt. Marjorie Perloff reminds us that the philosophical fascination with technology articulated in futurism and vorticism was translated into militaristic enthusiasm in the art community—"The war was celebrated by most of the poets and painters who enlisted as the culmination of a thrilling new adventure with technology."[10] But the overt connection between the new technologies of mass killing and their eugenic uses makes it clear that futurist and vorticist fascination with weaponry was neither purely aesthetic nor ideologically innocent. Marinetti's 1909 manifesto announces, "We will glorify war—the world's only hygiene"[11]—a sentiment translated in the 1914 war issue of *Blast* into Gaudier-Brzeszka's provocative language of population control, "THIS PALTRY MECHANISM, WHICH SERVES AS A PURGE TO OVER-NUMEROUS HUMANITY . . . THIS WAR IS A GREAT REMEDY." Gaudier goes on to code this superfluous humanity as proletarian, when he lauds the war for taking "AWAY FROM THE MASSES NUMBERS UPON NUMBERS OF UNIMPORTANT UNITS, WHOSE ECONOMIC ACTIVITIES BECOME NOXIOUS AS THE RECENT TRADE CRISES HAVE SHOWN US."[12] While we may be willing to reckon the texts of *Blast* as producing a mock-violent polemic designed to shock and provoke bourgeois sensibilities, it may not be prudent to absolutely absolve Gaudier's notion of mass killing as economic prophylaxis from what John Tytell describes as the "shocking recapitulation of the eugenics theory that was prevalent at the time." Tytell ascribes these theories to Winston Churchill, among others—"Winston Churchill was a believer in eugenics and the idea that the earlier stages of the industrial system had created work for an enormous mass of inferior Europeans who were less and less required as the system evolved." [13]

The Victorian coding of the masses as proletarian was transferred to the mass formations of World War I battlefields, which with their physical configurations of muddy, filthy, polluted trenches were easily figured in the public imagination as industrial slums. Paul Fussell argued that much of the disaster of the battle of the Somme—an engagement that the troops renamed "The Great Fuck-up"—was produced by "the class system and the assumptions it sanctioned." The officers took the largely ill-trained troops of miners and factory workers recruited from the Midlands and "assumed that these troops—burdened for the assault with 66 pounds of equipment—were too simple and animal to cross the space between the opposing trenches in any way except full daylight and aligned in rows or 'waves.' It was felt that the troops would become confused by more subtle tactics like rushing from cover to cover, or assault-firing, or following close upon a continuous creeping barrage." [14] The upshot was that nearly 60,000 soldiers—more than Americans killed in Vietnam in over a decade and a half—were killed in the battle of the Somme on a single day, the first day. [15] Twelve thousand are believed to have fallen in the first hour alone. This event also indicates the imputed erasure of consciousness that allowed these men to be reduced to mere bodies or collapsed into the collective and indeterminate pronoun of their numbers that in Ezra Pound's "Hugh Selwyn Mauberley" also transforms the name of the battle of the Somme into lower case—"Some quick to arm, some for adventure, some from fear of weakness, some from fear of censure." [16] The modernist conception of a mass psychology of intellectual inanition that William Chace describes as Pound's—"Lacking both perception and basic curiosity about the workings of the world, the masses could only subside into 'abuleia'" [17]—led William Butler Yeats to expel trench poetry altogether from his 1936 edition of *The Oxford Book of Modern Verse*; "Passive suffering is not a theme for poetry," he wrote in explanation. [18] The undifferentiated mass of the war dead was broken up into significant segments for the modernists only when the poets began to be killed, and their talent and art along with them. "And Henri Gaudier went to it, / and they killed him, / And killed a good deal of sculpture," Pound wrote in canto 16. The modernist turn against mass warfare hinged on a crude recognition of its lack of discrimination. Pound is said to have told Harriet Monroe that the real trouble with war was "that it gives no one a chance to kill the right people,"[19] and Wyndham Lewis, never afraid to outrage, asked "Why should Gaudier die, and a 'Bloomsbury' live?"[20]

The indiscriminate mass effects of the Great War's military technology—whose gas attacks killed livestock on French farms along with soldiers in the trenches—had to be strategically rerationalized in its aftermath and reconfigured into a form that spiraled its lethal turn toward even wider and more inexplicable mass destruction. Military thinking at the onset of the Second World War collapsed army and home front as a way of rationalizing the transformation of unarmed civilian populations into combatants with both infrastructural and psychological roles to play in war. But the shifting ground of the arguments for mass civilian killing also betrays their shiftiness. Civilians were quickly transformed from active war providers, factory workers and farmers whose strategic disabling was a pragmatic necessity, into signs or symbols of national value whose destruction in antimorale bombings would destroy in advance what the enemy ostensibly sought to protect and preserve. Gwynne Dyer writes, "Bombing civilians in cities—not by accident while trying to hit military targets but with the deliberate purpose of killing civilians and breaking their morale—was the final step in the brutal logic of total war." He goes on to find this logic extended to nuclear bombing: "Scientifically the atomic bomb was an advance into unknown territory, but militarily it was simply a more cost-effective way of attaining a goal that was already a central part of strategy: a means of producing results achieved at Hamburg and Dresden cheaply and reliably every time the weapon was used."[21] But Dyer's sense of continuity between conventional strategic bombing and the atom bomb may distort the structure of nuclear war—which, in its negation of the population's consent to participate, Elaine Scarry finds closer to the logic of torture than to war.[22] Dyer's continuity argument may also obscure concealed ideological motives behind the willingness to direct mass-death technologies against populations. The genocidal Nazi campaign to exterminate the entire population of unarmed European Jews made overt a hostility to population whose purely racist form exposed the fraudulence of pragmatic or functional rationales. The Third Reich's implementation of war for population control in the service of an extreme national racism may be construed as part of an ideological shift after World War I in conceptualizing the eugenic possibilities of war in terms of race rather than in terms of class. When, in his *Waste Land* vignette of Albert and Lil, T. S. Eliot figures the Cockney veteran's enlistment as a coitus interruptus insufficient to prevent his poor, ugly, toothless wife's multiparousness, he resonates to the World War I intellectual regret that mass warfare had not been a better form of proletarian population control. But soon after the Great War, a more global and explicitly racist view of populations and their effects from mass killing quickly asserted itself. Walter Benn Michaels tracks a garbled eugenics reference in Fitzgerald's *The Great Gatsby* to a 1920 book by Lothrop Stoddard called *The Rising Tide of Color Against White World-Supremacy*. Michaels writes, "The Great War, according to Stoddard, was a breeding disaster for the white race since, in killing millions of Nordic soldiers at an age when they were 'best adapted to fecundity' it had (like immigration) 'prevented millions more from being born and conceived.'" [23] The brutally overt articulation and military enactment of racism that sets the Holocaust apart from many other global atrocities allowed the racism that is usually concealed, disavowed, and repressed to be instantly recognized and confronted.

Indeed, John W. Dower, in *War Without Mercy: Race and Power in the Pacific War*, points out that Allied criticism of Nazi master-race ideology served to expose the Allies' own racial hypocrisies, which governed the treatment of blacks under Jim Crow laws at home and surrendered to racial fears in the face of growing Pan Asian unity abroad. The imbrication of race and population as locus for actuarial fears that justify mass warfare surfaced, if covertly, in official discourse. "In March 1945, a month before he died, President Roosevelt evoked in a negative way much the same image of Pan-Asian solidarity that the Asian leaders had emphasized in Tokyo in 1943," John Dower reports. "'1,100,000,000 potential enemies,' the president told a confidant, 'are dangerous.'" [24] These words represent a marvelous inversion of the *imagined condition* that Benedict Anderson finds essential to nationhood—namely, that in the mind of each member of even the smallest nation, "lives the image of their communion." [25] Racial fear imaginatively consolidates nations against their imagined relationship with a vast, uniformly hostile population. The collectivized image of an enormous pan-national population as an enemy was, as Dower argues, carefully crafted by the American propaganda apparatus during the war. In making the War Department film *Know Your Enemy—Japan*, director Frank Capra consistently supported governmental pressure to make the enemy not the Japanese leadership, but the

Japanese people themselves, who were represented as regimented, obedient, homogeneous, fanatical, and devoid of individual identity. "Such dehumanization," Dower writes,

> surely facilitated decisions to make civilian populations the targets of concentrated attack, whether by conventional or nuclear weapons. In countless ways, war words and race words came together in a manner which did not just reflect the savagery of the war, but contributed to it by reinforcing the impression of a truly Manichaean struggle between completely incompatible antagonists. The natural response to such a vision was an obsession with extermination on both sides—a war without mercy.[26]

In the Persian Gulf War, I wish to suggest that two tactics merged to produce a chilling new result. The United States employed the technology of the "death world" at the beginning of its offensive, not at the end, less to achieve specific political goals than as an exercise and display of pure power. But its justifications for the mass killing, which had to be activated only when civilians were killed—for example, when the Ameriyah facility in Baghdad was bombed—participated subtly but definitely in the discourse of race. The official White House press statement (reported in the *Los Angeles Times* on February 14, 1991) laid blame for the U.S. bombing of civilians in Baghdad directly on Iraq, by using the "human shield" argument, that any civilians killed in Iraq had been cynically put in the way of legitimate military targets in order to protect installations from U.S. military aggression. But in his pointed contrast between the East ("We don't know why civilians were at this location, but we do know that Saddam Hussein does not share our value in the sanctity of life") and the West ("America treats human life as our most precious value"), Marlin Fitzwater's official White House statement summoned up Orientalist contrasts between Islamic despotism and barbarism and Western democracy and humanism.[27] He implied, in effect, that sentimental America was more likely to mourn Iraqi civilians it killed "collaterally," than the heartless and inhuman Iraqis themselves. His statement concealed what reports in the *London Independent* later confirmed—namely, that the Pentagon knew that the Baghdad facility had been used as a shelter during the Iran-Iraq war and believed it was bombing the families of the Iraqi military elite.[28] The entire incident resonates to the strategy Edward Said identified a decade earlier when he referred to "the recent success of books, journals, and public figures that argue for the reoccupation of the Gulf and justify the argument by referring to Islamic barbarism."[29] This same Western rationalization about Third World populations—that humane subjectivity is underdeveloped and depressed in nonmodernized, non-Christian nations—in turn justified the refusal to count bodies or to give them individual burial in the Persian Gulf War. "U.S. journalists have reported seeing American and British troops shovelling the dead into shallow graves without identification or registration," the *Los Angeles Times* reported on March 12, 1991, a practice in patent violation of the Geneva Convention's articles 15, 16, and 17: "Article 17 requires that bodies be buried individually in marked graves, and only after careful examination to establish identity and cause of death."[30] Implicit in this article is the curious slippage in the double-meaning of the function of "counting" in the operation of the census, the verification of the material existence of populations, including dead populations, that simultaneously confers on them the dignity of significance: what is counted also "counts," or matters. Who does the counting is also of significance. In the end it was two environmental agencies that forced the government to produce its statistically disreputable estimates of Iraqi dead. Greenpeace and the Natural Resource Defense Council used the Freedom of Information Act to compel the Defense Intelligence Agency to make public its internal estimate of 100,000 Iraqi soldiers killed, 300,000 wounded—figures with an error factor of 50 percent or higher that render them statistically pretty meaningless.[31] This finding brings to its provisional close the narrative of modern technological warfare, which along with the explosion of communications technology, will remain the mark of the twentieth century. It has, alas, not been a progressive story of enlightened globalization in the face of world populations. If the mass war dead at century's beginning were proletarianized, the mass war dead at century's end are racialized. It is almost as though Western concern with "other" human populations lags far behind its growing concern with the environment. With only Greenpeace and other environmental agencies even caring enough to count, it is almost as though at century's end the death of populations has become significant chiefly as a problem of garbage.

# Border INSpection: Reflections on Crossing the U.S. Border

On a cold Sunday afternoon during the Gulf War, I was returning from Montreal to Rochester, New York, a trip that would take me through the U.S./Canadian border outside Watertown, New York. Still savoring the pleasant weekend I had spent with an exile friend—himself on intimate terms with the ins and outs of immigration control—I hardly thought about the violent experience of the border, the place where I had always felt the power of the law on my body and mind. It was, therefore, with a sense of cool forgetfulness, gingerly holding my newly acquired Resident Alien Card in my hand, that I encountered the primary inspector who, upon briefly examining my papers, sent me in for a secondary inspection.[1] Once inside the institutional space, covered with all the disciplinary warnings and posters that made me only more vigilant and apprehensive about the dangers of transgressing the immigration law, I could not but remember all my traumatic experiences at the border—the first time I arrived in New York City—I was alone, a boy of seventeen, and scarcely able to communicate with the inspector, or the time I had been kept in a claustrophobic room and body-searched in Detroit International, or still another time when I had to confess the status of my love relations at the Niagara check point to an agent who could not understand how I could be traveling with a female friend on a weekday while carrying a probationary "green card" that meant I was married. The secondary inspection for me, a Middle Eastern "subject," consisted of being asked to wait inside while my car was searched. For what? I wondered. Guns and bombs? What else could they expect to find in the car of a Middle Easterner?

While I was waiting, I distracted myself by watching the inspections of others, perhaps to comfort myself that I was not alone, that others had it even worse. First, I watched two blond-haired agents body-search a group of African-American youths (for drugs?). Then another Middle Eastern–looking man was subjected to the same inspection as mine. And finally, toward the end of my wait, another male inspector began a "flirtatious" inspection of two women who had been stopped perhaps for no other reason than to entertain the predominantly male staff.

During those thirty minutes of waiting, I could not but think critically about all the salutary theories of border and travel I had been seduced by, theories that claim uncritically that the border experience allows the "subversion of all binarism, the projection of a 'multicultural public sphere.'" [2] The border, I began to realize, was not a metaphor of transgression and hybridity but rather a place of policing and discipline, control and violence. As bell hooks has observed, for many people of color, travel and crossing borders "is not about play but is an encounter with terrorism," the "terrorizing force of white supremacy" that construes a person of color as contraband. [3]

As I reflected later on this incident, I began to wonder why we were being inspected differently. Was it our race and gender that made us symbolize different kinds of threat to American security? But could the law be so nakedly blunt about its modes of regulation? And if not, could it be that particular procedures of the law allowed inspectors to categorize us differently along such crude stereotypes as the terrorist, the drug dealer, and the "babe"? It was these questions that drew me to the topic of the politics of border control and immigration law, questions that are closely intertwined with my own autobiography—my anxiety to confront the terror of border crossing and my desire to ward off the fear and violence I always encounter at the border as an immigrant/exile from an "undesirable" nation mediate and inform my critical interest in U.S. immigration laws.

The disciplinary nature of border control and the elusive character of its procedures convinced me early on that the answer to my questions could only be found through an *ascending, archaeological* research project. By an ascending, archaeological research project, I mean, following Michel Foucault, a mode of analysis that considers the infinitesimal mechanisms of a discourse of power, their particular trajectories and specific histories, paying attention to their differential formations and micro-mechanical nature, an analysis that establishes how these mechanisms of power form a chain that is utilized and invested by the more general structures of discipline and control we encounter in places such as the border. [4] In what follows, then, I will provide a few examples of these micro-mechanisms by way of calling into question both the generalizing theories of travel that metaphorize the actual experience of border and social science studies of immigration law that rely on such binary categories as exclusion/inclusion or policing/transgression to explain the predicament of border control. I wish to argue instead for the importance of the specific practices of Immigration and Naturalization Service (INS) agents who are responsible for everyday applications of general laws, laws that are powerful precisely because they depend on principles of interpretation, discontinuity, and difference.

A crucial document to consider in describing the micro-mechanisms of border control is the U.S. Department of Justice's *Guide for the Inspection and Processing of Citizens and Aliens by Officers Designated as Immigration Officers*. This corpulent document describes the task of the inspector as one of "immeasurable importance in the protection of national interests, fostering of good will in foreign relations, and facilitation of international travel," positing thus the inspector as a metonym of national sovereignty (1). As the representative of his—the document unabashedly posits its user as male—national interest, the officer is asked to keep in mind the crucial importance of "courtesy, consideration, tact, and a genuine interest in people" as well as the need to project a positive "image of the United States to the nationals of other countries who come our way." Similarly, the *Immigration Detention Officer Handbook*, another manual published by the Department of Justice, reminds the INS agent that "the attitude with which [he] should exercise his authority is best defined by the old-fashioned word 'courtesy'" (chap. 2). "In the long run," the manual assures him, "courtesy will make the officer's job easier, and everyone, including himself, will feel better about it." Authority, in other words, is presented in the *Handbook* as the "humane and liberal administration of the Immigration and Nationality laws." Similarly, in the *Guide* the disciplinary practices of admitting or detaining "aliens" are given the respectable names of "pleasant service" and "courtesy" (i). Although immigration and customs inspection is by its nature a kind of policing, these manuals construe the agent as an affable gatekeeper more interested in assisting law-abiding citizens than in exercising his or her disciplinary power over "aliens."

It should come as no surprise, however, that the discourse of courtesy and humanity soon yields to that of regulation and control as these documents turn to the basic procedures of inspection, procedures that reveal the exclusionary practices of immigration law. The *Guide for the Inspection and Processing of Citizens and Aliens*, for example, begins its discussion of basic

inspection procedures by stating the policing authority of the agent by pointing out that sections 235 and 287 of the Immigration and Nationality Act grant
the inspector the right to question under oath and search without warrant
the person and effects of any person entering U.S. territory—at the border,
the Fourth Amendment does not apply, at least not to foreign nationals. The
manual is also quite blunt about the segregated character of its application,
delimiting its disciplinary practices to aliens alone. "The immigration laws,"
the *Guide* declares, "do not apply to United States citizens" and "examination under those laws should cease as soon as it is found that the applicant
for entry is a citizen" (1). Immigration law is founded on a profound, binary
distinction between citizen and alien, a distinction that implicitly associates
the "alien" with criminality, illegality, and transgression.

These manuals, furthermore, invest the agent with tremendous discre-
tionary power. Immigration enforcement laws are often too vague to define
the boundaries of legality and illegality, and thus the agents are expected to
use such tools as "behavioral analysis," "cool logic," and observational techniques, developed through "experience," to help them exercise their authority efficiently. Consider, for example, the following advice about establishing
citizenship by oral statement: "Pay careful attention to what the individual
says and the way he says it, as well as his actions and appearance. Experience
will quickly sharpen your ability to detect accents in speech and unusual statements which might indicate foreign origin" (*Guide*, 2). The category of "experience" is crucial here, because it makes evident that it is not so much
training and knowledge that makes one a good and efficient agent as "working the line."[5] Instructions such as these make evident the fluidity and flexibility of immigration procedures. In fact, the *Immigration Detention Officer
Handbook* clearly states that the agent's "attitude must not reflect a narrow,
rigid or arbitrary application of the law" (chap. 2). In outlining the basic
inspection procedures, these guides often emphasize the significance of "careful observation, study, and use of ingenuity" in detecting "law-breakers."
"Immigration inspectors," as Gilboy remarks, "possess extensive discretion
stemming from broad delegations of legal authority and from the organizational characteristics of enforcement" (575). Much of the immigration and
border regulations are about interpretations by particular agents, which in
most cases means the sanctioning of a whole range of cultural stereotypes in
the practice of border inspection—stereotypes that impose different kinds of
inspection, say, in the case of a Middle Easterner with a beard (a terrorist), a
Chicana with an accent (an illegal immigrant), or a young Ethiopian woman
(a drug courier).[6] As Gilboy's empirical research confirms, for example,

"categorization of an individual as from a 'high-risk' nation routinely results in the [primary] inspector treating the individual as referable with *no further inquiry* to take place *at* [the secondary inspection] *stage*" where the traveler is subjected to further questioning, baggage-search, and sometimes strip-search (582).

The scale of control in border inspection, I want to argue, is detail, the infinitesimal mechanisms that can distinguish between different appearances, clothing styles, gestures, accents, nationalities, and attitudes. Border inspectors, Gilboy remarks, "take great pride in their knowledge of their setting—for instance, in identifying the nationality of passengers by the height of the men, by the straightness of the inspection queue, or the existence of pushing in it" (583). No detail is unimportant in border inspection for its potential to help categorize people into types. Immigration examination forces on both the agent and the "alien" a detailed system of identification, description, and categorization. "Discipline," as Foucault points out, "is a political anatomy of detail."[7]

Detail in immigration inspection, however, is a function of interpretation or, more accurately, of the *authority* to interpret. Attention to particular details is not merely the effect of an organizational perception or characteristic enforced institutionally by a particular INS bureau, as Gilboy has argued. Rather, detail offers the disciplinary power a site to seize, control, and produce subjected bodies through the authority of interpretation that procedures of the law allow and encourage. In immigration inspection, disciplinary power is intertwined with the semantic significance of detail, the "truth" that it holds back. Border inspection, as a disciplinary form of examination, posits each traveler as a potential "case," a case that, as Foucault describes, "is the individual as he may be described, judged, measured, compared with others" (191). In such a fluid system of regulation, individual characteristics, interpreted through a complex network of cultural perceptions and stereotypes about "others" constitute a "hold" for disciplinary power.

An example of how the methods of disciplinary individuality are played out in the exercise of border control appears in a story titled "The Revenue Nose" in the government magazine *Customs Today*.[8] The story begins as follows:

Little did Customs Inspector Delmar Baker realize, as he began screening passengers at the Houston International Airport on June 26, 1989, that his observations would set in motion a cocaine smuggling investigation that would span four continents and result in the first-ever controlled delivery of cocaine between the United States and the Federal Republic of Germany. As the passengers were leaving an aircraft which had just arrived from Guatemala, Baker noticed that one of the women was in transit to Amsterdam. Normally such transit passengers are considered low risk and pass through Customs with little notice. But there was something about this passenger, traveling on a Guatemalan passport bearing the name "Funez," that just didn't seem quite right. Baker decided to refer the passenger to Customs Inspector Holt, who was working secondary. Through questioning, Holt determined that Funez was a teacher and was going to Amsterdam on vacation. The fact that Funez did not act like a teacher on a sabbatical, was nervous and was carrying only an overnight bag reinforced Holt's decision to refer her for a personal search. As Funez was escorted to the search room by Customs Inspector Dimple McArthur, she began to cry. A personal search revealed 32 packages of cocaine weighing seven kilograms in a smuggler's corset. Funez' Colombian passport in her true name of Blanca Dominguez was also found.

The article goes on to tell how this arrest, continued with "international cooperation," led to the stopping of a cocaine ring, and it ends with the following remark:

> And so it ended. The long arm of the law had reached across continents to dismantle a drug smuggling organization which had started in South America and stretched through to Europe and Asia. And all because Blanca Dominguez didn't seem right to Delmar Baker's revenue nose.

This story is interesting, above all, because it demonstrates how Immigration and Custom regulations involve a micro-practical understanding of laws and procedures, procedures that make it possible to classify and form categories that enable the law to extend its arms across the world. The construction of Blanca Dominguez as a describable, analyzable object becomes the determining factor not just in marking her with the sign "criminal," but, more important, in providing a hold for the disciplinary power. But the law works here because it doesn't work. She is brought under the gaze of disciplinary power, her body is subjected to its examination and control, not by the general regulations of the transit law, but through small techniques of observation and comparative systems of individuation. By observing her general appearance, analyzing her behavior, and comparing her with a "teacher on a sabbatical," the agent is able to single her out as a "criminal." Here "the examination, surrounded by all its documentary techniques, makes each individual a 'case,'" to use Foucault's words (191). Blanca Dominguez is a case that can be defined, described, judged, compared with others in her individuality, a disciplinary practice that can finally extract her "true" identity. Immigration procedures, in other words, make individuation, categorization, and observation a means of control and domination. Immigration inspection is thus the fixing of individual differences as the new modality of power. What matters in border control is not the law but the nose of the revenue, and what defines the parameters of disciplinary power is the individual as the effect and object of its knowledge.

The sanctioning of stereotype in the primary inspection and the emphasis on detail are of crucial importance in the context of the exclusion provisions of the Immigration and Nationality Act, which is intended to exclude "undesirable aliens." The broader implications of attention to detail are discernible here. What matters in the individualized exercise of immigration control, I want to argue, is not ultimately the isolated cases of lawbreakers, but the organization of surveillance and control to ensure a more general and automatic functioning of power. Section 212(a) of the Immigration and Nationality Act lists 33 classes of excludable aliens, 22 dealing with the "personally undesirable," and 6 concerning the "physically or mentally deficient." The agent is expect to "tentatively identify" these "undesirable aliens," who may range from a "mentally retarded" person to paupers, drug addicts, aliens "afflicted with any dangerous disease" or "physical defect," polygamists, bigamists, prostitutes, spies, rapists, murderers, anarchists, communists, and so on. This list is an interesting example of detailed political investment of the alien's body and mind as the law turns everything to account and tries to name every possible category of "undesirability." In listing these categories, most of which are hard, if not impossible, to determine upon border examination, the immigration law is not as interested in determining a mode of delinquency that an alien may conceal as it is in locating and seizing a site for the exercise of its power. The high volume of cases and the limited resources of INS make it impossible to identify and catch more than a very small percentage of "lawbreakers." The goal of border inspection, therefore, is not the total exclusion of "undesirables," but rather the establishment of a pattern of social control that constitutes a generalized mode of surveillance.[9] The idea, in other words, is not to identify prostitutes, the mentally ill, or drug addicts, but to make them sites where the law can extract the "truth" of prostitution, insanity, and addiction in order to impose on the average border crosser a "principle of compulsory visibility." It is for this reason that all who apply for permanent residency in this country are asked whether they belong to any of these "undesirable" categories in section 26 of their applications, questions that are always answered in the negative, but whose power of interrogation makes one feel the "search lights." Constantly reminding the "alien" of the "undesirable" categories both during the application process and on the ubiquitous warning posters in inspection and immigration offices aims to induce in the "alien" a sense of permanent and conscious visibility that guarantees a more economic, if not more efficient, operation of power. Border control subjects us to a field of visibility and forces us to assume responsibility for our own surveillance. In short, it makes us become the principals in our own subjection.

# PART III

# Fin de Siècle
# Fates, Mournings,
# and In-Betweens

# Strange Cases, Common Fates: Degeneration and the Pleasures of Professional Reading

## Hooligans and Fleshly Poets

To begin, consider two essays written by the Scottish literary journalist Robert Buchanan. Both invoke degeneration in order to condemn a popular author, though the authors condemned could hardly be less alike. In December 1899 Buchanan attacked Rudyard Kipling in "The Voice of the Hooligan," inaugurating a by-now-familiar line of Kipling criticism. "The Voice of the Hooligan" linked Kipling's literary ascendancy with the rise of militant jingoism and lamented the barbarizing effects of both on British culture. Kipling's "exaltation to a position of almost unexampled popularity," Buchanan argued, could be accounted for only by the fact that "in his single person [he] adumbrates . . . all that is most deplorable, all that is most retrograde and savage, in the restless and uninstructed Hooliganism of the time."[1] Late-Victorian fears of the "hooligan," as Geoffrey Pearson has shown, drew heavily on middle-class portrayals of the urban poor as a degenerate "race" whose physical and psychological health had been irreparably damaged by modern city life.[2] Buchanan extends this category to include those portions of the bourgeoisie whose appetites had likewise been brutalized by contemporary conditions. For Buchanan, the hooligan was the type of the modern degenerate, Kipling its most dangerous spokeman. His fiction pandered to "whatever is basest and most brutal" in modern man, quickening the decline of a once-great English people.[3] Under such influences, Buchanan warned, the nation was regressing to such an extent that it would soon be indistinguishable from the most primitive tribe.

Buchanan, when he is remembered, is sometimes remembered for this essay, though his name is more often linked with a piece published 28 years previous to it. In 1871, under the pseudonym Thomas Maitland, he attacked Dante Gabriel Rossetti in "The Fleshly School of Poetry," thereby earning himself some notoriety among readers of Victorian verse. Where Kipling offended with his violence and vulgarity, Rossetti alarmed with his sensualism and "intellectual hermaphroditism." The vocabulary of degeneration again comes into play, this time in connection with what Buchanan thinks of as Rossetti's perverse addiction to the senses and his confounding of gender categories. Fleshly poets are unnatural men, the critic argues. To support this contention, he reads Rossetti's artistic productions as symptoms that betray the pathological deviations of the artist's diseased body. In Rossetti's painting and poetry there is visible

> the same thinness and transparence of design, the same combination of the simple and the grotesque, the same morbid deviation from healthy forms of life, the same sense of weary, wasting, yet exquisite sensuality; nothing virile, nothing tender, nothing completely sane; a superfluity of extreme sensibility, of delight in beautiful forms, hues, and tints, and a deep-seated indifference to . . . all the thunderous stress of life, and all the straining storm of speculation.[4]

This is diagnosis rather than analysis, and so it is meant to be. In such critical discourse the question, as Barbara Spackman suggests, becomes "not *who* produced a text but *what*—what disease, what atavistic deformity, what hereditary fault."[5] The disease of the fleshly poet finds its counterpart in the disease of the fleshly poems, with body and text each displaying the same telltale "symptoms." Turn where we will in his poetry, Buchanan says, we find only Rossetti and his "sickness." No one of his poems is "quite separable from the displeasing identity of its composer," who cannot help but put "the most secret mysteries" of his being on display in "shameless nakedness."[6] In Kipling too Buchanan finds the same impulse to self-exposure, the same aversion to "anything that demands a moment's thought or a moment's attention," the same uncontrollable desire for sensual gratification, in this case the gratification associated with inflicting punishment, exerting mastery, or indulging brutal instincts.[7]

In "The Fleshly School of Poetry" Buchanan invokes modern degeneration theory's founding text, Benedict-Augustin Morel's *Traité des dégénérences* (1857), when he calls Rossetti's writerly excesses "morbid deviation[s] from healthy forms of life." Whether Buchanan actually read Morel is irrelevant; he probably did not. Nor did he need to, since by the 1870s Morel's definition of degeneration as "a morbid deviation from an original type" had long since passed into public usage on both sides of the Channel.[8] Indeed, the most striking feature of Buchanan's essays is the unself-conscious and untheoretical way they appropriate vocabularies of degeneration to make their points. Buchanan gives no indication that he might be working with anything other than widely understood paradigms that needed no further explication or justification. Much of the condemnatory power of the essays arises precisely from Buchanan's belief that he is merely speaking the language of common sense.

Buchanan also follows Morel in assuming that more than individual health is at issue. Despite their differences—and it is difficult to imagine figures more unlike than Rossetti and Kipling—these two writers are in the critic's view indicative of larger troubling trends in the culture. While, as forms of "deviance," fleshliness and hooliganism appear to have little in common, they represent for Buchanan the two end points at which a debased modernity has arrived. A similar claim is made by Arthur Waugh in his alarmist *Yellow Book* essay of 1894, "Reticence in Literature," where the "two excesses" into which modern English writing has fallen are further coded by gender: "on the one hand, the excess prompted by effeminacy—that is to say, by the want of restraint which starts from enervated sensation; and, on the other, the excess which results from a certain brutal virility, which proceeds from coarse familiarity with indulgence."[9] For both Buchanan and Waugh, bad writing has in effect become a matter of biology.

Public danger lurks in such texts. The degenerate artwork, symptom and sign of its author's pathology, in turn becomes an instrument of contagion, "diligently spreading the seeds of disease broadcast wherever [it is] read and understood."[10] Or is it rather, Buchanan worries, that the seeds of degeneration, already sown in the culture, simply await a fertilizing influence? Does the deviant artwork call forth an answering echo, awaken a degeneracy lying dormant in the public body? If so, then Rossetti and Kipling are less the causes of degeneracy's spread than its catalysts. Rossetti's hypersensualism, Kipling's libidinous hooliganism, Buchanan suggests with unease, find their counterparts within society at large. The problem of degeneration moves from the spasms of single bodies to the decay of the body politic and back again, and in attempting to negotiate these exchanges Buchanan's essays generate much frantic energy. What begin as excoriations of deviant individuals quickly become laments for the decline of civilization as a whole. The degenerate artist, by definition one who has fallen away from the common level of men, is paradoxically also Representative Man, the type of the modern age. In between artist and culture stands the degenerate text, at once symptomatic, infectious, and disturbingly mimetic.

## Degeneration and Common Sense

Buchanan's two essays help map out our terrain. He identifies three kinds of "morbid deviation," which are to his mind mutually implicated. The deviations are biological: both Rossetti and Kipling are victims of unspecified nervous disorders that make them write as they do. They are social: fleshliness and hooliganism name larger trends within the culture which depart from healthy forms of public life. And they are aesthetic: Rossetti's poetry perverts romantic sensibility while Kipling's fiction perverts the standards of classical realism. Also running through both essays is a largely inchoate critique of modernity itself as a kind of degeneracy.

I have situated Buchanan's essays alongside a body of knowledge I am calling degeneration theory, but it is important to be clear about what is involved here. Beginning at midcentury the study of degeneration occupied researchers across a number of scientific and humanistic disciplines. Much "technical" literature was produced on the subject, most notably in the fields of cellular biology, clinical psychiatry, and criminology. As the distances separating those three fields suggest, however, "degeneration" had no single fixed meaning or material referent. Indeed, meaning and referent notoriously changed according to the type of research being done. Even within disciplines there were disagreements about what the term meant and how it ought to be studied.

At the most general level, nearly everyone accepted Morel's definition of degeneration as a morbid deviation from an original and thus normative type. This formulation begged a number of questions (how did one define a type? what constituted deviation? how were morbid changes distinguished from healthy?) but it also proved highly portable. As a critical designation, degeneration moved with often disconcerting fluidity through a broad range of nineteenth-century intellectual disciplines. With it, theorists could trace the vicissitudes of single-celled organisms, map the genealogies of outworn families, or reveal the fate of nations. They could account for deviations in literary form or explain the behavior of crowds. The term became a component of debates over the growth of cities, the expansion of empire, the rise of criminal classes, the growth of mass culture, and the development of socialist and anarchist philosophies, not to mention the blossoming of decadent art. It also provided ways to make connections among these disparate phenomena. As Robert Nye notes, by the 1880s degeneration theory "served to provide a continuum between biological and social thought that makes nonsense of the usual efforts to distinguish between them, and was so culturally useful that it could explain persuasively all the pathologies from which the nation suffered." [11] Indeed, the power of the degenerative model rested largely in the way it linked the private with the collective, the individual life with the life of the people. Tying physical maladies, psychological disorders, and social disturbances together in a vast analogical universe, degeneration became, in Daniel Pick's apt phrasing, "the condition of conditions, the ultimate signifier of pathology." [12]

As such diversity implies, while allusions to degeneration abound in the latter half of the century, at no point did its "theory" possess anything resembling a coherent terminology or rational methodology. Such incoherence nevertheless did not inhibit—indeed probably spurred—the avalanche of treatises that appeared between 1850 and the turn of the century. That same incoherence also made it easier for "knowledge" about degeneration to be assimilated into the vocabularies of everyday life. As a model for the movements across time of individuals or groups, degeneration could also be mapped onto a variety of familiar narrative models of decline and fall. Tropes of degeneration were easily appropriated for use by nonspecialists. [13] As Buchanan's example suggests, one need not have studied the subject in order to cash in on the insights it appeared to offer.

Knowledge about degeneration thus became a form of "common sense" as Antonio Gramsci defines it. In Gramsci's formulation, common sense is "the 'folklore' of philosophy," or that "conception of the world which is uncritically absorbed by the various social and cultural environments in which the moral individuality of the average man is developed." [14] Like folklore, common sense is the repository of a "wisdom" that, though powerful and in many ways enabling, is "not critical and coherent but disjointed and episodic" (325). As a "generic form of thought common to a particular period," common sense is "diffuse, uncoordinated," lacking the rigor and coherence associated with true philosophical or scientific inquiry (331–32). (As Gramsci notes, and as the "scientific" study of degeneration bears out, science too can be a locus of common sense.) In uses such as Buchanan's, knowledge about degeneration is indeed deployed "disjointedly," though it is no less functional for all that.

For common sense is never simply a form of blindness. Inhering in its inchoate formulations is what Gramsci calls "good sense." The perceptions and responses that together make up a common sense "conception of the world" may be fragmented, diffuse, and therefore uncritical, but that does not necessarily make them false (327–28, 346). In other words, common sense may point toward pressing historical circumstances without being able accurately to name or even to recognize them. For Gramsci, the "spontaneous philosophy" of a given social group always involves a misrecognition of historical phenomena, yet it also serves to make those phenomena visible for more critical scrutiny. The contemporary problems that critics tried to address were real enough, even as the attempts themselves were reductive, misleading, and often regrettable. A charitable reading of Buchanan's essay on Kipling, for example, would see in it a sincere though muddled attempt to elucidate the connections between domestic class conflict and imperial ideology, a project taken up more coherently by Lenin a generation later. For many late-Victorian writers, degeneration helped to name a plethora of disturbances characteristic of modernity in the West. If their namings were finally misnamings, they still help us identify the disturbances.

Degeneration theory was one of many forms that bourgeois common sense took in Britain in the last half of the nineteenth century. Like other forms of common sense, it readily betrays its class allegiances. As all historians of the subject point out, the study of degeneration was invariably put in the service of an empowered middle class. It was an effective means of "othering" large groups of people by marking them as deviant, criminal, psychotic, defective, simple, hysterical, diseased, primitive, regressive, or just dangerous. Yet we should be wary of the urge to identify a "politics" of degeneration. While it is true that the study of degeneration buttressed a wide range of repressive practices, it also supported various kinds of social activism. Everyone agreed, for instance, that degeneration was intimately linked to poverty and urban blight, but that knowledge did not entail any particular political program. In testimony given before the British Parliament's Interdepartmental Committee on Physical Deterioration (1904), reformists and reactionaries cited the work of pathologists with equal fervor. The committee, charged with investigating "the causes and indications of degeneracy in certain classes of the community, and the means by which it may be arrested," concluded that degeneration resulted not from moral turpitude or an unfortunate gene pool but from poor housing, bad food, polluted air, and inadequate hygiene. Campaigns to sterilize the poor invoked the specter of the degenerate subject; so did movements for better housing, more humane labor laws, and improved medical care. These polarized responses do not negate the claim that degeneration is a class-specific discourse, since the kinds of philanthropy and reform suggested are themselves grounded in middle-class ideology. Nevertheless, we should resist the temptation to posit a monolithic patriarchy that subjugates all others (also monolithically conceived) by means of oppressive discourses. The uses of degeneration theory provide a striking instance of Foucault's power/knowledge nexus, but (as Foucault's work everywhere makes clear) the potential political deployments of knowledge are many and varied. If "knowledge is not made for understanding" but "for cutting," as he claims, it can nonetheless cut in several directions.[15]

Such fractures and discontinuities become most evident as we move away from technical discussions of degeneration and toward its myriad invocations in the popular realm. Popular usage could on occasion be highly informed—the works of Morel, Cesare Lombroso, Max Nordau, Henry Maudsley, and others were widely known and often cited—yet they were more often disjointed. Nevertheless, a relatively small cluster of issues was continually worried over by nearly everyone who invoked degeneration and its paradigms. As Buchanan's essays suggest, fears about the breakdown of individual identities were imbricated with fears about an ongoing and perhaps irreversible social decline. Cutting across both sets of anxieties were concerns about the proper functions of art in a well-ordered and healthy society.

That last issue—the proper social functions of art—turns out to be central to nearly all late-Victorian studies of degeneration. Degeneration theorists routinely became entangled in what have to be considered as forms of literary criticism. On one level, literary works were often brought forward as evidence of this or that type of degenerative illness (as Buchanan brings forward Rossetti and Kipling), while literature as a whole was, paradoxically, praised for its potentially therapeutic effects. Degeneration theorists from Morel through Maudsley, Lombroso, and Nordau (himself a novelist) viewed imaginative writing as the preeminent human activity while also considering it essentially pathological in nature.

To yoke imagination to disease is of course to invoke a model of literary activity with a long and complex history. Yet in many cases that model gained a new biological specificity in the last half of the nineteenth century. A brief comparison clarifies the difference. When in "The Decadent Movement in Literature" (1893) Arthur Symons notes that the "representative literature of to-day, interesting, beautiful, novel as it is, is really a new and beautiful and interesting disease," he is, despite his emphasis on novelty, in fact pointing out the continuities between his own historical moment and earlier epochs of "decadence." Contemporary literature "has all the qualities that mark the end of great periods, the qualities that we find in the Greek, the Latin, decadence."[16] By contrast, when in *Degeneration* (1895) Nordau argues that Pre-Raphaelite poets suffer from retinal irregularities that prevent them from seeing the world as it really is, and that such malformations are due to nervous exhaustion brought on by the stress of modern life, he is making a new kind of argument—one grounded, as Symons's is not, in a (mis)understanding of biology and genetics—about the "novelty" of modern literature.

Degenerationists became enmeshed in aesthetics in yet another way, since works of literature offered models of interpretative procedure that theorists were quick to appropriate in their attempts to decipher degeneration's complex signs. Because degenerative illness presented itself to the interested observer as a series of marks and symptoms to be interpreted, certain aggressive forms of reading were required to make sense of the evidence. The "text" to be read took many shapes—bodies, cells, cultures, nations, races, historical periods, as well as works of literature. Yet all were open to interpretation in similar ways and according to similar protocols. In any case, such texts had to be properly read, had in fact to be vigorously *over*read, before their damaging or therapeutic effects were revealed. From its beginnings, degeneration theory identified such vigorous overreading as the sine qua non of the discipline. This insistence on hermeneutic method—a method, moreover, associated with a specific emerging professional class, in this case physicians—links degeneration theory to other manifestations of the same impulse in the period, most notably Freudian psychoanalysis as well as nascent forms of professional literary criticism. If imaginative writing was often figured as a product of disease, that disease was made visible through the hermeneutic expertise of the professional critic, whose own writing was untainted by the various pathologies afflicting the artist.

The remainder of this essay considers more closely the nature of that hermeneutic expertise, since the diagnoses of biological, cultural, and aesthetic deviance offered by degenerationists were inseparable from the interpretive paradigms in which they were couched. In particular, I will be considering the emergence of a form of "professional" reading in the Victorian fin de siècle, one practiced with the greatest popular success by Nordau in his infamous *Degeneration*.

## Stigmata and "Strong Representation"

According to Morel, the degenerate subject was himself a text to be read, since he displayed the signs of his condition written unmistakably on his body. The droop of a lip, the curve of an ear, the twitchings of a hand all seemed to signify univocally, attesting to pathology. Morel labeled these marks "stigmata," another of his lasting contributions to the lexicon of the later nineteenth century. His successors developed increasingly elaborate taxonomies designed to classify and collate all possible combinations of these signs. The last half of Eugene Talbot's widely read handbook, *Degeneracy: Its Causes, Signs, and Results* (1898), for example, is taken up with detailed instructions on how to identify "The Degenerate Cranium," "The Degenerate Face and Nose," "Degeneracy of the Lip, Palate, Eye, and Ear," "The Degenerate Teeth and Jaw," and so on.[17] The psychiatrist Henry Maudsley, the most important English theorist of degeneration, firmly and succinctly tied sign to essence. "Without doubt," he wrote, "the character of every mind is written in the features, gestures, gait, and carriage of the body, and will be read there when, if ever, the extremely fine and difficult language is fully and accurately learnt."[18] As scientific methods became ever more sophisticated, the author of a popular handbook on degeneration confidently asserted, the body of the criminal deviant would be recognized for what it was, a mere "sign-board denoting the rottenness within."[19]

In postulating this correspondence between outer sign and inner being, degenerationists revealed their debt to older semiotic systems such as physiognomy and phrenology. Yet to a greater extent than these earlier "sciences," degeneration theory made apparent, often unwittingly, the troubling multivalence of bodily signs. Indeed, in practice the difficulty and not the ease of accurate interpretation was more likely to be apparent. "Hitherto I had noticed the backs of his hands as they lay on his knees in the firelight, and . . . I could not help but notice that they were rather coarse—broad, with squat fingers. Strange to say, there were hairs in the centre of the palm."[20] Jonathan Harker's initial description of Count Dracula—rank breath, protruding teeth and brow, scanty hair, pointed ears, abnormally thick eyebrows, pale skin, in addition to the squat fingers and hairy palms—would have placed him for Bram Stoker's first readers within degeneracy's purlieu. Indeed, the Count's outward appearance does correspond to a "rottenness within." Yet it is a rottenness that long goes undetected, despite the vampire's penchant for walking openly "through the crowded streets of your mighty London." Even to eyes as practiced as Professor Van Helsing's in the novel, Dracula is not immediately recognizable as a public threat, and much narrative energy is expended in determining where exactly on the spectrum of deviance "Nordau and Lombroso"—those two prominent theorists of degeneration— "would . . . classify him."[21]

As Van Helsing's experience suggests, despite claims that the body's stigmata spoke univocally, degeneracy's signifiers could in fact be notoriously hard to interpret. Only the trained professional observer could make sure distinctions between the truly healthy man and what Robert Reid Rentoul labeled the "faker." The faker had learned to mask the outward signs of his condition, to dissemble with his very body. To all appearance unmarked, at times "crafty and cunning enough to avoid breaking the law," the faker "act[ed] the part of the normal man or woman" even while harboring degeneracy's seeds within. The "ill-defined case of degeneracy"—telling adjective, that—was "by far the most dangerous," Rentoul claimed, because it made policing difficult and because it blurred the distinction between health and sickness. "The schoolmaster, the tailor, the parent" all might be diseased without anyone—even, sometimes, the victim—recognizing the fact.[22]

Morel had acknowledged the impossibility of reducing degeneracy to its physical signs. What he called "internal differences" also came prominently into play. These encompassed not just abnormalities of the body's interior—tissues, organs, nerves, skeleton—but also breakdowns in one's emotional or intellectual or moral being.[23] Such "mental stigmata" were by definition inaccessible to outside observers, locked away in the body's interior or in the even more remote processes of the psyche. Indeed, in the last analysis degeneracy was not reducible to *any* combination of its signs, whether outward and visible or inward and hidden. It was no accident that Morel lighted on the word "stigmata" to describe these phenomena, nor that the term enjoyed such wide currency among his successors. Like the marks left on the religious believer, degeneracy's stigmata were manifestations of an essence that was beyond human sense perception. Degeneration touched the body, saturated and transfigured it, but the thing itself could be located nowhere. It was never equivalent to any one of its symptoms, but was always located just beyond whatever mark was being interrogated. Degenerative insanity was "a fixed fact . . . more potent than all theories," according to W. W. Godding, yet "it will elude your most careful scrutiny with scalpel and microscope."[24] The body was a text inscribed with degeneracy's runes, a text that in its separate parts or as a whole might be deceptive, overdetermined, or even illegible, a text that would give up its truths only under the pressure of a professional scrutiny.

If the study of degeneration encourages certain aggressive forms of reading, it also associated itself with equally aggressive modes of writing. As a rule, degenerationists traded in what Alexander Welsh has called "strong representations": a making visible through narrative of what cannot be directly perceived.[25] Like professionals in other disciplines—the geologist who excavates the story of creation from the fossil record, or the barrister who persuades a jury that his account of a crime is accurate—the clinical psychiatrist worked to construct a compelling and "truthful" portrayal from an array of mute and often ambiguous "facts." Like the barrister, too, degenerationists were centrally concerned with revealing "character."

In one sense, their representations made character and disease synonymous. Because degeneration inevitably manifested itself in even the smallest gesture, no aspect of one's being could be considered apart from the disease. Degenerationists thus continually found themselves trying to untangle the thickets of motive, intention, will, and desire as they related to a self conditioned by countless social forces. This is territory traditionally occupied by the realist novel, which has almost always taken its most vital task to be the examination of individual character within a specific cultural milieu. (Welsh lists the High Victorian novel among the influential purveyors of strong representations.) Sounding uncommonly like George Eliot, Eugene Talbot warned his fellow scientists that the ultimate significance of a characterological trait could be determined only after a series of complex evaluations of the entire organism within its physical environment.[26] Given such strictures, it comes as no surprise that degenerationists availed themselves of novelistic techniques associated with High Victorian realism. Indeed, for many the realist novel became the normative "type" against which later literary "morbid deviations" were measured. In appropriating the discursive strategies of realist novelists, critics—and here Nordau is the best example—implicitly set their own critical discourse in opposition to the various "diseases" of much fin de siècle literature.

These realist strategies included a radical historicizing of character. Because degenerative disease revealed itself not simply as a state of being but also as a narrative, one that knitted together the stages of a single life as well as the lives of different generations, its study required an acute historical sense. Each individual carried not only the residues of all the acts of his own life but also those of the lives of his ancestors. "To search adequately into the unillumined region of a person's character," Maudsley argued, "in order to find out the motives of his conduct . . . would manifestly necessitate the complete unravelling of his mental development, if it did not compel us to undertake, in historical retrospect, an analytic disintegration of the mental development of the race from its beginning."[27] Like the earth itself in Victorian paleontology, the self could no longer be imagined as immutable. Instead it was riven by history, sedimented by innumerable strata of earlier lives and fates, molded into its present shape by an ineluctable and almost unimaginably distended past. Individuals were palimpsests, written over with the marks of ancestors near and remote. (We recall the popularity of Francis Galton's composite photographs in the 1870s and 1880s.) The scientist who would understand character, Walter Bagehot contended, must adopt the methods of the geologist, since "man himself has . . . become 'an antiquity.'" An attentive eye could read "in the frame of each man the result of a whole history of all his life, of what he is and what makes him so; of all his fore-fathers, of what they were and of what made them so." [28]

Though Bagehot does not draw directly on degenerationist paradigms, he stands as an important transitional figure between mid- and late-Victorian uses of biological paradigms for cultural study. His conception of individual identity as multiply determined by heredity and environment stands firmly in a British tradition of neo-Lamarckian thought that includes Herbert Spencer and T. H. Huxley. But he also anticipates some of the concerns of critics like Maudsley and Nordau who invoke degeneration as a dominant paradigm in their thinking. In this context Bagehot's *Physics and Politics* (1871) is worth pausing over for the proleptic light it throws on Nordau's book. Two concerns link Bagehot to Nordau: their shared interest in the possibility of theorizing national "character," and their belief that "literary" language is central to the formation of collective identities. For both Bagehot and Nordau, the key words are "style" and "imitation."

In *Physics and Politics* Bagehot takes a traditionally neo-Lamarckian view of character. He argues that human beings, like all successful organisms, thrive by continually accommodating themselves to their environments, thus preserving an ever-changing equilibrium with ever-changing milieus. At first these adaptations result from acts of volition, but by frequent repetition they become what Huxley termed "artificial reflex actions." Such reflexes, having been imprinted on the nervous system, are transmitted biologically to future generations. Thus "by born nervous organization," Bagehot writes, descendants possess what their forebears acquired only through the long process of habituation (8). In a memorable phrase that yokes Lamarckian biology to Aristotelean ethics, Bagehot claims that the wholly civilized man is literally "charged with stored virtue" (6).

Bagehot then extrapolates from this argument to posit the existence of national character. The transmission of acquired traits is "'the connective tissue' of civilization" (8) since it allows for continuity across generations, but this diachronic explanation does not account for a community's synchronous existence. In other words, Lamarckian biology explains why individuals are like their ancestors but not necessarily why they are like each other. Bagehot's response is to argue for the primacy of what he calls the "imitative instinct" in mankind. The "innate tendency of the human mind to become like what is around it" is one of the strongest parts of its nature (36). What binds us into communities, he contends, is ultimately our instinctual desire to be like one another.

The audacity of this argument is that Bagehot uses it to derive the existence of nations solely from physiological processes. He insists that imitation is instinctual, a response of the body that is not directed by rational reflection or choice. Unlike Ernest Renan, who claimed that communities are built on "consent, the desire to live together, the will to perpetuate the value of the heritage one has received in an undivided form," Bagehot dismisses all conscious activities (consent, will, rational desire) from the process of nation-making.[29] "We must not think that this imitation is voluntary, or even conscious," he warns. "On the contrary, it has its seat mainly in very obscure parts of the mind, whose notions, so far from having been consciously produced, are hardly felt to exist" (92–93). According to Bagehot, a nation's "character"—its ideology, history, customs, institutions—is written on the nerve tissues of its citizens, who are bound through their bodies to each other and to their collective past. In effect, Bagehot rewrites in biological terms Edmund Burke's argument that society is constituted by an unbreakable contract between the dead, the living, and the unborn. But where both Burke and Renan speak of a cultural heritage, Bagehot talks of a biological inheritance.

What is the medium through which imitation proceeds? The magic word for Bagehot is "style," and he has in mind the power of literary language to construct subjectivities and form character. Individuals are unconsciously moved to imitate whatever style has come to dominate their age. They do not think independently but rather "catch the words that are in the air, and the rhythm which comes to them they do not know from whence; an unconscious imitation determines their words, and makes them say what of themselves they would never have thought of saying" (33). Those airy words and rhythms must nevertheless originate somewhere, and so Bagehot looks to the poets, who for him become legislators of the nation in ways that Shelley did not dream.[30] "Some writer . . . not necessarily a very excellent writer or a remembered one," hits on a manner which all others feel compelled to imitate. This dominant style, which gives "a curious and indefinable unity" to a historical period, seems to appear entirely at random. "Of course there [is] always some reason" for its emergence, yet it lurks in so murky a region of the collective psyche as to be effectively inaccessible (88–89). For Bagehot, "style" is the Platonic essence that differently informs the various manifestations of the national character: political institution, law, philosophical system, religion, domestic arrangement, taste, dress, and the arts. Since they originate in physiological processes, none of these systems can be ultimately defended on the grounds either of its cultural usefulness or of its rationality. In the latter claim Bagehot again echoes Burke, though in the former he turns Burke on his head.

Regarding these conclusions, we can certainly agree with Christopher Herbert that Bagehot "carries out . . . about as systematic and lethal a deconstructing of Victorian habits of thought as one could well imagine" in the early 1870s.[31] Yet it is also true that within a brief time such modes of thought became the norm. Sociological investigations like Gustave Le Bon's *The Crowd* (1896), for instance, stress both the irrational nature of "group psychology" and the importance of rhetoric on the formation of collective identities; political theorists like Benjamin Kidd and Arnold White take for granted that politics is biology; psychiatrists like Maudsley begin from the assumption that character is physiologically determined; and cultural critics like Nordau wrestle with the suspicion that literary language exerts undue influence on a nation's psychic health.

As these examples suggest, however, a significant gap separates Bagehot from his successors. Bagehot explicitly offers his argument as evidence that civilization inevitably advances. Progress is made a function of biological law. Like the early Herbert Spencer, Bagehot sees Western Man moving ever upward as he continues to adapt successfully to changing social environments. This commitment to the ideology of Progress marks him as eminently Victorian. Yet as Sander Gilman and J. E. Chamberlin note, progress had its "dark side": the same "laws" that provide the ground of Bagehot's optimism could as easily be cited to support bleaker conclusions. In 1880 the zoologist Edwin Ray Lankester ridiculed equating change with progress, claiming that modern social conditions in fact made degeneration ever more probable. "It is well to remember that we are subject to general laws of evolution, and are as likely to degenerate as to progress."[32] Like Bagehot, Lankester argued that organisms adapt to their environments, but unlike him he believed that under the pressures of industrialization contemporary society had itself become pathological. Individuals could adapt only by disfiguring themselves. Maudsley echoed this conclusion, arguing further that a new and degenerate "species" of humanity—the "savages of a decomposing civilisation"—would eventually usurp the land. Asking rhetorically "what will be the end thereof?" Maudsley offers a Wellsian nightmare vision of the future:

Once the dissolution of things has got full start and way, it will be vastly quicker than the evolution has been; for the degenerate products of social disintegration will not fail, like morbid elements in the physiological organism or like the poisonous products of its own putrefaction, to act as powerful disintegrants, and to hasten by their anti-social energies the downward course. Not that humanity will retrograde quickly through the exact stages of its former slow and tedious progress . . . it will not in fact reproduce savages with the simple mental qualities of children, but new and degenerate varieties with special repulsive characters—savages of a decomposing civilisation . . . who will be ten times more vicious and noxious, and infinitely less capable of improvement. . . . [They will be] social disintegrants of the worst kind, because bred of the corruption of the best organic developments.[33]

This is degeneracy as a by-product of modernity. Among the "forewarning intimations" of Britain's "inevitable decline and death," Maudsley foregrounds the spread of degenerate writing. He divides such writing into three categories: "elaborate introspective self-analyses; thin and shrieking sentimentalities; emasculated sensualities."[34] Though his focus is on the clinical aspects of degenerative disease, Maudsley does not hesitate to cite certain forms of literary production as exemplum, symptom, and carrier of pathology.

In an 1895 *Fortnightly Review* essay Janet Hogarth makes this connection explicit by arguing that literary "style" had become a primary vehicle for the spread of degenerative practices. The diseased artist often "contrives to shroud the corpse of sensuality in the fair, white linen garment of a beautiful style." Such language seduces the unwary and "disarms [even] the hostile critic." In the modern world literature and disease have become synonymous, Hogarth claims, acknowledging that "it is a little depressing that the ravings of lunacy should on the surface bear such a strong likeness to what has hitherto been accepted as literature."[35]

## Nordau and the Uses of Professional Reading

Hogarth's comments appear in the context of a sympathetic review of Nordau's recently translated *Degeneration*. The signal popularity of this massive work—the first English edition went through seven printings in 1895 alone—attests to the period's fascination with the topic of degeneracy, but also to Nordau's dexterity at translating the discourses of clinical pathology into a pop vernacular. Nordau's canniest move was to situate his discussion squarely within the realm of everyday culture, with examples drawn not from the prison or madhouse but from the lecture hall and coffeehouse. More specifically, throughout most of its great length *Degeneration* presents itself as a work of *literary* criticism. To be sure, Nordau labored to appropriate the authority of science for his argument, but the argument itself consists almost exclusively of extended analyses of literary texts. Literature in fact comprises nearly the only "data" the book offers, yet Nordau nevertheless was able to find cases of degenerative illness everywhere he looked. Tolstoy, Ibsen, Zola, Swinburne, Baudelaire, Wilde, Nietzsche, and Verlaine provide the leading coordinates of the investigation, but *Degeneration* ranges encyclopedically across every literary style and movement of the day.

Nordau defended his hermeneutic procedures by arguing that no distinction need be made between reading bodily stigmata and reading texts. One "sure means of proving that the application of the term 'degenerates' to the originators of all the *fin-de-siècle* movements in art and literature is . . . no baseless conceit, but a fact," he writes, "would be a careful physical examination of the persons concerned, and an inquiry into their pedigree."[36] Crania would be measured, features classified according to well-established criteria. Yet such intrusive procedures (which Nordau ruefully admits would not be tolerated) are not the critic's only option. He also has recourse to other "vital manifestations" of disease—works of art, which "betoken degeneracy quite as clearly" as physical stigmata (17). The same organic defects that produce malformed earlobes also produce "the disorderly tumult" (21) of degenerative art. Nordau works tirelessly to establish the organic basis of all artistic activity, to trace idiosyncrasies of style back to their sources in the chemical vagaries of nerve cells or the misfirings of synapses. The degenerative writer cannot help but reveal himself in his every word, since his words reproduce his sickness. Thus whereas the healthy man tells us what he thinks, the sick man can only tell us what he is. The very desire to write becomes entangled with degenerative impulses of varyingly exotic nature: echolalia, logorrhoea, graphomania, impulsivism, rabachage, onomatomania.

Like many others, Nordau blames the spread of degeneracy ultimately on "the vertigo and whirl of our frenzied life" (42). The human organism was not built to bear the frantic pace of the modern world. To live now involves "an effort of the nervous system and a wearing of tissue" (39) unparalleled in history. The pandemic fatigue of the Western nations is one sure indication, Nordau argues, that humanity's Lamarckian "adaptations" have swung in the direction of pathology. "Under any kind of noxious influences an organism becomes debilitated" (16). Because artists tend to be most sensitive to external stimuli, they exhibit degenerative pathologies most clearly. In a critique of *Degeneration* Bernard Shaw summed up this part of Nordau's argument with his customary lucidity. Mr. Nordau's "message to the world," Shaw wrote, "is that all our characteristically modern works of art are symptoms of a disease in the artist, and that these diseased artists are themselves symptoms of the nervous exhaustion of the race by overwork."[37]

Yet Nordau's message is at once more textured and more insidious than Shaw was willing to credit. Nordau is concerned not simply with excoriating degenerate works of art, but also with showing how art in general operates to construct collective identities. Here two key terms—imitation and style—recur, though Nordau puts them to different uses than did Bagehot. According to the later writer, the imitative instinct comes into play only when organic exhaustion has reduced individuals to a state of hysteria. In Nordau's lexicon, "hysteria" is the last station on the road to degeneracy, afflicting more men (since they are more likely to be immersed in the vertigo and whirl of life) than women. The hysteric is characterized by an utter inability to resist suggestion, especially when it comes to him via the strong rhetorical patternings of literary language. One "result of the susceptibility of the hysterical subject to suggestion is his irresistible passion for imitation, and the eagerness with which he yields to all the suggestions of writers and artists" (26). In the modern world, the relation between writer and public exactly reproduces that between degenerate and hysteric. The former, organically disoriented by the frenzy of modernity, produces chaotic and "insane" (though still rhetorically effective) visions that the latter, weak and aboulic, takes as model and guide. For Nordau the "complete coincidence of [the] clinical picture of hysteria with the description of the peculiarities of the *fin-de-siècle* public" (26) marks the age as nothing else does.

Nordau possesses a profound reverence for the power of literary language, even (or especially) when that language is "diseased."[38] Like Bagehot, Nordau designates "style"—a particularly resonant word for a fin de siècle public familiar with the work of Ruskin, Pater, and Wilde—as the medium in which collective character is formed. What constitutes a degenerate literary style? For Nordau, degenerate works in all their varied forms—and there are many—share one overriding feature. They signify promiscuously. Nothing induces more anxiety in Nordau than the suspicion that language is not, as it ought to be, "clear, homogenous, and free from internal contradictions" (91). The healthy mind recognizes innate bonds between words and things, since "every word, even the most abstract, connotes a concrete presentation or a concept" (57). The degenerate writer refuses to respect such firm correspondences, and his texts as a result generate meanings with scandalous abandon. Every detail is overdetermined—"mystified" is Nordau's preferred term—

and thus capable of leading a hysteric public into unforeseeable realms. Attention is focused on the signifying power of language itself, not on what is signified. For "anyone who demands that words should be the media of definite thoughts" (136), such a situation is close to intolerable. Extreme cases of degenerative prose involve "the stringing together of wholly disconnected words" (94), a procedure that overthrows the logic of grammar, dissociates terms from their natural referents, and disrupts accustomed connections between ideas. "All is discrepant, indiscriminate jumble" (11).

In his own paranoid fashion, Nordau is groping toward a description of a kind of postrealist writing that Nietzsche defined more succinctly. With consummate irony (for he is in part describing himself) Nietzsche also claimed that the decadent modern imagination manifests itself as "style," a style that foregrounds a vitality of the word at the expense of organic form. Here is Nietzsche in *The Case of Wagner* (1888): "For the present I merely dwell on the question of *style*.—What is the sign of every *literary decadence*? That life no longer dwells in the whole. The word becomes sovereign and leaps out of the sentence, the sentence reaches out and obscures the meaning of the page, the page gains life at the expense of the whole—the whole is no longer a whole." [39] What Nietzsche calls "the *lie* of the great style" occurs when an "anarchy of atoms" pretends to an artistic wholeness it does not possess. (Thus Nietzsche can make the perverse claim that Richard Wagner is "our greatest *miniaturist* in music.")

Pace Nietzsche, and despite the bleak picture painted in *Degeneration*, Nordau retains an Enlightenment faith in the saving power of reason. Significantly, he invests this power in the critic, who stands apart from the unhealthy symbiosis of degenerate writer and hysteric public. Confronted with the "lisps and stammers" (557) of "stylized" writing, the critic's task becomes, if not to halt meaning's proliferation or unity's demise, then to identify these conditions accurately. It becomes a diagnostic task, in other words. In Nordau's view the physician and the literary critic perform identical interpretive operations, operations whose ultimate goal is to unearth truths hidden by a welter of confusing signs. Criticism "is the sacred duty of all healthy and moral men" (556) because it possesses enormous therapeutic value. Effective criticism reclaims lost souls. In present conditions, Nordau cautions, "the police cannot aid us" in "the work of protecting and saving those who are not already too deeply diseased" (557).

This Arnoldian belief in the efficacy of criticism requires Nordau to distinguish firmly between the imaginative works he cites and his own critical practices. Perhaps not surprisingly, the distinction refuses to remain properly distinct. Indeed, Nordau's text manages to suggest that the degenerative artist finds a shadowy double in the figure of the critic himself. Shaw was by no means the only reviewer to point out that Nordau's prose exhibited many of the same "pathologies" he identified in others. Graphomania and logorrhea come most readily to mind. Beyond these superficial correspondences, the pathologist-critic shared with his putative subject a sense of the world as a vast semiological field that could only be understood in the interrelations of all its elements. Both kinds of men were addicted, to lift Henry James's phrasing, to seeing one thing through another, and other things through that. This insight Nordau understandably represses, though its presence is felt whenever he stresses the innate "mysticism" of the deviant imagination. According to him, "the simplest word uttered" appears to the degenerate as "an allusion to something mysteriously occult": "In the most commonplace and natural movements he sees hidden signs. All things have for him deep backgrounds; far-reaching shadows are thrown by them over adjacent tracts; they send out wide-spreading roots into remote substrata. Every image that rises up in his mind points with mysterious silence, though with significant look and finger, to other images distinct or shadowy, and induces him to set up relations between ideas, where other people recognize no connection" (46). A more succinct account of the procedures of degeneration theorists could not easily be imagined. For Morel onward, the study of degeneration constantly threatened to teeter into "occult" practices as the hidden signs and mysterious silences of the body were compelled to yield up their secrets.

Yet by moving out to a larger context, we can also say that Nordau is here describing the practices of professional readers across a number of disciplines nascent in the period. A commitment to aggressive interpretation, to reading strongly against the grain in the service of hidden and ostensibly enabling truths, is common not only to the study of pathology but also to such recently consolidated hermeneutic practices as psychology, sociology, anthropology, criminology, and—as Nordau himself continually demonstrates—literary criticism.[40] What links together these and other like disciplines is their status, newly won in this period, as professional discourses. The late-Victorian doctor of pathology differs from the phrenologist or physiognomist of midcentury primarily in the institutionally conferred authority he enjoys. Thus, despite the highly visible connections between phrenology and degeneration theory, the two practices can be distinguished on the grounds of the latter's status as a professional discourse. Nordau himself trades heavily on such professional authority by calling attention to the way his literary readings are embedded within larger discourses of medicine and criminology.

His interpretations strive to be "professional," and thus authoritative, in a way wholly distinct from the belletristic tradition associated with more conventional critics of the period like George Saintsbury or Edmund Gosse.

The rise of "professional man" in turn coincides with the final consolidation of power during the nineteenth century in the hands of a capitalist bourgeoisie.[41] By definition professionals are middle class (and in this period male); their discourses are means by which middle-class life elaborates and extends itself. Certainly, degeneration theory provides an at times startlingly clear instance of this process. Nordau reveals the theory's class bias when he asserts that, despite degeneracy's rapid spread, "the *bourgeoisie* are sound" (2), an assertion his evidence seems everywhere to contradict. He theoretically locates the problem instead within an exhausted aristocracy and certain sections of a depraved working class. In practice, however, the label "degenerate" is attached to any aesthetic or political program that Nordau considers disruptive of middle-class ideals: degenerative practices "mean the end of an established order, which for thousands of years has satisfied logic, fettered depravity, and in every art matured something of beauty" (3). Nordau, like many of his brethren, designates all progressive political programs as ideologies of the pathological. Indeed, he suggests, given a certain level of intelligence, degenerate individuals are invariably driven to become either mystical poets or else socialists. Severe cases lead to anarchism or—it comes to the same thing for Nordau—a love for the poetry of Swinburne.

We can easily dismiss or ridicule Nordau, though such responses fail to account for the status his book enjoyed. Despite his desire for that book to be considered a work of science, *Degeneration* is instead an unusually clear articulation of what I have been calling the commonsense view of degeneration and of its relation to such diverse topics as sexual deviance, national character, class, literary style, interpretation, professionalism, and modernity. The book also reveals how thoroughly entwined degeneration theory was with the collective anxieties of the bourgeoisie in this period. Nordau is mean-spirited, his conclusions nasty and narrow, but that very nastiness often serves to foreground the fears he tries to ward off. Invocations of degenerative paradigms are invariably tied up with concerns about the decline and fall of the bourgeoisie. Indeed, though degeneration theory is overtly concerned with the Other, it covertly expresses the anxieties of a middle class worried about its own present status and future prospects.

# Neighbors, Strangers, Corpses: Death and Sympathy in the Early Writings of W. E. B. Du Bois

In the climactic mourning chapter of *The Souls of Black Folk* (1903), W. E. B. Du Bois describes the Atlanta funeral procession for his eighteen-month-old son.

> Blithe was the morning of his burial, with bird and song and sweet-smelling flowers. The trees whispered to the grass, but the children sat with hushed faces. And yet it seemed a ghostly unreal day,—the wraith of Life. We seemed to rumble down an unknown street behind a little white bundle of poesies, with the shadow of a song in our ears. The busy city dinned about us; they did not say much, those pale-faced hurrying men and women; they did not say much,—they only glanced and said, "Niggers!"
>
> We could not lay him in the ground there in Georgia, for the earth there is strangely red; so we bore him away to the northward, with his flowers and his little folded hands. In vain, in vain!—for where, O God! beneath thy broad blue sky shall my dark baby rest in peace,—where Reverence dwells, and Goodness, and a Freedom that is free?[1]

The scene records a stunning lapse of fellow feeling, an inability to see beyond the Black type to acknowledge a universal grammar of suffering. Du Bois's reproof here is muted and indirect: the abrupt cropping of the paragraph expresses typographically what cannot be conveyed by ordinary language. The moment is isolated, set apart; one must turn away from a human action that replicates the inhumanity of death. This figurative recoiling is confirmed by the immediate details of the parents' departure "northward" to bury their son. Du Bois maintains a "hushed" tone throughout, not because he is too numb to feel this slight keenly but in order to avoid responding emotionally to a display that has denigrated sentiment itself. For what is being represented by this scene is not just a lack of identification with Black pain, but the possibility that sympathetic actions have themselves become the pathway of estrangement. Where we expect to find instinctive recognition of another's feeling, we now find race hatred. It is not simply that sympathy is absent; it is that sympathy is supposed to be there. The encounter derives its dramatic force from the highly structured nature of funeral rites. In all cultures strict rules of etiquette govern expressions of grief and their reception. This denial of sympathy is a violation of custom, obvious to everyone. The air of suppressed violence in the scene arises from the expectation of sympathy, on the part of Black mourners and White bypassers alike. It is at the moment when they are invited to provide the most human of responses that the Whites "discover" their bigotry.

There is a special poignance in Du Bois's decision to locate his insights about sympathy in the funeral of his own son. Du Bois, like Emerson, demonstrates an ability to make personal tragedy resonate with collective and, in this case, political meaning. The scene implies that the act of sympathy may require not only the exclusion but the disappearance of certain groups. While we are meant to read the blood in Du Bois's red earth, the color is also intended as a racial property of the bodies buried there. Du Bois's image recalls a detail from an earlier moment of *Souls*: that the territory around Atlanta was "the ancient land of the Cherokees" (286). Describing the battles before the Indian retreat, Du Bois's conclusion confirms the theme of succession: "Small wonder the wood is red. Then came the black slaves. Day after day the clank of chained feet" (293). This is the history behind the theory of Social Darwinism. Arguments for the natural decline of nations, with superior replacing inferior in seasonal progression, are countered by a narrative of force and violence. If the red earth fails to jog our memories, we have the colloquial "pale-faced" to convince us of the parallel. "Observe the fate of the American Indian," Du Bois suggests, "and you will understand current speculation on the destiny of their Black counterparts."

For what is most peculiar about this later moment is its implication that death and "niggers" have become synonymous in White minds. The incident has a disturbing literalness if one takes into account contemporary child mortality statistics for Blacks—56 percent higher, according to demographers, than comparable statistics for White children in the urban north and south.[2] In light of these facts, Du Bois's image of the Georgia soil as an unmarked grave for Blacks and Indians expands to include the unrealized histories of the Black infant thousands. But the scene's metaphorical implications are equally disturbing: for Whites, Blacks cannot possess a ritualized relationship to death because they are identified with death.

This paper will explore the following series of propositions. That Americans at the turn of the century seriously debated the possible extinction of Black culture—a discussion carried out mainly in social scientific journals and books, but extending as well to other aesthetic, juridical, and religious arenas—and this dialogue of death only becomes meaningful, in all of its historical peculiarity, against the backdrop of two emerging forms of inquiry: the social scientific revision of death and social scientific accounts of sympathy as fundamental to sociality. Growing emphasis on the reception of death and on differences in cultural response and interpretation, accompanies increasing attention to the function of sympathy as a means of differentiation and exclusion. Death itself, its social versus universal significance, its reception within different communities, its typological uses in distinguishing the human from the inhuman, provides a critical impetus for Du Bois's interdisciplinary imaginings at the turn of the century. I want to highlight the status of *The Souls of Black Folk* as a "border text," my term for a book that crosses disciplinary boundaries while helping to define them, a designation I discuss in more detail below. His professional investment in the field of sociology led him to empirical confrontations with prevailing claims for Black extinction. His literary aspirations resulted in eloquent meditations on the meaning of death and on the beliefs and rituals surrounding it particular to his people. Du Bois's engagement with the subject of death culminated in reflections on a sacrificial rite whose enactment in this period was approaching "epidemic" proportions: lynching. The final section of my paper will consider the form that these reflections took.

*

The experience of Du Bois's funeral band suggests how Black identity, funeral rites, the darkness and grief occasioned by death, have come to form a procession of their own in White minds. This conflation of matter and mind, of Black bodies and sorrowful thoughts, recalls a line from one of Emily Dickinson's letters: "I have just seen a funeral procession go by of a negro baby, so if my ideas are rather dark you need not marvel."[3] This is obviously a pun. My interest lies in one consequence of Dickinson's ambiguity (is her mind stained by the ritual or its object?), the idea that race can "dark[en]" thought in the same way as grief, that physical difference—Blackness—is a calamity equivalent to any other misfortune. Yet it might be more accurate, and more in keeping with Du Bois, to say that physical difference most profoundly affects the reception of misfortune, which becomes apparent in this case when Dickinson's remark is restored to its own epistolary context, framed by the sympathetic expressions that precede and follow it. In the same letter, Dickinson describes with effusiveness her readiness to "sympathize with" her correspondent's "cold." In an earlier letter (to the same correspondent), she expresses great compassion for a friend who has lost her mother and feels it "keenly."[4] These sufferings (small and large) evoke outpourings of sentiment, while the funeral procession of the black baby is neatly confined to a play of words. This is not to deny the conventionality of my contrast (Dickinson is obviously responding to friends in one case, strangers in the other), nor to deny that Dickinson's remark may express genuine sadness over the baby's death. Least of all do I claim to draw any conclusions about Dickinson's "attitudes toward race" from this passing observation. My point is that the Black appears to occupy a representative status of stranger, which is defined against the other representative status of kin by the fact that it elicits emotional distance. It is not the affinity of suffering that elicits sympathy. It is the affinity of those who suffer. Sympathy has less to do with identifying what is universally human about a particular individual, than with universalizing a certain set of human particulars.

Du Bois's meditations on survival and sympathy were part of a wider context, which included novelist Pauline Hopkins's remark that "the dawn of the twentieth century finds the Black race fighting for existence in every part of the globe." She envisioned Africa, "stretching her hands to the American Negro, crying aloud for sympathy in her hour of trial." Hopkins's fears were echoed by the journalist Ida B. Wells, who saw rape charges against Black males as attempts to place them "beyond the pale of human sympathy" in order to justify their elimination through lynching.[5] According to these African-Americans writing at the turn of the century, it had become possible to exclude entire peoples from the claims of sympathy. This is consistent with reports from medical historians that nineteenth-century interpretations of responses to physical suffering were sharply divided along racial, ethnic, and class lines. The notion that certain groups were less susceptible to pain rationalized outrageous cruelties during the slave era and supported the withholding of anesthesia from certain patients (typically, Blacks, immigrants, and the lower classes) later in the century.[6] Such developments help to explain the regularity with which Du Bois laments (throughout writings from this period) the tendency to view Blacks as an undifferentiated collectivity—as if thinking in collective terms about humanity necessarily imperiled vulnerable social groups.[7]

*Race Traits and Tendencies of the American Negro* (1896) by Frederick Hoffman, a Prudential insurance statistician commissioned to assess the group's relative "insurability," seemed designed to confirm Du Bois's fears. This study of Black life expectancy contains a long section on "pauper burials," which Hoffman claims occur with marked frequency among Blacks (his figures for Washington, D.C., from 1888 to 1894, for example, estimate 84.36 percent of pauper burials to be Black, despite their comprising only 32.89 percent of the total population). Exaggerated statistics of this sort appear throughout the book. Less characteristic is the oddly lyrical and gloomy description that accompanies this data. "Whoever has witnessed the pauper funeral of a negro," he writes, "the bare pine box and the common cart, the absence of all that makes less sorrowful the last rites over the dead, has seen a phase of negro life and manners more disheartening perhaps than anything else in the whole range of human misery. Perhaps only the dreary aspect of the negroes' [burial ground], the low sad hills, row after row, partly washed away by the falling rains, unrelieved by a single mark of human kindness, without a flower and without a cross, only the pauper lot itself, may be more sad and gruesome than the display of almost inhuman apathy at the funeral."[8] This scene fulfills a claim advanced on the book's first page, where Hoffman announces that his controversial contribution to the nature-nurture debate will explain the notable lack of "that natural bond of sympathy," which might be expected to exist "between people of the same country, no matter how widely separated by language and nationality." The book is an eccentric blend of social psychology, liberal philosophy, reformism, statistical analysis, ethnological description, and racist dogma. This is unsurprising given an author whose publications over two decades included, in addition to *Race Traits*, a history of the Prudential Life Insurance company (1900), and a book on pauper burials in large cities (1917).[9] More noteworthy is the possibility that Du Bois had Hoffman's passage somewhere in mind while drafting his own funeral scene. Du Bois knew *Race Traits and Tendencies*, he reviewed it and refuted it more than once in sociological writings that appeared between 1896 and the 1903 publication of *Souls*.[10] The scenes are curiously compatible, that is if we consider Du Bois's as the mirror image of Hoffman's. One consequence of opening a dialogue between them is the exposure of the potent and meaningful sentimentality of Du Bois's scene. The "blithe" morning, the "bird and song," the "sweet-smelling flowers," take on an air of aggression when set against Hoffman's drama of nullification: "falling rains" and "bare pine box," "unrelieved by a single mark of human kindness," not even "a flower." Hoffman's scene is typical of the way in which their exclusion from sympathy was projected onto Blacks themselves as a "race trait" of carelessness and apathy. Charges of primitive insensibility (Blacks were often compared to the "uncivilized" peoples described by contemporary ethnographers) were used to excuse White atrocities such as lynching, castration, and near-cannibalism. It was as if these White antagonists were caught in some perverse state of sympathetic identification which made them helplessly susceptible to the barbaric atavisms of their victims. Needless to say, Du Bois recognized the dangerous subtext of Hoffman's allegations. Hoffman's thesis that Blacks can't mourn properly—they lack appropriate ritual modes and objects; loss with them does not translate into grief—is answered by Du Bois's record of White actions that deliberately destroy the ritual content of Black burials.

When Whites look at these mourners and mutter "Niggers," they are defining Blacks through their exclusion from sympathy as outside the borders of community. This is consistent with Du Bois's color symbolism in this passage. The first three color allusions are "red earth," "white poesies," and "niggers"—a term that thwarts the prospects of a red, white, and blue design. Blue is introduced at the passage's end in the form of a hope or plea ("where, O God! beneath thy broad blue sky shall my dark baby rest in peace?"), to remind us of a national promise unfulfilled. The note of dissonance, however, does not come from the Blacks who embody this execration. While the white poesies and red earth are labeled as objective parts of the scene, the color black is enclosed in quotes, an idiom that degrades its speaker.

To accept the possibility that we are being asked to read the social exclusion of Blacks here in terms of a foiled national symbol (the American flag) is to accept that the passage has implications for the relationship between sentimental bonds and nationality. The black hole in the flag (where the blue should be) signifies a potential gap between the impulse of sympathy and the rites of an American democracy, a gap that is overlooked in a contemporaneous analysis of race prejudice by the sociologist W. I. Thomas. Thomas suggests that "the dependence of cultural groups on signs of solidarity is seen in the enthusiasms aroused by the display of the flag of our country."[11] The key term here is culture, for America's uniqueness as a nation lies in the fact that it is not a single "cultural group" but a plurality of cultures. As Thomas assumes, sympathy is concrete and possessive, it expresses immediate attachments: to family, religion, ethnicity. In traditionalist nations like Italy, Germany, or France, the rites of citizenship are based on these bonds. A complex cultural affect complements national identity, often serving as an arsenal for aggressive nationalist agendas (as in Nazi Germany). In the United States, sentimental attachments have always existed in tension with the rational principles ("e pluribus unum" "inalienable rights") that are the foundation of national unity.

Du Bois's scene reminds us that in a heterogeneous nation with open borders, sympathy has the opposite of its traditional effect: it threatens rather than supports the collective identification of citizens. From this perspective, the scene stages the dilemma of social bonds in a pluralist democracy. It introduces two of the most obvious sources of human commonality, death and mourning, and the sympathetic response to it, and shows how both function to differentiate and exclude. Indeed, one could argue that the red, white, and black scheme of this passage also invokes (in more universal terms) the three elemental bodily products, but subordinates them to a more dramatically represented politics of color. White is the life source, the color of semen and mother's milk; red is menstrual blood or blood shed in war or hunting; black is feces, the sign of bodily dissolution.[12] It is no coincidence that convictions of the particularity of death (variations in mortuary practices both within and across cultures), and of the limits of sympathy's harmonizing effects are both especially heightened in this period. Du Bois's consistent declarations of distrust in the sentiments, and attraction to social science, are explained in part by his awareness that appeals to the emotion (of the kind on display in nationalist celebrations like parades and fireworks demonstrations, as well as in universal practices like mourning) have so often been vehicles of intolerance.

For Du Bois, there is an interplay between physical, emotional, and social losses: the death of the Black child; the overidentification of Blacks with funeral rites; the distorted response to Black grief are all of a piece. The failure to honor the proprieties of death rites and the disavowal of sympathy's liberalizing role together exemplify the loss of faith in universals that lent a special urgency to the development of the social sciences in this period. Writing in the powerfully moving language that characterizes *The Souls of Black Folk* as a whole, Du Bois captures in one astonishingly brief scene the complicated relationship between death rituals, the problem of the stranger, and the faculty of sympathy.

Let me emphasize how much of what we know about changing views of death at the turn of the century is encompassed by Du Bois's moment of mourning. There is first of all the distinction that had become current between death as a universal versus death as a social particular. As a universal event that "happens" to everyone, it was the great democratizer; as a social event, it expressed prevailing hierarchies and forms of estrangement. In his Durkheimian study, *The Collective Representation of Death* (1907), Robert

Hertz notes that in most cultures the death of a stranger or slave will "occasion no ritual," for "their death merely consecrates an exclusion from society which has in fact already been completed."[13] Du Bois's scene reminds us that all cultures define the borders between acceptable and unacceptable peoples by manipulating their associations with death: an association that was increasingly in this era thought to be an arbitrary one. W. I. Thomas cites testimony from a range of explorers (including Marco Polo, Charles Darwin, and David Livingstone) on cultures where death's symbolic hue is white. Thomas's catalog, drawn from places as diverse as Africa, India, and Australia, reflects a growing understanding of death as an event whose interpretation varies from one culture to another, with as great or greater consequences for the people left behind as for the deceased person.[14] Through elaborate discrimination of cultural practices and beliefs, typological classification of funeral rites, and philosophical speculation on the reception of death, social scientific analyses by authors such as W. E. Roth, Emile Durkheim, Robert Hertz, Nathaniel Shaler, and, later, Newbell Niles Puckett sought to submit this fundamentally incoherent event to rational method.[15]

Du Bois too portrays death as a problem of reception: a series of effects and affects, muting trees, silencing children, dimming song, conferring an aura of ghastly unreality overall. But sociologically, the most profound implications of his scene are compressed into the word that transforms a family mourning the loss of their only child into a statistic, the prejudicial magic that turns a group of individuals for whom death is an unexpected trauma into a collectivity for whom death is customary. The Whites play the role of serpent in an Edenic idyll of proper mourning. They represent the fall into a certain social scientific knowledge of humanity as universally insignificant and socially estranged. Death here is at once shrunken and enlarged: it is shrunken from a universal to a contemporary plane of explanation and meaning; it is enlarged as a society-centered rather than personal event. In one sense there is nothing particular to racial politics in the idea that death is routinized when it is viewed as something that is happening to a social group rather than to an individual. Such a difference is the basis for the rise of F. L. Hoffman's life insurance industry, whose redefinition of death, in collective and statistical terms, was its means of investing it with predictability and control. "Nothing is more uncertain than the duration of a single life," wrote Elizur White, a founder of the industry, "nothing is more certain than the duration of a thousand lives."[16] This view prepared the way for the commodification of death, which now possessed a value that could be determined by the laws of probability. In this way and more, death proved beneficial to the living: every death contributed to social progress (in the words of Charles Ellwood, an editor of the *American Journal of Sociology*, "Progress everywhere waits on death—the death of the inferior individual—and nowhere more so than in racial problems"),[17] and fostered the integration of the community. The act of mourning, according to contemporary analysts like Nathaniel Shaler, inspired "greater fellowship between men than any other basis of fellowship can afford," an idea that inevitably implied the reverse—that it exposed differences between them.[18] Because the distinction between the living and the dead is an absolute, arguably the most absolute distinction that can be made, death not only provided a metaphor for defining the status of outsiders but death practices themselves were an important means for differentiating aliens from like kinds or kin.

It is the failure to acknowledge the force of kinship that is at issue in Du Bois's scene: the inability of White pedestrians to identify with the grief of a mother and father. I consider it significant that the paradigm for sympathetic identification in Max Scheler's *The Nature of Sympathy* (1913) is likewise familial, two parents before "the dead body of a beloved child . . . who feel in common the 'same' sorrow, the 'same' anguish . . . they feel it together in the sense that they feel and experience in common not only the self-same value situation, but also the same keenness of emotion in regard to it." For their "friend . . . who joins them and commiserates," such sorrow can only be an "'external' matter."[19] What is critical about this moment for Scheler, and what makes it acutely representative of the status of sympathy in the modern world, is its self-enclosure. The scene is instructive for what it can't reveal about other potential sympathetic circumstances, for how it doesn't pertain, and in this sense it is best understood as an anti-example. Scheler's scene, like Du Bois's, implies that kinship is the final boundary of sympathy: they use mourning (a ritual designed to master the separation of the dead, sometimes by denial as in the idea of ghosts or visitations), in order to show how the sympathetic response—usually associated with harmony and inclusion, embracing another's experience and extending one's own—functions increasingly in the modern era to distinguish aliens from neighbors. Both scenes spin out into a series of impossibilities so far as feeling is concerned: the failure of friend (in Scheler) or stranger (in Du Bois) to empathize with one's pain replicates the distance felt by both sets of parents from their dead offspring. Du Bois's scene dramatizes a double betrayal: their betrayal by fate (which forges an insuperable border between themselves and their child) is seconded by the passing Whites (who express their separation from the community). It is telling in this regard that the Black parents turn away from their son at the moment of death (351), a fulfillment of a folk decree that anticipates the actions of the Whites.

The question of race remains implicit in Scheler, who offers this scene as exemplary, I believe, to illustrate the reliance of sympathy, in theory and in practice, on notions of similarity and difference. His elusive (and unparalleled) "community" of mourning parents highlights the extent to which liberal conceptions of sympathy have always invited the identification of affinities and exclusions. Sympathetic states described by writers like Adam Smith are really states of "infection," in Scheler's words, where the individual is overtaken or inhabited by another's point of view. The ascription of a kind of porousness to mental life is part of the general tendency of these theories to confuse emotional and physical experience. For the ease with which another's perspective can be internalized is directly related to the other's physical qualities of familiarity or resemblance. On the contrary, Scheler holds, emotional connection to another human being is facilitated, not precluded, by the recognition of difference: authentic sympathy requires a capacity for distance that is balanced by the imaginative access to others' experiences. The modern world is bereft of "communities of feeling," it provides little potential for genuine sympathy not because of its increasing heterogeneity (culturally, ethnically, nationally), but because the inability to confront, either in intellectual or in moral terms, the changing configurations of social relations results in the denial of what is profoundly common in human emotional life.

The very *idea* of sympathy is a problem for Scheler: his effort to chart the concept's history, to explore its sociological basis, is inspired by his belief that the need to construct a theory about sympathy signals its demise as a harmonizing social force. Scheler seems to intuit that theorists of sympathy have been unreflectively motivated by new global tensions arising from interracial, interethnic, and international contact (Scheler critiques Hume's "naive" position on prejudice, for instance, with reference to "the American race problem").[20] These hidden and not so hidden agendas can be traced from Hume's *Human Nature* (where sympathy is "a resonance between people's feelings, made possible by their identical constitution"),[21] to contemporaneous sociological definitions of sympathetic identification as inherent (e.g., F. H. Giddings's citation of interracial marriage taboos as proof of the natural yearning for "like kinds"),[22] to works of pseudosociology like *The Neighbor* by Nathaniel Shaler (Du Bois's geology professor at Harvard), which views sympathy as the highest faculty of human evolution. This last book is an example of what I think is a crucial aspect of interdisciplinary discussions from the turn of the century through our own time. I have called this the "border text," a work that at once defines and bridges divisions among professional disciplines (such as sociology, anthropology, psychology), and in turn, between these disciplines and more popular audiences. Marked by their accessible language and broad appeal, these texts cut across emerging specializations in ways that accentuate the process of specialization itself.[23]

Shaler's "natural history of human contacts" aims at a scientific account of neighborliness, arguing that a psychic resistance to aliens (a term that for Shaler includes Blacks, Jews, the wounded, and the dead) is the most basic of human responses. For illustration, Shaler recalls an apparition during a foggy morning walk in Tuscany: "an unclassifiable creature which looked like a cow walking on its hind legs," a sight that inspires "dread" until the subject is revealed as "a man in a cow costume . . . a fellow of our species," and the "sympathies" are activated. Shaler's apparition provokes a contrast between skins that are removable and skins that are not, between differences that can be dismissed as optical illusions and differences that are magnified by a reduction of physical distance. The man in the cow costume recalls the ancient Semites described by Robertson Smith in his study of kinship and sacrifice, who draped themselves in the skins of sacrificial victims as a means of securing "divine protection." This custom, in which Smith locates the origins of the "robe of righteousness," gives way to a practice of offering sacrificial substitutions—sometimes animals, sometimes social strangers— for members of the community. In keeping with this, one could say that a strange skin which is removable identifies a beneficiary of the sacrificial rite, while a strange skin that is not, identifies a victim.[24]

Shaler's thoughts on proximity and strangeness invite comparison with Du Bois's scene, a comparison illuminated by Orlando Patterson's understanding of slavery as "institutionalized marginality," a system designed to reconcile the contradictory charge of housing aliens within. Patterson cites, among expressions of this contradiction, the Cherokee description of slave identity: one possesses "the shape of a human being, but no human essence."[25] Shaler's man in the cow costume represents the opposite conundrum—a human being in essence despite his shape, whose reconciliation as human is signaled by his arousal of sympathy.

Du Bois's Black mourners pose a far greater dilemma for the spectators of his scene. They are neither human shapes without human essence nor human essences without human shape. To assume their conformity with the structural position of the slave would imply an intimacy and connection that is clearly absent here. This accords with Shaler's conviction that the tragedy of modernity is its terrible capacity to bring strangeness ever closer, without the formal means of keeping it within bounds. Whites can only voice their alienation weakly, through inadequate terms such as "nigger and the like," which are themselves "barriers to sympathetic advance." Shaler's inability to separate such categories from their subjects leads him to conclude, in a chapter titled "The Way Out," that a sympathetic humanitarianism will not reach its highest form until the disappearance of those who fail to inspire it.[26] A reconsideration of Du Bois's White onlookers as serpents in the garden of mourning will help to specify the historical claims of this passage. Shaler's argument marks Blacks with the quality of antique or remnant; they are the collective sacrifice to the development of a broadbased sympathy. Du Bois, in contrast, sees that Blacks in his time have become the special object of a uniquely modern point of view—the sociological imagination. His insight is supported by Ralph Ellison, who observes that sociology became "closely concerned with the Negro after Emancipation gave the slaves the status—on paper at least—of nominal citizens . . . the end of the slave system created for this science the pragmatic problem of adjusting our society to include the new citizens," an obsession that has sometimes caused Blacks to feel like "phantoms that the white mind seeks unceasingly, by means both crude and subtle, to lay."[27]

One might go so far as to classify the era's writers on sympathy along a continuum. Their theories range from confrontations with the vexed and complicated circumstances of sympathy, to a symptomatic registration of these circumstances. At the symptomatic end of the spectrum, we find Nathaniel Shaler, together with sociologists Franklin Giddings, Robert Park, and Albion Small. The critical end includes Max Scheler, whose antagonism toward the category of sympathy becomes more explicable in light of these other sentimentalizations, and Du Bois. Du Bois and Scheler are among sympathy's most powerful modern analysts in judging the faculty to be in crisis. Throughout *Souls* Du Bois tends to capture emotions in color (*awe* over his son's birth is "brown"; *hope* in the future prospects of Black John is "yellow"; *wonderment* on the part of the young Alexander Crummel is "blue and gold"). And there is no image that does more to register the combined material and emotional effects of color than the indeterminate (simultaneously colorful and colorless) color line itself. The book's color symbolism becomes a way of emphasizing that the role of emotions as social forces cannot be fully assessed without reference to the national and international drama of race relations.

The story of sympathy's downfall has a critical epilogue: the deliberate un-neighboring of Blacks. Du Bois notes the tie between sympathy and seg-regation in an 1899 volume of the *Atlanta University Publications*, speaking here, not incidentally, about the funeral business: "Segregated as a social group there are many semi-social functions in which the prevailing prejudice makes it pleasanter that he should serve himself if possible. Undertakers, for instance, must come in close and sympathetic relations with the family. This has led to Negroes taking up this branch of business, and in no line have they had greater success."[28] From the turn of the century to our own time, the policy of segregation has been implemented with increasing efficiency, cul-minating in a residential segregation so pronounced that some recent analysts have labeled it "American Apartheid."[29] Comparing the post-Emancipation prospects of Blacks to the expectations of European immigrants from the same era, Stanley Lieberson observes that there is an actual "deterioration in the position of blacks over time," a decline that is "hardly to be expected" if this position were mainly attributable to the institution of slavery and its aftereffects.[30] My claim is that we have in Du Bois's America, partly in re-sponse to the post-Emancipation gains and challenges of Blacks, an attempt to reinvent their "social death"[31] under slavery in a new, more intensely metaphorical form.

*The Souls of Black Folk* can be read as a book of the dead. "Herein lie buried many things" (209), Du Bois proclaims in the very first line, and he goes on to characterize Black American existence repeatedly as a "living death" (216, 349, 354, and so on). The Sorrow Songs are ghostly ("haunting melody" from the "dark past"), the first chapter opens with a staged ex-change between an animate White interlocuter and an inanimate Black sub-ject, and the veiled life of the "doubly conscious" Black (not "true self-consciousness, but the revelation of the other world") looks decidedly deadly. Eleven (out of fourteen) chapter epigraphs (both musical and literary) image graves, ashes, corpses, mourners—while two of the three chapters written expressly for the collection ("Of the Passing of the First-Born" and "Of the Coming of John") culminate in death and lynching.

The book's symbolic center is Du Bois's elegiac reflections on his son's death. They reveal how personal loss is at once deflected and sustained by an apprehension of its collective ramifications. Grief in *The Souls of Black Folk* takes on a monumental quality because individual death among certain groups can never be separated from the dilemma of group survival. Du Bois's account of the dread aroused by the infant's mulatto features is a way of ac-knowledging that all young Black lives are marked from the beginning by uncertainties about the larger group's perpetuation (350). In this sense, Du

Bois's treatise on mourning offers a significant contrast to its Emersonian analog, "Experience." For Du Bois, it is not the elusiveness of death that appalls, but the ease with which it envelops Black life, destroying an already provisional domesticity. The "fetid Gulf wind" that carries the son's illness, devastating the parental "dreams" and "plans," recalls passages from Du Bois's sociological works describing the perilous exposure of Black homes. Emerson's complaint is that we can never be sufficiently exposed to feel the effects of our exposure. Du Bois complains that there is no way for Blacks to avoid feeling the damage of their experience. Du Bois struggles to reconcile private grief and collective identification, to join Black elite and Black masses. This purpose is complicated by a demographic plot that implies disproportionately lower reproductive rates among the Black elite and distinguishes the relative values of different Black lives.

Du Bois's 1899 sociological work, *The Philadelphia Negro*, commissioned by White leaders convinced that the morbid condition of Philadelphia's Black community was responsible for a more general municipal malaise, provides another perspective on this death talk. Du Bois's assignment was to codify the urban eyesore that was Negro Philadelphia, on behalf of its eventual removal. But Du Bois's revisionary sociology ended up challenging the functionalist theory it was supposed to sustain, by exposing its hypocrisy. Du Bois's ironic retrospect on *The Philadelphia Negro* explains how the science of society was reconceived by his study. It became, in effect, "a Gospel of Sacrifice," with its new gospel text, "the mud sill theory of society: that society must have the poor, the diseased, the wretched, the criminal, upon which to build its temples of light."[32] He also challenged sociological practice by documenting a Black Philadelphia that no one had wanted to see: the thriving institutions of a Black middle class. The book is structured in terms of an immigrant thematics, portraying Philadelphia as a Negro Ellis Island, a racial gateway between feudal South and modern North. It also represents Du Bois's personal quest for professional legitimacy, his immigration ticket, as it were, into the newfound land of sociology. *The Philadelphia Negro* applies sociological theory and method to the circumstances of a stratified and self-identified Black community. To this end, it opens with a Weberian gesture designed to contain Du Bois's bias—Blackness—through an explanation of the decision to capitalize "Negro" throughout. The gesture, more importantly, signifies its author's intent to insert a live and articulate Black body (as opposed to a criminal or morbid one) into the social text of Philadelphia.

Despite Du Bois's revisionary aims, however, the book ends with a capitulation to a more subtle kind of death projection for the Black people. It shows how the Black middle classes had actively cultivated a certain social invisibility. It reveals them caught, like any ambitious immigrant group, in a dialectic of their own unmaking. The final chapter on Black-White intermarriage offers an assimilationist prophecy consistent with the utopian schemes of liberal sociologists who were predicting the gradual extinction of Blacks through a racial amalgamation that was already underway ("survival of the fittest" elaborated genetically).[33]

To confront *The Souls of Black Folk* in the wake of Du Bois's sociological work is to recognize how it transforms a dialogue of death into living art. This is exemplified by the book's attention to the regenerative aspects of folk ritual, mortuary rites in particular. As I have implied, the image of the Whites turning away from the funeral may indicate their unconscious replication of a Black folk decree (observed previously by the parents), that it is bad luck to look at death. This moment is linked to other chapter references—to omens, crosses, sacrifices, journeys, burial customs—which invoke a vast tradition of Black folk practice, representing an apparently alternative system of value. This alternative perspective is also captured by the musical notes of Sorrow Songs placed at the head of each chapter. As published *adaptations* of the original slave songs, brought into conformity with Euro-American tastes, they confirm the difficulty of preserving authentic oral culture. As oral inscriptions of the sufferings of slavery, whose own preservation seems tenuous, they embody the dilemma of Black cultural survival.[34] Eric Sundquist shows how these songs represent at once an elite language, legible only to those who read music, and a secret ethnic code, audible only to those who know how the songs "really" sound. Finally, the Sorrow Songs harbor the book's evolving prophecy concerning prospects for the unification of colored interests throughout the world. Because they are largely *composites* of various cultural voices, associated especially with the isolated inhabitants of the Sea Islands off the coasts of South Carolina and Georgia, they seem relatively immune to American influences. Songs of diaspora, without geographic bounds, they point to the cross-cultural foundations of African-American culture and to potential international alliances of the future.[35]

The dialogue of death is specific to an era: at this historical moment it was possible, especially in certain social scientific circles, to imagine Black culture in terms of decline and even extinction. But these associations have persisted in the twentieth century, as a variety of echoes in literary, social scientific, and popular-media sources. As a rule, neither historian nor social scientists of the American nineteenth and twentieth centuries have responded conceptually to these traces, in contrast to a contemporaneous African-American literature. African-American authors have read past the exaggerated (and refutable) statistics on the morbidity of Black culture to identify a consistent pattern of thinking. In so doing, they have reached a deeper sociological depth than social scientists themselves. Their work has been especially informed by Du Bois's famous formulation of Black double-consciousness, an intense dialectical condition of self and social awareness, which might be understood as a kind of sociological sixth sense. I think of Ralph Ellison's hero at the end of *Invisible Man* buried alive in a crypt of light; or of Richard Wright's *The Long Dream*, which chronicles the life of an undertaker's son. There may be no writer who captures the sociological implications of modern African-American life with more power than Toni Morrison, whose works are also richly evocative of a Black symbolic, centered in the possibilities of folk belief. Take *The Bluest Eye*, whose metaphor for the peripheral existence of Blacks ("on the hem of life") is death. As a domestic correlative to this condition of social death, Morrison's Black psyche is a permanently empty kitchen. No experience of possession, no amount of objects, no stocked and swollen cupboards and jars, can compensate for the foundational experience and ever-present threat of dispossession. The novel's lead character, a small, dark Hester Prynne, ends her days in "a little house . . . on the edge of town." Now a compulsive wastepicker, in fulfillment of her life as a repository for the waste of the town ("which we dumped on her and which she absorbed"), she is, for Morrison, at least one significant emblem of Black status in America. And consider *Song of Solomon*, which opens with the suicide of a life insurance agent and centers on the devitalized existence of a Black middle-class family called the Deads. Most recently, there is the work of playwright Suzan-Lori Parks, *The Death of the Last Black Man in the Whole Entire World* (1992) and *The America Play* (1994), a brilliant portrayal of a Black culture steeped in the rituals of death and mourning.[36] The nonliterary soundings of this theme are notably less self-conscious. There is the Moynihan report on the morbidity of the Black family; Andrew Hacker's *Two Nations*, which Orlando Patterson critiques in his response to the first Rodney King verdict for its "late twentieth-century prototypical Black who wanders on the margins of the White world, overwhelmed by his blackness, a slug on the salt of America's obsessive whiteness"; and media characterizations of Black males as an "endangered species." Finally, consider the label "Death Row Records," favored by rap artists such as Snoop Doggy Dog, which regionalizes the creativity of Black youth as a ghostly limbo, somewhere between deviance and a (possibly compensatory?) land of the dead.[37]

I want to emphasize that this reading of Du Bois's early work explores only one aspect of a rich and complicated endowment. I believe it to be an important one, but of course there are others well worthy of analysis. Let me end by sketching out, briefly, a line of inquiry I develop at greater length in my book-in-progress, "The Science of Sacrifice: American Literature and Modern Social Theory." One of my claims is that sacrifice, as both concept and event, is central to modern social scientific thought. We can recognize it as a fundamental category of exchange: what you have to give up in order to get what you want. In defining sacrifice as the condition of value, Georg Simmel contrasts it with the "naturalness" of aesthetic productions, whose charm derives from the "sacrifices ordinarily required to gain such things." Max Weber refers repeatedly to the "intellectual sacrifice" required of the religious believers he pities and envies. And Emile Durkheim offers vivid analyses of sacrificial rites at home (altruistic suicide) and abroad (self-mortification in the mourning ceremonies of the Australian aborigines).[38] While sacrifice in theory and in practice plays a significant role in turn-of-the-century social science (and this is as true of its American variant), a contemporaneous literature, I argue, *stages* sacrifice. It offers what might be called a corresponding sacrificial theater. These literary spectacles range from the feasting warriors of Frank Norris's *McTeague*, to the foot soldiers of Stephen Crane's *Red Badge of Courage*, sacrificed to their "bloodswollen God," from the wasted working class of Gertrude Stein's *Three Lives* to the female adolescents of Henry James's *Awkward Age*, imagined as sacrificial lambs. *The Souls of Black Folk*, Du Bois's magnificent fusion of sociological and literary method, includes conceptualizations of sacrifice as well as stagings of sacrificial action.

Du Bois's text is framed by rites of sacrifice. They begin with the Hebrew invocation of kinship in the "Forethought" ("I . . . am bone of the bone and flesh of the flesh," 209), an allusion to the sacrificial meal where all, human and god, become one substance.[39] They end with the "Afterthought," where Du Bois declares his book an offering in the "wilderness" (389). The chapter on his son recalls two biblical moments of sacrificial substitution. In one, blood drops are substituted for human bodies; in the other, God's body is sacrificed for the sins of the human collectivity. The chapter's title, "Of the Passing of the First-Born," alludes to the Passover story, where the Hebrews are commanded to mark their doorposts with lamb's blood, a sacrificial sign that ensures that the angel of death will "pass over" their homes and spare their firstborn sons.[40] Belief in the protective powers of the color red (persisting to this day in Jewish and Black, among other, folk traditions) can be traced back directly to this passage in Exodus. At the same time, characterizations of the son as a "revelation of the divine . . . his baby voice the voice of the Prophet that was to rise within the Veil" (351) associate his birth and death (as critics have duly noted) with the story of Christ.

The echoing lines near the chapter's beginning—"I saw, as it fell *across* my baby, the shadow of the Veil. . . . I saw the shadow of the Veil as it *passed over* my baby" (my italics, 350), seem to equalize the sacrificial symbols of crucifixion and passover. But of course they are not equivalent. The obstructed first sentence, where the infant's body, enclosed in commas, appears caught by the shadowy Veil (though perhaps also draped, as in royal robes), recalls a New Testament sacrifice that was.[41] The second sentence, a single breath suggesting immunity through unimpeded moment, highlights a Hebrew sacrifice that was not. These two biblical alternatives provide insight into Du Bois's view of Black American experience at this time: as a sacrificial possibility fulfilled or averted. The collective symbolic status glimmering through the death of this young Black hope (Du Bois notes how the entire race was "sacrificed in its swaddling clothes on the altar of national integrity," 238) is at once the work of an uncommon fate and an all-too-common agency. His uncommon fate is that of a Christian God whose suffering served to justify ever after, as Albert Camus observed, "the endless and universal torture of innocence."[42] The common agency, in Du Bois's words, is the "economic and social exclusion" that might well "succeed in murdering" Blacks "until they disappear from the face of the earth" (*Philadelphia Negro*, 388). Its brutal and extravagant extension is lynch law.

The link between his son's death and Christ's sacrifice evidently resonated for Du Bois with a form of sacrifice that preoccupied him in this period—lynching. I think we are meant to hear the "whistle" in Black John's "ears" at his lynching, as the completion of the "shadow . . . song" in the "ears" of the mourners at Burghardt Du Bois's funeral (377, 353). Surveying the Atlanta lands of the Cherokees earlier in *Souls*, Du Bois draws our attention to the spot "where Sam Hose was crucified" (285). The display of Hose's charred knuckles in an Atlanta storefront a month before Burghardt's death (Du Bois heard about it but avoided the spectacle) turned Atlanta, according to Du Bois's biographer, into "a poisoned well, polluted with the remains of Sam Hose and reflecting the drawn image of Burghardt."[43] The proximity of these two Black deaths highlights Du Bois's burden throughout this chapter, to reconcile his own analytical distance from a Black America stigmatized by high mortality with a firsthand experience that tragically confirms his own implication in it.

I hope I have made sufficiently clear that the stigma of excessive Black mortality, especially as it adhered after the turn of the century, was at least in part an expression of the very opposite concern: the surprising vitality of Black population rates. In the same 1908 *American Journal of Sociology* debate where he identified American "race friction" as a problem of international proportions, Du Bois labeled America's color line the war plan of besieged Whites, who had rightly deduced that the hard logic of bodies and numbers was bound to favor the world's darker peoples.[44] The practice of lynching confirmed the inversion that was taking place. For lynching was invariably imagined as an act of vengeance: a retribution for the White female victims of Black hypersexuality (or hyperfecundity), often exacted quite literally through the accompanying ritual of castration. The suspicion that Black population growth was in fact vigorous was manifested in reactions to the prospect of Black suffrage, a development that "ended a civil war by beginning a race feud" (*Souls*, 238).

Lynching was a monstrous inversion of the mortality issue, the proof that far from being fated, the elimination of Blacks required aggressive action, extending to the mutilation of their reproductive organs. Lynching also represented a monstrous fulfillment of the sympathy crisis: a frenzied unification of White sentiment, a segregated, incestuous sympathy gone wild. The lynch mob was the logical culmination of sympathy's rewriting as a circumscribed intragroup exchange. Here group identity was founded in the ritual sacrifice of social strangers. This aspect of sympathetic identification was especially apparent to James Elbert Cutler, a disciple of William Graham Sumner and author of the social scientific study *Lynch-Law* (1905). As a stage for the problems of mob behavior, intolerance, and social integration and a litmus test for the shortcomings of liberalism, it is easy to see why lynching caught the attention of contemporary social scientists. In this light, Du Bois's disclaimer, that lynching made him doubt the value of rational analysis, seems more a matter of personal experience than professional judgment. Still, Cutler's obvious sympathies for lynching, and the fact that his effort to explain lynching scientifically often amounted to explaining it away, serve to substantiate Du Bois's charge. There is no doubt that the resemblances between American lynchings and the violent, cannibalistic rites of uncivilized peoples were deeply disconcerting to the liberal practitioners of social science.[45] But Cutler views lynching as both an expression of social instability, and a critical means for managing social difference. Lynch law could not have escalated, he points out, were the majority of citizens out of "sympathy with the mob." Nor would lynching subside until the American legal system was relieved of its commitment to "abstract principles concerning the rights of all men" and brought into conformity with the "ethnic and societal factors involved in the race question."[46] Cutler's claim is fully consistent with the conclusions on sympathy reached by Nathaniel Shaler and F. H. Giddings. Political ideals were one thing, social facts another. Until they were reconciled, there would be collective effusions such as lynchings.

Undoubtedly, the most striking passage in *Lynch-Law* is Abraham Lincoln's account of those "sacrificed" in an exemplary rash of violence: "First . . . gamblers—a set of men certainly not following for a livelihood a very useful or very honest occupation. . . . Next, negroes suspected of conspiring to rise an insurrection . . . then, white men supposed to be leagued with the negroes; and finally, strangers from neighboring States . . . till dead men were literally dangling from the boughs of trees by every roadside, and in numbers almost sufficient to rival the native Spanish moss of the country as a drapery of the forest."[47] Lincoln's haunting description transforms lynched strangers into "rivals" even in death, now of the more "native" moss. Despite differences in content, Lincoln's list anticipates in its apparent oddity a much later assortment of victims by Rene Girard: "prisoners of war, slaves, small children, unmarried adolescents . . . [sometimes] the king himself."[48] These analytical attempts to discriminate the identities of typical victims can be seen as fragile borders, in their own right, against the chaos that is supposedly foreclosed by ritual violence. But they help to pinpoint just what is at stake in sacrificial designs. Sacrifice is always at least in part motivated by a threatened erasure of social distinctions. The victims are considered expendable because they are casteless, or have somehow abandoned the bounds of caste. As social strangers, or neighbors without strong allies, their deaths do not entail acts of vengeance.

In biblical Hebrew the generic term for sacrifice is "korban"—"to bring near"—which implies the effort to bring a God or gods closer to human experience.[49] It is clear from Du Bois's hopeless apostrophes throughout the chapter (alternately to Death, Fate, and God), that he has little faith in the prospects for such intimacy. Du Bois is an unwilling Abraham: he offers up his son with a resentful eye toward "all" that I have "foregone at thy command, and without complaint . . . save that fair young form" (354). Du Bois's resentment raises questions about resistance, and the place of sacrificial rites within the Black community itself. This is consistent with the sacrificial elements of Black folk religion as Du Bois portrays it in *Souls*, specifically the Obi worship of slavery days. It's unclear from Du Bois's description who the victims were, or how the particular aims of such "blood-sacrifices" were construed (341–43). But he seems intent on confirming the lingering impact of this vengeful spirituality. This theme is brought forth to the book's conclusion where he notes how "fire and blood, prayer and sacrifice, have billowed over this people, and they have found peace only in the altars of the God of Right" (387). American Blacks have been much sacrificed, he suggests, but they are not without their own forms of sacrificial agency. Du Bois's preoccupations with death and sacrifice form a central part of his legacy: to confront them is to recognize how the identification of a negative cultural typology can be a source of creative inspiration, critique, and ultimately, perhaps, even renewal. There is no stronger evidence of this final possibility than Du Bois's "After-thought," conveyed in the form of a sacrificial offering. "Hear my cry, O God the Reader; vouchsafe that this my book fall not still-born into the world wilderness" (389).

## What's Awkward About *The Awkward Age?*

The title of Henry James's 1899 novel *The Awkward Age* refers most directly not to the historical moment at which it was written and which it also represents, but to the problematical age of its eighteen-year-old heroine, Nanda Brookenham.[1] In his 1908 New York Edition preface to the novel, James locates its "scant but quite ponderable germ" in "the note one had inevitably had to take of the difference made in certain friendly houses and for certain flourishing mothers by the sometimes dreaded, often delayed, but never fully arrested coming to the forefront of some vague slip of a daughter."[2] Nanda, the "modern daughter" (*AA*, 106), is at that "awkward," in-between age— too old to remain upstairs, not quite old enough to be "down" in the "circle of free talk" (*AN*, 101) constituted by her mother's drawing room—and her descent in turn creates an awkward situation for the members of that circle. "The inevitable irruption of the ingenuous mind" into the "free circle" triggers a "mild revolution" requiring "some sacrifice in some quarter," an "interval," James says, "to be bridged," in which the "frankness" and "ease" of the already initiated adults' conversation must be compromised or, as Stuart Culver has put it, censored, if Nanda is to remain marriageable (*AN*, 100, 102–3).[3] In the Preface, James specifically defines this "interval" as the period between the first *exposure* to the socialized realm of talk for this "merciless maiden" and her marriage, a period that can be short or long depending upon whether the methods employed in "keeping the place tidy . . . for the young female mind" involve "some rude simplification" ("a girl," he points out, "might be married off the day after her irruption") or alternatively, more complex forms of "diplomacy" (*AN*, 100; *AA*, 170; *AN*, 102–3).

*The Awkward Age*, then, is "precisely a study of one of these curtailed or extended periods of tension and apprehension, an account of the manner in which the resented interference with ancient liberties came to be in a particular instance dealt with" (*AN*, 103). And James's insistence that the awkward social situation depicted—awkward in the sense of uncomfortable, embarrassing, requiring caution, lacking in ease or grace for its participants—is also a temporal interval suggests that we *should* read his title as in part a reference to the fin de siècle moment to which the book belongs. Indeed, in the Preface James repeatedly stresses his conviction that his "vague slip of a subject" was viable precisely insofar as it was topical, a timely glance at a social phenomenon of the moment worthy of Oprah (though perhaps not quite of Geraldo). *The Awkward Age* is in one sense a comedy of manners— albeit a highly experimental one—dependent for its effects on a detailed, some would say infuriatingly minute, observation of a particular social class in a particular national culture at a particular historical moment. But what, exactly, does it mean to comprehend one's historical situatedness *as* "awkward?"

In his Preface James remarks that the free intercourse of contemporary "talk" is "as far as possible removed" not only from that of "the nursery and the schoolroom" but also from "that of supposedly privileged scenes of conversation twenty years ago" (*AN*, 102)—a comment that not only links the two ages of his title, but that points as well to the disjunctions and discontinuities repeatedly experienced by the novel's characters. Mr. Longdon, the elderly bachelor and unrequited lover of Nanda's grandmother, Lady Julia, returns to society after a retirement of some years only to find himself unable to understand the manners and speech—especially the up-to-the-minute slang—of Mrs. Brookenham's circle. "I belong to a different period of history," he exclaims to Vanderbank, the circle's handsome and eligible young civil servant, after his first evening in London. "There have been things this evening that have made me feel as if I had been disinterred—literally dug up from a long sleep" (*AA*, 22). Later in the novel, Longdon, who remembers Van's mother from his earlier time, comments that "she herself, today, wouldn't know [Van]" nor he her—"There's a link missing"—before going on to admit that it's really "I . . . who have lost the link in my sleep. I've slept half the century—I'm Rip Van Winckle" (*AA*, 136). Modern society is repeatedly depicted in the novel as "disconnected altogether" from its past (*AA*, 120): "its origin[s]," like those of the cigarette case Van at one point contemplates giving as a present to Nanda, are "lost in the night of time" (*AA*, 129). When the "circle" descends on the country house of Mitchy, its *nouveau riche* "son of a shoemaker" (*AA*, 51), we quickly learn that the house—described in terms taken straight from the pages of *Tom Jones* or *Pride and Prejudice*—is only rented. Van in fact recalls having stayed there, "but not with Mitchy; with some people or other—who the deuce can they have been?—who had the place for a few months a year or two ago." Van takes it as a "charming sign of London relations" that he has "los[t] the whole thing," quite forgotten "to whom [he] ha[d] been beholden"—though he takes comfort in being sure that his former hosts' "minds are an equal blank. Do they even remember the place they had?" (*AA*, 126–28).

"You see," Van at one point says to Longdon, "we don't in the least know where we are. We're lost" (*AA*, 37). And this mode of experiencing the historical present as an awkward gap, an interval floating somewhere between origins and ends that are equally unlocatable, is obviously not without its disturbing implications, both for the novel's characters and for its readers. When Longdon asks Van, "What becomes of friendship" in modern London—and Longdon, we are told, "maintained the full value of the word"— Van responds blankly, "Friendship?" (*AA*, 28), the word, like so much else in the novel, apparently having lost its link to any discernible source or signified. Tzvetan Todorov, in what is probably still the most influential reading of *The Awkward Age*, finds in Longdon the traces of James's own nostalgic regret for a lost world of "full values." But James, as Todorov recognizes, is only partly committed to Longdon's position;[4] for James understands—and here I am paraphrasing Joan Scott—that full values, full by virtue of their secure place and presence in a teleology of origins and ends, are in fact both too full and too empty: too full because even when they appear to be fixed, they still contain within them alternative, denied, or suppressed possibilities; too empty because they have no original or ultimate, no natural or transcendent meaning.[5] *The Awkward Age* portrays a rapidly revolving world in which, as Nanda says, "everything changes. It's the law—what is it?—'the great law' of something or other" (*AA*, 289). And in a novel that consists almost entirely of "talk," historical change is felt most insistently as linguistic change, in and through the gaps that open up between words and the values previously invested in them. But where Longdon mourns the loss of the fixed and full meanings once attached to words like "lady" and "gentleman," and is shocked by Van's playful assertion that nowadays "everything" can be called "anything" (*AA*, 165), James seems mostly exhilarated by the historical contingency of words and values. When words lose their connections to "natural" or "transcendent" signifieds, they also acquire a capacity to take on new meanings, meanings which in turn have the potential to enable new forms of experience, new ways, for example, of *being* ladies and gentlemen.

"We live notoriously," James remarks in the Preface, "as I suppose every age lives, in an 'epoch of transition'" (*AN*, 103). And if I emphasize the crucial qualifying phrase here ("as I suppose every age lives"), as well as the scare quotes that surround "epoch of transition," it is because they suggest not only an ironic commentary on the urgent exceptionalism of so much fin de siècle rhetoric, but also the nature of James's own counterdiscourse of the century's end: eschewing the languages of apocalypse, decadence and/or nostalgia, *The Awkward Age*, I argue, refigures the disjunctions and discontinuities of the fin de siècle as the disorienting but potentially productive "awkwardnesses" of what James calls an "appealing 'modernity'" (*AN*, 102). Arnold's sense of being lost "between two worlds, one dead, / The other powerless to be born,"[6] typically evolves, by the century's end, into a flight from history—into narratives of collapse, exhaustion and degeneracy, hysterical visions of political and sexual anarchy, and their attendant nostalgic myths of some lost golden age of unity and "full value," or, alternatively, into apocalyptic anticipations of some new, more "authentic" totalizing order. Many of James's contemporaries viewed *The Awkward Age* as a decidedly decadent text: condemned as a "study of degeneration" permeated by "an atmosphere of mental and moral squalor," the book was also denounced as a "swamp" of "pessimism and unpleasantness and horrors" worthy of "the most unnatural French creations."[7] And subsequent critics have frequently associated the novel's elaborate, artificial style and its intricate, autotelic formal structure with another kind of antihistoricism—the fin de siècle cult of art for art's sake.[8] But if James in his preface jokingly acknowledges the charge that the novel had been pumped "gaspingly dry . . . not only of superfluous moisture, but absolutely . . . of breathable air" (*AN*, 114), it would be a mistake to interpret *The Awkward Age* as a withdrawal from history into the palace of art. As Jonathan Freedman has shown, reading James in the context of British aestheticism can in turn help us to recover "the fascinating volatility of aestheticist art," and to recognize the simultaneous existence of "an intense, even obsessive historicism" alongside the "desire to evade or annul history."[9] *The Awkward Age*, I believe, is precisely a case of "obsessive historicism," a book that embodies not a revolt against history, but its refiguration as the inevitable in-betweenness of historical process, and that finds in the missing links and disconnections experienced by its characters the potential for transforming the discursive and social structures within which we understand and make history.

To understand history, as I am arguing that James does, as a perpetually awkward situation—to see every age as a process, rather than an epoch, of transition—is also to make room for those alternative, denied, and repressed possibilities, the "complications," as James says, "almost beyond reckoning" (*AN*, 101), which the master narratives of history exclude in asserting the full, transcendent, and all too tidy values derived from the teleological imperatives of origins and ends. History for James is like one of those ungainly, "misplaced middles" (*AN*, 100) which he both rues and—although this has been less noticed—celebrates in the New York Edition prefaces. Ungainly, ill-proportioned, or outsized: this is another definition of awkwardness that needs to be brought into play here, for it suggests how James's apprehension of the historical present *as* awkward is inseparable from his practice of "appreciable, or more exactly perhaps . . . almost preposterously appreciative, overtreatment" of his fictional germs—a practice which in *The Awkward Age* transformed the scantiest of subjects into a "comparative monster," and which numbers it among "a group of productions . . . which have in common, to their author's eyes, the endearing sign that they asserted in each case an unforeseen principle of growth" (*AN*, 114, 98). The monstrosity of *The Awkward Age*—more than one reviewer found its length distressingly "inordinate" [10]—thus exemplifies the awkward processes by which the "propriety" of "a smooth general case" is "really all the while bristling and crumbling into fierce particular ones" (*AN*, 105). It also defines the novel as "a prime specimen of the way in which the obscurer, the lurking relations of a motive apparently simple, always in wait for their spring, may by seizing their chance for it send simplicity flying" (*AN*, 105). When James expresses his "wonder" at "what 'over-treatment' may, in the detail of its desperate ingenuity, consist of" (*AN*, 115), and his belief in "the truth of the vanity of the *a priori* test of what an *idée-mère* may have to give" (*AN*, 101), he anticipates Derrida's rejection of "the notion of an Idea or 'interior design' as simply anterior to a work which would supposedly be the expression of it." "To write," Derrida says, "is to know that what has not yet been produced within literality has no other dwelling place, does not await us as prescription in some *topos ouranios*, or some divine understanding. Meaning must await being said or written in order to inhabit itself, and in order to become, by differing from itself, what it is: meaning." [11]

In emphasizing this novel's monstrous hospitality to the details and differences that produce new meanings, and thus to history's "possible relations and extensions" (*AN*, 101), I do not mean to suggest that James fails to acknowledge how history inscribes human beings in the hurtful simplicities of the smooth general case; indeed, it is only by representing the social, cultural, and linguistic—and, I would add, aesthetic—forms that determine and sometimes thwart our lives that James is able to put those forms in awkward relation with the possibilities and desires they deny and suppress, possibilities and desires that in turn contain the potentiality to destabilize the dominant forms. As Susan Mizruchi has shown in her study of the links between *The Awkward Age* and emergent modern social science discourses concerned with controlling women's sexuality and reproduction, Nanda's story can be fruitfully read as an exemplification of the commodification of women in the age of mechanical reproduction [12]—the reproduction of a lady, one might say, in an age where women's beauty is advertised like "soap and whiskey," and where the marriage market demands "cash over the counter and letters ten feet high" (*AA*, 32). Isabel Archer is "ground in the . . . mill of the conventional";[13] Nanda is trapped by much more specific mechanisms of cultural, class, and gender inscription. Caught in between outmoded but still potent representations of feminine purity and the exposure attendant on her mother's more modern methods—at one point she describes herself, in rather startling terms, as "a sort of a little drainpipe with everything running through" (*AA*, 210)—Nanda is ultimately "spoiled" for Van: "to force upon him an awkwardness," she thinks at the end of the novel, "was like forcing a disfigurement or a hurt" (*AA*, 279, 286). Yet Nanda's awkwardness, however unpalatable it is to Van, also serves to articulate the gaps between inherited gender codes and the desires of the men and women who are bound by them. Nanda is, after all, a sort of "new woman" in embryo, who at one point thinks of herself as "the horrible impossible" (*AA*, 309), largely because the historical landscape she traverses as yet lacks any discursive terms for the new kind of femininity she is trying to articulate. Yet when she descends into the circle of free talk that defines James's text as well as her mother's drawing room, she enters a space or interval in which those codes—the marriage plot; normative models of masculinity and femininity; culturally prescribed narratives of sexual experience—are denaturalized and hence rehistoricized, a space, in other words, where the impossible is rendered possible. James reemphasizes the historicity of apparently "natural" cultural forms when he articulates, in preface and novel alike, his preference for the awkward, middle ground of English culture, with all the "muddle," "compromise," and "monstrosity" of its "eternal . . . false positions" (*AA*, 47, 50), to the comparatively "rude simplifications"—on the one hand the straightforward exclusion of the "ingenuous mind" from the circle of talk; on the other the complete reduction of that talk's freedom to the parameters defined by the girl's foregone inclusion—prevalent in France and America (*AN*, 103–4). James, in any case, is well aware that, as Van puts it, there are situations in which "'nature' [is] the greatest of falsities" (*AA*, 282). If Longdon initially wants to find in Nanda "an absolute revival" (*AA*, 95) of the original, "natural" Lady—the grandmother whom Nanda so uncannily resembles—he has, by the end of the novel, engaged her in a relationship that acknowledges and responds to her individual and historical difference. And however unsatisfactory Nanda's final retreat from London with Mr. Longdon may seem, it nevertheless constitutes a loophole through which she escapes her interval's preordained conclusion in marriage; it is also an example of what James calls "the triumph of intentions never entertained" (*AN*, 100).

The Awkward Age belongs to James's so-called experimental phase, the latter half of the decade of the 1890s during which he also published such notoriously ambiguous texts as *The Turn of the Screw, In the Cage, The Sacred Fount*, and *What Maisie Knew*. As I have already suggested, these fictions, including *The Awkward Age*, struck many readers as shocking, repulsive, and indeed "unnatural," especially in their relative frankness about sexual matters.[14] It is worth pointing out, for example, that *The Awkward Age*, along with *What Maisie Knew* and *The Turn of the Screw*, works to deconstruct the supposedly "natural" category of childhood innocence. Like Maisie, Nanda, as she herself discovers, always *knew*: "There never was a time when [she] didn't know *something* or other" (*AA*, 302). Moreover, each of these texts troubled contemporary readers by exhibiting the same "endearing" monstrosity, the same tendency to grow "by a rank force of its own," that characterizes *The Awkward Age*.[15] The "experimental phase" might well be called James's own "awkward age," for all the texts he produced in this interval are oddly poised between the traditional realism of his earlier work and the elaborate modern or postmodern affinities of *The Ambassadors, The Wings of the Dove*, and *The Golden Bowl*, the "major phase" novels he published in the first years of the new century. James was, moreover, between audiences during these years. Increasingly aware that he had lost favor with the mass audience that had made *Daisy Miller* a bestseller, James had attempted, in the early 1890s, to regain his popularity by abandoning fiction and writing for the theater. The results were disastrous: James, in what can only be called an excruciatingly awkward moment, was hooted from the stage on the opening night of the play (*Guy Domville* [1895]) he thought his best. When he returned to writing fiction, his experimentation was in part an effort to find and cultivate a new, more specialized community of readers; in the event his new directions often elicited, in his own words, "little *but* bewilderment—except indeed . . . denunciation."[16]

The James of these years is thus unmistakably a writer in transition, consciously engaged in disrupting the narrative conventions and teleology that had informed a book like *The Portrait of a Lady*, yet often palpably uncertain about the uncharted territory into which these oddly dislocated and dislocating texts seemed to be leading him. Since the publication of the volume of Leon Edel's biography devoted to what he calls James's "treacherous years," moreover, it has been impossible to ignore another kind of in-betweenness, the suspension, during this period, of James's putatively "normal" or "natural" gender affiliation. Edel argues that the experimental phase, especially the sequence of texts that includes *The Other House*, *What Maisie Knew*, *The Turn of the Screw*, *In the Cage*, and *The Awkward Age*, embodies a process of "imaginative self-therapy" in which James assumed the "safety disguise of a little girl" in order to work out unresolved psychological tensions, particularly his uncertainties about his own masculinity.[17] Edel's history is a familiar one—all too tidy, I should say—of crisis followed by resolution: the "self-analysis" enacted in the experimental phase leads, "after a period of crisis," to "restored . . . creative power," and to the renewed, re-masculinized mastery of the major phase.[18] Edel thus contains the awkwardness of these texts by seeing in them only a "safe" pathway to a restored, essentially unchanged masculinity, just as other critics have defused the power of the formal and generic monstrosities of the experimental phase by seeing in them only a temporarily misplaced middle through which James ultimately attains his predestined end in his mastery of the style and techniques of his major phase. If James's masculinity is "threatened" in this narrative, masculinity (or, for that matter, femininity) itself is not, for Edel unhesitatingly accepts the conventional division of gender (masculine/feminine) and the terms—especially the oedipal terms—through which our culture structures gendered identities as fixed, unalterable, and "natural."

My goal here then is in part to resist reading the awkwardness of the experimental phase proleptically, as merely a stage in a teleologically overdetermined master narrative of James's career. But it also involves a recognition of yet more senses of *awkward*—*awkward* in its root sense of "turned the wrong way," in its senses of "perverse" and "left-handed," which is to say, of course, *awkward* in the sense of "queer." It is, after all, Nanda, the exposed, compromised, horribly impossible possible, who holds, as Van remarks, "the strings of such a lot of queer little dramas" (*AA*, 287). Like Mr. Longdon in the novel's opening chapter, James in all his awkwardness is trying "to utter something that [is] too delicate not to be guarded and yet too important not to be risked" (*AA*, 28), an experiment for which Nanda's queerness provides an enabling site, though never a "safety disguise." In "The Future of the Novel," an essay published in the same year as *The Awkward Age*, James in fact advocates an openness to "experiments—queer and uncanny things" he calls them—as a necessary response to something like an awkward age in the history of the novel itself. Anglo-American fiction, James argues, has reached an impasse, its development blocked by "forms at once ready-made and sadly the worse for wear" that leave "whole categories of manners, whole corpuscular classes and provinces, museums of character and condition, unvisited," in effect unrepresentable.[19] If James, as one sympathetic reviewer wrote in 1899, was beginning in his experimental fictions "to exercise his dexterity upon the problem of saying the unsayable,"[20] it is because he recognized that the unsayable—"the revolution taking place in the position and outlook of women"; the "immense omission [of the subject of sexuality] in our fiction"; the lives of those "innumerable women" (and men?) "who, under modern arrangements, increasingly fail to marry, . . . fail, apparently, even, largely, to desire to"[21]—is a function of history, of the ways in which historically specific discursive and linguistic structures work to exclude as "unnatural" and hence unutterable alternative forms of knowledge, experience, and desire.

In his reading of *The Awkward Age* as, in essence, our first great postmodern novel, Todorov argues that the novel's linguistic awkwardness, the "conversational obliquity" that necessitates its characters' persistent efforts to "fill out [the] gaps" and "read in . . . the unsaid" (*AA*, 34), has "reached such a degree" that "it is no longer obliquity: the connecting lines between words and things are not merely loose or tangled—they have been cut." For Todorov, the effect of these linguistic gaps—figured in the floating pronouns, interrupted predications, and unfinished sentences that characterize the novel's talk—is to render the novel "an allegory of fiction writing" marked by "two contradictory feelings"—"regret for having lost the world, joy at the autonomous proliferation of language."[22] But language, in *The Awkward Age*, is never really autonomous; it is always in relational tension with the world, always by definition social and socialized; it is, precisely, the "awkward situation" in which history makes, and is made by, those who participate in its processes. Critiquing the tendency among historians, including many historians of sexual difference, to essentialize the category of "experience," Joan Scott argues that when "experience" is "naturalized" as "the origin of knowledge," questions "about the constructed nature of experience, about how subjects are constituted as different in the first place, about how one's vision is structured—about language (or discourse) and history—are left aside." To divorce experience from language, Scott insists, is to "preclude critical examination of the workings of the ideological system" and its "categories of representation":[23] "Experience is a subject's history. Language is the site of history's enactment. Historical explanation cannot, therefore, separate the two." To recognize that experience and history are "linguistic event[s]," on the other hand, is to understand not only that history "doesn't happen outside established meanings," but also that it is not "confined to a fixed order of meaning."[24] It is by "tracking 'the appropriation of language . . . in both directions, over the gap'" between the "'writings of legitimacy'" and "'the voices of the illegitimate,'" and by "situating and contextualizing that language," that "one historicizes the terms by which experience is represented, and so historicizes 'experience' itself."[25]

"Tracking 'the appropriation of language . . . in both directions, over the gap'" between the always-already said and the as yet unsayable, James in *The Awkward Age* is above all engaged in the historicizing of history. For James never wanted, like so many of the modernists who claimed this master as their own, to transcend, or to escape or awake from, history. Rather, through an awkward immersion in history—by allowing history's meaning, as Derrida would say, to differ from itself—he sought to uncover and explore the latent and alternative possibilities denied, often at great cost, by its master narratives of origins and ends. When Mrs. Brookenham worries aloud to Mitchy about the "abominable," "horrible" books that her son Harold spends his time reading, Mitchy responds in terms that James, I think, would be happy for us to apply to his own awkward monstrosity of a novel: "The worse things are, let me just mention to you about that, the better they seem positively to be for one's feeling up in the language" (*AA*, 61–62). Feeling up in the language and thus in history itself, James pulls from the inside out the small subjects and "queer little dramas" that may be said to figure his "unentertained intentions": the apparently "quiet instants," as he would write in *The Ambassadors*, "that sometimes settle"—and, I would add, unsettle—"more matters than the outbreaks dear to the historic muse."[26]

# PART IV

# Narrative
# Embodiment:
# Gender and Desire
# in History

# Fin de Siècle, Fin de Sexe: Transsexuality, Postmodernism, and the Death of History

When and how did history die? Was its passing a climactic and catastrophic one, tied to the unspeakable horrors of Auschwitz and Hiroshima, which shattered, once and for all, any lingering belief in the redemptive power of Western myths of progress? Or did it dissolve slowly and invisibly into a phantasmagoria of media images, into glossy simulations of a rapidly receding, ever more unknowable past? At what point in time did the idea of history itself become history, did it become possible to say, "That was then, this is now?" And how does this perception of a temporal gulf between "then" and "now," between the era of past history and *posthistoire*, tally with the claim that we no longer possess a historical consciousness? Is it history that has died, or merely the philosophy of history, and is there a difference? And finally, and most important for my present purposes, what is the connection between discourses of the end of history and the end of sex? How do our cultural imaginings of historical time relate to changing perceptions of the meaning and nature of gender difference?

I begin some tentative responses to these questions by noting the pervasiveness of images of transsexuality within much postmodern and poststructuralist thought. For example, in *The Transparency of Evil*, Jean Baudrillard writes, "The sexual body has now been assigned an artificial fate. This fate is transsexuality—transsexual not in any anatomical sense but rather in the more general sense of transvestism, of playing with the commutability of the signs of sex . . . we are all transsexuals."[1] Here transsexuality, or perhaps more accurately, transgenderism, serves as an overarching metaphor to describe the dissolution of once stable polarities of male and female, the transfiguration of sexual nature into the artifice of those who play with the sartorial, morphological, or gestural signs of sex. The media visibility of such celebrities as Madonna, Michael Jackson, and La Cicciolina becomes symptomatic for Baudrillard of a fascination with the exaggeration, parody, and inversion of signifiers of sexual difference that pervades the entirety of contemporary Western culture. Contemporary critical theory itself both echoes and intensifies such practices of gender bending and blending in its sustained conceptual challenge to the ontological stability of the male/female divide. While male theorists like Derrida, Deleuze, and Baudrillard himself profess their desire to "become woman" by aligning themselves with a feminine principle of undecidability and masquerade, so feminists are in turn increasingly appealing to metaphors of transvestism to describe the mutability and plasticity of the sexed body. Two of the most influential feminist theorists of recent times, Donna Haraway and Judith Butler, have sought in different ways to break out of the prisonhouse of gender by reconceptualizing masculinity and femininity as performative, unstable, and multiply determined practices.

"Fin de siècle, fin de sexe"; the epigram coined by the French artist Jean Lorrain to describe the symbolic affinity of gender confusion and historical exhaustion in the late nineteenth century seems even more apt for our own moment.[2] An existing repertoire of fin de siècle tropes of decadence, apocalypse, and sexual crisis is reappropriated through self-conscious citation, yet simultaneously replenished with new meaning, as gender emerges as a privileged symbolic field for the articulation of diverse fashionings of history and time within postmodern thought. Thus the destabilization of the male/female divide is seen to bring with it a waning of temporality, teleology, and grand narrative; the end of sex echoes and affirms the end of history, defined as the pathological legacy and symptom of the trajectory of Western modernity. Ineluctably intertwined in symbiotic relationship, phallocentrism, modernity, and history await their only too timely end, as a hierarchical logic of binary identity and narrative totalization gives way to an altogether more ambiguous and indeterminate condition. Indeed, this idea that history has come to an end has become perhaps the most ubiquitous and least questioned commonplace of postmodern thought, even as particular expressions of this motif vary in register from the nostalgic to the celebratory.

My aim in this paper is not to prove or disprove such claims—the end of history is clearly not a thesis that is amenable to empirical adjudication—but to investigate further the rhetorical mechanisms of their deployment and their varying political agendas. What does it mean exactly to talk about the death of history? To what extent does such a claim tacitly reinscribe the very logic of temporality that it seeks to negate? And to what extent does a perspective sensitive to gender issues either affirm or complicate the thesis of the end of history and the end of sex? Through a brief discussion of the work of Baudrillard and Haraway, two of the most influential diagnosticians of the postmodern moment, I will suggest that their writings are in fact imbued with large-scale visions of historical time that are in turn allied to their diverging views of the transgendered subject as either apocalyptic or redemptive metaphor. I then turn to the work of Italian philosopher Gianni Vattimo, which usefully explores the inevitable historicity of postmodern thought, though I will also argue that Vattimo fails to address adequately the different meanings and political valencies accruing to particular manifestations of this historicity. Finally, I will consider the significance of discourses of the end of history and the end of sex from the standpoint of feminist theory.

## (Trans)gendered Histories:
## Baudrillard and Haraway

Baudrillard's relentless polemic against the pathology of Western culture depicts a world overflowing with meaning and thus empty of it, a teeming promiscuity of information/communication that is obscene in its total transparency. Media saturation, computerization, the imperatives of consumerist and cybernetic logics, conspire to create a hallucinatory limbo of the hyperreal which has no exteriority, no point outside the network. Notions of history, reality, and linear time live on only as exoskeletal traces, fossilized remains endlessly replayed on the screens of our video terminals. Post 1968, politics has been revealed as a self-delusory project; all forms of liberation—sexual, political, aesthetic—engender only an escalation of networks of simulation which subsume, neutralize, or dissolve all meaning. Increasingly, the model of the code gives way in Baudrillard's work to that of the virus, signaling the invasive yet invisible multiplication of contagious signifiers engaged in constant proliferation.

In Baudrillard's later work, questions of gender and sexuality centrally define this nightmarish vision of an epidemic of signification. *The Transparency of Evil* mourns the reduction of sexuality to "the undifferentiated circulation of the signs of sex"[3] as the erotic falls prey to the logic of simulation through its own ubiquitous presence as spectacle. "After the demise of desire," Baudrillard writes, "a pell-mell diffusion of erotic simulacra in every guise, of transsexual kitsch in all its glory."[4] In Baudrillard's relentlessly heterosexual and -sexist universe, this loss of desire is attributed to the disappearance of sexual difference; we have become "indifferent and undifferentiated beings, androgynous and hermaphroditic,"[5] creatures without gender and hence without sex. Biotechnological research heralds a brave new world of cloning and parthenogenesis, of serial reproduction by celibate machines replicating like protozoa. Feminists in turn accelerate this confusion of gender categories by reducing the once inescapable destiny of being male or female to a matter of preference and rights. The figure of transsexuality thus becomes for Baudrillard a privileged metaphor of a general social process of implosion and de-differentiation which renders all terms commutable and indeterminate. The end of sex echoes and affirms the end of history, understood both as a problem of agency (the eclipse of the subject by the sovereignty of the object) and also of knowledge (the impossibility of imputing any meaning or direction to temporal processes).

Yet even as he insists that narrative has become impossible, Baudrillard's writings inscribe a metahistorical fiction of the first order, articulating a powerfully nostalgic narrative of the Fall. Harking back to an imagined era of referential plenitude, they emplot an exemplary parable of the decline of Western civilization from the standpoint of the latecomer, the one who comes after. At one point, Baudrillard writes, "We are merely epigones. . . . The highest level of intensity lies behind us. The lowest level of passion and intellectual illumination lies ahead of us."[6] Such a melancholic vision of cultural decadence is of course a recurring trope within the modern, the faithful and constant shadow of the overarching myth of historical progress. On the one hand, Baudrillard denies the possibility of a meaningful future, claiming that linear and progressive time no longer exist in an imploding universe where history turns back on itself in a necrophilic spiral of infinite regression. In the mythic no-time of TV that we all inhabit, history is flattened out into a smorgasbord of endlessly recycled images of the past. On the other hand, this very diagnosis explicitly posits a history that once *was* and is no more, expressing a profoundly historical sense of the current impossibility of history. Even as he insists that linear time has been replaced by reversibility and repetition, Baudrillard reinscribes a temporal schema structured around the triadic relation of a disappearing present, an absent future, and an authentically self-present, if no longer knowable, past.

This point can be highlighted by considering Donna Haraway's very different emplotment of historical time. Like Baudrillard, Haraway insists on the radical transformation of social relations engendered by cybernetic systems, biotechnological innovation, and an all-pervasive dissemination of media networks. She too argues that old oppositions of masculine and feminine, along with their corollary distinctions of private versus public, mind versus body, culture versus nature, no longer hold in the new world system she calls the informatics of domination. In this context she introduces her resonant symbol of the postmodern cyborg, a hybrid blend of male and female, organism and machine, that emblematizes the contemporary fusion and intermingling of previously distinct categories. We are all cyborgs now, she states, "The Cyborg is our ontology, it gives us our politics."[7] Haraway's transgendered cyborg, however, bears little kinship to Baudrillard's transsexual subject. An ironic and polyvalent symbol of both matrices of domination and possibilities of resistance, it gestures resolutely toward the future rather than gazing toward the past. Instead of demonizing technology and taking refuge in a nostalgic vision of an organic feminine, Haraway argues, feminists need to explore the new possibilities, pleasures, and politics made possible by transgressed boundaries and fragmented selves. The cyborg serves as a feminist icon for the postmodern era, an unruly child of technological systems that it simultaneously exploits and contests.

How, then, do cyborgs embody or subvert existing patterns of historical times? Haraway explicitly refuses the redemptive frame of Western progress narratives as well as the organicist myth of the Fall. The cyborg, she declares, is outside salvation history and has no origin story; it rejects the seductions of vanguard politics and teleological notions of agency. Yet even as it weaves its way through multiple perspectives, Haraway's manifesto (a quintessentially modernist genre which her text both ironizes and reproduces) expresses a deeply historical awareness of the irreversible and linear nature of time. Drawing upon Fredric Jameson's tripartite scheme of capitalist development, her argument insists on both the distinctiveness of our own epoch and the impossibility of returning to an earlier moment. "We cannot go back ideologically or materially," she writes; "it's not just that 'god' is dead, so is the 'goddess.'"[8] The "Manifesto for Cyborgs" is a text permeated by a strong sense of its own temporality, of the irrevocable historical transformation of our material and conceptual universe by cybernetic and biotechnological logics that have definitively severed us from our own past. Without minimizing the logics of domination shaping our own era, Haraway seeks nonetheless to recuperate both political agency and the redemptive promise of the future. Coding the transgendered subject of the postmodern as liberating icon rather than nightmarish catastrophe, she sees new and unimagined possibilities in hybrid gender identities and complex fusions of previously distinct realities. In its expectant and hopeful gesturing toward a "not yet" that may liberate women from the naturalized oppressions and dichotomies of the past, Haraway thus carves a resolutely utopian, forward-looking temporality out of social conditions often identified with the dwindling of political possibilities.

The texts of Baudrillard and Haraway, then, exemplify two very different political and philosophical responses to the de-differentiation of sexual difference as postmodern trope. Transsexuality, as Sandy Stone observes, currently functions as a hotly contested site of cultural inscription; this contestation expresses itself not simply in ongoing disputes between doctors, feminists, and transsexuals themselves, as Stone argues, but also in the more general cultural appropriations of the figure of transsexuality as a semiotically dense emblem in the rhetoric of fin de millenium.[9] Interpreted as historical symptom or philosophical symbol, this figure inspires a multiplicity of claims and counterclaims regarding its liberatory or catastrophic meanings. Nowhere is this more apparent than in two recent anthologies on gender and the postmodern body edited by Arthur and Marilouise Kroker, *Body Invaders* and *The Last Sex*.[10] Here celebrations of transsexuality as perverse artifice couched in the vocabulary of postmodern feminism and queer theory are juxtaposed with dark apocalyptic imaginings of docile bodies completely inscribed by intersecting grids of commodification and biotechnological control. While *Body Invaders* inclines toward a more pessimistic reading of the aestheticized body as a dystopian symbol of the omnipresent tyranny of simulation, *The Last Sex* euphorically celebrates this same free-floating aestheticism as the necessary precondition for a future transgender liberation and the emergence of a third sex. Thus the editors rhapsodically gesture toward a "new sexual horizon" that is "post-male and post-female"; their goal, they write, is to achieve the indeterminate state of "female, yet male, organisms occupying an ironic, ambivalent and paradoxical state of sexual identity."[11] If ends of centuries serve as privileged cultural moments for articulating highly charged myths of death and rebirth, senescence and renewal, in our own era such hopes and anxieties are writ large across proliferating representations of the transgendered body.

### The Paradox of Historicity: Gianni Vattimo

What interests me in these various writings, then, is not just the weighty yet conflicting meanings assigned to transsexuality in recent theories of the postmodern, but also the paradoxical reinscription of historicity in the very act of its disavowal. Even as they subvert conventional structures of sociological realism and philosophical narrative through fragmented and multiperspectival forms, the texts I have discussed simultaneously reveal a profound sense of locatedness in time, positioning themselves in relation to past and future histories that are richly endowed with both redemptive and dystopian meanings. This paradox is explored in some detail by a contemporary theorist of the condition of *posthistoire*, Gianni Vattimo. According to Vattimo, the defining feature of the modern is its narrative structuring of time as the progressive realization of an ideal of human emancipation; modernity is epitomized by a project of Hegelian overcoming that assumes the emancipatory value of the new as a means of transcending the errors of the past. Vattimo thus agrees with Lyotard and others that postmodernity signals the dissolution of such a unilinear narrative of history with its corollary notions of progress and overcoming. What has come to an end, Vattimo insists, is not simply a certain set of ideas about history, but history itself, insofar as history is inseparable from its rhetorical articulation as a metaphysically driven narrative.[12]

Yet Vattimo also recognizes the contradictory nature of such a claim; the elevation of the postmodern over the modern reproduces precisely that same gesture of historical overcoming, the valorization of the new and the now over the inauthentic past, that is endemic to the logic of the modern itself. The critique of history and modernity thereby reveals itself to be inexorably enmeshed within the very Enlightenment narrative it seeks to contest. As many writers have noted, the announcement of the end of metanarratives thus becomes another metanarrative, which assigns an ontological reality to history in the very act of its negation. Here Vattimo takes Lyotard to task for seeking to ground his own account of the postmodern through unproblematic procedures of historical legitimation. To argue that Auschwitz, or the terrors of Stalinism, have irrevocably dissolved the project of modernity is to endow such events with world-historical significance and hence to reaffirm the very philosophy of history that is ostensibly being called into question.[13] Vattimo's aim here is not to minimize the tragic and unspeakable events of the twentieth century, but merely to note that they cannot in themselves prove or disprove a progress narrative without recourse to a competing account, such as a view of the modern as exemplifying a historical logic of escalating domination. Similarly, Lyotard's insistence on the unrepresentability and singularity of Auschwitz as signaling the definitive dissolution of Western progress narratives would itself be seen by Vattimo as a profoundly historical affirmation of the irreversible change of consciousness brought about by a particular event. These events, in turn, never speak to us in their raw actuality, but always involve multilayered processes of mediation, interpretation, and emplotment.

According to Vattimo, then, the heritage of history and modernity cannot simply be transcended, because any such project must remain trapped in the very logic of overcoming that it seeks to contest. While archaism and progressivism, the idealization of the past and of the future, are both revealed as philosophically bankrupt positions, Vattimo simultaneously insists that we cannot go beyond metaphysics but can at best begin to recover from it as if from a sickness. Thus he advocates an alternative to Heideggerian *Verwindung*, a resigned and self-conscious acceptance of one's own necessary implication within historicism that thereby seeks to deflect much of its force. Yet Vattimo is, I would argue, insufficiently self-conscious in relation to his own philosophical story about a metahistorical subject that has lost its previous unconditional belief in the universal truth of history. First of all, such a sweeping narrative ignores alternative voices and traditions within the history of modernity itself; one might consider, for example, the ambiguous yet often contestatory relationship of nineteenth-century feminist discourses to dominant male-centered philosophies of history.[14] The repeated inscription of a single linear trajectory from modern totality to postmodern plurality within much contemporary theory simply reaffirms a reified and ultimately problematic construction of the homogeneity of the past. Second, this same narrative is in turn insufficiently attuned to the nonsynchronous relations of various social groups to the condition of historicity in our own time. Thus the present explosion of women's texts exploring issues of memory, temporality, tradition, and change seemingly contradicts the bland assertion that "we" no longer live historically. To assume that because history is not pure event, it can only be defined philosophically, to reduce the question of history to a problem in the self-critique of Western metaphysics, is surely to fall prey to a disabling theoreticism unable to address the multiple discursive sites at which the category of the historical is constituted as a social and pragmatic concern. Indeed, from a sociological perspective, one might speak not of the death of grand narratives but the proliferation of them, as ever more subordinate groups identify themselves as historical actors in the public domain.

Thus second-wave feminism, for example, has given rise to diverse and conflictual fashionings of historical time. One of its most familiar stories emplots the historical *Bildung* of the female subject as she liberates herself from the manacles of tradition and the constraints of the past in order to enter and transform the world as an autonomous, self-determining, modern individual.

An opposed and equally influential feminist narrative appropriates and re-writes the myth of the Fall, situating an authentic femininity in a nondiffer-entiated prelapsarian condition (nature, the organic, the preoedipal) prior to the alienating subject-object split of modernity. Both of these competing sto-ries have come to appear increasingly problematic in their construction of a historical metanarrative grounded in a normative ideal of femininity, as poststructuralist feminists have been eager to point out. Yet as my discussion of Haraway suggests, such critiques in turn engender their own developmen-tal stories and binary oppositions in describing how the naive essentialisms and binarisms of early feminist thought have given way to the more enlight-ened, sophisticated, and theoretically self-conscious perspectives of the pres-ent. Indeed, as M. J. Devaney has recently argued, the discourse of legitima-tion of much postmodernist thought often invokes a relatively uncomplicated idea of progress in its claims to refute the past errors of a univocal and monolithic entity variously defined as modernity/Enlightenment thinking/ the Western metaphysical tradition.[15]

Rather than seek simply to "transcend" narrative or teleology, then, feminism can perhaps more usefully acknowledge both its own inevitable enmeshment within rhetorics of emplotment and their changing forms, meanings, and effects. To argue that the evident failure of Western myths of progress renders any further appeal to history terroristic and totalizing is surely to remain trapped within a logic of identity that subsumes the chang-ing uses and elaborations of a particular paradigm within the binary logic of either/or: *either* metanarrative and hence a reactionary because totalizing politics, *or* linguistic fragmentation and (by questionable analogy) social free-dom. One might insist at this point that Western feminist metanarratives, however problematic in certain respects, *mean* differently from those of lib-eralism or Marxism, because of their own historically particular and relatively fragile relationship to institutional power and authority.[16] The politics of big historical stories is not, after all, given in their form, but depends upon the specific mechanisms of their deployment, circulation, and institutionaliza-tion. Such stories may, for example, help to engender symbolic solidarities and affiliations within disadvantaged groups eager for enabling myths of ori-gin or inspiratory utopias, even as they may in turn become regulatory mech-anisms of exclusion and totalization. Which of these will turn out to be the case can surely only be answered in contingent rather than absolute terms.

In his recent work, Vattimo both acknowledges yet minimizes the force of such oppositional voices in noting that the new visibility of social move-ments and minorities has irrevocably pluralized, and hence dissolved, the category of history. For Vattimo, like Baudrillard, the proliferation of histories signals the death of history, leaving only multiple images of the past projected from different points of view.[17] Yet this is surely to construct an over-simple relationship between the universal and the particular, as if the histories being written by women or postcolonial peoples, to take just two examples, comprised nothing more than a random plurality of local narratives, whose various truth claims remained inaccessible to meaningful adjudication. Yet many of these histories seek to contest and transform our view of the past by discovering its exclusions, oppressions, and hidden triumphs, to rewrite and extend, rather than negate history. The discourses of contemporary social movements such as feminism often seem in this respect to blur the clarity of the ubiquitous distinction between *grands* and *petits recits*. As narratives engendered by a profound sense of exclusion from conventional Oedipal genealogies, they question rather than affirm the notion of a universal subject of history; yet they also seek to reconfigure our understanding of both past and present in a manner that transcends the local. From the perspective of those whose view of historical knowledge is indissolubly linked to the pragmatics of everyday life and contestatory politics in the public arena, Vattimo's own metatheoretical pronouncements may speak more eloquently of the European philosopher's crisis of faith in a particular metaphysical tradition than of the status of history as such. As Judith Roof has noted, such a strategy does not undermine intellectual authority so much as reinscribe it; the truth that there is no truth, the knowledge that history no longer exists, becomes the new locus of the certainty, identity, and will to power that is ostensibly being displaced.[18]

## Conclusion

This in turn brings me back to my starting point: the figure of transsexuality or transgenderism as the site of deeply invested and symbolically charged rewritings of history and time. In counterposing the differing temporalities shaping the work of Baudrillard and Haraway, I do not seek to make them represent "male" versus "female" versions of the postmodern; any such move would oversimplify diverse and often conflicting representations of history on both sides of the gender divide. Yet particular cultural affiliations and identifications undoubtedly shape our imaginings of temporal processes; the obsessive relationship to a past historicity that marks the texts of Marxist and post-Marxist theorists such as Baudrillard, Jameson, Lyotard, and Vattimo engenders a narrative of loss that is by no means as universal as these writers often assume. Thus even a cursory glance at recent feminist writings reveals an array of rather different temporalities when it is woman, rather than man, who is envisioned as the imaginary subject of history. Even as they call into question existing Oedipal stories, such texts insist on the relevance of history as an ongoing concern rather than a defunct problematic for many women. Furthermore, as evidenced by my discussion of Haraway, the questioning of sexual difference does not inevitably signal a waning of the historical imagination; rather, it may help to generate powerful new feminist stories of possible futures, fueling imaginative projections of new worlds and alternative genealogies.

Such a claim itself, of course, paradoxically undermines the trope of transgenderism by drawing attention to the particular gender-political affiliations shaping the formation of cultural narratives of beginnings and ends. The end of sex is an idea whose truth is self-evidently symbolic rather than literal, yet even as metaphor it captures only one aspect of the contemporary cultural imaginary. Not all social subjects, after all, have equal freedom to play with and subvert the signs of gender, even as many do not perceive such play as a necessary condition of their freedom. As Arjun Appadurai has argued in a different context, we cannot grasp the complex cultural dynamics of our own time in terms of a single logic of either increasing homogeneity or heterogeneity; rather, we need to consider the diverse and often simultaneous movements between de-differentiation and re-differentiation that are played out across the force fields of cultural worlds.[19] Thus even as gender distinctions are irrevocably denaturalized through economic, political, and technological changes, so in turn the very question of women's specificity and difference has come to the fore as never before. The erosion of gender remains indissolubly linked to the affirmation of particular gendered identities, such that a conventional opposition of "equality" and "difference" within feminism reveals itself as an illusory and misleading antithesis.

In this sense, transgenderism remains a necessarily ambiguous figure for feminist theorists. I have questioned the view that symbols of gender crisis are inextricably linked to a loss of historicity and agency; in both the last fin de siècle and our own, this seems much more true of the feminized male than of the masculinized woman, whose ambiguous gendering is frequently charged with historical purpose and an exhilarating sense of new possibilities rather than with decadence and exhaustion. Thus the remarkable influence and impact of the Harawayan cyborg on the feminist imaginary undoubtedly bears witness to a widespread desire for inspiratory icons that do more than simply reproduce extant images of idealized femininity. Yet Susan Bordo introduces a useful note of caution into the feminism/postmodernism debate, suggesting that such celebrations of multiple and shifting identities may merely serve once again to elide the particularity of women and to deny the specificity of gendered embodiment. Furthermore, the very prominence of metaphors of transvestism and cross-dressing within contemporary feminism has been called into question by Eve Sedgwick and Michael Moon, who argue that this often careless appropriation works to elide the particularities of actual transvestite cultures and practices, including their intimate and ongoing linkage to the history of homosexuality.[20] The same is of course true of transsexuality; its elevation to the status of universal signifier ("we are all transsexuals") subverts established distinctions between male and female, normal and deviant, real and fake, but at the risk of homogenizing differences that matter politically: the differences between women and men, the difference between those who occasionally play with the trope of transsexuality and those others for whom it is a matter of life or death.

Gender, in this sense, remains both essential and impossible for feminism, which shifts between a radical questioning of the ontology of femininity and an insistence upon its real effects. Neither the idealization nor the demonization of recent theories of transvestism and transsexuality, it seems to me, does adequate justice to feminism's always-already conflictual relationship to the male/female divide. A similar oscillation between affirmation and negation also typifies the condition of history, which flickers persistently on our horizon in a movement of simultaneous doing and undoing. Clearly, our present imaginings of time differ markedly from nineteenth-century depictions of the purposeful unfolding of the laws of history. Yet in conceding the demise of Victorian evolutionism we do not negate, but rather affirm, our own sense of historicity, our recognition that certain assumptions and vocabularies are now no longer possible. The waning of nineteenth-century models of history does not necessarily signal a loss of locatedness in time nor of the desire to imbue cultural phenomena with meaning by locating them within larger temporal frames. The distinction lies, perhaps, in the fact that we have become more aware of the speculative nature of our stories, and of their inevitable plurality, rather than in the fact that we have gone "beyond" them. Narratives of the end of history are, I have suggested, in this sense symptomatic of the very historicity they seek to disavow.

To put it another way, the signifier "history" has more than one referent. Often, as in the case of Baudrillard and Jameson, the proliferation of diverse histories in our own era is acknowledged only in order to be negated. It is only because we no longer have access to a true history, the argument runs, that we are increasingly surrounded by impoverished simulacra of the historical. Quite apart from the epistemological problems posed by such sweeping distinctions between authentic and inauthentic forms of representation, this nostalgic narrative works to erase the power-laden logics of previous histories, including, I would insist, their problematic relationship to women and questions of gender. In renouncing this unilinear trajectory from the presence to the absence of history, we leave ourselves free to ask other kinds of questions. How do current apprehensions of historical time either appropriate, transform, or contest those of earlier eras? To what extent do these diverse apprehensions bear witness to conflicting visions of the politics of history on the part of particular cultural groups? How can we remain attentive to disjuncture and nonsynchrony in the experience of temporality while simultaneously acknowledging systematic connections and relations among discrete cultural practices? From such a standpoint, the thesis of the end of history merely repeats rather than subverts the ongoing myth of a universal history.

# Mourning and Misogyny: *Hamlet, The Revenger's Tragedy,* and the Final Progress of Elizabeth I, 1600–1607

I

In 1597, André Hurault, Sieur de Maisse and Ambassador Extraordinary from Henri IV, noted that although the English people still professed love for their aging queen, the sentiments of the nobility were such that "the English would never again submit to the rule of a woman."[1] There may have been more coincidence between high and low opinion than de Maisse thought. On the evening of Elizabeth's death six years later, the streets of London were lit by festive bonfires and punctuated by cries of "We have a king!"[2] The advent of an orderly and Protestant succession does not in itself account for such a celebratory spirit; in fact it was a significant transformation in the body politic, a re-incorporation and regendering of monarchy, that was being heralded. Rather than a seamless transition of power reminding all the populace that the corporate body of the monarch was immortal, unchanging, and unaltered by the demise of a particular sovereign, the death of Elizabeth marked a breach in the body politic as much as a continuation of it, and one that could be figured, at least by some, as a welcome discontinuity. The queen is dead—long live the king.

There were extensive and sincere eulogies, to be sure, heartfelt expressions of grief over the passing of Elizabeth, but during the last years of her reign the "political misogynism of the early years"[3] had also resurfaced strongly throughout her court and beyond its confines. It would not take many years of Jacobean rule to complicate the desire for a male sovereign, of course. As Christopher Haigh has noted, an idealized portrait of Elizabeth as a shrewd ruler and capable strategist emerged gradually over the first decade of James's reign, oftentimes in the form of a "coded commentary" on the defects of that reign.[4] But the recuperation and even reinvention of such a queen—Gloriana, the Virgin Queen, who had reigned for a remarkable span of forty-five years—seems a more complicated cultural process than Haigh's pragmatic account suggests. It is this process of accommodation and revision, marked as it is by an uncertain economy between mourning and misogyny, that I wish to examine here; I am interested not only in Elizabeth herself but also in the complex and ambivalent affective process that her death allows us to glimpse—a process that might be called mourning under the sign of patriarchy. Indeed, the possibility I wish to entertain is that, for the Renaissance, (male) mourning is sometimes difficult to dissociate from misogyny: that misogyny may in fact be an integral part of the mourning process when the lost object or ideal being processed is a woman, especially but not exclusively when that woman is a queen of England too.

Human emotions are no more free from historical and cultural construction than are genders or ideologies or gestures; that is to say, emotions and other forms of human affect have a history, or rather histories, since the differences traced by cultural historians, historical psychologists, and anthropologists must be charted along specific cultural, regional, communal, and geopolitical axes as well as temporal ones.[5] When dealing with a contemporaneous or "living" culture, however, affective life is relatively accessible: an anthropologist not only may be able to discriminate between a wink and a blink (to use Clifford Geertz's famous example)[6] but also may be able to postulate with some success, through interviews with informants, the "structures of feeling" that invest ostensibly common or shared human emotions with cultural difference.[7] But when fieldwork is limited to archival interrogations of past cultures, an impassable interpretive aporia is soon reached, such that the analysis of even public and recorded expressions of emotions is difficult and fraught with uncertainty—an uncertainty that increases considerably, needless to say, when one moves from the domain of gestures or externalized behavior to the domain of feeling. For example, we know—thanks in part to Jean de Léry's proto-ethnological account of his voyage to Brazil— that when a sixteenth-century Tupinamba covered his or her face and wept, it was in a ritualized gesture of welcome. But we do not and, in this instance, can never know what emotions were thereby expressed: whether it was joy, or humility, or proleptic sorrow (since any arrival foreshadows departure), or some combination of these and other affective registers that was both felt

239

and conveyed—conveyed, at least, when the party being welcomed was another Tupinamba, well-schooled in his or her own cultural codes, rather than
a Frenchman.[8]

Beyond such general caveats, it should also be noted that both mourning and misogyny, considered individually, pose interpretive challenges specific to late-sixteenth-century English culture. Misogyny presents an interpretive embarrassment of riches: it is everywhere, unabashed in its articulation
and so overdetermined in its cultural roots that individual instances sometimes seem emotionally underdetermined, rote and uninflected expressions
of what would go without saying if it weren't said so often.[9] By contrast, articulated expressions of grief are far less common. Private personal diaries, in
which one would expect to find subjective emotional responses recorded, are
themselves rare in the period; the expressions of individual grief which do
exist can easily strike the modern reader as remote and unfeeling, leading
even so astute a student of the past as Lawrence Stone to confuse historical
and cultural difference with absence and to declare that major bereavements
were not felt as such in the period, since "in the sixteenth and seventeenth
centuries interpersonal relations were at best cold and at worst hostile."[10] For
any inquiry into the entanglement or interaction of such forms of affect,[11]
Elizabeth clearly provides a salutary and strategic methodological focus, as a
woman who so fully commanded the political life of the nation and for such
an extensive period that she also inscribed herself deeply in the cultural
imagination of Renaissance England. The final progress of Elizabeth—the
cultural processing of her age, in both senses of that term—was completed
long after her funeral procession took place but begun some years before it,
when her aging body first announced the proximity of her last days; it was
enacted not in the streets of London or in the provinces but in the political
unconscious, and to catch a glimpse of it we have to broaden our field of
inquiry beyond the traditional resources of political history—journals and
letters written before and after the queen's death, or the histories of Greville
and Camden—and turn, among other places, to the Elizabethan and Jacobean stage. It has often been remarked that the resurgent political misogyny
of Elizabeth's court in the 1590s coincided with a dramatic increase, as it were,
of misogyny on stage; in the years after her death, as recent studies have also
begun to detail, the popular stage manifested an acute and complex investment in the imaginary reworking and resolution of Elizabeth's reign.[12] But
my own recourse to the popular theater is not solely motivated by such topical resonances. For anyone concerned, as I am here, with the cultural construction of emotions and other forms of affect, the popular stage represents

a unique historical resource, and one whose significance in its own time cannot be limited to the passive role of merely recording or reflecting early modern structures of feeling.

The symbolic economy of English culture—by which I refer not just to official efforts to manage and maintain dominant systems of belief but to the entire repertoire of cultural representations and practices, official and unofficial, that shaped the political, social, and psychological subject and defined his or her place in the cultural hierarchy—underwent a significant and radical transformation in the sixteenth century. The English Reformation itself was hardly a tidy affair, marked as it was by the succession of no fewer than five official state religions, each claiming the status of unrivaled and absolute truth, and all within the space of a single generation; one of the results was to displace and destabilize the very notion of the orthodox or the absolute, producing a skeptical if not cynical relativism evident, in court records, even among the lower classes.[13] During the same period, individuals commanded an increasingly greater access to heterodox ideas and ideologies, aided as they were by the rapid expansion of print culture and by what we think was a slow yet steady rise in literacy. But contemporary fears of an increasingly informed and hence more autonomous subject were not only focused on those who could read, and with good reason; as Tessa Watt has recently reminded us,[14] the boundary between oral and literate cultures in the period was highly permeable, such that ideas and ideologies were disseminated not only by direct and unmediated access to a printed text but also by diverse processes of re-presentation and representation, in official and unofficial forums ranging from the pulpit to the tavern. In the case of sixteenth-century London, however, what the debate over literacy obscures is a much more explosive expansion of the symbolic economy—the one produced by the fiercely contested emergence and rapid institutionalization of the popular stage.

The controversy provoked by the popular theater was largely ideological and political rather than aesthetic, and the reasons for this are relatively clear. Public drama was not customarily graced with the status of literature or, less anachronistically, of poesy. More important, in an age when the domain within which knowledge was produced and circulated was still a relatively contained system, any significant expansion of that domain, any significant difference in the degree to which ideas and attitudes could be disseminated, threatened to become a difference in kind as well—to alter the structure of knowledge by redefining its boundaries, to force a transition from a relatively limited and closed symbolic system to a more radically open economy of knowledge and representation. That the emerging institution in question was, at best, quasi-illicit only exacerbated the dilemma of its emergence. Combated throughout its history by the city, licensed but hardly controlled by the court, the Elizabethan public theater emerged from and appropriated a place within the fissures and contradictions of the cultural landscape;[15] although it rapidly became, in Jean Howard's words, "one of the chief ideological apparatuses of Elizabethan society,"[16] it was neither the product nor the organ of the state but rather the result of a historically determined collusion between artisanal entrepreneurs and a socially diverse and astoundingly large audience. And unlike other expansions of the discursive domain in the period, literacy was not the price of admission to the theater, a fact which gave the stage a currency and accessibility rivaled only by the pulpit, which it threatened to eclipse.[17]

Unlike the pulpit, of course, the stage was an affective rather than a didactic forum; the ideas and ideologies, stories and histories real (whatever that might mean) and imaginary that it made available, and hence appropriable, for a significant portion of the population were also dramatically embodied, and by modes of theatrical representation that were themselves significant departures from English dramatic tradition.[18] The shift away from the morality tradition and its abstract personification of states-of-being and toward the particular, discursive, and theatrical embodiment of affective characters demanded and produced new powers of identification, projection, and apprehension in audiences, altering the threshold not only of dramatic representation but also of self-representation, not only of the fictional construction of character but also of the social construction of the self.[19] As a forum for the representation, solicitation, shaping, and enacting of affect in various forms, for both the reflection and, I would argue, the reformation of emotions and their economies, the popular stage of early modern England was a unique contemporaneous force. It may well have participated in what many before me, from Weber and Elias to Foucault, have posited as a fundamental reshaping of the political, social, and psychological subject during this period; it certainly served as a prominent affective arena in which significant cultural traumas and highly ambivalent events, such as the death of Elizabeth, could be directly or indirectly addressed, symbolically enacted, and brought to partial and imaginary resolution.

As I noted above, misogyny is generally on the rise in the drama of late Elizabethan and early Jacobean years, but it intersects with mourning in certain plays and genres more fully and forcefully than in others. Revenge tragedy has long been recognized, on the one hand, for the speed with which it becomes virtually synonymous with stage misogyny[20] and, on the other, for its generic and sometimes profound investment in recognizably Renaissance processes of mourning—revenge, after all, is the private response to socially unaccommodated grief—but typically these traits have been considered in isolation from one another, in separate studies and only insofar as they duplicate Renaissance habits of thought articulated elsewhere, in medical or philosophical discourse. Yet it is in late Elizabethan and early Jacobean revenge tragedy that the aging and posthumous body of Elizabeth is most fully engaged and problematized, in an apprehensive interplay of mourning and misogyny, revisionary desire and aggression, idealization and travesty. Remarking on a process of sovereign incorporation more literal than the psychic one that Freud describes in "Mourning and Melancholia," Hamlet notes that even "a king may go a progress through the guts of a beggar" (4.3.30–31);[21] he does so from within a play that infuses a new undercurrent in the subgenre to which it belongs. From 1600 to 1607—from Shakespeare's *Hamlet*, that is to say, to Middleton's *The Revenger's Tragedy*[22]—the various bodies of the queen go a progress, if not through the guts of a beggar then through the visceral responses of those slightly better off, who could afford the price of admission to experience, in the popular theater, the very age and body of *her* time.

## II

In 1600 the Virgin Queen was 68 years old, and contemporaneous accounts of her appearance detail the degree to which she was showing her age. In that same year, however, the Rainbow Portrait was issued, placing in circulation a new image of an unaging and youthful Gloriana. Yet the contradiction between the age inscribed on the queen's body and the highly sexualized aura generated by the cult of Elizabeth over the years and reinvoked in such late portraits was more complexly wrought than any distinction between reality and image can encompass; presenting or representing her body—"showing her age," to recall my own colloquial expression in a fuller register—necessitated a full and overdetermined embodiment of this sovereign contradiction. Although prospects of childbearing and marriage were long past and a Protestant successor was waiting in the wings, the aging of Elizabeth during the last decade of her reign was still a highly fraught political, physical, and symbolic issue, as she herself well knew.

"I think not to die so soon," Elizabeth told the French ambassador in 1597, ". . . and am not so old as they think."[23] De Maisse had already recorded, in journal entries from previous audiences, some of Elizabeth's efforts to counter what "they think," to embody in her age an alluring and captivating appeal:

> She was strangely attired in a dress of silver cloth, white and crimson. . . . She kept the front of her dress open, and one could see the whole of her bosom [*gorge*], and passing low, and often she would open the front of this robe with her hands as if she was too hot. . . . Her bosom [or throat; *gorge*] [24] is somewhat wrinkled as well as {one can see for} the collar that she wears around her neck [*col*], but lower down her flesh is exceedingly white and delicate, so far as one could see.
>
> As for her face, it is and appears to be very aged. It is long and thin, and her teeth are very yellow and unequal, compared with what they were formerly. . . . Many of them are missing so that one cannot understand her easily when she speaks quickly. Her figure is fair and tall and graceful in whatever she does. [25]

The queen's behavior was apparently not exceptional; in an entry that records a subsequent audience, de Maisse tells us:

> She was clad in a dress of black taffeta. . . . She had a petticoat of white damask, girdled, and open in front, as was also her chemise, in such a manner that she often opened this dress and one could see all her belly, and even to her navel [*tout l'estomac jusques au nombril*]. [26] . . . When she raises her head she has a trick of putting both hands on her gown and opening it insomuch that all her belly can be seen. [27]

As Louis Montrose has noted in detail, Elizabeth's display of her bosom was a complex register of cultural and sumptuary symbolism, signifying her status as a maiden and as a nurturing and bountiful mother, a "virgin-mother—part Madonna, part Ephesian Diana," whose "conspicuous self-displays were also a kind of erotic provocation." [28] In private the signs of age in the queen's face were apparently left unobscured by cosmetics, heightening the incongruity between advanced age ("her face . . . is . . . very aged . . . long and thin") and the exposed bosom of a maiden ("lower down her flesh is exceeding white and delicate"). In the public domain this incongruity was lessened and mystified to a certain degree by the circulation of painted images of the unaging sovereign body, but even here the line between image and reality, idealized portrait and the physical lineaments of age, is difficult to draw. Anthony Rivers, a Jesuit priest, reported that at Christmas celebrations in 1600 Elizabeth was painted "in some places near half an inch thick." [29] The queen was painted on canvases more than once; she was herself one of those canvases, a painted image no less than the Rainbow Portrait was.

Of course few outside the court saw either the Rainbow Portrait or the queen's holiday face, but it would be a mistake to conclude from this that Elizabeth's erotic displays and painted selves were either inconsequential or mere vanity, given all that was at stake in the sovereign aura. They were efforts to imbue the aging natural body of the monarch with the ageless aura of the body politic, which, as Marie Axton notes, "was supposed to be *contained within the natural body of the Queen.*"[30] Elizabeth's attempt to reinvest her final years with the erotic dynamics of courtship and desire—with the dynamics of Petrarchan romance that had so fully informed her earlier reign[31]—was an effort to close the gap or internal fissure that was, in the 1590s, increasingly apparent between the queen's two bodies. It was an ambivalent enterprise at best, especially where cosmetic portraiture or face-painting was concerned, as Thomas Tuke's "Treatise Against Painting" makes clear. According to Tuke, the painted woman, like the monarch, has two bodies; but the painted woman is an idolatrous and even curiously transvestite parody of the incorporated monarchical body, one that violates categories of gender and grammar as well as prerogatives of divine creation:

> She is a creature that has need to be twice defined . . . though she be the creature of God, as she is a woman, yet is she her own creatress, as a picture. Indeed a plain woman is but half a painted woman, who is both a substantive and an adjective, and yet not of the neuter gender: but a feminine as well consorting with a masculine, as ivy with an ash.[32]

Tuke and other commentators also describe the poisonous effects of the mercury-based cosmetics used in the period; as Laurie A. Finke has noted, such descriptions serve as both medical warnings and ideologically potent metaphorical images, vividly registering "all the horrors, both visual and olfactory, of [a] putrefying corpse."[33] In such treatises a cosmetically enhanced visage figures as a sign not of sexual allure but of the skull beneath the skin— or rather, sexual allure and the skull are combined in a conundrum that *is* the aging female body, for in a period that linguistically coded sexual climax as a form of death, "dying" the face introduces a third register to the common Renaissance pun. The painted lady does not disguise death or obscure the skull beneath her painted flesh; she is a *memento mori* herself, without need of demystification.

Even aside from the necessity to paint "near half an inch thick," however, the erotic dynamics of Elizabethan rule had always entailed a certain ambivalence and danger, involving as they did the construction of an ambiguous desire for the queen, not as monarch but as woman. An incident in 1600 documents Elizabeth's continuing success, even in her later years, in thus constructing her subjects' desires and illustrates some of the danger involved as well. On June 3 of that year, Elizabeth's secretary William Waad wrote to Cecil concerning the antic disposition of one Abraham Edwardes, a "Kentish man born, and . . . a mariner," who first came to Waad's attention when he sent "so passionate a letter to her Majesty" and was subsequently arrested and imprisoned "for drawing his dagger in the presence chamber." Rather than charging Edwardes with attempted regicide, Waad counseled his removal to Bedlam Hospital, noting that "the fellow is greatly distracted, and seems rather to be transported with a humour of love, than any purpose to attempt anything against her Majesty."[34]

Waad provides a curiously one-dimensional, even proto-Freudian interpretation of the scene. Edwardes's display of love in the form of a drawn dagger seems at least to combine sexual and other potential forms of physical aggression and violence; whatever the case, his act was in itself a violation of the queen's presence, and one that is tempting to relate to Hamlet's audience with another queen, when he needs to remind himself to use verbal rather than physical violence in Gertrude's chamber: "I will speak daggers to her, but use none" (3.2.387). It is relatively certain that some version of *Hamlet* was being presented on stage by 1600, and the play may have made its first appearance as early as 1598 or 1599, so topical allusion in the usual sense of the phrase is not at issue. Juxtaposed with Hamlet's royal audience, however, Edwardes's "humour of love" does allow us to see the queen—Elizabeth or Gertrude—through period eyes, shifting critical focus from the long-romanticized melancholy of the Dane to the aging yet erotic body of the queen, and in a manner that supplements recent suggestions that *Hamlet* is a play keenly aware of its *late* Elizabethan status, in which the impending transfer of power "from one monarch to another had to be rethought in view of the aging body of the queen."[35]

### III

Cecil seems to have followed Waad's advice: Abraham Edwardes was not prosecuted as an attempted regicide, despite appearances and the ease with which a case could have been made, but was instead confined as an antic lover, overly receptive to the queen's graces. *Hamlet* may serve to condition our surprise at such peculiar and lenient treatment. In the play Hamlet's own role as an antic lover is debunked rather than confirmed by the crown, but regicide is similarly displaced from his and our attention by the eroticized and aging figure of the queen. Mourning for a dead king, even revenge, is displaced or at least overlaid and complicated by misogyny toward a queen who is too vital, whose sexuality transgresses both her age and her brief tenure as widow.

Hamlet's first appearance onstage sets the pattern. Isolated by the mourning clothes he refuses to abandon and more aggressively distanced from the court by his barbed comments and asides (and perhaps by his stage position as well),[36] Hamlet styles his grief as that which "passes show":

> Seems, madam? Nay, it is. I know not "seems."
> 'Tis not alone my inky cloak, good mother,
> Nor customary suits of solemn black,
> Nor windy suspiration of forc'd breath,
> No, nor the fruitful river in the eye,
> Nor the dejected haviour of the visage,
> That can denote me truly. These indeed seem,
> For they are actions that a man might play;
> But I have that within which passes show,
> These but the trappings and the suits of woe.
>
> (1.2.76–86)

What you see is what you get: surface and depth, appearance and reality, stage posture and being coincide and cohere fully in a proclamation of sincerity that marks all around him as theatrical dissemblers. When alone onstage, however, Hamlet immediately reveals that all is not as it seems:[37]

> Fie on't, ah fie, 'tis an unweeded garden
> That grows to seed; things rank and gross in nature
> Possess it merely. That it should come to this!
> But two months dead—nay, not so much, not two—
>
>        . . .
>
>      Why, she would hang on him
> As if increase of appetite had grown
> By what it fed on; and yet within a month—
> Let me not think on't—Frailty, they name is woman—
>
> (1.2.135–46)

Grief over his father's death is overlaid and supplanted by obsessive disgust over what has failed to die, here figured as the unweeded garden of Gertrude's sexual appetite; it is the incestuous "dexterity" of the queen (1.2.157), that indeed occupies the core of Hamlet's being and "denote[s him] truly," as a generalized sign of the bestial inconstancy of all womankind. Like son, like father: at the first mention of his "seeming-virtuous queen," the Ghost forgets his purpose and digresses upon Gertrude's lust and lewdness, her taste for "garbage," and it is only the morning air that reminds him that his time is short, and that he has yet to inform Hamlet of the details of Claudius's crime. The vengeful charge of the ghost is itself focused not on the past crime of regicide but on the ongoing sexual transgression: "Let not the royal bed of Denmark be / A couch for luxury and damned incest" (1.5.82–83). Even in the later Mousetrap scene, Claudius is hardly the observed of all observers; throughout the Player Queen and King's prologue, Hamlet's attention is on Gertrude alone, this part of the Mousetrap functioning clearly to catch the conscience not of the king but of the queen.

This obsessive concern with Gertrude is hardly news; a long history of Oedipal readings begins here, typically effacing the sovereign cast of Hamlet's obsessive misogyny—Gertrude as queen—by an exclusive focus on the domestic scene, viewing the play as one more family romance—Gertrude as mother—only incidentally staged in terms of state hierarchies and monarchical sexuality. Performances governed by this critical tradition often portray Gertrude as a young queen, sometimes played by an actress who is, if anything, younger than the actor playing Hamlet. Quite recently, however, critics have suggested that the aging widowed queen of the play resonates strongly with the aging virgin queen on the throne. As Peter Erickson has remarked, "Gertrude represents the convergence of three issues—sexuality, aging (3.4.68–70), and succession—that produced a sense of contradiction, even breakdown, in the cult of Elizabeth in the final years of her reign. . . . The latent cultural fantasy in *Hamlet* is that Queen Gertrude functions as a degraded figure of Queen Elizabeth."[38] What I earlier called the conundrum of the aging female body, with its overdetermined registers of sexuality and death, unites the two monarchs. Aspects of the two that might seem to distinguish them—Gertrude's status, for example, as both widow and mother—also contribute to the association of royal bodies when viewed in a sixteenth-century context. Elizabeth styled herself, of course, as the sovereign mother of her subjects; she also presided over a period in which widows occupied an increasingly anomalous and threatening position, whether they remarried or remained single. As independent yet marriageable women, they recovered the one position of power available to most women in early modern patriarchal society—the social space on the threshold of marital alliance, which Elizabeth had occupied so masterfully throughout her reign—but this time without parental strictures and oftentimes with enhanced economic power as well, derived from the estates inherited from their husbands. Remarriage might seem to resolve the threat posed by female independence, bringing the woman back into the fold of patriarchal hegemony, but as Barbara J. Todd has demonstrated, in the later part of the sixteenth century the reverse was true: remarriage raised fears of greater independence, and of a kind where economic and sexual hierarchies are difficult to disentangle. After about 1570, wills began to restrict widows' access to inherited estates if they remarried, and the economic grounds for such restrictions are often overlaid with sexual anxieties. "The remarriage of any widow," as Todd puts it, "confronted every man with the threatening prospect of his own death and the entry of another into his place."[39]

Gertrude's transgression is not merely against her first husband, however. What distracts Hamlet from his almost blunted purpose is Gertrude's *aging* sexuality, conceived at times as a contradiction in terms, at times as a violation of her own body akin in its unnaturalness to a rebellion in the body politic: hers is a passion that "canst mutine in a matron's bones" (3.4.83), at once unimaginable and yet impossible not to imagine and visualize in graphic detail. At her age the queen's sovereignty should extend to and rule over such desires—"You cannot call it love; for at your age / The heyday in the blood is tame" (3.4.68–69)—and if not, such passion is a mutineer, a traitor, a figure of "rebellious hell." The heyday in Gertrude's blood can be denigrated but cannot be exorcised from Hamlet's mind or her matron's bones or her chamber, where she lives "In the rank sweat of an enseamed bed, / Stew'd in corruption, honeying and making love / Over the nasty sty!" (3.4.93–95).

Where modern productions sometimes efface the transgression of aging sexuality, the stage apparatus of the Elizabethan theater would have necessarily heightened the incongruity and contradiction embodied in Gertrude's figure. Gertrude is verbally inscribed with a sexuality that, according to Hamlet, transgresses the sovereign and aging body of the queen; onstage such a transgression would have been at once refigured and reproduced as a contradiction between the object and means of theatrical representation, the aging but sexually marked discursive body of the queen given its theatrical embodiment not by means of verisimilitude but by means of a homologous, highly sexualized contradiction of a different order.[40] On the Elizabethan stage the skull beneath the painted skin, the mutineer in the matron's bones, would be represented not by an aging actress but by a boy, whose sexual register onstage and in the acting company was also ambivalently marked, differently but equally overdetermined, and to a considerable extent indecipherable from our own historical vantage point.[41]

According to Freud, melancholy is produced by an incapacity to acknowledge or properly mourn death; distinguishing between Freud's nearly synonymous use of the terms *incorporation* and *introjection* to describe the mourning process, Nicolas Abraham and Maria Torok have defined incorporation as the sign of this interminable mourning.[42] The temporizing process of incorporation intervenes, as Jacques Derrida explains, whenever, introjection is blocked or fails for whatever reason:

> Sealing the loss of the object, but also marking the refusal to mourn, such a maneuver is foreign to and actually opposed to the process of introjection. I pretend to keep the dead alive, intact, *safe (save) inside me,* but it is only in order to refuse, in a necessarily equivocal way, to love the dead as a living part of me, dead *save* in me, through the process of introjection, as happens in so-called normal mourning.[43]

Even if we accept such terms as relevant for other times and cultures—and some such distinction between resolved and irresolvable mourning does seem valid, whether for a play like *Hamlet* or even for more distant cultural contexts—we must still historicize them. For example, English culture in the last half of the sixteenth century witnessed an intense Protestant campaign against both the expression of grief and the expression of comfort or condolence toward those in mourning. As G. W. Pigman has shown, sixteenth-century treatises on mourning regard grief as a sign of "irrationality, weakness, inadequate self-control, and impiety"[44]—the latter succinctly registered in Jonson's "Of Death":

> He that feares death, or mournes it, in the iust,
> Shewes of the resurrection little trust.[45]

Manuals on grief and bereavement counseled angry remonstration against the bereaved rather than sympathy or comfort, producing an ideologically charged cultural climate whose ramifications are difficult to determine with any rigor but which should at least condition modern critical responses to the maimed rites of mourning in a play such as *Hamlet.*[46] The degree to which such strictures affected how people *felt* grief in the period is of course uncertain; for a brief period of time, however, they clearly altered the decorum of bereavement, casting a moralizing and religiously charged pall over traditionally available expressions of grief, whether public rites or private rituals and practices. The result for Elizabethan England may well have been a higher ratio of socially induced melancholy in Abraham and Torok's revised sense of that term, fostering a psychic culture of incorporation rather than introjection.[47]

Hamlet's melancholy, however, is of an entirely different order: produced as much by Gertrude's sexual vitality as by his father's death, it is the result not of an interminable or encrypted mourning but of a "prevented" mourning in the rhetorical sense of the term—a mourning before the fact, over a vitality that one wants to be or imagines or finally produces as past and dead. It is an all-too-fully proleptic mourning,[48] and misogyny is the sign of this prolepsis: a response to what should be dead but isn't, an aggressive and often counterproductive effort to resolve this dilemma. What is sexually vital in the aging queen becomes variously figured as its opposite, a sign of death. The Player Queen presents one aspect of this sign, and in doing so clarifies the degree to which Gertrude's sexual desire and behavior do not merely distract Hamlet from his ostensible object of mourning—the king— but are fully folded into it, as an emblem of death to the male order of state and marital hierarchies. "A second time I kill my husband dead, / When second husband kisses me in bed" (3.2.179–80). Twice in the play, Hamlet himself configures signs of female sexuality-in-age as *memento mori*, registering not vitality but corruption and death. To Ophelia, whose youth presumably belies the need for cosmetics, he castigates painted women as transgressive and presumptuous usurpers of divine creation: "God hath given you one face and you make yourselves another" (3.1.144–46); in the graveyard scene Yorick's skull prompts not reflection on human or even male mortality but a triumphant reading and declaration of *female* mortality: "Now get you to my lady's chamber and tell her, let her paint an inch thick, to this favor she must come" (5.1.186–89).

Although a commonplace of Renaissance misogyny, Hamlet's move from Yorick's skull to that of the painted lady is also a great deal more. It is the last instance of the pattern I briefly outlined earlier, in which an obsessive misogyny displaces or supplants grief over a male figure, and as such it marks a significant moment in the gynophobia of the play. After this moment Gertrude is no longer vilified and villainized for *her* sexual transgression but is instead represented as the victim of *Claudius's* pandering lust:

> He that hath kill'd my king and *whor'd my mother*,
> Popp'd in between th' election and my hopes,
> Thrown out his angle for my proper life . . .
> (5.2.64–66; *my emphasis*)

The change is a dramatic one: grammatical object rather than subject, victim rather than sexually transgressive agent, Gertrude no longer precipitates a misogynistic digression; she is no longer the source of obsessive concern that displaces revenge but instead has become one among several motives for revenge. This is not, it should be noted, the only difference in the Hamlet we encounter in act 5; he reveals a new and calm assurance in the working of divine providence as well, a transformation that has sometimes been ascribed to what happens offstage, characterized as a sea change produced by the fortuitous events onboard the ship bound for England. The muting of misogyny cannot be so ascribed, but may be located in the graveyard scene itself.

Why should the proleptic death of "my lady," Hamlet's or Shakespeare's painted queen, be figured into a moment of mourning for a court jester? What partial resolution of misogyny is enacted by such a complex and composite figure? In a play where mourning is characteristically prolonged or disrupted by prematurely foreshortened or "maimed" rites, Hamlet's encounter with Yorick's skull provides a subtle if economical glimpse of successful mourning in action, of what Abraham and Torok define as introjection rather than incorporation. Hamlet's caustic and easy cynicism over the leveling effect of death earlier in the scene, when the bones tossed up by the gravedigger are anonymous, ceases when Yorick's skull surfaces and is named. The thing Hamlet holds in his hand recalls and makes present in his mind the living figure, the vital memory from his childhood, even though the two Yoricks register at first as sheer contradiction, and what is alive in memory and imagination seems reduced to this, the decayed skull, in a moment of visceral revulsion:

> Alas, poor Yorick. I knew him, Horatio, a fellow of infinite jest, of most excellent fancy. He hath bore me on his back a thousand times, and now—how abhorred in my imagination it is. My gorge rises at it. (5.1.178–82)

Successful mourning requires a resolution of the contradiction between what is still vital in the memory and what is dead; rather than deny or avoid the contradiction, Hamlet heightens it by projecting the living memory onto the skull, lips onto the death's head, and exacerbates his revulsion by planting an imaginary (recollected) kiss on the grotesque, composite overlay. He then shifts from commentary to direct address:

> Here hung those lips that I have kissed I know not how oft. Where be your gibes now, your gambols, your songs, your flashes of merriment, that were wont to set the table on a roar? Not one now to mock your own grinning? Quite chop-fallen? (5.1.183–86)

The Yorick in Hamlet's mind would have mocked his own death, even his own death's head; that was, after all, his profession. The Yorick in Hamlet's hand is somber, serious, grinning but "quite chop-fallen." The moment of direct address, however, is also the moment of full introjection of that which is vital, making the living memory not only a part of Hamlet but also the part he now plays, literally in the face of death; the memory is made present not only in mind but also in body and behavior, embodied and given voice and new life onstage, as Hamlet becomes Yorick, the jester mocking his own grinning.

Why such a moment is interrupted by Hamlet's final piece of misogyny, and with such a satisfied and resolute tone, is unclear unless we press the peculiarities of the scene further. The exhumation of Yorick's skull is accompanied by a curious exhumation of the past as well, a precise but perplexing concatenation of dates—not only the odd concurrence of Hamlet's birth, Fortinbras senior's death, and the sexton's entrance into his profession but also the number of years Yorick has lain in the grave—that has drawn critical attention largely because it identifies Hamlet as 30 years old, and we all want him to be younger than that. But Hamlet's present age is hardly the final equation the scene produces; Yorick's tenure in the grave, 23 years, dates instead a specific moment in the past, Hamlet's age when Yorick died, and it is hardly an insignificant number. Seven was not only the canonical age of reason. In the Renaissance it was also the age of transition from childhood to youth, and from a culturally ungendered to a culturally gendered world: it was the breeching age, when the smocks in which children of both sexes were dressed gave way to gender-specific clothing, and boys were passed "out of the hands of women" and into "the hands of men."[49] The reference is highly veiled, to say the least, enough to make us suspect an overly imaginative critical ingenuity at work—were it not for the fact that, a decade later, *The Winter's Tale* repeats and confirms this aspect of Shakespeare's gestational lexicon:

> Looking on the lines
> Of my boy's face, methoughts I did recoil
> Twenty-three years, and saw myself unbreech'd
> In my green velvet coat, my dagger muzzled,
> Lest it should bit its master, and so prove
> (As [ornament] oft does) too dangerous.
> (1.2.153–58)[50]

Hamlet is not the only Shakespearean male who, in a moment of sexual and gender crisis, looks back to recall himself unbreeched. Here the speaker is Leontes, already in the throes of his developing jealousy, and he reproduces the chronology exactly: 30 years old, he too recoils exactly 23 years to remember an early modern version of a preoedipal phase.

If the confrontation with Yorick's skull produces the one clear instance of successful mourning in the play, then more than Yorick's death is being mourned. What Hamlet holds in his hand is no mere *memento mori;* it is also, perhaps preeminently, a memento of passage into the world that he, like Leontes, is now dismayed by.[51] Passage into the gendered world of sexuality, the world the aging queen refuses to pass beyond, is also being mourned and perhaps even effaced for the moment, when Hamlet returns to Yorick's time and finds there a world where his own gendered identity has not yet been produced, so that signs of adult sexuality—especially in women—can be misrecognized, transvalued, and even laid to rest. "Let her paint an inch thick, to this favour she must come. Make her laugh at that" (5.1.187–89).

Recently Judith Butler has suggested that Freud's account of the formation of gender identity in *The Ego and the Id* needs to be read alongside his comments on melancholy. Freudian gender identity, according to Butler, is itself a melancholic structure formed around a taboo against homosexuality that precedes the heterosexual incest taboo:

> Gender identification is a kind of melancholia in which the sex of the prohibited object is internalized as a prohibition. . . . If the melancholic answer to the loss of the same-sexed object is to incorporate and, indeed, *to become* that object through the construction of the ego ideal, then gender identity appears primarily to be the internalization of a prohibition that proves to be formative of identity.[52]

For the Victorian age and its aftermath—the period responsible for the invention of homosexuality and its taboo—Butler's revisionary reading is both apt and brilliant.[53] We are only beginning to recover some sense of earlier economies of sexual practices and cultural prohibitions, and we know next to nothing about the psychological strictures of early childhood in the Renaissance. Despite the fact that its psychological resonances are lost to us, however, the rite of passage known as the breeching age may well have constituted a significant moment of gender formation, analogous—at least insofar as it marks a transition into a more rigidly gendered world—to Butler's melancholic structure. Historically specific, officially and culturally inscribed, the breeching age would have represented a moment crucial not to the early or primary formation of the psychological subject (whatever that might mean in the early modern period) but to the gendered codification of the cultural and political subject. For boys and girls it meant the adoption of gendered clothing; for boys, unlike girls, it meant passing "out of the hands of women" and into "the hands of men": moving out of a period when full dependency upon women was culturally maintained as the norm and into male and patriarchal adulthood.

Historically speaking, the more rigidly hierarchical the system of patriarchy, the more rabid and chronic are its expressions of misogyny. They are of course more fully, explicitly, and officially licensed, but the reasons are structural as well. The patriarchal hierarchy of early modern England was grounded in an explicit and officially promulgated ideology of male supremacy and autonomy. As Janet Adelman has recently shown, however, such autonomy was everywhere contradicted by inescapable and everyday signs of male dependency upon women;[54] some of the more virulent outbreaks of misogyny in the Renaissance are aggressive expressions of this contradiction, and I would include here the affective conflation of mourning and misogyny I have been tracing. In some respects such a conflation should not surprise us. Rage or anger are common components of grief in many cultures,[55] most often directed toward the deceased when the survivor's dependence on that figure is greatest—and most virulent when such dependency is itself a source of ambivalence. In a rigidly hierarchical patriarchy like Renaissance England, the death of an influential woman—whether proleptically or posthumously mourned—would mark the fullest encounter with such ambivalence, when male autonomy would be exposed, in grief itself, as male dependency—as one of the fundamental contradictions of patriarchal society.

If Hamlet could indeed regress beyond the breeching age he would resolve the contradiction, but only by abandoning the patriarchal mystifications of male autonomy and by embracing full dependency upon women. Other than for a brief moment of imaginary resolution, of course, such a regression is impossible. In the scene that follows his encounter with Yorick's skull, Hamlet does indeed embrace his own dependency in an unprecedented and surprising manner, placing his fate in the hands of a special providence, but the divinity that shapes his end is the Christian god, the ultimate patriarch. Like other Shakespearean males, Hamlet achieves a partial if suicidal resolution of the contradictions of patriarchy by constructing a world that is not so much ungendered as free from gender differentiation—a world that is all male.[56]

## IV

"That woman is all male," Vindice declares in *The Revenger's Tragedy*, "whom none can enter" (2.1.111).[57] Elizabeth, of course, styled herself as a bit of both, acknowledging that she had "the body of a weak and feeble woman, but . . . the heart and stomach of a king";[58] after her death, however, Cecil would complain that she had been "more than a man, and, in troth, sometime less than a woman,"[59] and Ben Jonson would ascribe her lifelong status as the Virgin Queen to a membrane so tough that no man could, indeed, enter her.[60] Elsewhere in *The Revenger's Tragedy*, the Elizabethan register of misogyny is less veiled. An encyclopedic compendium of motifs, roles, and plots from the revenge tradition—enough so that modern editors may be wrong to punctuate the title as a *singular* possessive—the play also serves as a dramatized interpretation of the Elizabethan undertones I have been tracing in *Hamlet*, making explicit and clarifying the degree to which the partially resolved cycles of mourning and misogyny in the earlier play functioned as a processing of Elizabeth herself, the aging sexuality of the Virgin Queen recast in the degraded figure of the sovereign and remarried widow.

The play opens, as it were, in the graveyard scene of *Hamlet*: a long-delayed revenger stands on stage, musing on mortality and his own grief, a skull in his hand. Although Vindice too has lost a father and blames the lecherous duke for that death as well, the current object of his mourning and motive for revenge, inexplicably put off for some nine years, is a woman who out of love for him spurned the duke's advances and was poisoned for her refusal. Hers is in fact the skull that he holds, although he will withhold the name until the opportune moment. Vindice begins by addressing this as-yet-anonymous skull as an icon of the purity and chastity his lover died to preserve, but it quickly becomes a curiously ambivalent icon for contemplation, meditation, and revenge. Viewing the "ragged imperfections" and "unsightly rings" of the skull, Vindice recalls and imaginatively reinvests the "face / So far beyond the artificial shine / Of any woman's bought complexion" (1.1.20–22), but the dichotomy between true and painted beauty, the chaste virgin and (all other) cosmetically enhanced sirens, does not hold for long. Seeking terms appropriate for praising her chaste beauty and beautiful chastity, Vindice cannot master such culturally charged oxymorons without recasting them as contradictions. So beautiful was she, he continues as if in praise, that she could do what painted beauties could not: provoke desire in men otherwise inaccessible to sexual allure, so that

> the uprightest man (if such there be,
> That sin but seven times a day) broke custom
> And made up eight with looking after her:
> O she was able to ha' made a usurer's son
> Melt all his patrimony in a kiss.
>
> *(1.1.23–29)*

As Peter Stallybrass has noted, Vindice's praise undoes and contradicts itself in the process of enunciation, finally making it clear that it is only in death that she is truly "beyond the artificial shine," only as a skull that her "memory [can] be reconstituted outside the realm of bought complexions."[61] Clear to us, at any rate, for one of the remarkable aspects of this opening speech is its unbroken air of praise, as if Vindice at this point were entirely deaf to the entanglements of his own mourning and misogyny.

Such deafness is especially striking in Vindice, who can easily make Hamlet sound like a protofeminist. Women in general he defines as intrinsically permeable bodies, subject to what might be called a fully recursive incontinence: they let everything in (that woman is all male—i.e., no woman at all—whom none can enter) and they let everything out. Women's bodies and hence their characters are commonly described as "leaky vessels" in the period, as Gail Paster has shown,[62] but Vindice brings to this commonplace a freshness verging on obscenity at one point in the play when, disguised as a mercenary malcontent, he offers to procure his own sister for the duke's son Lussurioso (presumably the only way to gain the inner circle at court). Asked simply if he knows how to keep a secret, Vindice responds

> My lord!
> Secret? I ne'er had that disease o'th' mother,
> I praise my father. Why are men made close
> But to keep thoughts in best? I grant you this,
> Tell but some woman a secret over night,
> Your doctor may find it in the urinal i'th' morning.
> (1.3.79–84)

Modern editors are particularly chary in their glosses on these lines, reluctant to articulate Vindice's gross economy of tongue and genitalia, seeds planted in the ear and elsewhere, in a leaky vessel that cannot help but "piss away" whatever is sécreted (or secréted) within it.

When the skull returns to the stage in act 3, Vindice has applied cosmetics to it and supplied it with a shawl; his "chaste lover" is thus costumed as a whore, her death's grin smeared with poison, for the pièce de résistance of Vindice's revenge will be to let the duke be undone by his own lust, visited upon the courtesan Vindice has promised to supply him. Fully reconstituted in the realm of bought complexions, his lover can also now be named: she proves to be none other than Gloriana, the namesake of Elizabeth's idealized royal persona. In 1607, of course, Middleton could afford a more explicit topicality; Elizabeth had been dead for some four years, and her absence from the throne allowed for more license in theatrical representation, supplying Middleton an objective correlative not so much lacking as politically unavailable in Shakespeare's play. It is in this scene that Vindice most strongly recalls Hamlet in the graveyard, but where Hamlet reinvested Yorick with flesh in his imagination—"Here hung those lips that I have kissed I know not how oft"—Vindice literalizes this process to produce a theatrically viable spectacle:

> Here's an eye,
> Able to tempt a great man—to serve God;
> A pretty hanging lip, that has forgot now to dissemble;
> Methinks this mouth should make a swearer tremble.
>
> (3.5.54–57)

Within the confines of the play, making his chaste lover the vehicle of her own revenge means subjecting her to the fate she died to avoid: she is the painted lady, the courtesan, the whore; unlike Hamlet's imagined and recollected kiss, hers will be literalized, the kiss she refused the duke in life will be granted him in death, with Vindice playing the panderer. The ideal lover and the painted lady are one, and both are revealed to be fully male constructions. I will paint her an inch thick, for she was always destined to come to this. Vindice himself paints the woman—whether an inch, or half an inch thick—who in life was beyond the artificial shine, and his mourning for her now resolves itself into a quite conscious misogynistic regard:

> And now methinks I could e'en chide myself
> For doting on her beauty, though her death
> Shall be reveng'd after no common action.
> Does the silkworm expend her yellow labors
> For thee? For thee does she undo herself?
> Are lordships sold to maintain ladyships
> For the poor benefit of a bewitching minute?
>
> (3.5.68–74)

Vindice's revenge *of* his dead lover has become a literal travesty of her chastity, a revenge enacted *upon* her in the name of mourning.

As the skull of Gloriana, the travesty extends to Elizabeth as well. During her reign, however, Elizabeth was the primary actor in the cult of Gloriana and actively appropriated Petrarchan poetics to construct the desire of her subjects. Vindice's travesty turns those poetics upon the memory of Elizabeth in a radical sense, returning her to the traditional status of the Petrarchan lady by making her so fully the object rather than the actor or subject of male desire. Gloriana is a "property" (3.5.100), a stage prop; not even the overdetermined sexuality of the boy actor can peep through this representation of sovereign sexuality fully mastered and fully violated. The violation may not be the final act in the long process of misogynistic mourning for Elizabeth, but it is arguably a climactic one; the only good woman may be a dead woman in *Hamlet*, but *The Revenger's Tragedy* does not even offer this posthumous recovery. In the travesty of Gloriana, the dead queen is proved all woman at last, not only entered by the duke's tongue as he kisses her "like a slobbering Dutchman" (3.5.62) but also possessed and mastered by Vindice, who thus proves himself all male, not at all dependent upon or in the hands of women.

But this resolution of one of patriarchy's fundamental contradictions, through such an extreme reassertion of gender difference, cannot hold either. In most revenge plays the revenger's actions gradually obscure the difference between themselves and the typically lecherous murderers they oppose, and Vindice follows suit in this regard, announcing at the end of the play that there is "one enemy left alive. . . . 'Tis time to die, when we are ourselves our foes" (5.3.107–8). First, however, he undoes himself by undoing the sheer differentiation between the closed body and world of men and the porous and leaky realm of womankind. At play's end he has not only succeeded in his revenge upon the duke but has also managed to produce the deaths of all the duke's sons and much of the court as well, and has managed to make it look as though they slaughtered one another. The duke's death has remained a mystery, but here Vindice cannot keep his mouth shut; proud of his accomplishments, he cannot keep his own secret and even squeals on his brother and sometime accomplice as well:

> 'Twas somewhat witty carried though we say it:
> 'Twas we two murder'd him.
>
> *(5.3.96–97)*

Although one of the people avenged by Vindice in the course of the play was the wife of the good lord Antonio, who killed herself after being raped by the duke's youngest son, the good lord summarily orders both brothers carted off for execution. Vindice ends the play as the leaky vessel he thought to distinguish himself from, dribbling away his secret, his carefully constructed maleness, and his life.

Such a denouement is so uncharacteristic of theatrical misogyny in the period and so explicit that it allows one to entertain, at least, the possibility that Middleton conceived this play with all its excesses not as yet another, and in many ways culminating, instance of stage misogyny but as a critique and critical examination of the tradition. Even so, the elaborate travesty of Gloriana remains one of the few things not undone in the process. Other heads brought on the Elizabethan and Jacobean stage register a visual pun, recalling the scaffold of execution by overlaying it upon the scaffold of theatrical representation; Middleton achieves an overlaid meaning no less spectacular but of a different order, by making Vindice so fully possess the skull of Gloriana—the maidenhead, according to the implicit logic of his pun, of the Virgin Queen herself.

## Once Upon a Time, Not Long Ago, O

**Artaud Speaks:**

When O was a young girl, above all she wanted a man to take care of her.

In her dream, the city was the repository of all dreams.

A city which was always decaying. In the center of this city, her father had hung himself.

This can't be true, O thought, because I've never had a father.

In her dream, she searched for her father.

She knew that it was a dumb thing for her to do because he was dead.

Since she wasn't dumb, O thought, she must be trying to find him so that she could escape from the house in which she was living, which was run by a woman.

O went to a private detective. He called O a dame.

"I'm looking for my father."

The private eye, who in one reality was a friend of O's, replied that the case was an easy one.

O liked that she was easy.

And so they began. First, according to his instructions, O told him all that she knew about the mystery. It took her several days to recount all the details.

At that time it was summertime in Dallas. All yellow.

O didn't remember anything in or about the first period. Of her childhood.

After not remembering, she remembered the jewels. When her mother had died, a jewel case had been opened. The case, consisting of one tray, had insides of red velvet. O knew that this was also her mother's cunt.

O was given a jewel which was green.

O didn't know where that jewel was now. What had happened to it. Here was the mystery of which she had spoken.

The private eye pursued the matter. A couple of days later, he came up with her father's name.

"Oli."

The name meant nothing to her.

"Your father's name is Oli. Furthermore, your father killed your mother."

That's possible, O thought, as if thinking was dismissing.

The detective continued to give her details about her father: he was from Iowa and of Danish blood.

All of this could be true because what could she in all possibility know?

When O woke up out of her insane dream, she remembered that her mother had died eight days before Christmas. Despite the note lying beside the dead body in which the location of the family white poodle was revealed, the cops were convinced that the mother had been murdered. By a man unknown. Since it was now Christmas, these cops had no intention of investigating a murder rather than returning to their families, Christmas warmth, and holiday.

O realized, for the first time in her life, that her father could have murdered her mother. According to the only member of her father's family whom she had ever met, a roly-poly first cousin whose daughter picked up Bowery bums for sexual purposes (according to him), her father had murdered someone who had been trespassing on his yacht.

Then, her father had disappeared.

O became scared. If her father had killed her mother, he could slaughter her. Perhaps that's what her life had been about.

During this period of time, O lived and stayed alive by dreaming. One of the reveries concerned the most evil man in the world.

It was at a fancy resort that was located in the country, far from the city: O stood on one of the disks, as if on a giant record, which jutted out of a huge cliff. Shrubbery was growing out of parts of the rock. Each record lay directly over and under another record, except for the top and the bottom. The one on which O perched thrust farther into a sky that was empty, for that record was a stage.

In the first act of this play, O learned that evil had entered the land. That the Father, who was equivalent to evil, was successfully stealing or appropriating his son's possessions. Both of them were standing behind O. Then, the father began to torture his son. He inflicted pain physically. O actually saw this older man point three different machine guns at her. Each of them was different. O understood that he wanted to scare, rather than to shoot, her.

He laughed. And then disappeared.

O hated him more than it was possible to hate anyone.

Either the next day or some days later, the young woman began to search for the older man. She and his son were partners, co-mercenaries, in this venture; in fact, it was the son who taught O that to be a successful detective, one has to get rid of fear.

For some reason unknown to O, she was always frightened of people.

The father left one clue to his whereabouts. *DN.*

Nobody seemed to know whether *DN* were the initials of someone, of something, whether the letters were part of a language no human could understand. O and the son believed that *DN* was the name of a coffee joint . . .

. . . . . . . . . . . . . . . . . . . . . . . . . . . . . . . . . . . . . . . . . . . . . . . . . . . . . . . .

. . . . .They entered a deserted western town. The coffee joint found in the loneliness, whose name was *a street,* within all the yellow didn't have a name . . .

. . . . . . . . . . . . . . . . . . . . . . . . . . . . . . . . . . . . . . . . . . . . . . . . . . . . . . . .

. . . . .They traveled to a ranch. The main building, which at first they didn't notice because it wasn't noticeable, was one story, white peeling paint. In its right side, a cafe-in-the-wall.

A girl was feeding her dog-horse, 'cause it was as large as a large horse, a plate of raw hamburger. She used to be married to the son; now, she was living on this ranch and happy.

This is the second clue.

One didn't need to find any more because the man for whom she had been looking walked right up to her. In all that was openness, there was no one but those two. O realized that all that had happened to her had only because she was attracted to this man. To this father. And she hated him because he was violent.

It was at this point that O began to teach him how to change violence into pleasure.

Now O decided that she wanted to go where she had never been before:

### O Speaks:

The revolution had yet to begin in China. At that time, the word *revolution* meant nothing to us because the same governments owned everything. There seemed nowhere left to go. All of my friends, including me, before we reached old age were dying and, until we died, living in ways that were unbearable because that's what living was. Unbearable.

I had no interest in politics.

I had come to China as I usually came: I had been following a guy.

I had believed we were in love.

It didn't matter, the name of this unknown city to which I came. All the unknown cities, in China, held slums which looked exactly like each other: each one a labyrinth, a dream, in which streets wound into streets which disappeared in more streets and every street went nowhere. For every sign had disappeared.

The poor ate whatever they could put their hands on.

Right before the revolution, the Chinese government told its people that the recession was over. This lie made the poor unable to distinguish between economic viability and disability. Some of them walked around with needles sticking out of their bodies.

Many of the women were whoring for money.

W, my boyfriend, said that if I loved him, I would prostitute for him. I knew that W got off on women who were whores. I didn't know whether or not he had deep feelings for me and, if so, what those feelings were. I used to wonder, again and again, why I ran after men who didn't care for me.

It was my mother, not my father, who dominated my waking life. When she was alive, my mother didn't notice or, if she had to, hated me. She wanted me to be nothing and something worse because my appearance in her womb, not yet in the world, caused her husband to leave her. What my mother who was ravishingly beautiful, charming, and a liar, had told me. While she had been alive.

*Absence* isn't the name only of the father.

Every whorehouse is childhood.

The one in which W placed me was named *Ange*.

Outside the whorehouse, men fear women who are beautiful and run away from them; a ravishing woman who's with a man must bear a scar that isn't physical. My mother was weak in this way; her weakness turned into my fate.

Inside the brothel, the women, however they actually look, are always beautiful to men. Because they fulfill their fantasies. In this way, what was known as *the male regime*, in the territory named *women's bodies*, separated its reason from its fantasy.

Since I was the only white girl in this brothel, the others there, including the Madame who had once been a male, hated me. They sneered at my characteristics, such as my politeness. What they really detested was that economic necessity hadn't driven me into prostitution. To them, the word *love* had no meaning. But I didn't become a whore because I loved W so much I'd do anything for him. Anything to convince him to love me. A love I was beginning to know I would never receive. I entered the brothel of my own free will so that I could become nothing because, I believed, only when I was nothing could I begin to see.

I had no idea what I was doing.

When I entered the house, Madame took away all of my possessions, even my tiny black reading glasses. It was as if she was a prison matron. She said that, because I was white, I thought that I deserved to possess commodities. Such as happiness. That I was too pale, delicate, to be able to bear living in this place.

The other girls thought that I could leave this cathouse whenever I wanted.

But I couldn't walk away because inside the whorehouse I was nobody. There was nobody to walk away.

I was now a child: if I rid myself of childhood, there would be nothing left of me.

Later on, the girls would accept me as a whore. Then I would start to wish that I loved a man who loved me.

There were many prescients in the slum. The whores, in their spare hours, visited these fortune-tellers. Though I soon started accompanying my friends, I was too scared to say anything to these women who often had once been in the business. I would stand in the shadows and rarely ask anything, for I didn't want to confess anything about myself. When I, at last, did inquire about a future, I asked as if there were no such thing. I felt safe only knowing the details of daily life, johns and defecations, all that was a dream.

As if dreams couldn't be real.

Fortune-tellers wandered around the streets outside *Ange*.

The one fortune, *mine*, which I remember, was based on the card of the Hanged Man:

The woman who was reading the cards still took tricks.

"Does that mean that I'm going to suicide?" I asked.

"Oh, no, O. This card says that you're a dead person who's alive. You're a zombie."

But I knew better. I knew that the Hanged Man or Gérard de Nerval was my father and every man I fucked was him.

My father was the owner of Death, of the cathouse. Sitting in his realm of absence, he surveyed all that wasn't.

The cards showed me clearly that I hated him. When a message travels from the invisible to the visible world, that messenger is emotion. My anger, a messenger, would lead to revolution. Revolutions are dangerous to everyone.

But the cards said worse. They told us, the whores, that the revolution which was just about to happen, due to its own nature or origin, had to fail. As soon as it failed, as soon as sovereignty be it reigning or revolutionary disappeared, as soon as sovereignty ate its own head as if it was a snake, when the streets turned to poverty and decay but a different poverty and decay, all my dreams which were me would be shattered.

"It's then," the fortune-teller said, "that you'll find yourself on a pirate ship."

The cards that I remember told me that my future is freedom.

"But what'll I do when there's no one in the world who loves me? When all existence is only freedom?"

The cards proceeded to show images of stress, illness, disease . . .

I had been in the cathouse for a month. W hadn't once visited me, for he had never cared about me.

I was a whore because I was alone.

The fortune-teller had told me that I would be free after I journeyed into the land of the dead.

I was trying to get rid of loneliness and nothing would ever rid me of loneliness until I got rid of myself.

## Artaud Speaks:

O said, I want to go where I've never been before.

I was living in a room that was in the slum. I was still sane.

I was just a boy. All I saw was the poverty of those slums. In order to counteract the poverty that was without and within me, I ran to poetry. Especially to the poetry of Gérard de Nerval who wanted to stop his own suffering, to transform himself, but instead hanged himself from a rusty picture nail.

I had no life. I only loved these poets who were criminals. I began to write letters to people whom I didn't know, to those poets, not in order to communicate with them. To do something else.

Dear Georges, I wrote.

I have just read, in *Fontane* magazine, two articles by you on Gérard de Nerval, which made a strange impression on me.

I am a limitless series of natural disasters and all of these disasters have been unnaturally repressed. For this reason, I am kin to Gérard de Nerval who hanged himself in a street alley during the hours of a night.

Suicide is only a protest against control.

Artaud.

The alleyways were lying all around me. They ran every which way so haphazardly that they stopped. There was the brothel.

I would watch man after man walk through its doors. Men went to this brothel, not in order to have the sexual intercourse they could have on the outside, but to enact elaborate and tortuous fantasies which, one day, I'll be able to describe to you.

I'll be able when there's human pleasure in this world.

Day after day I would look through one of my windows into one of theirs. There, I first saw O who was naked. My eye would follow her, as much as it could, trying to clear away for her everything that was before and behind her.

I would die for her. Whenever a man hangs himself, his cock becomes so immense that for the first time he knows that he has a cock.

One day, O came out of the brothel. I saw her stand on the edge of its doorway and look away. Obviously, she was terrified. Finally, one of her feet peeped over the doorframe's bottom. I had no idea what was mirrored in those eyes. Three times her feet darted back and forth across that doorstep.

As soon as she was fully outside, she began to turn in the same ways the winds do through the sky. Perhaps she was meeting the outside, the sky, for the first time. Perhaps, in the staleness of the brothel, O had been a *she* and now she was another *she* who wasn't distinct from air. I watched this girl begin to breathe. I watched her encounter poverty for the first time, the streets which my body was daily touching. The streets whose inhabitants ate whatever they could and, when they no longer could eat, died.

These streets reminded O of her childhood. For when she had been a child, she had always been alone. Even though she'd a half-sister who was now married to a European armaments millionaire. Every summer, O's mother, so she would never have to see her, sent O to a posh summer camp. A camp of girls.

There, the girls passed through the latest dances in each other's arms in the hour before they were ordered into dinner while O watched them. She knew that she couldn't dance. For the first time in her life, in the whorehouse, O was safe because, here, there were no humans.

In the whorehouse, she had become naked.

Now that O felt safe, she had the strength to return to her childhood. To poverty. I watched O walk down street after street, searching for who she would be. I knew that when she had found what she had had to find, she would belong to me.

### O Speaks:

The first time W and I slept together, I knew that he didn't love me. But I didn't know why. The nausea and confusion that resulted left me shreds of belief to which I could cling: I clung to belief that in the future W might start to love me.

Like a child who's not able to believe that her mother doesn't care about her.

I remained in that brothel. One day W came back to tell me that he wanted me to meet the woman he adored even more than his own life. To meet her, he was going to take me out of the brothel for the day.

They had been together many years before he met me. He said. That she had left him. It had been his fault: he wasn't good to her. She returned to him in China and now, he wanted to be as good to her as it was possible for a human to be.

Though she had come back to him, she still wasn't sure whether she wanted to be with him and this made him love her more.

I didn't know who I was to W, why he was telling me about the woman whom he worshipped.

I could cling to my nausea. Maybe nausea, then, is something. A man's body. I followed him out of the brothel. Into those streets which I had started to explore by myself.

A bird was flying through the sky.

His girlfriend was as white as me. But she was beautiful and rich. As soon as I met her, I knew that I didn't exist for her in the same way that I didn't exist for W, that she didn't know how to love. She was one of those owners. She was somebody.

I could love W which she never could, but what did he want? Did he want all that I would be able to give him?

After dinner, he brought his girlfriend and me back to the brothel and he tied me to my bed. Needles inserted into the flesh just below the lower lashes kept the eyes open. In front of me, W made love to her. First, with his fingers. Delicately playing with her outer labia. They turned from pale pink to blood red. Opened to my eyes as his fingers disappeared. Some were in her mouth. He was bending her over and then he turned around, her cunt juice dripping so much that I could see it on his fingertips, and put his cock, which was in my mind, into that cunt that must have been open, wanting, screaming for pleasure, whether she loved him or not, she was being fucked inserted thrust into pummeled bruised and all that comes out is pleasure, the body is pleasure, I have known pleasure, and I am watching the endless pleasure, as it comes again again again, that I have known and now I am being refused.

Rich, she could never know what my pleasure was, and so I changed.

Throughout all of the dinner and the sex I was forced, also by myself, to watch, I was wearing the red lipstick which my mother had worn. My mother always walked around her house naked, touching her own body. She wore her menstrual blood on her mouth. In her house, there were no men, for my father had left her before I was born.

Since I never knew you, every man I fuck is you. Daddy. Every cock goes into my cunt which, since I never knew you, is a river named Cocytus. I said that I'm only going to tell the truth: When you, Cock of all Cocks, you, the only lay in the world, and I know for I'm supposed to live, not die, for sex, when you took a leave of absence ejaculated disappeared skipped out and vanished before I was born, you threw me, and I hadn't yet been born, into even another world.

The name of that world was China.

Who can understand China's teeming populaces, its children, its marching, student soldiers?

## Artaud Rewrites His First Letter
## to Georges Le Breton:

I am a violent being, full of fiery storms and other catastrophic phenomena. As yet I can't do more than begin this letter, begin it again and again, because I have to eat myself, my own body is my only food, in order to write. But I don't want to talk about myself. I want to discuss Gérard de Nerval. He made living: a living world. He made a living world out of myth and magic. The realm of myth and magic that he contacted was that of a Funeral. His own death and funeral.

I'll talk about death, my death, later.

The tarot card in the realm of Nerval is the Hanged Man. Heidegger, under the same sign, reversed himself and turned away from Hitler. Trying "to come to terms with his . . . past in the Nazi movement," he explained that "the very possibility of taking action" or "the will to rule and dominate" was "a kind of original sin, of which he found himself guilty." Instead of *Dasein*, he placed emphasis on *Sein* or an essentially reverent contemplativeness that might open and keep open the possibility of a new paganism in which no sovereignty could arise, no sovereignty out of the ashes of Hitler's aborted revolution.

Reverent contemplativeness is the Hanged Man in the realm of Nerval. Contemplativeness is the act of turning inside out, reversing, traveling the road into the land of the dead while being and remaining alive. Contemplativeness is seeming to do nothing. In other words, the Hanged Man card, to me, represents the slight possibility that this society in which human identity depends upon possessing rather than on being possessed, this society in which I'm living, could change.

Gérard de Nerval was a sailor who descended into oblivion and, as he did, wrote against oblivion. He hated his own cockhead and so he descended into the Cocytus, into oblivion, three times until his cockhead floated bloody on those waters. In other words, he hanged himself.

## O Speaks:

I spent day after day walking the streets, looking for W whom I would never again find.

## The Letter Continues:

I am Gérard de Nerval who hanged himself at midnight on a Thursday by his own hands. The other one died in Paris or announced that his death was going to happen, he announced that he was going to die from loneliness.

I, Gérard de Nerval, who write in the teeth of the utilitarian concept of the universe, will hang myself from an apron string tied to a grating. There will be nothing left.

At this moment, I, Gérard de Nerval, want to talk about the difference between hanging and the Hanged Man:

I, Antonin Artaud, hanged myself and I haven't died.

I'm living in a slum in China and I'm going to become sexual.

## O Speaks:

If W's not around, I don't want to be a whore.

## Artaud Speaks:

I entered the brothel so that I could meet O. The Madame stopped me to ask where I was going. I said that I was going to serve O.

She told me that I had to give her money so I could be with O. Because I don't have any money, I was thrown out of the whorehouse.

I found myself in a marketplace where everything was being sold for everything else. Some of the poor who were there didn't have any limbs. Others were willing to do anything sexually for money. The children said that a third of them would die, the next harvest, if there weren't enough beans. I decided that I had to stop the hell in which I was living.

I knew that they had thrown me out of the whorehouse because I refused to give O money.

I wanted O to love me.

Their denial of my sexuality planted in me the seeds of rebellion. There would be other women and men like me in that slum. Ones who would do whatever had to be done in order to change everything.

## O Speaks:

I no longer want to be a whore.

## Artaud Speaks:

It was at this time that the revolutionaries, both male and female, met in what light came from the quarter moon.

"We're poor," they said. "We need to get our hands on weapons."

"A white man just gave us some money for weapons, probably in order to save his own neck."

Though I had no interest in such tools, I agreed to undertake the machine gun delivery, dangerous at least, in return for the exact amount of cash I needed to buy O so that I could give her her freedom.

In this way, I cut my cockhead off so blood out of a heart I had never known started to flow.

## O Speaks:

How long will this reign of masochism continue?

## Artaud Addresses This Version of His Letter to O:

Everywhere he went, de Nerval would take with him a scummy apron string which had once belonged to the Queen of Sheba. De Nerval told me this. Or it was one of the corset strings of Madame de Maintenon. Or of Marguerite de Valois.

From this apron string which was tied to a grating, he hanged himself. The grating, black, partly broken, and stained by hound excretion, was located at the bottom of the stone stairs which lead to the rue de la Tuèrie. There's a straight drop from that stair platform downward.

As de Nerval swung there, a raven hovered over, as if it was sitting on his head, and cawed repeatedly, "I'm thirsty."

They were probably the only words the old bird knew.

I, Antonin Artaud, am now an owner, for I own the language of suicide.

Why did Gérard de Nerval hang himself from an apron string? Why is this society which is China insane?

To learn why Gérard madly offed himself, I shall enter his soul:

Gérard was a man like me. He wrote this: "le dernier, vaincu par (Jéhovah) / Qui, du fond des enfers, criait: 'O tyrannie!'"

Gérard was *le dernier* because, when he wrote that, he was just about to suicide, he was writing his own suicide note to God the Tyrant whose very existence was putting Gérard in hell. That is, Gérard suicided because of the existence of God: Gérard opposed the tyrant God by cutting off his own head. For God is the head, *le génie*. Gérard cut off his own head with a woman's apron string so now he is a woman so now he has a hole between his arms. Every soul is nothing. The soul of Gérard de Nerval has taught me that nothingness is the abyss of horror out of which consciousness always awakes in order to go out into something in order to exist.

A hole of the body, which every man but not woman including Gérard de Nerval and myself has to make, is the abyss of the mouth.

I have found this language which is why I can write this letter to you, O. You see, Gérard, who was naked like you are, gave me a language that doesn't lie, for it spurted out of the hole of his body.

You're naked so I know you've got a body.

When Gérard cut off his head, he made all that was interior in him exterior: today all that's interior is becoming exterior and this is what I call *revolution* and those humans who are holes are the leaders of this revolution.

I have gotten to know Gérard de Nerval and he was a revolutionary both before and after he hanged himself from an apron string. He hanged himself from a woman's string in order to protest against political control. Suicide is only a protest against control. I repeat that. After he castrated himself, language came pouring out of him.

I am evidence that this is true.

Now I am Gérard de Nerval after he castrated himself because consciousness in the form of language is now pouring out of me and hurting me and so I can be with you. I shall own you, O.

## O Speaks:

Now I knew W would never come back to me and take me out of the brothel.

Being aware that he would never love me was equal to knowing that he never had.

I was no longer safe so I became sick. I hovered at death.

It was at this time that the student revolutionaries, more professionally armed than any of the cops around them, burst into the English embassy which was located next to the slum. Though paying in serious injury and death, they successfully annihilated the government building.

When my health returned, I learned that W partly owned the cathouse. I had known that he was rich. I no longer cared what W felt about me: all I wanted was for him to be absent from me.

I wanted W to remain absent from me: I didn't want anything to change.

It had been W who had first given the terrorists the money to buy weapons. Perhaps he hadn't known why. Perhaps there was a need in him to disrupt and destroy. I didn't know W and I don't. When the revolutionary raid on the English had succeeded, probably he had become frightened. *For the first time in his life*, he had realized that to be rich and white is to be vulnerable. So when the revolutionaries had returned to him to ask for more funds, he had refused.

They started to beat him up. They almost killed him.

As soon as I learned what had taken place, I stopped hating W for not returning my love.

In a skirmish prior to the explosion of the English embassy, a young boy who had run guns to the revolutionaries had one of his arms severely injured.

With the other hand holding the money that he had earned by working for the terrorists, he walked into the brothel. He found the Madame and gave her the amount she had requested as the price of my purchase.

I knew nothing about the purchase of my freedom.

Behind my bedroom door, Artaud told me that he had come back for me.

"I'm still sick. I don't want to see anyone."

He forced himself into my room so I hit him. He fell down to the floor on the arm that had been broken. When he cried out, I was surprised.

"You're just a boy so how could you be hurting so badly?"

His arm was bent the wrong way for a human.

Now I understood that someone could hurt more than me. Reaching down, I lifted up his body, onto my thigh, as much as I was able. I only wanted to fuck with him. Pain was the same, for him at that moment, as sexual pleasure. For me, every area of my skin was an orifice; therefore, each part of his body could do and did everything to mine.

We wondered at our bodies.

### Artaud Rewrites His Letter:

When I saw O, I wanted to protect her because she worships her cunt.

### O Speaks:

I never saw Artaud again.

Weakened not only by the beating but also by the desertion of his rich girlfriend, W began to go mad.

He learned that the young boy and I had fallen in love. He began to follow Artaud, through the slum's streets which now reeked of more and more revolutionaries, into alleyways which were blind. In one of those, he shot the young poet and left him for dead.

In those days, there were too many bodies for there to be such a thing as murder.

When I heard this, I no longer cared what happened to W. I quit that whorehouse. For me, there were no more men left in the world.

I had been searching for my father, in a dream, and found a young and insane boy who was then killed.

I stood on the edge of a new world.

# "The Sex Appeal of the Inorganic": Posthuman Narratives and the Construction of Desire

> You are seduced by the sex appeal of the inorganic.    —Barbara Kruger

> The computer takes up where psychoanalysis leaves off.
> —Sherry Turkle, *The Second Self* (309)

> During the Post-Body Age, we're going to get songs like: She shut me down / wiped me clean / made me blanker than a banker's screen / But that's alright / There's no end in sight / I'm programmed well against that risk / with 47 copies of myself on disk.
> —Otter, in the independent zine *Dropout* (22)

Recent popular culture often seems to agree with Jean Baudrillard that "the year 2000 has already happened" and therefore it is "not necessary to write science fiction" any longer, since we now live in such fictions.[1] A similar assumption underlies the increasingly widespread belief that we are on the verge of a "post-body" or "posthuman" age, of not only desiring machines but a literal desire *for* machines or to *be* a machine, codified in such popular magazines as *Future Sex* and *Mondo 2000*. Specifically, popular culture is the site of two conflicting stories about what happens to traditional conceptions of the body in the context of these new technologies. I contend that popular narratives about the obsolescence of the body interrupt more traditional stories about gender and sexual identity, but at the same time this apparent break with the humanist past is often ideologically recontained, especially when it takes the form of what Arthur and Marilouise Kroker call "the disappearing body." I will situate these popular narratives in relation to the scientific narratives that legitimate them and in relation to attempts by critics to narrativize the possible outcomes of new technologies.

Let me begin with this untitled photograph by Barbara Kruger, of two mismatched gloves arranged to suggest a couple holding hands, framed with the caption "You are seduced by the sex appeal of the inorganic" (Figure 1). On the most immediate level, this image evokes a familiar critique of consumer culture and the "pseudo-satisfactions" of the commodity form, a critique of manufactured desire that can be traced back at least to Marx's comment that capitalist production creates subjects for its objects at the same time that it creates objects for its subjects.[2] Subjects learn to adapt themselves to the needs of the production process, not vice-versa. However, there is a more disturbing reading of this image as typifying the mutations of late capitalism, a reading that can be arrived at most easily through a contrast between Kruger's representation of the body as commodity and the same representation in surrealist art, specifically the motif of the mannequin.

Fredric Jameson argues that for the surrealists the mannequin thematizes the transition from a precapitalist political economy, in which objects retain "the half-sketched, uneffaced mark of human labor, of the human gesture" and therefore "remain . . . potentially as mysterious and as expressive as the human body itself," to a capitalist economy in which "the human body itself comes before us as a product."[3] In contrast, the effect of Kruger's image is derived from the postmodern context created by late capitalism's "expansion . . . into hitherto uncommodified areas" and the resultant elimination of "the enclaves of precapitalist organization" previously "tolerated and exploited in a tributary way."[4] The result, as Jameson argues, is a lack of depth, which makes objects "totally incapable of serving as a conductor of psychic energy" and therefore precludes "all libidinal investment in such objects."[5] But Kruger's photograph suggests that this extension of the commodity structure does not necessarily foreclose on libidinal investments or reduce such investments to the level of pseudo-satisfactions; instead, the persistence of such investments in objects that seem inappropriate to receive them results in a redefinition of desire as "inorganic" and in a critique of the expressive qualities Jameson attributes to "*the* human body" as a universal form. In a similar critique, Deleuze and Guattari famously suggest replacing "that organization of the organs called the organism" with the figure of the "body without organs."[6] The contrast between this redefinition of embodiment and the surrealist fetish, with its residual nostalgia for the body as a site of unalienated labor, is perhaps clearest in postmodern feminist artist Cindy

277

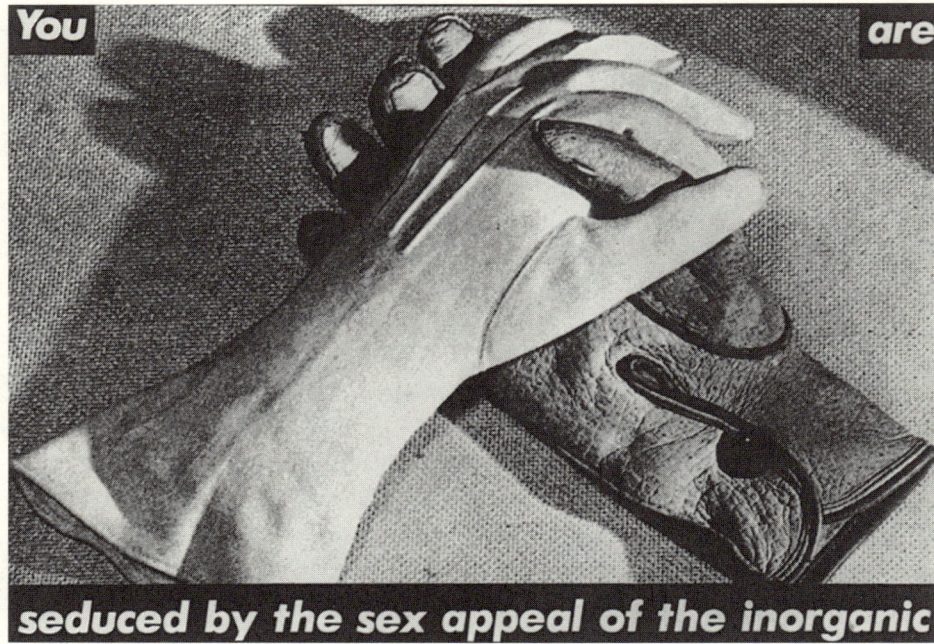

You are

seduced by the sex appeal of the inorganic

**Figure 1.** Untitled photograph by Barbara Kruger, 1982. Courtesy of Barbara Kruger.

Sherman's recent series of photographs of rearranged mannequin bodies, mixing male and female parts.[7]

New computer and communication technologies are central to the extension of the commodity structure that Jameson associates with the cultural logic of late capitalism. As Bill Nichols puts it, "Just as the mechanical reproduction of copies revealed the power of industrial capitalism to reorganise and reassemble the world around us, rendering it as commodity art, the automated intelligence of [computer] chips reveals the power of postindustrial capitalism to simulate and replace the world around us, rendering not only that exterior realm but also interior ones of consciousness, intelligence, thought and intersubjectivity as commodity experience."[8] These new technologies also result in the reorganization and reassembly of the experience of embodiment and desire, as Sherman's photos of the disassembly and reassembly of gendered bodies suggest. While the title of one recent scientific book on artificial intelligence research declares its project as *How to Build a*

*Person*, on a more popular level cyborg imagery also often literalizes social constructionist theories of the body as denaturalized in ways that permit intervention and reconstruction.[9] But as N. Katherine Hayles points out, this redefinition of embodiment depends upon the extension of the commodity structure that Nichols defines: "As the body increasingly is constructed as a commodity to be managed, designed, and parceled out to deserving recipients, pressure builds to displace identity into entities that are more flexible, easier to design, less troublesome to maintain."[10] If this extension of the commodity structure obviously makes possible new forms of control and domination, what new forms of resistance might also be produced?[11]

In the Cartesian tradition, the body, along with animals and machines, is associated with the quality of extension and therefore with the category of space. In contrast, the mind is associated with the abstract and purely conceptual realm of reason. But this dualistic structure is challenged by emergent technologies that call into question any definition of the human, such as genetic engineering, artificial intelligence, expert systems, electronic communities, and by new computer interfaces such as virtual reality. In particular the development of the human-computer interface promises to disrupt the mind-body dualism by giving the conceptual realm phenomenal form, through the creation of virtual spaces where knowledge and information can be experienced and manipulated in concrete, sensory ways. In a different and possibly more productive way than Nichols could in 1986, the emergence of virtual reality technologies reframes the question of how new media affect experiences previously encoded as "interior" and "exterior," without losing sight of the problem of commodification. In an essay called "Through the Looking Glass," a computer researcher named John Walker appropriated the term "cyberspace" from the cyberpunk science fiction writer William Gibson. Walker used the notion of cyberspace to argue that the human-computer interface should not be conceptualized as a dialogue with another person but instead as an act of entering another world, the virtual space on the other side of the computer screen.[12] The response to this conceptual shift was to create hardware designed to collapse the distance between the user and the screen, such as head-mounted displays and datagloves that translate the movement of the hand into a kind of computer-animated mouse. The result is an "exteriorization of mind,"[13] so that "knowledge that was accessible only through formal processes can now be approached concretely."[14] The conceptual realm therefore begins to take on qualities previously attributed only to bodies. As another researcher succinctly put it, while "print and radio tell" and "stage and film show," "cyberspace embodies."[15]

But when the domain of the mind can be experienced in terms previously reserved for the category of the body, what happens to the experience of embodiment? This question defines what is at stake culturally in the development of these new technologies. Both contemporary theory and popular culture attempt to narrativize this mutation in the relation between mind and body, perhaps most visible in cyborg imagery, as Donna Haraway has argued. Bruce Sterling's 1985 novel *Schismatrix* popularized the term "posthuman" as a description of the effects of advances in genetic engineering and cybernetics (133), and this novel can be read as a response to John Varley's 1977 novel *The Ophiuchi Hotline*.[16] At the end of Varley's novel, a character explains that the possibility of manipulating genetic structures means "you will have to cease defining your race by something as arbitrary as a genetic code, and make the great leap to establishing a racial awareness that will hold together in spite of the physical differences you will be introducing among yourselves."[17] Veronica Hollinger argues that this notion of the posthuman in popular science fiction should be understood in relation to poststructuralist critiques of expressive subjectivity and postmodern critiques of the universally human.[18] I add that the "physical differences" made culturally visible by new technologies should be understood in relation to already existing differences of sex, gender, and race. While Varley's novel acknowledges the challenge these "physical differences" pose to traditional definitions of humanity, the novel tends to remain optimistic about the possibility of an overarching "racial awareness" or metanarrative that could subsume these "physical differences." In contrast, Sterling's novel tends to present these differences as permanent and irrecuperable within any definition of humanity. These popular narratives and their different definitions of the term "posthuman" provide a basis for understanding the narrative forms taken by the attempts to explain the implications of new technologies in contemporary culture generally. For example, this term provided the title for an art exhibit that toured Europe between June 1992 and May 1993.[19]

One of the favorite posthuman stories about the body circulating in our culture today is that it will simply disappear, and the posthuman will be synonymous with what Hans Moravec calls the "postbiological."[20] This narrative is legitimated by the scientific culture surrounding artificial intelligence research (AI), like Moravec's. For example, scientists who support this research defend its assumptions against humanist critiques of technology by accusing their critics of "carbon-based chauvinism."[21] In this narrative, the mind not only takes *on* qualities associated with the body, but the mind also takes *over* those qualities, supposedly making actual bodies obsolete.

However, there is another story about the collapse of the mind-body dualism and its outcomes. In this second story, what disappears are not material bodies but an abstract notion of *the* body as the naturalizing ground of a unitary and universalizing notion of the self. The disappearance of "the body" is then followed by a reconstruction of embodiment, and only the alternative models of historical experience generated by that reconstruction deserve the name "posthuman."[22] As Haraway puts it, technologies that disrupt the mind-body dualism "highlight our need for stories of shape-shifters."[23] My epigraph about the post-body age exemplifies this second narrative, in its attempt to imagine what kind of popular culture a post-body age might generate. What becomes obsolete here is not the body but another story about it, the psychoanalytic narrative of gendered subjectivity. In the pop songs of the post-body age, castration anxiety is replaced by the possibility of a systems crash and a loss of information or processing capability: "she shut me down / wiped me clean / made me blanker than a banker's screen." With the body figured as a storage medium, anxiety is no longer an appropriate affective response to this threat: "that's alright / There's no end in sight / I'm programmed well against that risk / with 47 copies of myself on disk."[24]

Science fiction novelist Melissa Scott offers a more directly feminist version of this second narrative in a recent novel expropriating cyberpunk representations of virtual reality. This novel suggests that the implantation of prosthetic devices in the body to permit a direct neural interface with computer networks will most strongly appeal to "the underclasses, the women, the people of color, the gay people, the ones who were already stigmatized as being vulnerable, available, trapped by the body."[25] In other words, as Haraway also suggests, there are social subjects who are already accustomed to thinking of their bodies as constructed, usually by others, and therefore as "available" to reconstruction—that is, there are already existing traditions of shape-shifting that might provide an alternative to the narrative of the disappearing body as a paradigm for the effects of new technologies.

Popular culture is one site where the implications of these two narratives are tested and contested. A series of related questions emerge.[26] Do the technologies of posthumanism participate in a narrative of disembodiment or one of "refigured embodiment?"[27] And given the extent to which the mind-body dualism is gendered and racially determined, with the masculine and Europe aligned with universal reason and the feminine and the colonies with the particularity of the body, what are the ideological consequences of such narratives? [28] Will new technologies disrupt the Cartesian dualism and the ideologies of cultural identity that are structured by it? Or will those ideologies determine in advance the forms taken by new technologies and the consequences they can have? What happens to differently sexed bodies when bodies in general are reimagined as informational structures that can be saved, copied, merged, morphed, or cut and pasted? Predictably enough, perhaps, it is when new technologies are popularly represented as having sexual consequences that the contradictions surrounding them and their cultural implications become most clearly visible. Currently, virtual reality technology has been generating considerable interest in the possibility of "teledildonics," to use a phrase popularized by Howard Rheingold. [29] Figure 2 is a photograph from the technoporn magazine *Future Sex*, depicting what virtual reality sex equipment might look like.

However, in some of the most powerful popular representations of the human-computer interface, such as cyberpunk science fiction, the narrative of the disappearing body in posthuman culture often seems to reproduce, even intensify, the mind-body dualism, not disrupt it. Bruce Sterling defines the cyberpunk movement through its attitude toward technology, which is represented as "pervasive, utterly intimate. Not outside us, but next to us. Under our skin; often, inside our minds." [30] But the paradigmatic cyberpunk novel *Neuromancer*, by William Gibson, seems to emphasize a different relationship between technology and the body. This novel imagines the possibility of a direct interface between the human nervous system and computer networks, allowing characters to jack into the cyberspace matrix, defined as a "consensual hallucination," a "graphic representation of data abstracted from the banks of every computer in the human system." And for the users who work inside this consensual hallucination, "the elite stance involved a certain relaxed contempt for the flesh," usually referred to as "the meat" or, for those unfortunate enough to lose their access, as "the prison of [their] own flesh." [31] Cyberspace can seduce through, or *as*, transcendence of the body. I have argued elsewhere that the narrative of *Neuromancer* is organized not around the characters' desires to abandon their bodies, but rather their desire to take control of how their bodies are "hardwired"—a desire to reformat or upgrade themselves, so to speak. [32]

Nevertheless, the reading of Gibson's novel as endorsing the "elite attitude" of devaluing the body as meat has proven popular, if reductive. For example, a graphic novel loosely based on Gibson's work, entitled simply *Cyberpunk*, narrates the extension of consciousness into cyberspace as a desire for the disappearance or forgetting of the body. In Figure 3 a character who

**Figure 2.** The cover of *Future Sex*, no. 2 (1992). Courtesy of *Future Sex* magazine, a registered trademark of Kundalini Publishing, Inc.

**Figure 3.** Scott Rockwell and Darryl Banks, *Cyberpunk*, vol. 1, no. 1 (Sept. 1989): 5, 6. Courtesy of Scott Rockwell and OCO Enterprises Inc.

has just jacked into the matrix asserts that "if I could leave my *meat* behind and just live here, if I could just be *pure consciousness*, I could be happy." A purer form of Cartesian thought would be hard to imagine. However, this same character also goes on to point out that experiencing cyberspace requires special software "just to convince you that you're *physically* there," so that the "nice thing . . . is you can also convince yourself that you are anything you want to be"; this sequence depicts the character morphing his cyberspace icon or avatar from a faithful representation of his organic body into an abstract, mechanical shape. This text then combines both narrative desires, to transcend the body and to refigure it. The plot finally privileges disembodiment, as the main character downloads his consciousness into the cyberspace matrix once and for all, but the narrative also contains its own counterdiscourse.[33]

In his book *Mind Children*, AI researcher Hans Moravec proposes a purely cognitive definition of the mind that makes it not only reasonable but unavoidable to imagine downloading human personalities into a computer or robot body. In the future, Moravec asserts, it will "be easy to bring to life anyone who has been carefully recorded on a storage medium. This process would make it possible both to make copies of individuals and to "merge memories from disparate copies into a single one," including copies of different people. As he puts it, "concepts of life, death, and identity will lose their present meaning as your mental fragments and those of others are combined, shuffled, and recombined into temporary associations, sometimes large, sometimes small, sometimes long isolated and highly individual, at other times ephemeral, mere ripples on the rapids of civilization's torrent of knowledge. There are foretastes of this kind of fluidity all around us."[34] Indeed, it is becoming a commonplace to suggest that once the information superhighway brings 500 channels of cable TV into American homes, "the thing we will pay a premium for is point of view,"[35] so that there will be a market for expert systems capable of filtering information, usually referred to as interface agents or "digital butlers."[36] Suggestions that "famous people will license their tastes and attitudes to be simulated by these programs" are beginning to circulate in the popular press, with journalists imagining that "if one wanted to watch the news reports and television shows or read the books that interest, say, John Kenneth Galbraith—or David Letterman, Madonna, or Rush Limbaugh—he or she could just point and click."[37] Nichols's comments about the capacity of new technologies to render "consciousness . . . as commodity experience" prefigure this franchising of personality as an expert system mediating between users and the universe of data that confronts us.

As Sherry Turkle puts it, the culture of artificial intelligence research is "deeply committed to a view that thought does not need a unitary agent who thinks." It is in this sense that Turkle suggests "the computer takes up where psychoanalysis leaves off," taking "the idea of a decentered self" and making "it more concrete by modeling mind as a multiprocessing machine."[38] However, this critique is only accomplished through the transcendence of not only bodily limits but the body as such, as if the body could not be thought outside a concept of organic unity. Gilles Deleuze and Felix Guattari's attack on "the organic organization of the organs," the ideology of the body as self-enclosed system, indicates the possibility of developing alternatives to this conception of embodiment as the necessary grounding for the unitary nature of individual consciousness.[39] Popular culture provides one important site for such alternatives, which do not necessarily take the form of Deleuze and Guattari's "body without organs," however.[40]

David Tomas optimistically conflates these two narratives of disembodiment and refigured embodiment, suggesting how inextricably they are merged in both the popular and the critical imaginations, when he argues that "advanced information technology . . . has the potential to . . . overthrow the sensorial and organic architecture of the human body . . . by disembodying and reformatting its sensorium in powerful, computer-generated, digitalized spaces." Tomas here updates Marshall McLuhan's vision of simultaneously enlarging "the domain of sex by mechanical technique" and possessing "machines in a sexually gratifying way."[41] But other critics find in cyberpunk fictions only a delibidinizing of the body to produce a "sexualized machine."[42] In contrast, Allucquere Rosanne Stone emphasizes the tension between these two narratives. While she also argues that cyberspace and computer-mediated communication involve the decoupling of the subject from the body, Stone complicates the AI narrative of disembodiment by claiming that this very decoupling makes cyberspace "a locus of intense desire for refigured embodiment." At the same time, she suggests that this refiguration is often purchased at the price of "freedom *from* the body," and that cyberspace therefore often appears only as a "concretization of the psychoanalytically framed desire of the male."[43] That reading is dramatically supported by a two-page advertisement for a new type of computer mouse that appeared exclusively in the technoculture magazines *Mondo 2000* and *Wired*. The images in Figure 4 associate the undisciplined body of the preoedipal infant, a body not yet captured in and unified through self-representation, with the freedom provided by high-tech computer equipment. These images certainly qualify Donna Haraway's assertion that "the

Feels Good.

Lots of mice feel good, but not as good as MouseMan—the world's first left- and right-handed, and cordless radio mice. In a survey of 2,000 experienced mice users, 77% agree MouseMan feels better than anything they've ever tried. At computer dealers everywhere. 1-800-231-7717

**Figure 4.** Logitech Corporation ad for MouseMan, a computer mouse, in *Wired* 1.1 (1993): 28–29. © 1993 Logitech Inc. Used by permission.

functional privileged signifier in [cyberspace computer networks] will not be so easily mistaken for any primate male's urinary and copulative organ" and that cyberspace will provide a "non-mirror stage" and a "different grammar of gender."[44]

Haraway famously argues that "cyborg imagery can offer a way out of the maze of dualisms in which we have explained our bodies and our tools to ourselves."[45] However, her argument seems to depend upon the assumption that this technology and its popular imaging will not or cannot be "psychoanalytically framed." Sexualized representations of technology pose this problem most directly. To what extent do such representations escape psychoanalytic framing? While acknowledging that in some cases "technology makes possible the destabilization of sexual identity as a category," Mary Ann

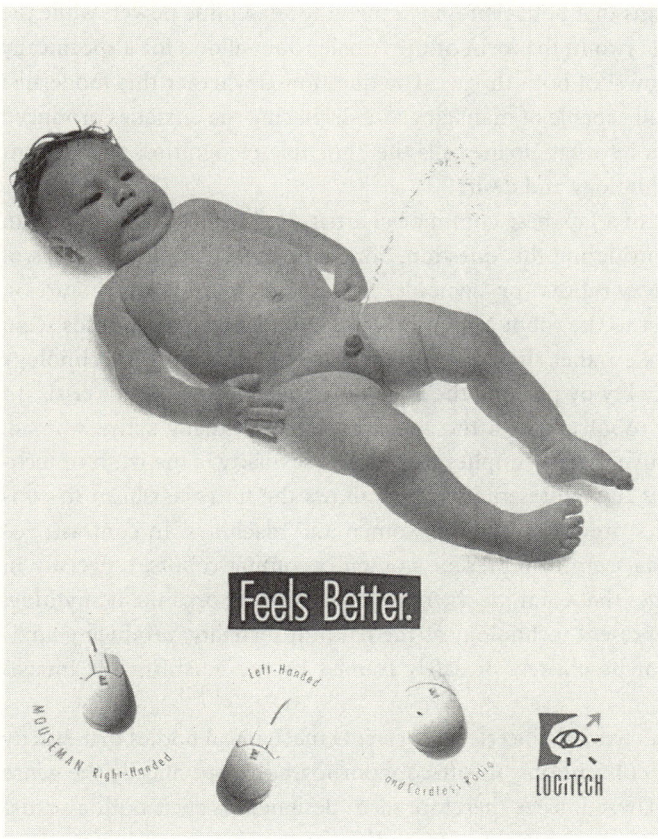

Feels Better.

MOUSEMAN Right-Handed

Left-Handed

and Cordless Radio

LOGITECH

Doane points out that there has been an "insistent history of representations of technology that work to fortify . . . conventional understandings of the feminine," a history in which anxiety about technology "is often allayed by a displacement of this anxiety onto the figure of . . . woman."[46]

Andreas Huyssen offers a similar analysis of the robot woman in the film *Metropolis*; he argues that "the fears and perceptual anxieties emanating from ever more powerful machines are recast and reconstructed in terms of the male fear of female sexuality, reflecting, in the Freudian account, the male's castration anxiety."[47] At the same time, the mechanical woman represents a femininity safely under male control and therefore the possibility of dispensing with actual women, in a classically fetishistic operation. In this representational framework, the analogy between technology and female sexuality confirms that both represent a threat to masculine power, while the conflation of the two in the form of the female robot allows for a specifically fetishistic disavowal of both threats. The question is whether this modernist framework is still capable of managing and displacing the anxieties produced in male subjects by what Doane calls the "horrible recognition of the compatibility of technology and desire."

The work of a Japanese commercial artist, Hajime Sorayama, offers an occasion for considering this question. Sorayama specializes in paintings of what he calls "sexy robots" or "gynoids," as opposed to androids (Figures 5, 6, 7). In contrast to the robot Maria in *Metropolis*, Sorayama's gynoids seem designed to evoke rather than dispel male anxieties about both technology and female sexuality by pushing the logic of fetishism to a point of crisis. In *Metropolis*, the robot takes on the appearance of a sexually active woman; the film's narrative thereby implies that female sexuality is the truth of technology, and it is this representation that allows the film's fetishism to contain the anxieties produced by both women and machines. In contrast, Sorayama's gynoids seem to represent women becoming robots, especially in the case of images that combine the mechanical and the organic. If anything, these images represent technology as the truth of sexuality, producing anxieties that cannot be entirely or safely framed by the fetishism the images evoke.

Sorayama's work deliberately represents mechanical bodies that exactly conform to the conventions of soft-core pornography, specifically the genre of the pin-up. These images therefore seem designed to elicit both a sexual response and an uncomfortable recognition of the inappropriateness, perhaps even obsolescence of that response. As the introduction to an American collection of Sorayama's paintings puts it, "These sexy ladies have a soul of steel. . . . We all know what they're saying. They're beauties from a futurist fantasy, longing for a little contact. But contact may be just what they're not going to get. Gaze on this steel perfection and all you'll see is your own reflection. . . . And even their secrets are nothing but the secrets of the Age of Technology."[48] Isn't this an account of a heterosexual male viewer beginning to think back through and finding himself confronted with the history of his own fetishistic desire, his own tendency to project male lack onto the ambiguously phallic mother? I do not intend to make any premature, celebratory claims for this "reflection" on the construction of heterosexual male desire, but I do want to argue that images like these make possible narratives of gendered subjectivity that differ significantly from classic psychoanalytic paradigms, differences that any cultural criticism of this cyber-porn must take

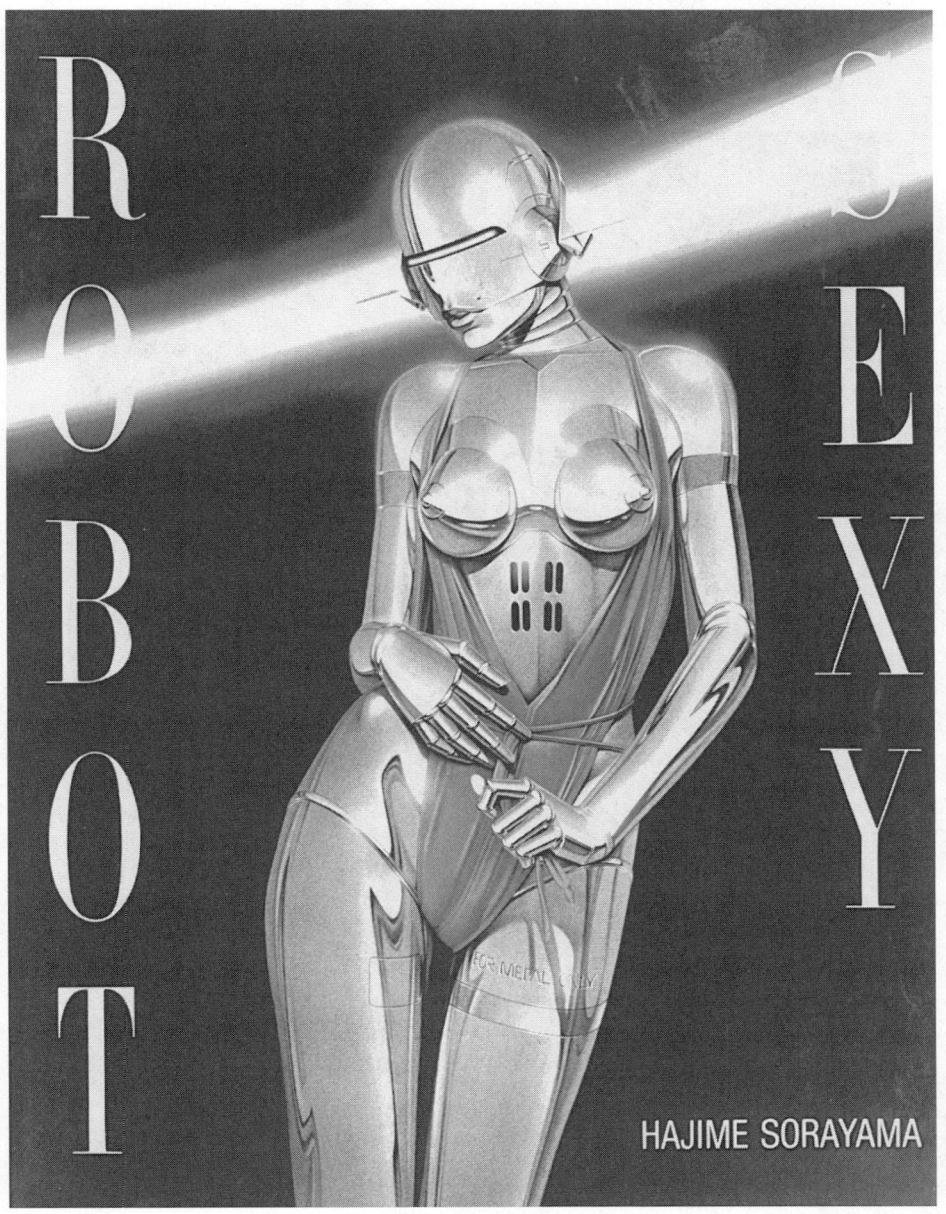

**Figure 5.** Cover of Hajime Sorayama, *Sexy Robot*. © Sorayama/Uptight Co. Ltd., 1996. Courtesy of Uptight Co. Ltd. and Artspace Company K&Y, Los Angeles.

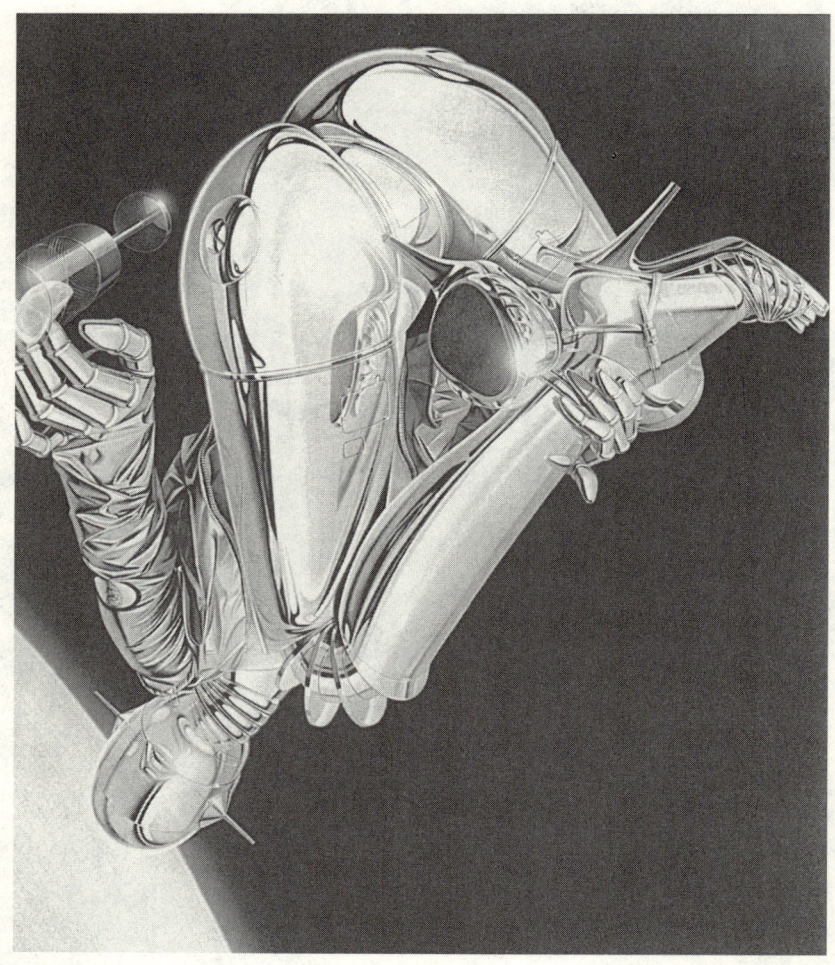

**Figure 6.** Hajime Sorayama, from *Sexy Robot*. © Sorayama/Uptight Co. Ltd., 1996. Courtesy of Uptight Co. Ltd. and Artspace Company K&Y, Los Angeles.

**Figure 7.** Hajime Sorayama, from *Hajime Sorayama*. © Sorayama/Up-
tight Co. Ltd., 1996. Courtesy of Uptight Co. Ltd. and Artspace Company
K&Y, Los Angeles.

into account, though these differences can only be understood in relation to psychoanalysis.[49]

Sorayama's images suggest an eroticizing of the fascination with the Real, understood as a failure to achieve symbolization, which Slavoj Žižek sees as the defining characteristic of the postmodern.[50] Of course, this fascination is by no means incompatible with classic psychoanalytic accounts of fetishism. In a famous passage, Gilles Deleuze distinguishes fetishistic disavowal of maternal castration from simple denial, since disavowal consists of "radically contesting the validity of that which is," as in the statement "the woman does not lack a penis."[51] But this simultaneous definition and refusal of castration nevertheless installs castration as "that which is" and therefore remains within the Oedipalizing boundaries of a male fantasy of phallic identification with the mother and the disappointment that results. In contrast, Sorayama's gynoids tend to reveal the basis of fetishism in male, and not female, lack. Disavowing the absence of the maternal phallus allows male subjects to retain preoedipal maternal attachments by enabling an oscillation within heterosexuality, between investment in the feminine as an object choice and identification with the phallic qualities associated with women through the agency of the fetish. Sorayama's images complicate this fetishistic framework in two ways. First, these images make it impossible to determine whether the sexy robot is a fetish object or a woman who has been fetishized. Is the robot body to be regarded as an object that replaces and supplements the body of an actual woman? Or are these images to be read as depictions of women whose bodies take on phallic qualities by being represented as mechanized?

The possibility that the robot body might provide the support for a phallic identification points to the second way that these gynoids complicate any attempt to fetishize them. Treating the robot body fetishistically, as a displacement of the phallus, does not and cannot achieve the desired goal of defending against castration anxiety. In the case of these images, fetishistic defenses against female sexual difference require the heterosexual male spectator to not only confront but identify with technologies that themselves generate castration anxiety. As Andrew Ross points out in a reading of cyberpunk fiction, the technologies of body modification associated with sexy robots and other cyborgs are "castrating in ways that boys have always had nightmares about."[52] The feminized robot body, the very object that seems to offer reassurance against the threat female sexuality might pose to men, only conjures up the specter of another form of castration, posed by the technology of the robot body itself. In this way, the representation of the feminized robot reflects back upon and implicates the male spectator (Figures 8 and 9). What Sorayama likes to call "that metallic feeling" here signifies not phallic mastery or self-possession but instead marks the role of technology in the construction of any subjectivity, where technology figures as an absence, an agency that is not part of the self, but an absence that is not necessarily or easily organized along gender lines (which of course does not mean that technology *cannot* end up organized in ways that reproduce traditional gender narratives).

Žižek argues that fantasy should not be understood simply as the construction of phantasmatic objects but instead provides "the frame enabling us to desire" at all.[53] I am arguing that Sorayama's gynoids enable forms of desire that accommodate libidinal investments in male lack, rather than a phallic ideal. These images, in my reading, imply that female subjectivity no longer represents the psychic location "at which the male subject deposits his lack." In Kaja Silverman's words, images like these produce "the confrontation of the male subject with the defining conditions of all subjectivity, conditions which the female subject is obliged compulsively to reenact, but upon the denial of which traditional masculinity is predicated: lack, specularity, and alterity."[54] Like the collective fetishism of sadomasochistic practices, the kind of images alongside which Sorayama's work is usually sold, his gynoids point to a different "sexual organization of social risk."[55]

The work of a British expatriate writer living in Thailand, Richard Calder, clarifies the narrative implications I've been claiming for Sorayama's images. In a series of short stories and one novel, *Dead Girls*, Calder combines the narration of both fetishistic investments in technology that reproduce traditional constructions of gendered subjectivity with a counternarrative of denaturalizing imitation produced through identification with fetishized technology. Calder's work suggests the possibility of rethinking sexual and cultural identities, especially masculine ones, from the point of view of the fetish object. These stories presuppose the emergence of a literary movement called the Second Decadence in the 1990s, which includes the return of the dandy as a cultural type and a preference for the artificial over the natural.[56] This movement provides the cultural background for the development of female automatons or dolls, which Calder refers to as gynoids.[57] European firms like Tiffany and Cartier, Dior and Chanel, all develop their own specialized lines, while Southeast Asian companies bring out cheaper knockoffs of these deluxe models, thereby participating in what is described as "the deathwish of Europe" (*Dead Girls*, 161).

One of Calder's stories, "Mosquito," reads like a cyberpunk version of

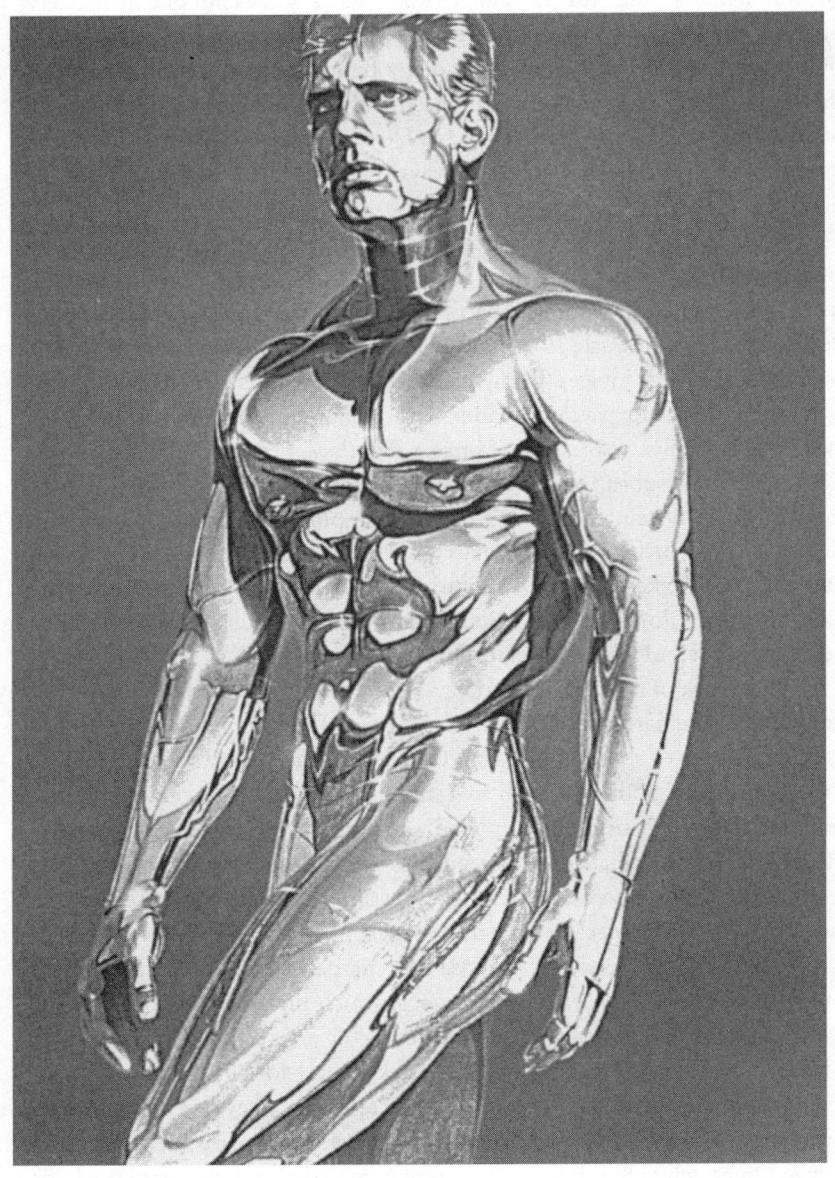

**Figure 8.** Hajime Sorayama, "Iron Man." © Sorayama/Uptight Co. Ltd., 1996. Courtesy of Uptight Co. Ltd. and Artspace Company K&Y, Los Angeles.

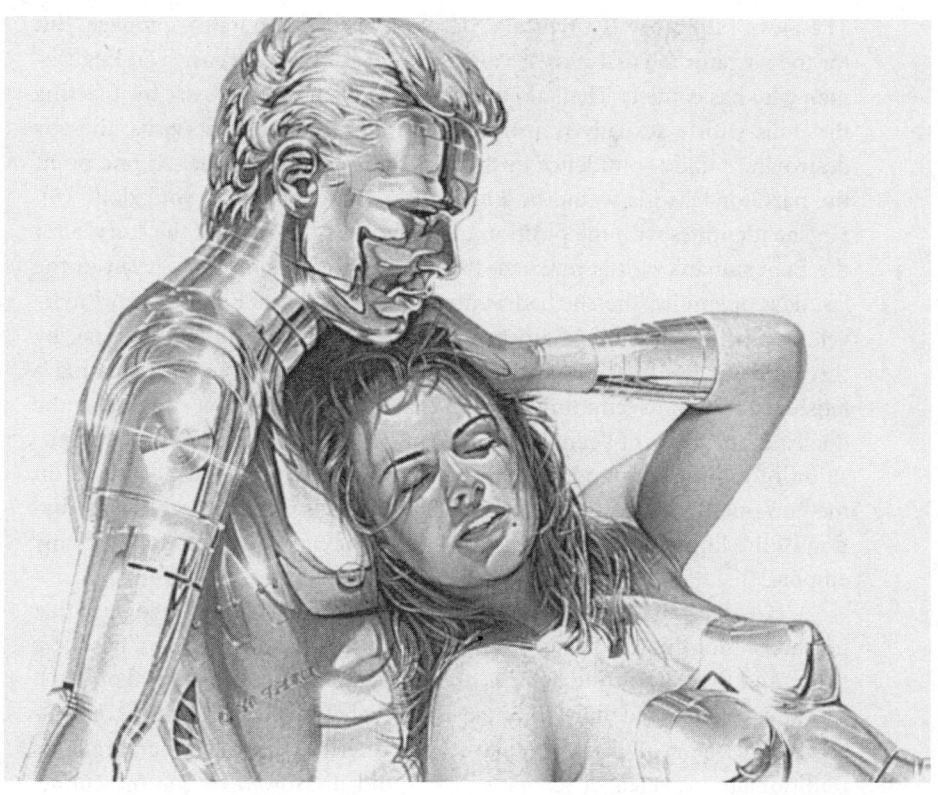

**Figure 9.** Hajime Sorayama, "Full Metal Love." © Sorayama/Uptight Co. Ltd., 1996. Courtesy of Uptight Co. Ltd. and Artspace Company K&Y, Los Angeles.

David Henry Hwang's play *M. Butterfly*.[58] The story is set in Thailand and narrated by the title character, a sex worker and pre-op transsexual who specializes in impersonating these European dolls. He/she has therefore decided not to have an actual sex-change operation after undergoing what he/she calls "the more radical surgery" needed to create the appearance of a doll. The reason, he/she explains, is that "only a man could imitate a doll. Women, it was said, were too real. For dolls are not women; they are man's dreams of women. Made in man's image, they are an extension of his sex, female impersonators built to confirm his prejudices, sexual illusionists" (6). In a word, fetishes.

This technology of female impersonation functions in at least two ways.

297

The plot of the story is a typical cyberpunk tale of corporate espionage. But for the narrator the real story involves his/her falling in love with an Englishman who has come to Thailand to cripple the illicit doll industry by infecting the dolls with a sexually transmitted and ethnically specific virus, thereby destroying public confidence in them as a safe-sex technique. At one point the narrator tells his would-be English lover, "I want to be your doll" (8). He/she identifies with the position of the fetish. At the end of the story, after the Englishman's plot is revealed, the narrator reflects on how "even in the last days of empire" he/she had wanted to be part of the Englishman's "marvellous world, that land of satisfied desire, part of its genuineness" (11). By this point, it becomes clear that the narrator is not only impersonating a fetishized notion of femininity but also the orientalized other of Europe; the dualistic categories of "genuine" and "imitation" are aligned with the opposition of Europe/Asia and masculine/feminine. When the narrator says, "in me he would find a real doll," the point is that it is only through the mediation of the Englishman's desire that the narrator can be a "*real* doll" (10; my emphasis).

However, the Englishman's betrayal leads the narrator to recognize that he/she is "not the real thing," "not even a poor fake," but just a "fake of a fake," and that "it was the dollworld, not [England] I was enamored of" (11). The story offers a redefinition of masculinity that involves the same compulsive reenactment of "lack, specularity, and alterity" that Silverman argues is traditionally expected of female subjects and disavowed by the masculine. The narrator's doubling of imitation, the impersonation of female impersonation or its technology, undoes the distinction between the original and the imitation, revealing the "genuine" to be a phantasmic ideal, which is what both heterosexual masculinity and British national identity are represented as in this story. By accepting the fictional nature of Europe's originality, the narrator decolonizes his/her mind, without reasserting an authentic "native" identity, and this same act of psychological decolonization is performed in relation to the "straight mind" and the narrator's initial need to have his phantasmic femininity validated by a real man. The narrator's performance as a gynoid results in the unlearning of his/her assumptions about the secondary or derivative status of the feminine, homosexuals, and formerly colonized peoples in relation to the norm of European masculinity.

In Calder's story, both the technology that produces the gynoids and the technology that allows the narrator to impersonate a gynoid are represented in terms of a concept of imitation that "does not copy that which is prior, but produces and *inverts* the very terms of priority and derivativeness," a concept of imitation whose gender implications have been elaborated by Judith Butler. If, Butler argues, "heterosexuality is an impossible imitation of itself, an imitation that performatively constitutes itself as the original, then the imitative parody of 'heterosexuality' . . . is always and only an imitation of an imitation, a copy of a copy, for which there is no original." [59] In "Mosquito," both the gynoids and the narrator embody such imitative parodies, as the narrator acknowledges both when he describes the gynoids as "sexual illusionists" and when he describes himself as "a fake of a fake." The result is "to expose heterosexuality as an incessant and *panicked* imitation of its own naturalized idealization." [60] As the Englishman tells the narrator of Calder's story, "you stole our copyrights, our names," the worst thing that can happen to a Europe that has become only an "an empire of style" (10, 8). This story suggests that the strategy of subversive mimicry that Butler famously defines implies precisely the "radical contesting of that which is" that Deleuze attributes to fetishism. Butler's notion of performative identity implies an understanding of oneself and one's sexuality on the model of the fetish, a supplement whose replacement of the "original" ideal indicates the impossibility of being that "original." [61]

I would argue that this counternarrative of claiming the position of the fetish as a strategy of subversive mimicry can be explained, at least in part, by contrasting Norbert Wiener's contribution to the development of cybernetics after World War II with that of Alan Turing. Where Wiener conceived of cybernetics deterministically, as a science of control and communications and as a deliberate reaction against quantum physics and the uncertainty principle, Turing is best known (at least on a popular level) for the Turing test, which established criteria for determining when artificial intelligence would be achieved. Turing presented this argument in his 1950 essay "Computing Machinery and Intelligence." In this essay Turing argues that a computer could only be determined to possess intelligence if it could discursively pass as human—that is, if it could carry on a conversation with human beings convincingly enough that no one would realize they were talking to a machine. Given the recent publication of Turing's biography, the fact that Turing was gay has become more commonly known as well. [62] In 1952, he was arrested for gross indecency and forced to undergo "organotherapy" for a year, a treatment that involved injections of female hormones. Presumably as a result of these events, Turing committed suicide in 1954. What is less widely known about Turing is the fact that his 1950 essay does not simply propose conversation as a test for artificial intelligence. Instead, he takes a detour through another "imitation game," based on gender. In this game, a man and a woman are concealed from a questioner, who attempts to determine which of the two is the man and which is the woman. Turing suggests that the man try to deceive the interrogator about his gender and the woman try to convince the interrogator that she is in fact a woman. Turing then asks, "What will happen when a machine takes the part of [the man] in this game? Will the interpreter decide wrongly just as often when the game is played like this as he does when the game is played between a man and a woman? These questions replace our original, 'Can machines think?'" [63]

This "imitation game" presents gender as a performance that can either be denaturalizing ("deceptive") or naturalizing ("truthful"), and the artificiality of gender identity provides an analogy for artificial intelligence, or its discursive performance. Given this representation of gender, it seems reasonable to inquire whether and to what extent Turing can be read as a queer theorist, and to what extent the whole project of artificial intelligence, of creating machines that can pass for human, is informed by Alan Turing's experience of the epistemology of the closet. Turing actually defines the criterion for AI research not as the ability to carry on a conversation, as his test is popularly remembered, but instead as the ability to impersonate a man trying to impersonate a woman, as the fake of a fake. Virtual reality interfaces require technologies of location that ensure "warranting," the connection between a discursive space in a computer simulation and the physical space or body of the operator.[64] But at the same time they make visible and call into question the social technologies and discursive formations already in place for similarly constructing what Judith Butler calls culturally intelligible bodies. It is precisely this crisis in embodiment, associated today with queer theory, that Turing's essay inaugurates for cybernetics.

Turing's essay might then be placed in a genealogy that would begin with Oscar Wilde's assertion that "what people call insincerity is simply a method by which we can multiply our personalities." [65] What does this statement imply except that the same deep commitment to the view that "thought does not require a unitary agent who thinks," which Sherry Turkle locates in the scientific culture of AI research? [66] Turing's essay might then provide the missing link between statements like the one I quoted from Wilde and Wayne Koestenbaum's recent claim, in an essay on Wilde and "the birth of gay reading," that "one can acquire reality only by faking it. Men can acquire masculinity only by mimicking it. . . . Mechanical reproduction is *not* second-rate: there is nothing wrong with becoming a clone, wanting to be famous for fifteen minutes, striving to be sexy through mimicry, or commodifying one's life, body, and work. To consider replication degrading is, literally, ho-mophobic: *afraid of the same*."[67]

The two narratives, the two constructions of desire that I have discussed as responses to the technological disruption of the mind-body dualism, often coexist uneasily but necessarily in the same texts. While I find myself describing the narrative of refigured embodiment and strategic mimicry produced by identification with the position of the technological fetish as a counternarrative, it has not yet been decided which of these two stories will ideologically subsume and contain the other. What it might mean to embark upon a "post-body age" is still in doubt. It is precisely the tension between these two narratives that makes intervention in the forms new technologies will take and the cultures that are growing up around them possible at all.

# Fin de Siècle and the Technological Sublime

As a bridge to the longer analysis of David Cronenberg's film *The Fly* (1986) that I will make in this essay on fin de siècle narrative and the technological sublime, I interpolate a short piece of text that meditates on the technologization of narrative's body. A Mr. James Stephenson, writing in 1907 for *Star Story* magazine, and thus dated somewhat after the nineteenth-century fin de siècle, but not too late I hope to qualify as an exemplar of the technological sublimity I am tracing, makes these astonishing remarks in his article, "Electrical Desire":

> And is it not the case that in our new electrifying age desire is everywhere and always to be discerned? Is it not clear that the new avenues of communication and their byways always operate on our human core of desire? Why, think to the great moment when Alexander Graham Bell made his discovery. He said into his telephone—"Watson, come here. I want you." Over the wire went the human cry of desire, and the chance to bring it into fulfillment.

Writ very small, this parable of transformative technology represents the fin de siècle technological sublime. Both 1900 and 2000 have been summoned up or narratively represented via the conjuring of an unrepresentable technology, an incorporation of a bodily yearning for apocalyptic sublimation. In the immediate post-1900 "electrifying age" the phone call is rendered as the quintessential expression of desire mediated technologically. I'm not sure if Stephenson was deliberately positing an exquisite homoerotic scenario, a glimpse that certainly casts a salutary glow over a founding moment of

American capitalism. Regardless, the narrative still *embodies*, suggests the retention of the bodiedness of narrative even as it is extruded through the electronic mediations that figure it mass-culturally. The trajectory "I want you" is indeed the ghost voice, the volatilized voice, within narrative formation. "Reach out and touch someone" is hardly a happy narrative translation of this phenomenon within narrative I refer to, but the latter exists side by side with the ideological inscriptions of advertising, as a possibility of narrative, although not, of course, its essence. In what follows, I will sketch a more current example of the technological sublime, but viewed through this same lens, namely, that the narrative of a century's end and consequent rebirth is now epitomized by a technologized apotheosis, a bodied narrative I refer to as the technological sublime.

*The Fly* may seem to burst all boundaries of decency and present something more akin to a body bag than a corporeally distinct dead body, but in its *disjecta membra*—its dismembered parts so nicely collected by the protagonist, Seth Brundle (Jeff Goldblum), into the "Brundle museum of natural history," housed in his medicine cabinet—it gives us a foretaste of narrative's body in the age of technological reproduction. As a mass-cultural narrative, the film belongs to several social genres, among them the horror film and the science fiction film, and it works as it does by playing off the recognizable codes of those movie types. *The Fly* is obviously in an intertext already, since it is a remake of the Vincent Price classic, and harkens one to many narrative connections, from *Frankenstein* (the book and the movies that are its spawn) to *Paradise Lost*, with a stop at Charles Laughton playing Quasimodo in between. What has seldom been suggested is that *The Fly* is a genuinely fin de siècle text, and it is under that apocalyptic rubric I shall engage it.

The technological sublime of *The Fly* focuses primarily on genetic science, whose ubiquity in the public eye extends from the Genome project and its struggles for funding to the recent first step in the cloning of human embryos as a technique in reproductive technology. Mapping the human genetic code involves not only the isolation of the individual bits of genetic material but also the construction of a sort of narrative about those bits—a story about a projected future, which in an immediately capitalized way has import on all aspects of social life. In tandem with the more rarefied genetic scientists who want to map the code either because it is there, or for specific medical purposes, has arisen a genetic code mapping industry, already able to sell genetic tests to prospective employers or prospective insurers. This is narrativity with a vengeance, and *The Fly* makes a narrative reply to it in relation to the closure of the century.

Seth Brundle hates vehicles—he has been subject to motion sickness since he was a small boy, when he used to "puke on his tricycle." The teleportation system he has devised is a way around that dislike of movement—it seems to be a transport method that strips away motion itself, in favor of the instantaneity of travel. When Brundle is describing the miraculous effect on the world of his invention, and the way he will be described by the grateful world citizens, he says he will be "the one who ended all concepts of transport, of borders." The problem is contained in the incredible ironies of that self-description, because the transport that is ended is the transport of metaphor, and the borders closed down are the very borders that give us the bodily outline we like, with some illusion, to call "ourselves." By film's end, Seth Brundle has indeed transported himself, made a metaphor of himself, until the borders of even the molecular genetic level have proven permeable, have been transported.

People eat meat in *The Fly*—Seth and Veronica (Geena Davis) go out for a cheeseburger to consolidate their project of collaboration—the journalist Veronica to record Seth's experiment "from the inside out," as she puts it to her employer on *Particle*, a science magazine, the ambiguously named Stathis Borans (John Getz). Seth doesn't want to tell Veronica what has gone wrong with the teleportations of animate objects thus far—"not while we're eating," he says, while Veronica retorts, with reference to the cheeseburgers they are clutching—"it can't be worse than this!" The whole teleportation project takes place in our familiar contemporary world, whose anxieties assault us even, or especially, while we are eating—the flesh of mass-produced hamburger is not going to bear much contemplation. The worries about contamination, infection, and poison are all too environmentally and medically omnipresent, and the degeneration of the body in *The Fly* speaks to these. The flesh is being invaded, but from where? A self-evident subtext of the film is the social shock effect of the HIV virus, and Seth Brundle's decomposition mimics all too harrowingly the depredations of the disease. Fear of AIDS is only one strand in the narrative body of the film, however, since it seems to be subsumed, terrible as it is, under a more general terror of genetic reproducibility.

Seth Brundle is innocent of the flesh, in more than one way. The scene of his first sex with Veronica is a crystallization of this problematic of knowledge and a harbinger of its difficulties. We see them in a languorous postcoital moment, Seth rolling over onto his back and embedding a piece of circuitry below his shoulder, which Ronnie gently removes. So far, it's an amusing anecdote of the absentminded genius, so sublimely unconcerned with ordinary human relations that he has bits of stray technology amid his sheets, the way other people might have cracker crumbs. But that moment of what might be called inscription, or branding, allies Seth's body with a machine part, suggesting in miniature the process that will ultimately leave us the unbearable final picture of Brundle-Fly's infusion with the third telepod, in the final scene. Of course we know that it is through just this sore and punctured grid of skin that the telltale fly hairs make their first appearance, after Brundle has unwittingly fused with a housefly at the molecular genetic level—they "transported" together, and transportation is also fusion. The wound is fresh and thus less resistant to the new fly genes, but the patch of skin marked by the piece of circuitry is the site of a mating that echoes the more straightforwardly sexual one Ronnie and Seth have just completed.

This uncanny imprinting of the computer on Seth's body also signals the uneasy alliance of knowledge between the computer and the human subject—although the computer, as Seth rightly describes it, is "confused," and only knows what it has been told by the human who programs it, the computer is also inscrutable, prepared to make judgments and to initiate active sequences that are horrific in their human consequences, although merely successful to the computer—"fusion of brundle-fly with telepod successfully completed," the glowing screen reads drily, while we have been shocked almost primordially by the resulting, tragic hybrid. Throughout the film the computer screen comes to fill the frame to show the change in scene, or to effect the cut—generally, these super-closeups of the screen occupy all of it, so that we, as the audience, are reading the movie screen as if it were translated into a gigantic computer monitor, a laptop with a giant monitor. There are no such closeups of the human face, except when Seth Brundle-Fly stares mordantly into the mirror, and then he is framed by the rim of the medicine cabinet. Although one shock cut moves from this super-intimacy with the computer screen down to Brundle-Fly's grotesque webbed hands, so that we know he has been staring into the screen just as we have, more often the screen is telling the tale, on its own. The most common readout across the big, impersonal green face is the phrase "initiate active sequence," another way of saying that the computer is also narrating to us, while it narrates Seth into Brundle-Fly. The sequences are frightfully absorbing for all but the teller—the computer is, a bit like Hal, imperturbable. There is more than a suggestion of Seth's face, and by extension our faces, staring into the face of God—a God without the slightest personal interest in the active sequences as they relate to human beings, but a God created by those same human beings as a form of systems manager. The uncertainty about the narrative's "body" persists throughout the film, as the issue of "who" is in the position to tell or be told the story emerges obsessively. When the screen is nothing but a pulsing cyberspace, the horror-show bodies on display are just epiphenomena of the truer narrative—the unfolding narrative of the genetic code.

The paradoxes of the flesh in a postmodern technological age begin to be explored when Veronica passionately declares that she could "eat Seth up—the flesh makes people crazy." What Seth realizes is missing from the computer sequence in his first unsuccessful tries to teleport is some understanding of this fleshly craziness. The reason inanimate objects can go through without a hitch is that their recreation is purely combinatorial, an information sequence process, a repetition of their codes. Flesh, however, is accorded a kind of "poetic" status in the film, in that it is the "poetry of steak" Seth resolves to teach the computer. To send a silk stocking from point A to point B is to translate it so perfectly that the simulacrum is the copy is the original. What the computer has been doing with Seth's data about animate objects, like the baboon it pulps against the telepod porthole, is "interpreting, translating, rethinking," rather than reproducing. At least in our social ideologies, there is a salient difference. The poetry of steak requires not the mere interpretation of a synthetic something, but a reproduction, a destruction, and a recreation.

*The Fly* takes us into three kinds of reproduction and shows us how they are all intertwined. The first is sexual reproduction, in the film's case, technologically unassisted; the second is representational reproduction, represented here by the movie's self-reflexivity as a copying medium, and in which the camera is analogous to the computer; and the third, which might be called social reproduction, the continual self-reproduction of the socius, as Bourdieu terms it. What begins in *The Fly* as a supremely ingenious way of getting things from place to place soon outstrips those limits entirely—the telepods are not only designer phone booths, as Ronnie refers to them before she knows what they do, they are reproduction chambers, telewombs of sexual, social, and simulacral reproduction. While the computer, it was thought, was reading the information sequences of the objects in the pod and then reconfiguring that information in a sequence at the other pod, in order to do this a reproduction is required, a reproduction that mimics childbirth, that mimics re-presenting, that mimics that copying of social relations.

*The Fly* cannot help but take up the vestigial mythologies of the body provided by Christianity, and these are weirdly blended in the confusions over reproduction levels (and narrative levels). As played by Jeff Goldblum, and courtesy of a certain haircut, Seth Brundle resembles the chromolithographs of Jesus sold at Walmart and K-Mart—this is before Brundle-Fly comes to fore. Seth is analogous to Jesus in a variety of ways, or at least the film narrative has metaphysical fun with the crossover of theology into cyberspace; in his programming of the computer and then sending himself through, he is God as the Nutty Professor, deciding to take on human form, thus bifurcating himself and yet retaining the attributes of one entity. The transport process that goes so awry involves Seth in that mystery of bodily incarnation evoked by Jesus, as if, with his discovery, Seth were an avatar of the Second Coming. Post-teleportation the film continually hints at these links, as when Seth ends his monomaniacal diatribe at the cafe with an exasperated "Waiter!—Jesus Christ," or when Ronnie calls out to Seth in his super-prolonged sexual state, "Wait, oh god, wait!" The trinitarian mystery that is so baffling—how it can be that Father, Son, and Holy Ghost are distinct and separate, and yet one, fused and inseparable, is given ghoulish palpability in Brundle-Fly's intense desire to teleport with Ronnie and her unborn fetus, so that the three of them would become fused and indissoluble. But fused in what sense? Would the resultant triad of Brundle-Fly, Ronnie, and baby Brundle-Fly/Ronnie become cognizant of its one-in-threeness, as, presumably, the triune godhead of the trinity is presumed to be? Or does one just imagine a nightmare blend-in at a Dairy Queen in techno-hell, where no individual narrative flavor retains consciousness of its narrative supremacy? To paraphrase Carson McCullers's *Member of the Wedding*, who would be the I of their we? The metaphysics of this fusion state may seem a relic of postmodern "encyclicals" that never were, but the improbable juxtaposition of these narrative questions with the socioeconomic vocabulary of technological capitalism, happening at a faster and faster rate now, turns the court cases and the medical ethics decisions into referenda on this movie.

Veronica plays a protean role in this set of religious resonances. Her name alludes to that mystical relic of the middle ages, Veronica's veil, a cloth that was used to wipe Jesus' face during the procession to the Crucifixion and that later displayed on its surface a perfect image of Jesus' face, a Shroud of Turin done in proto-photographic blood. This Veronica also wields various veils—one might say that her photojournalistic reporting on videotape of Seth's experiments held the modern representational veil of video up to him; there's also quite the bloody veil of her dream. By the last scene of the movie Veronica has gone from being Fay Wray in the grip of a giant Brundle-Fly to the Madonna, radiant in blue, calling out to the Fly to intercede with him before he deposits his corrosive enzymes on the head of Stathis Borans, already crippled from his exposures to fly juice.

The metaphor of the body invaded and rearranged on the genetic level is so powerful that it works as a template for a range of issues—the social text of the film is a dense field. Each further metamorphosis Seth Brundle-Fly undergoes as he becomes more Gregor than Seth is correlated to an episode from our common social text. A case in point is the scene that has Seth and Veronica out for a happy outing to celebrate what they think is the benign result of his teleportation. Suddenly, in this rather underpopulated film, the streets are thronged, and Seth and Veronica are joining the millions for a cup of espresso. The intimations of Fly-dom begin with the enormous amounts of sugar Seth heaps into his cup, a crystalline powder akin to the yuppie drug of choice in the 1980s. Convinced that teleportation itself is responsible for his feelings of manic energy and superiority, Seth's language becomes a verbal catalog of every promise held out by the "Me Decade." "It's given me a chance to be me," he natters on, sounding like a particularly fervent guest on Sally Jesse, or like Werner Erhard, back when he had good days. "Not to wax messianic," he waxes, "it makes a man a king—I feel like a million bucks." Every desperate social cliché of overweening egotism and the culture of narcissism spills out—evidence, perhaps, as well, that David Cronenberg is Canadian. The erstwhile mild-mannered Seth becomes Superman-Fly, who is at this moment much less than the piteous spectacle of self-knowledge he will later become. Seth unwittingly becomes a spokesman for a corporate ethos he otherwise knows nothing about, translating the surcharge of insect energy he is beginning to feel into the monetary discourse of the monstrous "me."

Things darken in the social mirror almost immediately. After a lovemaking bout he insists that Ronnie go through teleportation to be able to keep up with him; sexual prowess is now the linchpin of his bodily superiority, and he now translates the transport experience into a drug revel. "It's like a drug," he assures Ronnie, "we'll be the perfect couple, the dynamic duo." His frenzy can only be called Dionysian *manqué*: enraged that Ronnie has dared to question the nature of his sexual energy, he threatens her with a fear of being "destroyed and recreated." But Seth, becoming Brundle-Fly despite himself, shouts with Nietzschean hyperbole that Ronnie must be afraid "to penetrate beyond the veil of the flesh and enter the plasma pool!" His offer to move beyond the body into a swirling collective at the cellular level where individuality is dissolved has overtones of prophecy, but is also inevitably limited by the social discourse surrounding it, so that his invitation has none of the visionary power he might feel, but sounds like a cross between Walt Whitman's body electric and a genetic health club membership ad. Nonetheless, the veil of the flesh has proven to be just that, a veil cast up by the narrative of the plasma pool, a mere side effect of its codes, a readout or printout of its hieroglyphs. We are just an inexpensive bodily envelope bearing a solid-gold address.

What Seth has taken on, unwittingly, I have been trying to show, is a foray into reproduction and, as it happens, self-reproduction *malgré lui*. In response to this, the lines of sexual difference begin to be drawn ever more starkly, accounting for his descent into blue-collar machismo in the next circle of Brundle-Fly hell. Throwing on a leather jacket and dismissing Ronnie as a "drag," Seth heads out into the night in search of a "real" woman, one who will enter the vertiginous universe of sexual empowerment (and male dominance) with him. Not understanding his newfound strength, but not caring to mute it either, Seth is flush with macho glory as he wins Tammy for the night in an arm-wrestling contest. To the sounds of a horrendous scream uttered by the man whose arm he has snapped, Seth declares nonchalantly, "Yes, I build bodies—I take them apart and I put 'em back together." At this junction we realize Seth is inhabiting familiar textual terrain—he is Victor Frankenstein and his monster, cohabiting. While that text left its two as a haunted pair in a chase to the icy ends of the earth, Seth Brundle is the scientist who has devised re-creation as the very basic alphabet of life, become the monster of his own begetting. That this monstrosity should wear such everyday garb of masculine self-assertion is part of the social reproductive text of the film. Seth chooses relatively gullible and compliant Tammy for his own teleportation sex mate, but she is reluctant to go through just on the strength of his urging. Ronnie comes to warn her, and Seth angrily replies to Tammy's question about who Ronnie is with the retort "Oh, I live with my mother, too." His anger at Ronnie's intrusion on his masculine grandiosity takes the form of a fury at women as mothers, but the grotesquerie of this staple of male dependency rage is far more grotesque in this new terrain of narrative technological reproduction. He does live with his mother, because he is his own mother, his own father, and his own child, too, for that matter. Additionally, although he doesn't know it yet, Ronnie is his mother, because she is pregnant with a Ronnie/Brundle-Fly composite, whose Brundle-Fly genetic part is the "being" Seth is rapidly becoming.

The sticking point of the narrative logic as it cascades forth with these implausible genealogical riddles is the nature of the fetus as the narrative terminus. While that fetus is only half Seth's genetically, the logic drives us to an understanding of the reproduction as entailing a copy, or a simulacrum, of Brundle-Fly, while Ronnie's genetic contribution drops out of narrative sight. This is hardly an oversight on the part of the film, in my view, but yet another replication of the social text. Note that in anti-abortion rhetoric the fetus is narrated as male almost exclusively, and the passion of many male adherents of right-to-life positions rests on the presumption that the fetus in jeopardy is, or could be, them. An examination of the language of Operation Rescue shows how powerful this gendering of the fetal imaginary is, so that the injury done to the fetus in aborting it is construed as a masculine narcissistic wounding. This psychic narrative loops back in time with all the vertiginous qualities of Cronenberg's film, making fetuses homuncular copies of already adult men, who then grieve for their own putative aborting.

The terror of reproduction and reproductive technologies in toto is let loose in the film in its concentration on the abortion issue. To my knowledge it remains the only film—or at least the only mainstream Hollywood film— that has ever narrated abortion from the subject position of the woman contemplating it. This goes beyond the television movie narratives that have represented the decision on the part of sympathetically portrayed female characters, to interior subjective narrative that forces the audience inside the woman's mind, in the case of *The Fly* into Ronnie's very dream. We are deliberately "tricked" by the film into reading the sequence as "real," at first, so that her trip to the hospital for the abortion appears to be diegetic. As she lies, terrified, in her hospital bed we cower in our seats as well, even the anti-abortionists among us having been horrified by the thought of the Brundle-Fly fetus. Ronnie's dream is a charged arena of the social fears about women's control, or lack thereof, of reproduction, intersecting with the male-inflected world of science, medical technology, and social authority. Like a sleepwalker she is wheeled down a bright pink hospital corridor, until we see her in the procedural room attended by a gynecologist played by the director, who is thus facetiously placed at the literal site of horror, the vaginal Medusa.

Fetuses are frightening creatures in their own right, because they are so different; on another level, they can seem to be something other than fetuses where fear about loss of male control is strongest. The truly monstrous image we are presented with in Ronnie's shocker dream is theoretically not a whit less monstrous than the fetus we are asked to suspend disbelief she is actually carrying, but as a phallic monster or a penis-baby, it is hideously scary. The assumption is that one aspect of abortion in the social imaginary is the extrusion of male authority, abortion as castration of the symbolic male presence presiding at reproduction. This is extremely important to the logical economy of the film, because the antiseptic and innocent-seeming transport experiment has turned into a gene-splicing, reproductive mechanism that can, through an act of reading, shuffle the deck of the genetic code and come up with a new hand. Reproduction is stolen away, while at the same time a gender coding myth is enforced—the computer becomes male, and the telepods female. *The Fly* permits us to see that what is lost at one point in the system will have to crop up again in monstrous metamorphosis at another place. The throbbing phallus baby is, and forgive the antiquated theoretical language, a floating signifier spliced out by the disturbance created in the realms of sexual and social reproduction. If the bathwater is thrown out, the baby will be found somewhere. Thus the film is littered with references to the phallus, as when Ronnie is buying clothes for her then-new lover Seth, and the jealous Stathis Borans confronts her in the men's department. When she says that Seth is doing remarkable work and that, as his chronicler, she is "on to something huge," Borans shouts, "What's huge—his cock?" Borans flaunts cigars as suggestively as Clarence Thomas might have, where the cigar is not just a cigar, but an image of the tactics and strategies of power that have the phallus to back them up. The towers of Monolith Publishing are hilariously phallic, and Stathis is also (almost) hilariously emasculated in the final scene, losing arms, legs, and other members with abandon. Seth's gradual metamorphosis as Brundle-Fly is marked by the shedding of his human members, as he loses teeth, ears, fingers, and ultimately his penis, small as a mushroom and less formidable, relegated to a jar in the medicine cabinet of bodily curios.

It does not take long for Seth to realize that he is suffering from a disease, a "disease called life." Explaining to Ronnie on one of her terrifying house calls that he now knows why he is subject to such grandiloquent decay, he refers to his metamorphosis as a disease with a purpose, to turn him into something else, Brundle-Fly. Here is a rebirth that must take place through total destruction, giving a new twist to Seth's earlier boast that he wasn't afraid to be destroyed and re-created. Moreover, this literally means that Seth has died to the flesh and come back to life, because where did he go when he was teleported into himself? The valences of these sequences in relation to AIDS are of course overwhelmingly poignant, and pertinent.

When Seth has discovered the nature of his disease—a disease for him, but for the computer's active sequence, just another successful fusion in paradise—and before the subjectivity of Brundle-Fly begins to take command, he passes through an antic, almost surrealistically humorous period as a kind of underground man. Holed up in his apartment, he uses his scientific persona to watch himself and document the changes of this rare discovery, himself as an unprecedented genetic experiment. All his impulses to catalog and taxonomize are devoted to Seth's extraordinary efforts to produce himself as an object of study, a narrating narrative body. In one scene Seth is ebullient, almost dizzy with the grotesqueness of his own being, and he stages a mock children's science show for Ronnie's videocam, demonstrating to the boys and girls out there how he eats his food now—by emitting a substance over his doughnuts he says is colloquially referred to, by the single species member of Brundle-Fly, as "vomit drops." His hideous face still manages a toothy grin, and his transforming torso is still donned in a T-shirt, a sign of his link to human mass culture. He is like, and he knows he is like, and he spoofs being like, a crazed breakfast cereal commercial come to video life. Seth's insertion into a simulacrum of TV as an Incredible Hulk/Mr. Wizard celebrity indicates the narrative level of representation or aesthetic reproduction the film also explores. No one is exempt from the image circuit, not even a housebound housefly extraordinaire. This narrative level accords Seth a new, mass-cultural identity that is reproduced along the circuits of the media. We watch in rather agonized nausea through the lens of Ronnie's camera, as the scene slowly changes to Stathis Borans watching this same video tape on Ronnie's VCR. She has played it for him as a proof of the transformation, and as Stathis watches in disgust he little realizes he is being tutored in the mode of his own mutilation.

Let me advert here to one of the most remarkable scenes of the film, the height of its convergence of personal and political narrativity. Ronnie has come to tell Seth that she is pregnant but will be having an abortion; however, he is so much a Fly at this stage that she cannot really tell him, there being no Seth left to tell. Instead, Brundle-Fly delivers his own eulogy:

"Have you ever heard of insect politics? Insects don't have politics. They're very brutal—no compassion, no compromise. We can't trust the insect. I'd like to become the first insect politician."

Ronnie asks, "What are you saying?"

"I'm saying I'm an insect who dreamed you as a man, but now the dream is over, and the insect is awake. . . . I'll hurt you if you stay."

Ronnie exits, while we are left to witness Brundle-Fly's choking insect sobs. While there may be bathos in this (and a little bathos in my opinion never hurt anybody), there is also politics. Seth has been innocent of more than sex, and it is important for bringing the narrative ontologies of reproduction together that the locus of Brundle-Fly transformation is the border of Canada and the United States, a little pre-NAFTA, but still symbolic of the fusing borders of late or global technological capitalism. Seth had considered himself a scientist without portfolio, unbeholden to the corporations who would presumably have manufactured his teleportation invention. Bartok

Systems controls his research, but he has never really been part of their corporate structure. Seth has an almost childlike conviction that the system he has developed will be used for transport only, that it will help to annul cultural borders and boundaries. Just as he discounts his own contribution, by saying that he is a systems management man who farms out the really hard pieces of work to scientists even more reclusive than he (the romantic genius notion of science), so he ignores the presence of the real systems management, that in effect predetermines the catastrophic outcome of his experiment in space and time. James Watson, the famed geneticist and co-cracker of the genetic code, has been working for the Genome project, the attempt to map out completely every single human gene particle. This project is being fought over by scientists who want more government funding devoted to it, and by a technology corporation called Genome that wants to undertake the mapping as a private project with patent protection. Both groups refer to the process of identifying all the human genes as reading the language of the human being, with the molecular-genetic code as a kind of script. The goals of the groups diverge, though; Watson argues for the efficacy of the project as offering hope for genetically transmitted diseases, while Genome wants to be able to sell information on genetic codes to those who want to buy, on that new information superhighway. Both groups use millennial language to sell this technological sublime. The film is investigating precisely this: how control of the Particle level, as in *Particle* magazine, becomes part of the Monolith, the mega-control of life as corporate, intellectual, property. The uses of technology do not (usually) belong to those who conceive them at the particle level; they belong, ultimately and permanently, to the monolith, for whom the loss of Seth Brundle and the ghastly spit-out at the finish have no more meaning than these do for the computer's implacable screen. Brundle has been involved in a Faustian trade-off, without his knowledge—the corporation owns his intellectual labor and will determine what to do with it, until Brundle's dreams of effortless travel will be unrecognizable in their remoteness. What Brundle has stumbled on, because he works in a corner of the corporate empire, is a way to decode the entire living world, a device that operates as a super reading machine, as a super reproductive machine. Brundle may become the fly that fell to earth, but that is a mere wrinkle in the corporatization of the technology of life.

Something that cannot be accounted for in the systems of narrative reproduction I have been discussing is the phantom excess or commensurability, the volatility, of this narrative body. I am forced to give that volatility a name in the context of this film, where it is love (allow me to provisionally call it that) that offers the volatilization. Sexual reproduction may sometimes coincidentally occur as the result of what sometimes is "an act of love," but that has nothing to do with the process or its outcome; simulacral reproduction seems immune to the realms of love and the reproduction of social relations to rely on ideologies of love for its own purposes. The bombastic pathos of the end of the movie, however, highlights love as an uncomfortable extra circulating through these systems. What else can account for Ronnie's inability to kill off the despairing new mutant, Brundle-Fly-Telepod, or for that unnameable being's sacrificial placing of the rifle to its own head?

Ronnie's narrative is the most difficult one to suppress or repress. At one point she says to Stathis Borans, in arguing why her research with Seth is so important: "I'm the only recorder of this event from the inside out." Those words come literally true, as her recording is also reproductive. For much of the first part of the film Ronnie is the recorder, and frames and sets up scenes through her camera superimposed on the film's point of view. When she finds out she is pregnant, her place behind the camera comes to a halt. The narrative has been extended inside her—she is recording it from the inside out, a telepod or transporter of Seth's genetic narrative. At the film's end, with the death of Brundle-Fly-telepod, Ronnie's story is still left over. We almost forget that the fetus is still inside her, that the narrative of reproduction has not been officially halted. The death of Brundle-Fly-Telepod is as much a self-sacrifice as Gregor Samsa's quiet death was: the human machine puts itself abjectly to death, it practices insect politics. For Seth Brundle the monstrous task of self-knowledge has ended on a trebly Oedipal note. What is clear in the sexual politics of the narrative is that Cronenberg never intended to make a sequel featuring the impossible baby, as if that route could finesse the mother Ronnie and continue on with male self-reproduction in the form of Seth II. Instead, what is left is Ronnie's narrative, from the inside out, discontinuous, with no way left to report it.

*The Fly* shows us that every act of narration leaves its mark, leaves its trace, if not as openly and monstrously as the transformations of Seth Brundle. Seth Brundle is read by the computer and fused with a housefly—"We weren't even properly introduced," he points out. The technologies of narrative have moved even to the submolecular level, where strangely enough, metaphor can also be seen to inhere. Love entered in for Seth Brundle as he hoped to become the first insect politician, an emissary from the reading machine, and it kept him fixated on preserving the last bit of "himself" introjected into Ronnie's body. This was an illusion, of course, the illusion that Seth Brundle could still exist, unread and uncoded, and led to his attempt to form the most nuclear family ever conceived, by transporting himself and Ronnie in the telepod to fuse their three into one. This is another of love's lost illusions. Where should the love that I am talking about come in, then? And what rough beast comes stalking to the telepod to be born? The imponderability and the impossibility of the millennial new man, the fly-Christ-woman-telepod that hovers at the threshold of the new century, is a narrative abyss and a technological one. The terror is that our technology, which cinema has best represented since its invention in 1894, is no longer a representable one, or a narratizable one. *The Fly* as film acknowledges its own superfluity in the face of that sublime terror and fades out on a human, female, face.

# Reference Matter

## Bercovitch: Games of Chess

I want to express my thanks to the organizers of the splendid Conference on Narrativity for which this essay was originally prepared—in particular to Larry Reynolds and Robert Newman—and to the colleagues and friends who offered criticism and encouragement at various points in its development: Daniel Bell, Emily Budick, Stanley Cavell, Wai-Chee Dimock, Donald Fanger, Philip Fisher, Marjorie Garber, Eugene Goodheart, Steven Greenblatt, Lawrence Lipking, Rael Meyerowitz, Susan L. Mizruchi, Robert Nozick, Hilary Putnam, Margaret Reid, Peter Rudnytzsky, and Doris Sommer. I am grateful to the Huntington Library for providing a fellowship that allowed me to read through Renaissance manuals on chess and related materials on the game.

1. Georg Simmel, diary excerpt from *Fragmente und Aufsätze*; quoted in Kurt Wolff, introduction to *The Philosophy of George Simmel*, trans. and ed. Kurt Wolff (New York: Free Press, 1950), xx–xxi.

2. I assume that this division is conceptual as well as institutional, and that the conceptual issues warrant debate in their own right. The institutional question involves an entirely different set of factors, which may well constitute the *de facto* rules of the game. These factors include (1) the traditional function of Departments of Literature, which has been to provide society with a cultured elite, and (2) the shifting concept of "cultured" over the course of this century (which in turn expressed a shifting concept of the elite) from classics to national languages to modern literature and most recently (with the expansion during the past few decades of academic constituencies) to contemporary literatures and cultures. Cultural studies may be the logical next step in this (quite rapid) process in re-definition of a literary education. In that case, English departments will stand in

the same relation to cultural studies that classics now has in relation to English. It is plausible to see such an institutional development as part of a more general cultural and pedagogic movement toward a democratic aesthetics. If indeed this represents a historical process—so that the transition I speak of will seem in due time to be as logical, even natural, as the transition from theology to literature now seems—there is no reason not to think that cultural studies will develop methods of analysis just as sophisticated as those of modern formalists. Such methods might well enlist among its theoretical forebears Emerson's summons in "The American Scholar" to a poetics of the ordinary: "that which has been negligently trodden underfoot," "the literature of the poor, the familiar and the low," "the philosophy of the street," "the meaning of household life." *Essays and Lectures*, ed. Joel Porte (New York: Library of America, 1983), 403–14.

3. I am indebted for these references, and for the discussion of the cultural variability of death, to Susan L. Mizruchi's chapter on W. E. B. Du Bois in her forthcoming book, *The Science of Sacrifice: American Literature and Modern Social Theory*.

4. In this sense, my concept of universal might be termed absolutism by another name. I have no objection to this inference, provided that absolutism is redefined in the terms of noncoherence I set out below.

5. T. S. Eliot, "Hamlet and His Problems," in *The Sacred Wood: Essays on Poetry and Criticism* (London: Methuen, 1960), 100; Georg Lukács, *The Historical Novel*, trans. Hannah Mitchell and Stanley Mitchell (London: Merlin Press, 1962), 11. In each case, the concept of objectivity places the insisted-upon particular (emotive in Eliot's case, historical in Lukács's) within a closed system. I explore the different meanings of closure that this suggests later in the essay. But I want to add here that my critique (here and elsewhere through the essay) is meant to register the importance of the critics I cite to the sort of literary and cultural studies I envision. Thus Eliot and the New Critics are important precisely because they made the analysis of particulars the grounds of aesthetic appreciation. The complex detail is the alpha and omega of the Brooks-and-Warren method. *The Waste-Land* programmatically unites the Metaphysicals with chess games, London music halls, Jesse Weston, and the closing rituals of urban pubs. But this insistence on "the concrete universal" was an Arnoldian touchstone. It served as a wall against, rather than a bridge to, history and society. The New Criticism inherited and reinforced the dissociation of Culture from culture, especially in its literary aspects (hence renamed "writing," "propaganda," "ideology"). The phenomenal rise of textual analysis at midcentury had its counterpart in the decline of literary history. As a literary concept, the particularity of the text functioned here to prove that art could transmute base materials into gold (through the alchemy of complexity, ambiguity, paradox, etc.); consequently, art constituted a world of its own, either as a refuge from cultural mediocrity or else as a weapon against it. That quasi-religious distinction became as absolute in its way for many twentieth-century formalists as Augustine's separation of the City of Man from the City of God. On that basis, the New Critics turned close reading into a moral

critique of modern society, French semioticians developed a scientific aesthetic that vindicated the romantic contempt for bourgeois banality, and the Russian formalists made stylistic analysis a vehicle of political opposition. The classic touchstones (in these very diverse shapes) enclosed the gardens of literary academia from the wasteland of secular industrial states, from Stalinist communism to the philistine West.

6. Ludwig Wittgenstein, *Philosophical Investigations*, trans. G. E. M. Anscombe (New York: Macmillan, 1953), 31e–32e (no. 66); Jorge Luis Borges, "Chess," in *Borges: A Reader*, ed. Emir Rodriguez Monegal and Alistair Reid (New York: Dutton, 1981), 10–11.

7. Ludwig Wittgenstein, *Tractatus Logico-Philosophicus*, trans. C. K. Ogden (London: Routledge, 1989), 189; Eytan Bercovitch, "When Explanation Fails: Nalumin Discontinuity and Anthropological Understanding" (paper presented at the annual meeting of the American Ethnological Society, St. Louis, April 16, 1988). The paper itself advances a distinctive approach to culture, which is elaborated in "Mortal Insights: Victim and Witch in the Nalumin Imagination," in *The Religious Imagination in New Guinea*, ed. Gilbert Herdt and Michele Stephen (New Brunswick, N.J.: Rutgers University Press, 1989), and "The Agent in the Gift: Hidden Exchange in Inner New Guinea," *Cultural Anthropology* 9 (1994): 498–536. I have a deep and special theoretical debt to these essays and to the outlook and method they set out.

8. Raymond Williams, *Marxism and Literature* (Oxford: Oxford University Press, 1977), 53. My point is not that these cultural critics neglect the aesthetic dimensions of the text, but that a valuable contribution to aesthetics is marred by the metaphysics of social science, as in this scholarly exchange which the editors of a massive recent anthology, *Cultural Studies*, cite as proof of the "conflictual," "eclectic" directions in the field: "One speaker described his practice of *using* Milton's poem 'Lycidas' to teach . . . theoretical reading strategies. . . . [This was] vigorously attacked by some members of the audience who claimed that [the speaker was] . . . bludgeoning [his] students with instruments of patriarchal oppression and that . . . women students [in particular] were quite possibly being irreversibly damaged. . . . [Other cultural critics, however, pointed out that] after a decade in which thousands of young men have died prematurely in the course of the AIDS epidemic and thousands of others have mourned them, 'Lycidas' is quite probably a resource as rich and useful as many that could be named." Lawrence Grossberg, Cary Nelson, and Paula Treichler, eds., *Cultural Studies* (New York: Routledge, 1992), 20; my italics. This is an extreme example, but I cite it for purposes of polemic, not ridicule. (One might find comparable extremes in late Victorian debates about the canonical value of Dickens, or in New Critical debates about the complexity of Whitman.) In fact, in my view, both of the unlikely contexts offered for "Lycidas" could be well deployed for teaching purposes. The rules of patriarchy play a role in Milton's poetry, and these have continued to effect our own rules of sexuality. What I object to is the shift in focus, signaled by the terms "using" and "useful." Does "Lycidas" victimize women or benefit AIDS

victims? The value of the poem depends on its placement (false consciousness or utopian) within interpretive rules that pertain to a different, essentially progressivist and materialist contest, a zero-sum game of social progress in which "Lycidas" is appropriated either as an "instrument" or as a "resource" in the struggle for "gender liberation." I believe that ideological criticism should *resist* such endgame strategies.

9. Fredric Jameson, *The Political Unconscious: Narrative as Socially Symbolic Act* (Ithaca, N.Y.: Cornell University Press, 1981), 19.

10. I refer to Kant's "liberation" of aesthetics from "the constraint of the understanding," in *The Critique of Judgement*, trans. James C. Meredith (Oxford: Clarendon Press, 1969), 19–52. Here art is defined as "the rapid and transient play of the imagination . . . [unified] in a concept (which for that very reason is original, and reveals a new rule which could not have been inferred from any preceding principles or examples) that admits communication without any constraint of rules." This "Transcendental Aesthetic" (as Kant termed it in *The Critique of Pure Reason*) became the source of a variety of definitions of the work of aesthetics. The most frivolous of these has become a pillar of current "art appreciation": "The 'Transcendental Aesthetic' . . . has largely to do with sense experience in contrast with reason. . . . [It takes] a view of art as the occasion for aesthetic gratification and almost nothing else. . . . [It] distances art as something deep or dangerous or difficult or dark, and connects it with the faculty of taste rather than with passion or fear or feeling or hope. . . . [Aesthetics, in short, is a matter] of taste, pleasure, and gratification, and, hence . . . almost quintessentially . . . subjective and personal." Arthur C. Danto, *Beyond the Brillo Box: The Visual Arts in Post-Historical Perspective* (New York: Farrar Strauss, 1992), 168. This is the dead-end endgame of aesthetics, as distinct from the Infinity endgames of Schiller and Coleridge, for whom (in different ways) Kant's ideas serve to connect free play to the game at large—subjectively, by quickening the cognitive faculties, and objectively, by reaching beyond these boundaries to moral absolutes.

11. Michel Foucault, "What is an Author?" in *Language, Counter-Memory, Practice*, trans. Donald F. Bouchard and Sherry Simm (Ithaca, N.Y.: Cornell University Press, 1980), 116.

12. Wolfgang Iser, *The Fictive and the Imaginary: Charting Literary Anthropology* (Baltimore, Md.: Johns Hopkins University Press, 1993), 257–80.

13. Roland Barthes, *The Pleasure of the Text*, trans. Richard Miller (New York: Hill & Wang, 1975), 7, 42–43.

14. Roland Barthes, "Inaugural Lecture, Collège de France," in *A Barthes Reader*, ed. Susan Sontag (New York: Hill & Wang, 1982), 461–62.

15. Ferdinand de Saussure, *Course in General Linguistics*, trans. Roy Harris, ed. Charles Bally and Albert Sechehaye (New York: Philosophical Library, 1959), 88–89. Cf. Pierre Bourdieu, *The Logic of Practice*, trans. Richard Nice (Stanford, Calif.: Stanford University Press, 1990), 66.

16. W. H. Auden, "In Memory of W. B. Yeats," in *The Collected Poetry* (New York: Random House, 1945), 50.

17. John Graham, *The Literature of Chess* (Jefferson, N.C.: McFarland, 1984),

81. The term gambit comes from the Italian *gambitare*, "to set traps." There are clear parallels between the opening-game gambit and the middle-game sacrifice; and as metaphor or analogy, they might be used interchangeably if we allowed the gambit to open up questions of beginnings as well as questions of endings. The problems with (and the attractions of) this comparison may be found in I. A. Horowitz's *Chess Opening: Theory and Practice* (New York: Simon & Schuster, 1964); A. S. Suetin, *Modern Chess Opening Theory* (New York: Pergamon Press, 1978); Reuben Fine, *The Ideas Behind the Chess Openings* (New York: McKay, 1970); Max Euwe and H. Kramer, *The Middle Game* (New York: Bell Books, 1965); Paul Keres and Alexander Kotov, *The Art of the Middle Game* (New York: Penguin, 1964); Vladimir Vukovic, *The Chess Sacrifice* (New York: George Bell, 1968).

18. There are other mistaken options, of course: for example, my opponent is essentially a bad player (he was *bound* to lose); or I somehow *forced* the exchange (I was *fated* to win; or I was playing a winning game all along without quite knowing it). The modernist favorite, however, is the cruel absurdity of the game itself. I don't see *why* I had to lose, and so I conclude that I never really had a chance: "[Life is] an electronic computer, which plays chess and calculates any number of moves in advance. A man *must* play chess with an electronic computer, cannot leave or break the game, and *has* to lose the game. His defeat is just, because it is effected according to the rules of the game; he loses because he has made a mistake. But he could not have won." Jan Kott, *Shakespeare Our Contemporary*, trans. Boleslaw Taborski (New York: Norton, 1974), 109. Modernist variations on this theme range from Hemingway's Frederick Henry's endgame meditations on the "traps of the game," in *A Farewell to Arms* (New York: Scribner's, 1927), 242–64, to Bob Dylan's 1960s protest song, "Only a Pawn in Their Game."

19. Thomas Middleton, *A Game of Chess*, in *Works*, ed. A. H. Bullen (New York: AMS Press, 1964), 7:7.

20. Walt Whitman, "Song of Myself" (1855), in *Whitman: Complete Poetry and Collected Prose*, ed. Justin Kaplan (New York: Library of America, 1982), 87.

21. D. H. Lawrence, *Studies in Classic American Literature* (New York: Doubleday, 1951), 178–79; Whitman, "The Sleepers" and "Song of Myself," 112–13.

22. William Faulkner, *Light in August* (New York: Random House, 1932), 439–40.

23. The postmodern equivalent would present the dying Christmas as a self-referential collage made up of the commonplace of Fate, the mythology of the cross, the stereotypes of race, and the jingoism of American justice. The act of memory, then, lies in the holy-erotic pleasure of the text.

24. Jürgen Habermas, *The Legitimation Crisis*, trans. Thomas McCarthy (Boston: Beacon Press, 1975), 105, 108; Hans-Georg Gadamer, *Truth and Method*, trans. Joel Weinsheimer and David G. Marshall (London: Sheed & Ward, 1975), 383–88.

25. Wittgenstein, *Philosophical Investigations*, 32e (no. 66).

26. The references to chess in this essay come from a variety of sources. The single best history is still H. J. R. Murray, *A History of Chess* (Oxford: Oxford University Press, 1913), but it has been supplemented by Jerzy Gizycki's *History of*

*Chess*, trans. A. Wojciechowski, D. Ronowicz, and W. Bartoszewski (London: Abbey Library, 1972); Harry Golombek, *Chess: A History* (New York: Routledge, 1976); and Richard Eales, *Chess: The History of a Game* (New York: Oxford University Press, 1985).

27. Sir Philip Sidney, *A Defense of Poetry*, ed. Forrest G. Robinson (Indianapolis: Indiana University Press, 1970), 58.

28. Samuel Beckett, *End-Game: A Play in One Act* (New York: Grove Press, 1958), 5, and *Watt* (New York: Grove Press, 1958), 5. See also the chess game annotated in *Murphy* (New York: Grove Press, 1938), 243–45, whose opening move, P-K4, is "the primary cause of all White's subsequent difficulties."

29. Hilary Putnam, "Beyond the Fact / Value Dichotomy," in *Virtue and Taste: Essays on Politics, Ethics, and Aesthetics*, ed. Dudley Knowles and John Skorupski (Oxford: Blackwell, 1993), 135.

30. Wittgenstein, *Philosophical Investigations*, 46e–47e (no. 108); and *Philosophische Grammatik* (London: Blackwell, 1969), 184, and *Zetel* (London: Blackwell, 1969), 320, trans. in Arthur Kenny, *Wittgenstein* (London: Penguin, 1973), 20, 177.

31. *Wittgenstein and the Vienna Circle: Conversations Recorded by Friedrich Waismann*, ed. Brian McGuinness, trans. Joachim Schulte and Brian McGuinness (Oxford: Oxford University Press, 1979), 103–4. I select this latter passage for analysis partly because it provides in itself an interesting case of recommencement. Waismann's accuracy has been questioned, and Wittgenstein, we know, disclaimed the philosophy of the Vienna Circle; and yet this particular passage seems an accurate representation of how he used the chess analogy. Anthony Kenny places special emphasis on it in what remains the single best discussion of the subject. See his *Wittgenstein*, 10, 160–61 ff.; see also 74–77, 93, 142, 154, 157. A subtler and more rigorous formulation of the questions involved (systems, arbitrariness, and agency) comes in Wittgenstein's comparison of chess to language games and philosophical propositions in *Philosophical Investigations*, 52e–53e (no. 136).

32. Clifford Geertz, "Common Sense as a Cultural System," in *Local Knowledge: Further Essays in Interpretive Anthropology* (New York: Basic Books, 1983), 89.

33. Noam Chomsky, *Language and Mind* (New York: Harcourt Brace, 1972), 7; Wittgenstein, *Philosophical Investigations*, 80e (no. 197), 81e (no. 205), 82e (no. 206), and 115e (no. 365).

34. Arnold Davidson, "Sex and the Emergence of Sexuality," *Critical Inquiry* 14 (1987): 27; Stanley Cavell, *This New Yet Unapproachable America: Literature After Emerson After Wittgenstein* (Albuquerque, N.M.: Living Batch Press, 1989), 34, 48, 43–46; Kenny, *Wittgenstein*, 171.

35. Wittgenstein, *Philosophical Investigations*, 46e–47e (no. 108). See also: 15e (no. 31), 17e (no. 33), 22e (no. 47), 81e (no. 200), 104e (no. 316), 108e (no. 337), 150e (no. 563).

36. George Simmel, *On Individuality and Social Forms*, ed. Donald N. Levine (Chicago: University of Chicago Press, 1971), 354.

37. Leo Tolstoy, *The Death of Ivan Ilych and Other Stories*, ed. David Magarshak (New York: New American Library, 1960), 104; Stanley Cavell, *The Claim of Reason: Wittgenstein, Skepticism, Morality, and Tragedy* (Oxford: Clarendon Press, 1979), 496.

38. Eales, *Chess*, 18–38.

39. The Petrarchan connection is intriguing in its own right, as well as in relation to Renaissance colonization. Lucena's love-chess sonnet is part of a tradition that reaches back (in English literature) to John Lydgate and Chaucer's *Book of the Duchess*, and forward through Pope's translation of *The Odyssey*. In medieval poetry, the queen (called "Fez," after her predecessor, the Persian vizir) is notably restrained, almost too compliant, perhaps in response to the criticisms of the displacement of the vizir-counselor. These criticisms are echoed as late as William Caxton's popular 1483 translation of Jacobus de Cessolis's Latin treatise, which complains that "women can kepe no counceyl." *The Game of Chess*, facsimile ed. (London: Scolar Press, 1976), Biii verso. Shakespeare may be invoking this dual tradition in Elinor's warning in *King John* against Constance's ambition to "be a queen and check the world" (2.1.123); clearly, he adopts the Petrarchan tradition in Miranda's chess game with Ferdinand in *The Tempest*. There's a provocative connection from this perspective between the role of the queen in the New Chess vis-à-vis the conspicuous absence of women chess players (hence my use here of the male pronoun), and Virginia Woolf's contrast, in *A Room of One's Own*, between women as writers and as subjects of literature. It may be relevant that, with the advent of the New Queen, women chess players (a medieval commonplace) become increasingly rare, and that, for all the New Queen's power, the technical term for chess pieces after the Renaissance is "chessmen." A fascinating instance of the ambiguities this archaic term entails may be found in Thomas Hardy's *A Pair of Blue Eyes*.

40. Hans Wichmann and Siegfried Wichmann, *Chess: The Story of Chesspieces from Ancient to Modern Times*, trans. Cornelia Brookfield and Claudia Rosoux (London: Paul Hamlyn, 1964), 64.

41. Eales, *Chess*, 207. I am grateful to Doris Sommer for the observations about Lucena's wordplay.

42. Arjun Appadurai, "Disjuncture and Difference in the Global Cultural Economy," *Public Culture* 2 (1990): 1–2, and "Global Ethnoscapes: Notes and Queries for a Transnational Anthropology," in *Recapturing Anthropology: Working in the Present*, ed. Richard G. Fox (Santa Fe: University of New Mexico Press, 1991), 191–92, 209.

43. Benjamin Franklin, *Writings*, ed. J. A. Leo Lemay (New York: Library of America, 1987), 929.

44. Benjamin Franklin, "Morals of Chess," in *Writings*, ed. Albert H. Smyth (New York: Haskell House, 1970), 8:359; Paul Thième, "Chess and Backgammon (Tric-Trac) in Sanskrit Literature," in *Indological Studies*, ed. Ernest Bender (New Haven, Conn.: Yale University Press, 1962), 204–17.

45. The roots game is a telling current variation. To discover where you're re-

*ally* from, as a hyphenated American, even to retain (or adopt) a different language or set of customs, is to turn an endgame into a recommencement. This has been announced (of course) as a *new* approach, but it's a cultural reflex that can be traced back to the very meaning of "discovery," as this definition of Columbus's voyage was invented by U.S. mythographers of the New World. Elsewhere "discovery" for Europeans was an endgame puzzle, proceeding from Terra Incognita to India to the ancient site of Eden to the continents of South and North America. All of these claims proved susceptible to empirical validation, as the U.S. "discovery" emphatically does not. That *symbolic* moment (in which a historical event becomes a spiritual imperative) requires you to start all over again, both on your own behalf (self-discovery) and on the community's. A cultural *locus classicus* for this recommencement is the Puritan New England rhetoric of mission: "city on a hill" (always invoked with anxiety, in the future tense, as "we shall be," but perhaps not), "errand into the wilderness," "New England *Way*," and so on. The classic aesthetic demonstration of this symbolic strategy is the procession of "romances" that constitute the canonical American Renaissance. I think first of Hawthorne's *The Scarlet Letter*, a search for roots that ends with angst-ridden prophecies of things to come (both Arthur's and Hester's). But one might think equally of the ending to Thoreau's *Walden* ("I have several more lives to live. . . . The sun is but a morning star"), or of Whitman's "Song of Myself" ("Missing me one place search another, / I stop somewhere waiting for you"), or of Melville's *Moby-Dick* ("the devious-cruising Rachel . . . in her retracing search . . . only found another orphan"). In Poe's grotesque inversion of this strategy, *The Narrative of A. Gordon Pym*, the endgame blank on the map returns us to an imposter called Mr. White. Citations are from the Library of America editions: *Walden*, ed. Robert F. Sayre (1983), 579, 587; *Moby-Dick*, ed. Thomas Tanselle (1983), 1408; "Song of Myself," ed. Justin Kaplan (1982), 101.

46. Ralph Waldo Emerson, "The American Scholar," and "Circles," in *Essays and Lectures*, ed. Joel Porte (New York: Library of America, 1983), 53, 403–5, 407, 411. The association of "star-spangled banner" with a "new constellation" was a commonplace of the times.

47. Emerson, *Nature* and "Circles," in Porte, *Essays and Lectures*, 5, 405.

48. The origins game is, of course, a variation on the telos endgame. Here, the sacrifice of history is expressed as a transcendent starting point, whether theological, as in the Christian Word, or nationalist, as in antiquarian *Ur*-myths. Both of these make-believe forms contribute to the dominant U.S. myth of America. I referred earlier to the roots game. It may be pertinent to current literary and cultural studies to elaborate its variations as the melting-pot endgame and the multicultural endgame. The melting-pot posits telos through the rejection of origins for a new origins (and/or telos) called "America": "What has held the American people together in the absence of a common ethnic origin has been precisely a common adherence to ideals of democracy and human rights . . . the republic embodies ideals that transcend ethnic, religious, and political lines. It is

an experiment . . . in creating a common identity for people of diverse races, religions, languages, cultures." Arthur M. Schlesinger, Jr., *The Disuniting of America: Reflections on a Multicultural Society* (New York: Norton, 1992), 110. The multicultural endgame finds its most sophisticated expression—three centuries after St. John de Crevecoeur's American Studies classic ("What is an American?" in *Letters from an American Farmer*), which Schlesinger cites—in the theories of Jean-François Lyotard. Here, the ideal is a "common adherence" to a Kantian "idea of a society of free beings" *through* the "pragmatic intersection of . . . an indeterminate number of language games." Jean-François Lyotard, *Just Gaming*, trans. Wlad Godzich (Minneapolis: University of Minnesota Press, 1984), 77–78. Those who quarrel in the name of "America," with the social implications of that reversal should compare the ideal multiplicity of interests in *The Federalist Papers* with Lyotard's "politics of Ideas in which justice is not placed under a rule of convergence but rather a rule of divergence. I believe that this is the theme that one finds constantly in present-day writing under the name of 'minority.' Basically, minorities are not social ensembles; they are territories of language. Every one of us belongs to several minorities, and what is very important, none of them prevails. It is only then that we can say that the society is just." *The Postmodern Condition: A Report on Knowledge*, trans. Geoff Bennington and Brian Massumi (Minneapolis: University of Minnesota Press, 1979), 95. A separate essay would be needed to explain the U.S. incorporation of this French connection, from Crevecouer through Tocqueville to Lyotard and Derrida.

49. In terms of my chess analogy: (1) The *Volksgeist* variation of the origins game is like the "retrograde" endgame puzzle, which involves a game's past, rather than its future (e.g., a checkmate situation is given with a missing piece on square $x$; you have to figure out what piece it is and from where it is moved. (2) Leon Trotsky's *world revolution* teleology resembles the *cases conjugées* endgame, devised by the Dadaist Marcel Duchamp: Why, under certain conditions (only pawns and kings left in the game) is the black king *obliged* to move to square $x$ on one side of the board if the white king, at the other end of the board, moves to square $y$? (The answer involves a theory of relationship between empty squares which have no apparent connection.) (3) The *American recommencement game* differs from these in the full variety of ways listed in Sam B. Girgus's survey of "The New Ethnic Novel and the American Idea," *College Literature* 19 (1994): 57–72. One example of many is Bharati Mukherjee's interview with Bill Moyers, on "The World of Ideas," PBS, 24 June 1990: "What America offers me is romanticism and hope. I'm coming out of a continent of cynicism and irony and despair in many ways—a traditional society where you are what you are according to the family that you were born into, the caste, the class, the gender, and suddenly I found myself in a country where I can choose to discard that part of my history that I want and invent a whole new history for myself. In doing that we, of course, very painfully, sometimes very violently murder our old selves and that's an unfortunate, perhaps, inevitable process. I want to think that it is a freeing process

in spite of the pain—in spite of the violence—in spite of the bruising of the old self to have that freedom to make mistakes, to choose a whole new history for one's self is exciting."

## White: Storytelling

1. Fernand Braudel, "The Situation of History in 1950," in *On History*, trans. Sarah Matthews (Chicago: University of Chicago Press, 1980).

2. Roland Barthes, "The Discourse of History," trans. Stephen Bann, in *Comparative Criticism: A Yearbook*, vol. 3, ed. E. S. Schaffer (New York: Cambridge University Press, 1981), 16.

3. Roland Barthes, "Introduction to the Structural Analysis of Narratives," in *Image, Music, Text*, trans. Stephen Heath (New York: Noonday, 1977), 123–24.

4. Barthes, "Discourse of History," 6.

5. Georg Lukács, "Narrate or Describe?" in *Writer & Critic and Other Essays*, ed. and trans. Arthur D. Kahn (New York: Grosset & Dunlap, 1970), 143. Hereafter cited parenthetically in the text.

6. David Carr, *Time, Narrative, and History* (Bloomington: Indiana University Press, 1986).

7. C. Vann Woodward, "A Southern Romantic," review of *Judah P. Benjamin: The Jewish Confederate* by Eli N. Evans, *New York Review of Books*, April 14, 1988, 6–9.

8. Karl Marx, *The Eighteenth Brumaire of Louis Bonaparte, with Explanatory Notes* (New York: International Publishers, 1969), 8.

9. Louis Hjelmslev, *Prolegomena to a Theory of Language*, trans. Francis J. Whitfield (Madison: University of Wisconsin Press, 1961), 47–60.

## Stewart: Traherne's Centuries

1. Saint Augustine, *Confessions*, trans. R. S. Pine-Coffin (London: Penguin, 1961), 269–77. The discussion of time suffuses book 11 of the *Confessions*.

2. See Giambattista Vico, *The New Science*, trans. Thomas Goddard and Max Harold Fisch (Ithaca, N.Y.: Cornell University Press, 1970), 74–79 and 260; Benedetto Croce, *Theory and History of Historiography*, trans. Douglas Ainslie (London: George Harrap, 1921), 108–11; Samuel Taylor Coleridge, *Biographia Literaria*, ed. J. Shawcross (Oxford: Clarendon Press, 1907), 2:49–50; Friedrich Nietzsche, "Truth and Falsity in an Ultramoral Sense," in *Philosophy of Nietzsche*, ed. Geoffrey Clive (New York: New American Library, 1965), 503–15; Jean-Jacques Rousseau, *Essay on the Origin of Languages Which Treats of Melody and Musical Imitation*, trans. John H. Moran, in *On the Origin of Language: Jean-Jacques Rousseau, Essay on the Origin of Languages; Johann Gottfried Herder, Essay on the Origin of Language*, trans. John H. Moran and Alexander Gode (New York: Frederick Ungar, 1967).

3. Thomas Watson, *The Hekatompathia or Passionate Centurie of Love* (1582), facsimile reproduction and introduction by S. K. Heninger Jr. (Gainesville, Fla.: Scholars' Facsimiles and Reprints, 1964).

4. See, for example, Alastair Fowler, *Spenser and the Numbers of Time* (London: Routledge, 1964), esp. 237–57; Frances A. Yates, *The Occult Philosophy in the Elizabethan Age* (London: Routledge, 1979); Ernst Robert Curtius, *European Literature and the Latin Middle Ages*, trans. Willard R. Trask (New York: Harper & Row, 1953); and Joseph Leon Blau, *The Christian Interpretation of Cabala in the Renaissance* (New York: Columbia University Press, 1944).

5. Croce, *Historiography*, 108–10.

6. Thomas Crump, *The Anthropology of Numbers* (Cambridge: Cambridge University Press, 1990). This work has been helpful to me throughout the construction of this essay.

7. For a description and account of the film, see Philip Morrison and Phylis Morrison and the Office of Charles and Ray Eames, *Powers of Ten: A Book About the Relative Size of Things in the Universe and the Effect of Adding Another Zero* (New York: W. H. Freeman, 1982).

8. Saint Augustine, *De Musica*, trans. W. F. Jackson Knight (London: The Orthological Institute, 1949).

9. See David Summers, *The Judgment of Sense: Renaissance Naturalism and the Rise of Aesthetics* (Cambridge: Cambridge University Press, 1987), 134–35.

10. See Crump, *Anthropology of Numbers*, 8. Crump takes this concept of the "nombre marginal" from L. Gerschel, "La conquête du nombre: Des modalités du compte aux structures de la pensée," *Annales E.S.C.* 17 (1962): 691–714.

11. See Angus Fletcher, *Colors of the Mind: Conjectures on Thinking in Literature* (Cambridge, Mass.: Harvard University Press, 1991), 174.

12. Curtius, *Latin Middle Ages*, 59n.

13. Fowler, *Spenser*, 38.

14. S. K. Heninger Jr., *The Cosmographical Glass: Renaissance Diagrams of the Universe* (San Marino, Calif.: Huntington Library, 1977), 94, quoted from Henry Cornelius Agrippa, *Three Books of Occult Philosophy*, trans. [J]ohn F[rench?] (London, 1651), 232.

15. Curtius, *Latin Middle Ages*, 503.

16. Heninger, *Cosmographical Glass*, 92.

17. Fowler, *Spenser*, 38n. "Thus, 1000 is the cube of 10, and itself a cosmic number relating to the firmament of fixed stars."

18. Of particular relevance are these models in relation to the structure of the Dobell manuscript of Traherne's centuries. John Malcolm Wallace, in "Thomas Traherne and the Structure of Meditation," *ELH* 25, no. 2 (June 1958): 79–89, claimed an Ignatian structure for the *Centuries*. His argument was based on his reading of Louis Martz's book *The Poetry of Meditation* (New Haven, Conn.: Yale University Press, 1954). Yet Martz himself in his authoritative work, *The Paradise Within: Studies in Vaughan, Traherne, and Milton* (New Haven, Conn.: Yale University Press, 1964), traces the influence of Augustine, especially his *De Trinitate*, on Traherne (and of the Platonic and Neoplatonic influences on both of them), and goes on to claim that Traherne's *Centuries* "seem to accord in general" with the method of contemplation found in Saint Bonaventure's *Itinerarium Mentis in*

*Deum*, 35–102. A. L. Clements, in *The Mystical Poetry of Thomas Traherne* (Cambridge, Mass.: Harvard University Press, 1969), claims a number of influences on Traherne, including the Bible, Plato, Plotinus, Augustine, Dionysius the pseudo-Areopagite, Pico della Mirandola and Marsilio Ficino, Richard of St. Victor, Saint Bonaventure, Meister Eckhart, Henry Suso, John Rysbroeck, Julian of Norwich, and Jacob Boehme. Much of this is just speculation (as is his claim [on page 14 of *Paradise Within*], refuted by the *Commentaries of Heaven*, that Traherne was more sympathetic to Aristotle than to Plato in his view of form and matter). Elsewhere Clements turns to a broad analogy, leading him to conclude that the overall pattern of the *Centuries* follows the standard Christian model of Creation-Fall-Redemption. Sharon Cadman Seelig's *The Shadow of Eternity: Belief and Structure in Herbert, Vaughan and Traherne* (Louisville: University Press of Kentucky, 1981) suggests that Traherne's "ecstasy" does not much resemble any of the logical patterns of Christian meditation (105–15). And A. Leigh DeNeef's *Traherne in Dialogue: Heidegger, Lacan and Derrida* (Durham, N.C.: Duke University Press, 1988) claims that the structure of the Dobell sequence fits all four patterns: Bonaventure's, the conventional stages of Christian mysticism, Ignatius's, and the Christian soul's movement from innocence to fall to redemption (139). Traherne himself gives an interesting gloss on his method of composition in the *Select Meditations*, perhaps giving evidence of a more eclectic plan. In meditation 15 of the "Forth Century" he adds a small lyric that begins, "O Sing, O Soar, O faint, O pant of Breath! / O Saint Rejoyce . . ." Meditations 16 and 17 are blanks, but at 18 Traherne writes, "Here Aphorism and there a Song: here a suplication and there a Thanksgiving. Thus do we bespangle our way to Heaven." The presence of blanks is intriguing. We also find them in the *Centuries of Heaven* in the Second Century, where meditation 88 is blank. Because the *Select Meditations* seem to be a fair copy, there is a conscious use of the blank. In other words, the careful marking of space in the text makes a simple error in numbering unlikely. Although a conjecture, one might deduce that this blank represents the reality of some other measurement, such as a day, and that perhaps the centuries were written over 100 day spans. All references to *Select Meditations* are from Osborn MS b.308, Beinecke Library, Yale University, cited throughout for reasons based on the physical condition of the text by meditation rather than page number.

19. Malcolm Day, *Thomas Traherne* (Boston: Twayne Publishers, 1982), argues this connection between the structure of Hall's *Centuries* and the short extemporal meditations of David in the Psalms (106–7).

20. Martin Zeiler, *Centuria Variarum Quaestionum, Oder Ein Hundert Fragen, von allerlen materien und Sachen*, Samt Unvorgreifflicher Antwort (Ulm, 1658), and *Centuria III. Variarum Questionum. Oder das Dritte Hundert Fragen* (Ulm, 1659). Alexander Ross, *A Centurie of Divine Meditations Upon Predestination and its Adjuncts wherein are shewed the comfortable uses of this doctrine. To which are annexed sixteen meditations upon God's Justice and Mercy* (London, 1646).

21. For background to Traherne, see the following editions of his work: the early editions edited by Bertram Dobell are *The Poetical Works of Thomas Tra-*

*herne* (London: Dobell, 1903) and *Centuries of Meditations by Thomas Traherne* (London: Dobell, 1908). Standard editions are Thomas Traherne, *Centuries, Poems, and Thanksgivings*, 2 vols., ed. H. M. Margoliouth (Oxford: Clarendon Press, 1958); Thomas Traherne, *Christian Ethicks*, ed. Carol L. Marks and George R. Guffey (Ithaca, N.Y.: Cornell University Press, 1968); and Thomas Traherne, *Poems, Centuries and Three Thanksgivings*, ed. Anne Ridler (London: Oxford University Press, 1966). For secondary texts, see Day (cited at note 19) and Seelig, DeNeef, Clements, Martz, and Wallace (cited at note 18), and the following: Stanley Stewart, *The Expanded Voice: The Art of Thomas Traherne* (San Marino, Calif.: Huntington Library, 1970); Kenneth John Ames, *The Religious Language of Thomas Traherne's Centuries* (New York: Revisionist Press, 1978); A. M. Allchin, Anne Ridler, and Julia Smith, *Profitable Wonders: Aspects of Thomas Traherne* (Oxford: Amate Press, 1989); Slawomir Wacior, *Strategies of Literary Communication in the Poetry of Thomas Traherne* (Lublin: Redakcja Wydawnictw Kul, 1990); Franz K. Wohrer, *Thomas Traherne: The Growth of a Mystic's Mind*, Salzburg Studies in English Literature (Salzburg: Institut for Anglistik und Amerikanistik, Universität Salzburg, 1982); Queenie Iredale, *Thomas Traherne* (Oxford: Basil Blackwell, 1935); Alison Sherrington, *Mystical Symbolism in the Poetry of Thomas Traherne* (Brisbane: University of Queensland Press, 1970); Richard Douglas Jordan, *The Temple of Eternity: Thomas Traherne's Philosophy of Time* (Port Washington, N.Y.: Kennikat Press, 1972); Barbara Kiefer Lewalski, *Protestant Poetics and the Seventeenth-Century Lyric* (Princeton, N.J.: Princeton University Press, 1979), 352–87; and Joan Webber, *The Eloquent "I": Style and Self in Seventeenth-Century Prose* (Madison: University of Wisconsin Press, 1968), 219–47.

22. The *Commentaries of Heaven* are in the British Library, Add. MSS 63054. The most important accounts of the *Commentaries* can be found in Allan Pritchard, "Traherne's *Commentaries of Heaven* (With Selections from the Manuscript)," *University of Toronto Quarterly* 53, no. 1 (fall 1983): 1–35, and Julia Smith, "Traherne from His Unpublished Manuscripts," in Allchin, Ridler, and Smith, *Profitable Wonders*, 38–51. Julia Smith is now working on an edition of the *Commentaries*. I am grateful for our conversation regarding Traherne in October 1993. I would also like to acknowledge the assistance of the manuscript librarians at the British Library and the gracious help of the Reverend George Usher at St. Mary's Rectory, Credenhill, who shared his knowledge of Traherne's church and its history with me, opening St. Mary's under difficult circumstances in June 1993, for the church had been recently damaged by an arsonist and was officially closed.

23. See *A Collection of Meditations and Devotions in Three Parts by the First Reformer of the devotions in the Ancient Way of Offices* (Susanna Hopton), afterwards reviewed and set forth by the late Learned Dr. Hickes (London, 1717). For further background on Hopton, see Julia Smith, "Susanna Hopton: A Biographical Account," *Notes and Queries* 38, no. 2 (June 1991): 165–72.

24. See James J. Balakier, "Thomas Traherne's Dobell Series and the Baconian Model of Experience," *English Studies* 7, no. 3 (June 1989): 233–47.

25. The Ficino Notebook is British Library MS Burney 126. Carol L. Marks (Sicherman) has described Traherne's unpublished works and the influences of his studies upon his writings in the following important articles: Carol Marks Sicherman, "Traherne's Ficino Notebook," *The Papers of the Bibliographical Society of America* 63 (1969): 73–81; Carol Marks Sicherman, "Thomas Traherne's Commonplace Book," ibid., 58 (1964): 458–65; Carol Marks, "Traherne's Church's Year-Book," ibid., 60 (1966): 31–72; Carol Marks, "Thomas Traherne's Early Studies," ibid., 62 (1968): 511–36; Carol Marks, "Thomas Traherne and Hermes Trismegistus," *Renaissance News* 19 (1966): 118–31; and Carol Marks, "Thomas Traherne and Cambridge Platonism," *PMLA* 81 (1966): 521–34.

26. Numerical composition in Ficino is discussed in Josephine L. Burroughs's translation of Ficino's "Five Questions Concerning the Mind," in *The Renaissance Philosophy of Man*, ed. Ernst Cassirer, Paul Oskar Kristeller, and John Herman Randall (Chicago: University of Chicago Press, 1956). Burroughs's introduction is on 185–92; the translation itself, on 193–212. See also Michael J. B. Allen, trans. and ed., *Marsilio Ficino: The Philebus Commentary* (Berkeley: University of California Press, 1975) and Pico della Mirandola, *Heptaplus*, trans. Douglas Carmichael, in Pico della Mirandola, *On the Dignity of Man; On Being and the One; Heptaplus*, with introduction by Paul J. W. Miller (Indianapolis, Ind.: Bobbs-Merrill, 1940), 85–174. Traherne quotes from Pico's *De dignitate hominis* in the fourth century of the Dobell manuscript (74–78), and many aspects of Pico's thought are relevant to his writings, including the *Heptaplus* as a narration on the six days of creation; Pico's three chief zones of cosmology: the intelligences or angels, the heavenly bodies, and the corruptible earthly bodies; and Pico's transposition and recombination of Hebrew letters in his study of the cabbalistic method. In the *Commentaries of Heaven*, Traherne compares Aristotle and Plato and argues that Plato was superior to Aristotle, "And the reason is apparent for Plato delighting much in *Jewish traditions* (which he had imbibed partly from the Pythagorean philosophie, partly from his personal conversations with Jews and Egyptians in the Oriental parts) he thereby obtained great notices of *Divine Mysteries* especially such as related to the origins of the universe, the Spiritual Nature and Perfection of God, the Immortalitie of the Soul, etc." (f.129v). In the earlier *Select Meditations*, however, Traherne shows some contempt for Plato. He praises Plato for asking the "marvellous question," "Whether Things were Holy because they were commanded or therefore commanded because they were Holy," (Meditation 49) but then goes on to say that "the Heathen answered not his own question: for it was too deep for his Intelligence" (Meditation 50).

27. See James M. Osborn, "A New Traherne Ms." *TLS*, October 6, 1964. There are references to "Soften the Kings heart, Teach our Senators Wisdom," in I/82 and "The Government of A Church Established by Laws," in III/24. Other, sketchier autobiographical evidence in the *Select Meditations* dates the manuscript to the period of Traherne's appointment at Credenhill: "nor ever am I happy till I return home" (III/30); "when I see a little Church environed with Trees, how many Things are there which mine Eye discerneth not. . . . Especially I who have

been nourished at universities in Beautifull Streets and famous Colledges and am sent thither from God almighty the aer of Heaven and Earth to teach Immortal Souls the way to Heaven" (III/83).

28. It is perhaps not far-fetched to suggest as well that Traherne had a model for breaking off his writing at the fifth section in Ficino. See Allen, *Marsilia Ficino*, 10: "Ficino had given public lectures on his translation [of the *Philebus*], praised by Alberti. Alberti and Landino asked him to elucidate the theories he had developed in the *Philebus* commentary. After Ficino had announced to his listeners that the *Philebus* is divided into twelve sections, without any warning he interrupts his exposition after the fifth section; and although subsequently—twice in fact—he showed his regret at not having been able to complete his exposition, we see him contenting himself with illustrating it with apologues, an odd conclusion for the treatise."

29. Quoted in Theodor E. Mommsen, "St. Augustine and the Christian Idea of Progress: The Background of *The City of God*," in *Medieval and Renaissance Studies*, ed. Eugene F. Rice (Ithaca, N.Y.: Cornell University Press, 1959), 265–98, 295. For Augustine's concept of the "six ages," dividing world history according to the six days of Creation wherein the Christian era is an age of senility and decay leading to a seventh age when time comes to an end, see G. J. Whitrow, *Time in History: The Evolution of Our General Awareness of Time and Temporal Perspective* (Oxford: Oxford University Press, 1988), 80.

30. See Stephen Toulmin and June Goodfield, *The Discovery of Time* (New York: Harper & Row, 1965), 60–61. J. J. Scaliger, in *De emendatione temporum* (1583), had calculated the system of Julian days as beginning at noon on January 1, 4713 B.C.—his estimation of the date of creation. See Whitrow, *Time in History*, 137. Plato had claimed in the *Timaeus* that the battle between the Athenians and Atlantans had occurred 8,000 years before.

31. In his *Christian Ethicks* Traherne gives a similar account of the history of the world in chapter 15: "Of Faith." He says that there can be no "certain knowledge" of the "actions of free agents" except by "history and tradition": "That the World was made so many years ago, that Man was created in an estate of Innocency, that he fell into Sin, that GOD appeared, and promised the seed of the Woman to break the Serpents Head, that there was a Flood, that Sodom and Gomorrah was burnt by fire, that all the world spake one Language till the Confusion at Babel, that there were such men as Julius Caesar, or Alexander the Great, or such as Abraham, and Moses, and David; that the children of Israel were in Egypt, and were delivered from thence by Miracles; that they received the Law in the Wilderness, and were afterwards settled in the Land of Canaan, that they had such and such Prophets, and Priests and Kings; that Jesus Christ was born of the Virgin Mary, that he was GOD and Man, that he died and rose again, that he ascended into Heaven, and sent the Holy Ghost down upon his Apostles. Nay that there is such a City as Jerusalem" (107–8). Traherne goes on to say that the histories of peoples, the determination of the gospels, the accounts of miracles, the existence of emperors, church fathers, and places such as Judea, Rome, and Con-

stantinople are revealed "by the Light of History and received upon Trust from the Testimony of others" to be as clear as "mathematical demonstration, or [what] had been seen with our Eys" because of faith and the reliability of Christian typology. He concludes, "AMONG other Objects of Felicity to be enjoyed, the Ways of GOD in all Ages are not the least considerable and illustrious. . . . Ages are as long and as Wide as Kingdoms" (111).

32. It is worth noting that the *Select Meditations* manuscript, which from all evidence seems to be a fair copy, is written so that there are 33 lines of text on each page.

33. Unfortunately, there is a dearth of reliable documents regarding the facts of Traherne's life. Furthermore, much of Traherne's writing on infancy and childhood should be framed in Christian and Neoplatonic, rather than strictly autobiographical, terms. A current project to systematize the archives of the city of Hereford should be of help. Although Gladys Wade's biography, *Thomas Traherne* (Princeton, N.J.: Princeton University Press, 1944), is not always reliable, it does set forth a picture of the violent circumstances of Traherne's childhood in Hereford in light of the general religious and political circumstances of the town in the seventeenth century.

34. It is suggestive of his later interest in cabala that the flyleaf of one of Traherne's early notebooks from Brasenose College has two simple codes (387). One code covers only the vowels, using a kind of tailed Greek as a base. One stroke across the tail corresponds to "a," two strokes to "b," and so on. The second code on page 387 involves a correspondence between letters and numbers (a = 1, e = 2, i = 3, o = 4, u = 5, m = 6, n = 7, r = 8, c = 9)—Traherne wrote "1627" or "amen." (Recounted in Marks, "Thomas Traherne's Early Studies," 514.)

35. See Michael Ponsford, "Men After God's Own Heart: The Context of Thomas Traherne's Emulation of David," *Studia Mystica* 9, no. 4 (winter 1986): 3–11. Ponsford especially focuses on Traherne's *Thanksgivings*, where Traherne explicitly desires "that I were as David" (many of the "Thanksgivings" are pastiches of the psalms) and how the third century links Traherne to a poetics of imitation in the seventeenth century.

36. On the poetics of the Psalms, see Pius Drijvers, *The Psalms, Their Structure and Meaning* (New York: Herder & Herder, 1964); Robert Alter, "Psalms," in *The Literary Guide to the Bible*, ed. Robert Alter and Frank Kermode (Cambridge, Mass.: Harvard University Press, 1987), 244–62; Douglas K. Stuart, *Studies in Early Hebrew Meter* (Missoula, Mont.: Scholars Press for the Harvard Semitic Museum, 1976); Leopold Sabourin, *The Psalms: Their Origin and Meaning*, 2 vols. (New York: Society of St. Paul, 1969). Sabourin explains that "the alphabetic psalms are 9–10, 25, 34, 37, 111, 112, 119, and 145. They follow a literary device in which half-lines, lines, verses, or stanzas begin successively with a different letter of the Hebrew alphabet. In Psalm 119 the letter is repeated eight times throughout the 22 alphabetical stanzas. Psalm 9–10 originally formed a single alphabetical poem in which every second, third, or fourth verse began with a successive letter of the alphabet" (26–27). Crump, *Anthropology of Numbers*, 110–11, also discusses

Psalm 119, emphasizing that the Hebrew letters are also used as numbers here and that Psalm tradition will play a part in the development of cabala.

37. Percy Osmond, *The Mystical Poets of the English Church* (London: Society for Promoting Christian Knowledge; New York: Macmillan, 1919), 243: "Traherne is lavish in the use of the first person singular, a device which on a careless reader may leave an impression of monstrous conceit; but it should be noted that, in a section where the self-revelation becomes especially intimate, he adopts the third person." This technique is especially complicated in the *Select Meditations* manuscript where Traherne sometimes does write in the first person about himself, as he does in the passage I quote in note 27. He refers as well to his "brother" and "SH" (Susanna Hopton) and writes in meditation 93 of the first century, "know lady of our Happiness in being Redeemed," thereby perhaps addressing these centuries as well to Hopton. Yet there is also a recurring metaphor in the *Select Meditations* of Traherne himself as "the bride of Christ." In these passages of poetry and prose, Traherne, in a remarkable poem making up Meditation 17 of the second century, concludes, "I on Thy Turtle [Dove] shall with joy Behold / Angelique Life / Throughout her Skin / Shall clad thy wife and make her Shine within." Meditation 18, which follows, makes a direct appeal to God, "O my God would She See thy Goodness! How should her soul be ravished! Thy goodness and thy wisdom seen, would make thy Bride of Heaven and Earth a Queen!"

## Thomas: Turner's "Frontier Thesis"

1. William Cronon, "Revisiting the Vanishing Frontier: The Legacy of Frederick Jackson Turner," *Western Historical Quarterly* 18 (1987): 160. Some of the debate is collected in George Rogers Taylor, ed., *The Turner Thesis* (Boston: D. C. Heath, 1949). For fascinating appraisals by two revisionist historians of the West see *The Frontier in American Culture: Essays by Richard White and Patricia Limerick*, ed. James R. Grossman (Berkeley: University of California Press, 1994).

2. Frederick Jackson Turner, "The Significance of the Frontier in American History," in *The Frontier in American History* (New York: Henry Holt, 1920), 38.

3. Tiziano Bonazzi, "Frederick Jackson Turner's Frontier Thesis and the Self-Consciousness of America," *Journal of American Studies* 27 (1993): 162.

4. Michael P. Malone, "Beyond the Last Frontier: Toward a New Approach to Western History," *Western Historical Quarterly* 22 (1989): 410. Malone's claim that the frontier for Turner is a space of "social atomization" is commonplace. I argue that it is also for Turner a space for the creation of reconstructed *communitas*. See also Gerald Thompson, "Frontier West: Process of Place," *Journal of the Southwest* 29 (1987): 364–75.

5. Quoted in Wilbur R. Jacobs, *The Historical World of Frederick J. Turner* (New Haven, Conn.: Yale University Press, 1968), 135.

6. Martin Sklar, *The Corporate Reconstruction of American Capitalism, 1890–1916* (New York: Cambridge University Press, 1988), 26.

7. James Harvey Robinson, "The Original and Derived Features of the Consti-

tution," *Annals of the American Academy of Political and Social Science* 1 (1890): 203.

8. "The Figure of Columbus," *Atlantic Monthly* 69 (March 1892): 409. This anonymous reviewer urges that Americans need to supplement their understanding of the Teutonic origins of their civilization by reestablishing "our connection with Latin Christianity in all its forms" (409). The Spanish-American War derailed that project.

9. Herbert Baxter Adams, "The Germanic Origins of New England Towns with Notes on Cooperation in University Work," *Johns Hopkins University Studies*, 1st ser., 2 (1882): 1.

10. Robert H. Wiebe, *The Search for Order, 1877–1920* (New York: Hill & Wang, 1967).

11. Woodrow Wilson, "Bryce's *American Commonwealth*: A Review," in *Bryce's "American Commonwealth": Fiftieth Anniversary*, ed. Robert C. Brooks (New York: Macmillan, 1939), 181.

12. Albion W. Tourgée, "Reform versus Reformation," *The North American Review* 293 (1881): 305–19.

13. Woodrow Wilson, "The Study of Administration," *Political Science Quarterly* 2 (1887): 197–222.

14. Albion W. Tourgée, "The Twentieth Century Peacemakers," *The Contemporary Review* 75 (1899): 888.

15. David W. Noble, *The Paradox of Progressive Thought* (Minneapolis: University of Minnesota Press, 1958).

16. Arthur M. Schlesinger, "The City in American History," *Mississippi Valley Historical Review* 27 (1940): 43–66. Turner was not unaware of the importance of cities. In 1922 he proposed writing an essay on "the significance of the city in American history."

17. David M. Potter, *People of Plenty* (Chicago: University of Chicago Press, 1954).

18. David W. Noble, *The End of American History* (Minneapolis: University of Minnesota Press, 1985). For an excellent supplement to Noble's book that focuses on the history of the American West, see David M. Wrobel, *The End of American Exceptionalism* (Lawrence: University Press of Kansas, 1993). Turner's claim that the United States avoided European class conflict was challenged during the Depression. See Charles A. Beard, "The Myth of Rugged American Individualism," *Harpers*, December 1931, 13–22, and "The Frontier in American History," *New Republic*, February 1, 1939, 359–62, and Louis M. Hacker, "Sections—of Classes?" *Nation*, July 26, 1933, 108–10. Nonetheless, as Noble points out, even Beard maintained a vision of American exceptionalism.

19. Henry Adams, *History of the United States of America* vol. 1, *During the First Administration of Thomas Jefferson* (New York: Charles Scribner's Sons, 1891–96), 156.

20. G. W. F. Hegel, *Lectures on the Philosophy of History*, trans. J. Sibree (New York: Colonial Press, 1900), 85–87.

21. John T. Juricek, "American Usage of the Word 'Frontier' from Colonial Times to Frederick Jackson Turner," *Proceedings of the American Philosophical Society* 110 (1966): 33. The new use of "frontier" by no means completely drove out the old. In the same year that Turner presented the frontier thesis, Senator Thomas J. Geary of California defended his 1892 bill extending the exclusion of Chinese and severely punishing Chinese illegally caught in the United States by detaining the expense needed to maintain "guards and inspectors upon our frontiers and at our different seaports, in order to prevent the infraction of our laws by a race of people who never have shown any respect for them." "Should the Chinese Be Excluded?" *North American Review* 158 (1893): 61.

22. Frederick Jackson Turner, "The First Official Frontier of the Massachusetts Bay," in *The Frontier in American History*, 41.

23. Juricek, "The Word 'Frontier,'" 10–11.

24. Victor Turner, *From Ritual to Theatre* (New York: Performing Arts Journal Publications, 1982), 84, and *The Ritual Process* (Chicago: Aldine Publishing, 1969), 128. Sacvan Bercovitch draws heavily on Turner's notion of liminality to describe how an American *communitas* is forged out of a "Ritual of Consensus" in *The American Jeremiad* (Madison: University of Wisconsin Press, 1978), 132–75 and 204–5n.

25. Charles H. Pearson, *National Life and Character: A Forecast* (London: Macmillan, 1893).

26. Joseph Conrad, *Heart of Darkness* (New York: St. Martin's Press, 1989), 22.

27. James Westfall, "Profitable Fields of Investigation in Medieval History," *American Historical Review* 8 (1913): 490–504, and Joseph L. Wieczynski, *The Russian Frontier* (Charlottesville: University of Virginia Press, 1976).

28. Warren I. Susman, *Culture as History* (New York: Pantheon, 1984), 25.

29. Richard Slotkin, *Regeneration through Violence: The Mythology of The American Frontier, 1600–1860* (Wesleyan, Conn.: Wesleyan University Press, 1973). Although critical of the "myth" of the frontier, Slotkin to a large extent remains captive to Turner's construction of it. For instance, he accepts Turner's definition of the frontier, as a permanent fixture of American culture, not a late-nineteenth-century construction, going so far as to claim to identify "one of the *cultural archetypes* which emerged from the historical experience of the American *colonial* frontier to function as myth in our culture" (9, my emphasis).

30. Richard Slotkin, *Gunfighter Nation: The Myth of the Frontier in Twentieth-Century America* (New York: Atheneum, 1992), 26.

31. Ibid., 55.

32. My emphasis on metaphoric displacement as a space for reconstructing history has some similarities with Paul de Man's argument about "modernity" in "Literary History and Literary Modernity," *Blindness and Insight* (New York: Oxford University Press, 1971), 142–65. I am certainly indebted to de Man's criticism of the privileged status given to the symbol in studies of romanticism. But I am more strongly influenced by Hans Blumenberg's work on metaphor. See especially "An Anthropological Approach to the Contemporary Significance of

Rhetoric," in *After Philosophy: End or Transformation?* ed. Kenneth Baynes, James Bohman, and Thomas McCarthy (Cambridge, Mass.: MIT Press, 1988), 421–58. One important aspect of Blumenberg's work is his awareness that the concrete metaphors that we use matter. This commonsensical point complicates attempts, like Hayden White's, to explain the enduring status of powerful historical texts like Turner's by formalizing their content. See White's *Content of the Form* (Baltimore, Md.: Johns Hopkins University Press, 1987). If, indeed, the form of Turner's narrative allows for perpetual reconstruction, it also designates a specific place for the frontier. That designation opens his narrative to demystification.

33. See Peter Novick, *That Noble Dream* (New York: Cambridge University Press, 1988), 72–85, and John David Smith, *An Old Creed for the New South* (Westport, Conn.: Greenwood Press, 1985).

34. On Von Holst, see Eric F. Goldman, "Hermann Eduard Von Holst: Plumed Knight of American Historiography," *Mississippi Valley Historical Review* 23 (1937): 511–32.

35. Henry W. Grady, "The New South," in *Life of Henry W. Grady Including His Writings and Speeches*, ed. Joel Chandler Harris; reprint, 1886 (New York: Haskell House Publishers, 1972), 85.

36. Thomas Dixon Jr., *The Clansman* (Lexington: University Press of Kentucky, 1970), 54, 47.

37. Woodrow Wilson, *Division and Reunion, 1829–1889* (New York: Longmans, Green, 1893). Also in 1893 Wilson published a review attacking the bias of James Ford Rhodes's treatment of white Southerners. "Anti-Slavery History and Biography," *Atlantic Monthly*, August 1893, 272–74. Turner also faults Rhodes (24). On Turner and Wilson, see documents collected by Wendell H. Stephenson, ed., "The Influence of Woodrow Wilson on Frederick Jackson Turner," *Agricultural History* 19 (1945): 249–53. In addition, Turner was a powerful influence on Ulrich B. Phillips, whose *American Negro Slavery* (1918) is credited with authoritatively making the Southern perspective on race a national perspective until after World War II. In 1902 Turner hired Phillips to teach Southern history at Wisconsin, and when Turner died Phillips wrote his memorial for the American Historical Association's annual report. These connections should not, however, lead us uncritically to condemn Turner on the issue of race. What they suggest is that the reconstructive potential of Turner's narrative opens it to different political appropriations. Indeed, Phillips's youthful descriptions of Turner's influence highlight, not a specific content, but a spirit of endless renewal. "The best of this is that [Turner's] disciples are not content (the good ones) to walk in his steps, but are eager to blaze paths of their own." Turner's "great function" was "to stimulate and exhilarate young scholars in a way to make them stimulate others, and so on in a ripple which though it must lessen in the lapse of time and the spread of space, never quite reaches an end." Quoted in Merton L. Dillon, *Ulrich Bonnell Phillips* (Baton Rouge: Louisiana State University Press, 1985), 17.

38. W. E. Burghardt Du Bois, "Strivings of the Negro People," *Atlantic Monthly* 80 (August 1897): 195. In *The Souls of Black Folk*, Du Bois drops the

specific reference to Banquo's ghost, while retaining the lines from *Macbeth*. In *Souls* the first two sentences of the quotation read: "The swarthy spectre sits in its accustomed seat at the Nation's feast. In vain do we cry to this our vastest social problem." Du Bois also revises "thirty years" to "forty years." *The Souls of Black Folk* (New York: Penguin, 1989), 7. On Du Bois and Turner, see William Toll, "W. E. B. Du Bois and Frederick Jackson Turner: The Unveiling and Preemption of America's Inner History," *Pacific Northwest Quarterly* 65 (1974): 66–78. See also Kathleen Diffley, "Home on the Range: Turner, Slavery, and the Landscape Illustrations in *Harper's New Monthly Magazine*, 1861–1876," *Prospects* 14 (1989): 175–202.

39. David J. Weber, *The Spanish Frontier in North America* (New Haven, Conn.: Yale University Press, 1992). Weber is indebted to Herbert Eugene Bolton, who established the study of "Spanish Borderlands." Insofar as individualism was a sign of progressive democracy Chinese were seen as a blocking force because they were associated with feudal forms of collectivity. On the frontier with China, see note 21.

40. Victor Turner, *Dramas, Fields, and Metaphors* (Ithaca, N.Y.: Cornell University Press, 1974), 232–33.

41. Renato Rosaldo, *Culture and Truth* (Boston: Beacon Press, 1989). My understanding of Victor Turner and the recent challenge to him is heavily indebted to Donald Weber's "From Limen to Border: The Legacy of Victor Turner for American Studies" (paper delivered at the annual meeting of the ASA, Boston, November 7, 1993).

42. In the twelfth century Hugh of St. Victor wrote: "The man who finds his country sweet is only a raw beginner; the man for whom each country is as his own is only strong; but only the man for whom the whole world is as a foreign country is perfect." He is cited by Tzvetan Todorov, citing Edward Said, citing Erich Auerbach, to express the position of the displaced intellectual. Tzvetan Todorov, *The Conquest of America*, trans. Richard Howard (New York: Harper & Row, 1984), 250.

43. On the liberal logic of "both/and," see Sacvan Bercovitch, *The Office of "The Scarlet Letter"* (Baltimore: Johns Hopkins University Press, 1991). According to Victor Turner, *Blazing the Trail* (Tucson: University of Arizona Press, 1992), 49, "The most characteristic midliminal symbolism is that of paradox, of being *both* this *and* that."

44. The need for a global narrative to replace the exceptionalist one spawned by Turner's legacy has been especially felt in studies of the American West. For instance, Malone, "Beyond the Last Frontier," 424, urges that the word "frontier" be replaced by the term "globalization." See also Spencer C. Olin Jr., "Towards a Synthesis of the Political and Social History of the American West," *Pacific Historical Review* 55 (1986): 599–611. For an attempt to analyze the notion of "frontier" at times in relation to the notion of "border," see the special issue "Frontiers," *Oxford Literary Review* 14 (1992). Contributions are mostly from a series of seminars on the topic at the University of Sussex under the auspices of the College

Internationale de Philosophie. The volume was also affected by the "Borderlines" conference at Sussex in March 1991. According to editor Geoffrey Bennington, "frontiers" were defined in a seminar on Kant as "the place where violent lawlessness of the 'state of nature' returns inevitably to haunt the supposed lawfulness of political organization, this 'return' in fact originally constituting the concept of a 'state of nature.'" As a result, Bennington wonders, "if a radical political thinking would not have to attempt to start from the relations *between* States as a condition for anything like 'the' state in the first place." Bennington, "Frontiers: Two Seminar Sessions," 198, 199. It is unclear, however, what German term Bennington refers to in Kant to develop his definition of "frontier." Indeed, although the volume is full of etymological investigations, I discovered none devoted to "frontier" itself.

45. W. E. B. Du Bois, *The Souls of Black Folk* 1, 13, 35. An example of understanding the frontier as a metaphoric space on the color line occurs in a Frenchman's autobiographical account of an exchange year in Virginia in the 1950s. A diner called Steve's is described as "sort of a frontier post between the white and black sections of town." Phillipe Labro, *The Frontier Student*, trans. Williams R. Byron (New York: Ballantine, 1988), 81.

## Knapp: Rogue Nationalism

1. Joseph Hall, "An Holy Panegyric" (1613), in *Works*, ed. Philip Wynter, 10 vols. (1863; reprint, New York: AMS Press, 1969), 5:103. The ideology of England's sublime littleness is more fully discussed in my *Empire Nowhere: England, America, and Literature from Utopia to The Tempest* (Berkeley: University of California Press, 1992).

2. Bishop Cuthbert Tunstall, as reported in John Foxe *The Acts and Monuments [The Book of Martyrs]*, ed. Josiah Pratt, 3d ed., 8 vols. (1563–83; London, 1870), 4:666–67; Nicholas Sander, *A Treatise of the Images of Christ* (Louvain, 1567), preface, cap. 98; Thomas Harding, *A Rejoindre to M. Jewels Replie* (Louvain, 1567), C1a.

3. The first formal announcement of the break, the Act in Restraint of Appeals (1532), begins, "Whereas by diverse sundry old authentic histories and chronicles, it is manifestly declared and expressed, that this realm of England is an empire." For the history of the belief that England counted as an empire, see Walter Ullman, "'This Realm of England is an Empire,'" *Journal of Ecclesiastical History* 30 (1979): 175–203.

4. Thomas Dorman, *A Proufe of Certeyne Articles in Religion, Denied by M. Juell* (Antwerp, 1564), 112a.

5. Queen Elizabeth (1559) in response to a petition from her Catholic bishops, in John Strype, *Annals of the Reformation . . . in the Church and State of England, 1728–1735*, 6 vols. (New York: Burt Franklin, 1966), 1.1.218.

6. Franklin L. Baumer, "The Church of England and the Common Corps of Christendom," *Journal of Modern History* 16 (1944): 12. For the largely unrealized

proposals by English churchmen to achieve an international confessional unity, see 12–21.

7. Edwin Sandys, *Europæ Speculum. Or, A View or Survey of the State of Religion in the Westerne Parts of the World* (Hague, 1629), 188–89. The text is end-dated April 9, 1599; it was also first published in 1605 in an unauthorized edition as *A Relation of the State of Religion*.

8. Dorman, *Proufe*, 118b; Anthony Gilby, *An Answer to the Devellish Detection of S. Gardiner* (London, 1547), 69b; John Hooper, *Early Writings*, 201, quoted in Catherine Davies, "'Poor Persecuted Little Flock' or 'Commonwealth of Christians': Edwardian Protestant Conceptions of the Church," in *Protestantism and the National Church*, ed. Peter Lake and Maria Dowling (London: Croom Helm, 1987), 83; Edmund Spenser, *The Faerie Queene*, 2.1.19, 3.1.24, 1.7.50, and 1.2.9.

9. [William Allen], *A True, Sincere, and Modest Defense of English Catholics* (1584), in *The Execution of Justice by William Cecil and A True, Sincere, and Modest Defense of English Catholics by William Allen*, ed. Robert M. Kingdon (Ithaca, N.Y.: Cornell University Press, 1965), 234; Dorman, *Proufe*, 5b.

10. Richard Bancroft, *A Sermon Preached at Paules Crosse* (London, 1588 [1589]), 3. Cf. Bishop John Pilkington (1573), who asks a correspondent to "pause awhile with me, and mourn over this our church at this time so miserably divided, not to say, wholly rent in pieces." Pilkington to Rodolph Gualter, in *Zurich Letters*, ed. Hastings Robinson (Cambridge, 1842), 287; and the introductory epistle to a puritan *Dialogue, Concerning the Strife of Our Churche* (London, 1584), which begins by reminding its readers "that in this our Church of England, there hath been a schism for sundry years, which of late is grown so strong, that unless the Lord look upon us in great mercy, it will in short time bring forth a very lamentable desolation" (3). In 1590, in *A Short Treatise Against the Donatists of England, Whome We Call Brownists* (London, 1590), A3v, George Gifford reported that "there are, some say, at the least fifty several sects" in England.

11. In *A Treatise Wherein Dicing, Dauncing, Vaine Playes or Enterluds With Other Idle Pastimes etc. Commonly Used on the Sabboth Day, Are Reproved* (1577?; reprint, ed. Arthur Freeman, New York: Garland, 1974), A1b, the preacher John Northbrook maintains that "there be now so many adulterers, unchaste and lewd persons and idle Rogues" in England only as a result of "naughty education and bringing up"; "such as impute this thing to the new learning and preaching of the gospel are shamefully deceived."

12. Edward Hext (1596), in *Tudor Economic Documents*, ed. R. H. Tawney and Eileen Power (London: Longmans, Green, 1924), 2:341–42; [Richard Verstegan], *A Declaration of the True Causes of the Great Troubles* ([Amsterdam], 1592), 60, 58. King James (1616) himself later declared that "Beggars and Rogues . . . so swarm in every place, that a man cannot go in the streets, nor in the high ways, nor any where for them." Quoted in Dale Randall, *Jonson's Gypsies Unmasked* (Durham, N.C.: Duke University Press, 1975), 55 n. 114. The historian R. H. Tawney's famous remark that the Elizabethans "lived in terror of the tramp" appears in his *The Agrarian Problem in the Sixteenth Century* (London: Longmans, Green,

1912), 268. According to Catholics, the Reformation had spawned these social problems in various ways: by precipitating a general decline in morality and civility; by ruining the monasteries, which had cared for the poor; and by allowing clerical marriage, which on the one hand expanded the population and on the other made it impossible for the clergy to afford the Catholic level of "hospitality for the poor." [Robert Parsons], *An Epistle of the Persecution of Catholickes in Englande*, trans. G. T. (Douay in Artois [Rouen], [1582]), 17.

13. For the apparent increase in vagrancy, see A. L. Beier, *Masterless Men: The Vagrancy Problem in England, 1560–1640* (London: Methuen, 1985), 14–28, and Paul Slack, *Poverty and Policy in Tudor and Stuart England* (London: Longman, 1988), 43–45, 49–50, and 93–94. According to both historians, the major causes of this increase were overpopulation and the displacements resulting from enclosures; but Slack agrees with contemporary assessments that the dissolution of the monasteries and holy orders along with the Protestant attack on voluntary poverty helped worsen the plight of England's poor. *Poverty and Policy*, 13, 206; 23. See also John Pound, *Poverty and Vagrancy in Tudor England*, 2d ed. (London: Longman, 1986), 1–22.

For a recent compendium of traditional claims about the rise of English nationalism, see Liah Greenfeld, *Nationalism: Five Roads to Modernity* (Cambridge, Mass.: Harvard University Press, 1992), 27–87. Like most of her predecessors, Greenfeld has a Whiggish faith in the "uninterrupted" and thus "inevitable" (40) development of English nationalism that blinds her to any social problems or expressions of concern for England's internal integrity during the Renaissance. Nor does this Whiggism allow her to consider any religious stumbling blocks: she maintains that "the affinity between Protestantism and the idea of the nation guaranteed . . . the lack of religious opposition to nationalism" at the time (53). Greenfeld is untraditional, however, in her extreme secularization of the period: she argues, for instance, that by the time of the Revolution "it was the association with nationalism which made religion at all meaningful" (75).

14. John Norden, *A Progress of Piety* (1590–91, 1596) (Cambridge, 1847), 114, 116, 175–76.

15. Ibid., 178.

16. For the history and literature of the Renaissance English belief in a vagabond "underworld," see Frank Aydelotte, *Elizabethan Rogues and Vagabonds* (1913; reprint, New York: Barnes & Noble, 1967); A. V. Judges, *The Elizabethan Underworld* (1930), rev. ed. (London: Routledge & Kegan Paul, 1964); Normand Berlin, *The Base String: The Underworld in Elizabethan Drama* (Rutherford, N.J.: Fairleigh Dickinson University Press, 1968); Beier, *Masterless Men*; and Arthur F. Kinney, ed., *Rogues, Vagabonds and Sturdy Beggars: A New Gallery of Tudor and Early Stuart Rogue Literature* (Amherst: University of Massachusetts Press, 1990).

17. John Awdeley, *The Fraternitie of Vacabondes* (1565), in Kinney, *Rogues*, 91–101; Thomas Harman, *A Caveat for Common Cursitors* (1566), in ibid., 109–53; Thomas Dekker, *Lanthorne and Candle-light* (1608), in ibid., 213–60; [John Webster?], *New and Choise Characters*, by Sir Thomas Overbury, ed. W. J. Paylor (Ox-

ford: Basil Blackwell, 1936), 73 (for Webster's authorship, see xvi–xxiv). In *Martin Mark-all, Beadle of Bridewell* (1610), Samuel Rid observes that Dekker's "volumes and papers" on the rogues are "now spread everywhere"; quoted in Judges, *Elizabethan Underworld*, 386.

18. J. A. Sharpe, *Crime in Early Modern England, 1550–1750* (London: Longman, 1984), 101–3; see also Beier, *Masterless Men*, 57–58, 123–45. For a more qualified position on organized roguery, see Slack, *Poverty and Policy*, 102, and Pound, *Poverty and Vagrancy*, vii–viii; Beier, *Masterless Men*, 91, also notes that there were some large gangs of vagabonds, and that "itinerant tradesfolk . . . showed occupational solidarity." I agree with Pound that there must have been *some* truth to the rogue pamphlets: some organized roguery, some recognizable rogue types, and probably more cant.

19. Robert Greene, *A Notable Discovery of Coosnage* (1591), ed. G. B. Harrison (1922; reprint, New York: Barnes & Noble, 1966), 36.

20. Ibid., 37; Dekker, *Lanthorne*, 213. Cf. *The Defence of Conny catching*, by Cuthbert Cunny-catcher (1592), ed. G. B. Harrison (1922; reprint, New York: Barnes & Noble, 1966), 11–12; and S[amuel]. R[owlands]., *Greenes Ghost Haunting Conie-catchers* (London, 1602), A2b.

21. For touring players regarded as vagrants, see Virginia Crocheron Gildersleeve, *Government Regulation of the Elizabethan Drama* (1908; reprint, New York: Burt Franklin, 1961), 21–31.

22. See, for example, Muriel C. Bradbrook, *The Rise of the Common Player: A Study of Actor and Society in Shakespeare's England* (Cambridge, Mass.: Harvard University Press, 1962), 37–38, and Andrew Gurr, *The Shakespearean Stage, 1574–1642*, 2d ed. (Cambridge: Cambridge University Press, 1980), 28–29. For the text of the 1572 act, see *The Statutes of the Realm* (London, 1810–28), 4:590–98; see also 4:899–902. Cf. T.G., in *The Rich Cabinet furnished with Varietie of Descriptions* (London, 1616): "Player is afraid of the statute, for if he have no better supportation than his profession, he is neither admitted in public, nor if he be a roamer dares justify himself in private, being a flat rogue by the statute." Reprinted in *The English Drama and Stage Under the Tudor and Stuart Princes, 1543–1664*, ed. William Carew Hazlitt (Kensington, 1869), 229. The Oxford scholar who authored a Twelfth-Night play at Oxford in 1603 felt it necessary to begin by asserting, "We are no vagabonds, we are no arrant / Rogues that do run with plays about the country." *Narcissus* (MS 1603), ed. Margaret L. Lee (London, 1893), 5.

23. In his *Second and Third Blast of Retrait from Plaies and Theaters* (1580), Anthony Munday ignores the exclusions of the vagabond statutes: "As for the players in these days which exhibit their games for lucre sake . . . , they are of the most part of men either of authority, or learning held for vagabonds, & infamous persons; they may aptly be likened unto drones, which will not labor to bring in, but live of the labors of the painful gatherers. They are therefore to be thrust out of the Bee-hiue of a Christian Common-weal" (121–22). J. Cocke, in John Stephens's *Satyrical Essayes Characters and Others* (London, 1615), similarly overlooked the distinction, but playing in the permanent theaters seems to have be-

come more reputable than it had been in Munday's time, because an attack by John Webster forced both Stephens and Cocke to backpedal considerably: a second edition of the *Essayes* that same year devoted sixteen prefatory pages to Webster's supposed "mistaking of approved and authorized Actors for [the] counterfeit Runagates, or country Players, inveighed against by the Characterist" (A6v). For other defensive alterations as well as the text of Webster's response, see E. K. Chambers, *The Elizabethan Stage*, 4 vols. (Oxford: Oxford University Press, 1923), 4:255–58.

24. The phrase appears in a posthumously published work by the Elizabethan puritan Thomas Cartwright, *A Confutation of the Rhemists Translation* (London, 1618), 75.

25. For similar pronouncements by officials, see Chambers, *Elizabethan Stage*, 4:307–8, 315–16, 318, 320, 322, and 340.

26. Stephen Gosson, *Markets of Bawdrie: The Dramatic Criticism of Stephen Gosson* (contains *The Schoole of Abuse* [1579], *An Apologie of the Schoole of Abuse* [1579], and *Playes Confuted in Five Actions* [1582]), ed. Arthur F. Kinney (Salzburg: Institut für Englische Sprache und Literatur, Universität Salzburg, 1974), 99.

27. In his *Histrio-mastix* (1633), Wiliam Prynne famously remarks that the licensing system of the Elizabethan vagabond statutes exempted players "only from the punishment, *not from the infamy*, or style of *Rogues and Vagabonds*" (496).

28. Robert Greene, *The Repentance of Robert Greene Maister of Artes* (1592), ed. G. B. Harrison (1922; reprint, New York: Barnes & Noble, 1966), 26.

29. Thomas Dekker, *The Belman of London* (London, 1608).

30. Robert Greene, *A Disputation, Betweene a Hee Conny-catcher, and a Shee Conny-catcher* (1592), ed. G. B. Harrison (1922; reprint, New York: Barnes & Noble, 1966), 40.

31. For rogues compared to players, see Dekker, *Lanthorne*, 228, 240, 244, 247, 250, 251, 252, 254, 255, 256, and 260. Unlike play-rogues, however, the actual rogues reveal themselves only at night: "Now when the stage of the world was hung in black, they jetted up and down like proud *Tragedians*" (258).

32. The practice is reported by the player William Kemp in *Kemps Nine Daies Wonder* (1600), quoted in Bradbrook, *Rise of the Common Player*, 105, in the context of his denying any "acquaintance" with two cutpurses who followed him during his famous dance from Norwich to London. In his *Works*, ed. R. B. McKerrow, 5 vols. (1903–10; reprint, ed. F. P. Wilson, London: Blackwell, 1958), 1:213, Thomas Nashe (1592) claims that "in plays, all cozenages . . . are most lively anatomiz'd." Cf. Henry Chettle in *Kind-Harts Dreame* (1592), where a thieving landlord complains that plays "open our cross-biting, our conny-catching, our trains, our traps, our gins, our snares, our subtleties: for no sooner haue we a trick of deceit, but they make it common, singing Jigs, and making jests of us, that every boy can point out our houses as they pass by" (E3v). In his *Short Apologie of the Schoole of Abuse* (1579), in *Markets of Bawdrie*, 130, Stephen Gosson argues, however, that the open roguery of the player makes him *worse* than other criminals: "A thief is a shrewd member in a common wealth, he empties our bags by

force, these ransack our purses by permission; he spoileth us secretly, these rifle us openly; he gets the upperhand by blows, these by merry jests; he sucks our blood, these our manners: he wounds our body, these our soul."

33. Thomas Middleton and Thomas Dekker, *The Roaring Girl*, ed. Paul Mulholland (Manchester: Manchester University Press, 1987), 5.1.131–32. Although the first English play to offer an extended exposé of the rogue underworld, Dekker's was not the first to be based on the life of an actual rogue; the cutpurse Dick Evans inspired the now-lost *Cutting Dick* (c. 1600). See Arthur Melville Clark, *Thomas Heywood: Playwright and Miscellanist* (1958; reprint, New York: Russell & Russell, 1967), 28–29.

34. In Thomas Dekker, *The Whore of Babylon* (c. 1606), ed. Marianne Gateson Riely (New York: Garland, 1980), 1.2.129–31, the king of the Holy Roman Empire tells Queen Elizabeth's representative in the play, Titania, that she should no longer separate herself from the Catholic church: "The language which she [i.e., the Church] speaks goes through the world / To prove that all the world should stoop to her, / And, save yourself, they do."

35. Again, see my *Empire Nowhere*.

36. I don't mean to distinguish sharply between poets and issues of power on the one hand and players and issues of community on the other. But playing was inherently more communal an activity than writing poetry, and players were therefore more likely than poets to treat issues of community as professionally significant.

37. Christopher Marlowe, *Tamburlaine the Great* (acted c. 1587), ed. J. S. Cunningham (Manchester: Manchester University Press, 1981), 4.1.6. The same speech labels Tamburlaine a "rogue" (4).

38. *The Lamentable Tragedie of Locrine* (c. 1585–94; pub. 1595), ed. Jane Lytton Gooch (New York: Garland, 1981).

39. Although critics have long noted that Shakespeare drew on rogue literature to fashion Edgar's disguise as "poor Tom," they have generally overlooked the same basis for Shakespeare's characterization of Hal, whose ambivalent fraternizing with rogues seems directly modeled on Greene's pamphlet confessions and self-defense. "The odd mad-caps I have been mate to, not as a companion, but as a spy to have an insight into their knaveries, that seeing their trains I might eschew their snares: those mad fellows I learned at last to loath, by their own graceless villainies, and what I saw in them to their confusion, I can forewarn in others to my country's commodity." Greene, *Notable Discovery*, 7–8.

40. Samuel Rowley, *When You See Me, You Know Me* (1604, pub. 1605) (Oxford: Oxford University Press, 1952); Michael Drayton, Richard Hathway, Anthony Munday, and Robert Wilson, *I Sir John Oldcastle* (1599, pub. 1600), in *The Oldcastle Controversy: Sir John Oldcastle, Part 1 and The Famous Victories of Henry V*, ed. Peter Corbin and Douglas Sedge (Manchester: Manchester University Press, 1991), 36–144.

41. According to Henry IV, for instance, "insurrection" never lacks "moody beggars, starving for a time / Of pell-mell havoc and confusion" *Henry IV, Part 1*

5.1.79–82, in *The Riverside Shakespeare*, ed. G. Blakemore Evans et al. (Boston: Houghton Mifflin, 1974). For other contemporary history plays that associate vagabondage with rebellion, see *The Life and Death of Jack Straw* (c. 1590) (Oxford: Oxford University Press for the Malone Society, 1957) and also Shakespeare's *Henry VI, Part 2* (c. 1590–91), in which the "valiant" or sturdy beggar Jack Cade proclaims his ambition to become England's king (4.2).

42. Cuthbert Cunny-catcher, *Defence*, 64. Cuthbert is the first to complain that the rogue detectors are actually wasting their time on a relatively insignificant evil: "We Conny-catchers are like little flies in the grass, which live: or little leaves and do no more harm: whereas there be in England other professions that be great Conny-catchers and caterpillars, that make barren the field wherein they bate" (9). Cf. Rowlands, *Greenes Ghost*, A4b–B1a, and Rid, *Martin Mark-all*, 391–92.

43. John Fletcher (and Philip Massinger?), *Beggars Bush* (c. 1613–22), ed. John H. Dorenkamp (The Hague: Mouton, 1967); Thomas Middleton, Samuel Rowley, John Ford, and Thomas Dekker (?), *The Spanish Gypsy* (1623), ed. Edgar C. Morris (Boston: D. C. Heath, 1908).

44. Anne Barton, *Ben Jonson, Dramatist* (Cambridge: Cambridge University Press, 1984), 205–6.

45. Ben Jonson, *Bartholomew Fair*, ed. C. H. Herford, Percy Simpson, and Evelyn Simpson, in *Ben Jonson*, vol. 6 (Oxford: Oxford University Press, 1938), 1.6.37 and 4.6.106.

46. John Selden, *Table-talk* (1689), ed. Sir Frederick Pollock (London: Quaritch, 1922), 119–20.

47. The definition of a "Neuter," in Johann Wigand, *De Neutralibus et Mediis*, anon. trans. (London, 1562), A6r. In 1625, "Irenaeus Rodoginus" complains that extremists regularly try to stigmatize moderates as "Neutrals, neither *hic*, nor *haec*." See his *Differences in Matters of Religion, Betweene the Easterne and Westerne Churches* (London, 1625), D2r–v.

48. Galatians 3:28 (King James version).

49. John Awdeley, *A Godly Ditty or Prayer to be Song unto God for the Preservation of His Church, Our Queene and Realme, Against All Traytours, Rebels, and Papisticall Enemies* (London, [1569?]); *The Cruel Assault of Gods Fort* (London, [c. 1560]); and *The Wonders of England* (London, [1559]).

50. Even the archbishop of Canterbury, John Whitgift, fell victim to the smear of vagrancy. Martin Marprelate caustically referred to him as his Grace of Cant. or John of Cant., as in the phrase (and roguish characterization) "let John Cant. cast his cards and consider." See William Pierce, ed., *The Marprelate Tracts: 1588, 1589* (London: James Clarke, 1911), 123. In return, an antimartinist tract spread a rumor that while "wandering . . . in the manner of a *Gipson* [i.e., gypsy], for that he would not be known, [Martin] was taken, and truss'd up for a rogue." *Martins Months Mind* (London, 1589), E1v.

51. Awdeley, *Godly Ditty* and *Fraternitie*, 92.

52. The most influential work to turn the traditional polemic against monks and friars into an attack on the Catholic clergy generally was Simon Fish's *A Sup-*

*plicacyon For the Beggers* (c. 1529). Fish maintained that the Catholics were "another sort" of beggar from the "impotent" and therefore deserving poor: they were "strong, puissant, and counterfeit holy, and idle, beggars and vagabonds" who had "craftily crept" into England and had now grown "not only into a great number, but also into a kingdom" of their own (1).

53. Meredith Hanmer, *The Jesuites Banner* (London, 1581), ☞ 2a, C1b. Addressing the House of Commons in 1581, Sir Walter Mildmay characterized the Jesuits as "a rabble of vagrant friars newly sprung up and coming through the world to trouble the Church of God; whose principal errand is, by creeping into the houses and familiarities of men of behavior and reputation, not only to corrupt the realm with false doctrine, but also, under that pretense, to stir sedition." Quoted in Sir John E. Neale, *Elizabeth I and Her Parliaments, 1559–1581* (1958; reprint, New York: Norton, 1966), 383–84. In *The Plea of the Innocent* (London, 1602), 108, the puritan Josias Nichols referred to the Jesuits as "these vagabond and roguing Priests." In his *Answere to a Letter of a Jesuited Gentleman* (London, 1601), 118, the loyalist Catholic Anthony Copley called them "Ubiquitaries," who "range lawless over all, regarding neither Prince nor people, friend nor stranger, grace nor nature, but only to serve their own turns, and maintain their own common-wealth."

54. *Lanthorne*, 216. The closest a rogue writer comes to identifying the rogues with religious dissidents is an exception that proves the rule. In *Martin Mark-all* (1610), Samuel Rid imagines that his fellow detectors have put such pressure on England's rogues that the rogues have decided to emigrate to a vagabond utopia—"Thievigen," which Rid borrows from Joseph Hall's *Mundus Alter et Idem* (1605). Located near the South Pole, Thievigen, Rid explains, is filled with such misfits as "your idle vagabonds that after war will betake themselves to no honest course of life . . . , but especially seditious and rebellious subjects in a commonwealth, schismatical and heretical seducers in the Church, as Brownists, Papists, Jesuits, and suchlike." Judges, *Elizabethan Underworld*, 403. Yet even in this fictive and distanced setting, the rogues and the schismatics are merely compared, not conflated.

55. This transformation has been overlooked by the play's most influential reader in recent years, Jean-Christophe Agnew, who claims, in *Worlds Apart: The Market and the Theater in Anglo-American Thought, 1550–1750* (Cambridge: Cambridge University Press, 1986), 119–21, that the Induction to *Bartholomew Fair* heralds the alliance between two secularizing forces, the theater and the marketplace. In their *Politics and Poetics of Transgression* (London: Methuen, 1986), Peter Stallybrass and Allon White argue instead that "the very notion of contract which the Induction proposes is subverted in the play which follows" (70), but they do not believe that the play recommends any alternative to contractual social relations other than a "grotesque, saturnalian" one (71).

56. Richard Brome, *A Jovial Crew: or, The Merry Beggars* (c. 1641), ed. Ann Haaker (Lincoln: University of Nebraska Press, 1968).

57. Ben Jonson, *The Gypsies Metamorphosed* (*A Masque of the Metamorphosed*

*Gypsies*, 1621), in *Ben Jonson: The Complete Masques*, ed. Stephen Orgel (New Haven, Conn.: Yale University Press, 1969), 316–73. For a good introduction to the masque, see Randall, *Jonson's Gypsies Unmasked*. As Randall notes, Jonson's "Egyptians" are counterfeit: the Patrico speaks of using "the noble confection / Of walnuts and hog's grease" to change his "complexion" (1120–22).

58. In his dedication to the first edition of *A Jovial Crew* (1652), Brome states that the play "had the luck to tumble last of all in the epidemical ruin of the scene" (26–27). In *The Jacobean and Caroline Stage* (Oxford: Oxford University Press, 1956), 3:71–72, G. E. Bentley argues that Brome means the play "was performed on the last day the company acted before they were suppressed by Parliament's order, 2 September 1642."

59. On the more absolute nationalism that accompanied the civil wars, see Hans Kohn, "The Genesis of English Nationalism," *Journal of the History of Ideas* 1 (1940): 69–94; and Greenfeld, *Nationalism*, 40–41 and 73–78.

60. For the "Ordinance of the Lords and Commons against Stage-plays and Interludes" (September 2, 1642), see Hazlitt, *English Drama and Stage*, 63; for the ordinances against players (October 22, 1647; February 9, 1648), see 64–67. One contemporary news-book claimed that the members of Parliament felt "*Plays* must be lash't down, / For fear themselves be *whipt* about the *Town*." Quoted in Hyder Rollins, "A Contribution to the History of the English Commonwealth Drama," *Studies in Philology* 18 (1921): 291.

## Norris: The (Lethal) Turn of the Twentieth Century

1. Patrick J. Sloyan, "U.S. Tank-Plows Said to Bury Thousands of Iraqis," *Los Angeles Times*, September 12, 1991, A1.

2. John H. Cushman Jr., "Pentagon Seems Vague on Iraqi's Death Toll," *New York Times*, February 3, 1991, K10.

3. Elaine Scarry, "Introduction," in *Literature and the Body: Essays on Populations and Persons*, ed. Elaine Scarry (New York: Oxford University Press, 1988), ix.

4. Frances Ferguson, "Malthus, Godwin, Wordsworth, and the Spirit of Solitude," in Scarry, *Literature and the Body*, 113.

5. Susan Jeffords, "Rape and Resolution in Bosnia" (paper given at "A Day of Peace," May 15, 1993, University of California, Irvine), 13.

6. Ibid., 18.

7. Ferguson, "Spirit of Solitude," 106.

8. Matthew Arnold, *Culture and Anarchy*, ed. J. Dover Wilson (Cambridge: Cambridge University Press, 1971), 203.

9. Fredric Jameson, "'Ulysses' in History," in *James Joyce and Modern Literature*, ed. W. J. McCormack and Alistair Stead (Boston: Routledge & Kegan Paul, 1982), 134.

10. Marjorie Perloff, *The Futurist Moment* (Chicago: University of Chicago Press, 1986), xxi.

11. F. T. Marinetti, "The Founding and Manifesto of Futurism 1909," in *Futurist Manifestos*, ed. Umbro Apollonio (London: Thames & Hudson, 1973), 22.

12. Wyndham Lewis, ed., *Blast 2* (Santa Barbara, Calif.: Black Sparrow Press, 1981), 33.

13. John Tytell, *Ezra Pound: The Solitary Volcano* (New York: Anchor Press, 1987), 119.

14. Paul Fussell, *The Great War and Modern Memory* (London: Oxford University Press, 1977), 13.

15. Martin Stephen, *Never Such Innocence* (London: Buchan & Enright Publishers, 1988), 6.

16. Ezra Pound, *Personae: The Collected Shorter Poems of Ezra Pound* (New York: New Directions, 1971), 190.

17. William M. Chace, *The Political Identities of Ezra Pound & T. S. Eliot* (Stanford: Stanford University Press, 1973), 44.

18. *Oxford Book of Modern Verse 1892–1935*, ed. William Butler Yeats (New York: Oxford University Press, 1937).

19. Tytell, *Ezra Pound*, 120.

20. Wyndham Lewis, *Blasting and Bombardiering* (London: Eyre & Spottiswoode, 1937), 182.

21. Gwynne Dyer, *War* (New York: Crown, 1985), 84, 96.

22. Elaine Scarry, *The Body in Pain* (New York: Oxford University Press, 1985).

23. Walter Benn Michaels, "The Souls of White Folk," in Scarry, *Literature and the Body*, 185.

24. John W. Dower, *War Without Mercy: Race and Power in the Pacific War* (New York: Pantheon Books, 1986), 7.

25. Benedict Anderson, *Imagined Communities* (London: Verso, 1983), 6.

26. Dower, *War Without Mercy*, 11.

27. "Fitzwater's Remarks: 'Loss of Civilian Lives is Truly Tragic,'" *Los Angeles Times*, February 11, 1991, A15.

28. Allan Nairn, "When Casualties Don't Count," *The Progressive*, May 1991, 16.

29. Edward W. Said, *Covering Islam* (New York: Pantheon Books, 1981), xiii.

30. Holly Burkhalter, "Some Bodies Don't Count," *Los Angeles Times*, March 12, 1991, B11.

31. "How Many Iraqi Soldiers Died?" *Time*, June 17, 1991, A4.

### Behdad: Border INSpection

My choice of the topic of border inspection has to do with a desire to address our own late-twentieth-century anxiety about the figure of the "illegal alien." The nineteenth century's end was marked with a profound anxiety about the disappearing exotic, the blurring of the "civilized" and the "primitive," the "modern" and the traditional—issues that I address in my *Belated Travelers* (Durham: Duke

University Press, 1994)—our century is ending with new fears about the blurring of borders and boundaries, the "intrusion" of the "threatening immigrant," and the emergence of the exclusionary discourse of immigration. Given the proliferation of anxious literature about these issues, I felt a sense of critical urgency to address some of these current predicaments. Living in California and speaking first about this topic in Texas, states where the everyday issues of border and immigration haunt the popular consciousness, I could not but feel intellectually responsible to broach these collective fears and cultural anxieties that have produced what I call "the politics of exclusion" at the turn of this century. I wish to thank Larry Reynolds, Shawn Maurer, and Robert Newman for inviting me to the extremely stimulating conference at Texas A&M University where I presented an earlier form of this essay.

1. Every traveler entering U.S. territory is inspected by a primary inspector who examines the traveler's entry documents—such as passport, Resident Alien Card, and so on. If the primary inspector suspects that the traveler is not eligible to enter the United States, then he or she refers that traveler for secondary inspection, which may involve anything from further standard questions about the person's intention for traveling to the United States to a baggage and body search.

2. The quotation is James Clifford's (see "Traveling Cultures," in *Cultural Studies*, ed. Lawrence Grossberg, Cary Nelson, and Paula Treichler [New York: Routledge, 1992], 109), but the idea is shared by many cultural and literary critics. For a discussion of travel as a privileged *trope*, see my "Traveling To Teach: Postcolonial Critics in the American Academy," in *Race, Identity, and Representation in Education*, ed. Cameron McCarthy and Warren Crichlow (New York: Routledge, 1993), 40–41.

3. bell hooks, "Representing Whiteness in the Black Imagination," in *Cultural Studies*, 343.

4. For a brief discussion of this approach, see Michel Foucault's "Two Lectures," in *Power/Knowledge: Selected Interviews and Other Writings 1972–1977*, ed. Colin Gordon (New York: Pantheon Books, 1980), 78–108.

5. This point is also made by Janet A. Gilboy, who demonstrates how the agency's concerns and responsibilities shape the nature of categorization and practical decision making. See "Deciding Who Gets In: Decisionmaking by Immigration Inspectors," *Law & Society Review* 25, no. 3 (1991): 571–99.

6. I disagree with Gilboy's claim that the categorization of travelers into types by immigration inspectors is a function of organizational knowledge and institutional criteria. I counter that such categorization is just as likely to be a function of cultural prejudice.

7. Michel Foucault, *Discipline and Punish: The Birth of the Prison*, trans. Alan Sheridan (New York: Vintage Books, 1977), 139.

8. *Customs Today* 27, no. 3 (summer 1992): 16–18.

9. Perhaps one could even argue that immigration control depends on a certain level of what Foucault calls "useful delinquency" and "controlled illegality"

as effects of its functioning for it to justify not only its institutional significance as a "political observatory" but also its discriminatory mode of regulation.

## Arata: Strange Cases, Common Fates

1. Robert Buchanan, "The Voice of the Hooligan," *Contemporary Review* 26 (1899): 776–77.

2. See Geoffrey Pearson, *Hooligan: A History of Respectable Fears* (New York: Schocken, 1984), esp. 69–75. In 1885 Dr. James Cantlie of Charing Cross Hospital argued that a distinct form of degenerative illness—he proposed calling the condition "urbomorbus"—was endemic to lower-class urban life. See *Degeneration Amongst Londoners: A Lecture Delivered at the Parkes Museum of Hygiene* (London: Field & Tuer, 1885), 24. See also J. Milner Fothergill, *The Town Dweller: His Needs and Wants* (London: H. K. Lewis, 1889).

3. Buchanan, "Voice of the Hooligan," 777.

4. Robert Buchanan, "The Fleshly School of Poetry: Mr. D. G. Rossetti," *Contemporary Review* 18 (1871): 335–37.

5. Barbara Spackman, *Decadent Genealogies: The Rhetoric of Sickness from Baudelaire to D'Annunzio* (Ithaca, N.Y.: Cornell University Press, 1989), 1.

6. Buchanan, "Fleshly School," 340, 338.

7. Buchanan, "Voice of the Hooligan," 783.

8. On Morel's importance, see Daniel Pick, *Faces of Degeneration: A European Disorder, ca. 1848–1918* (Cambridge: Cambridge University Press, 1989), 44–59, 189–201; and Robert A. Nye, *Crime, Madness, and Politics in Modern France: The Medical Concept of National Decline* (Princeton, N.J.: Princeton University Press, 1984), 121–26. Oscar Wilde usefully discusses the status of the term "morbidity" in late-Victorian cultural criticism in "The Soul of Man Under Socialism" (1891), in *The Artist as Critic: Critical Writings of Oscar Wilde*, ed. Richard Ellmann (Chicago: University of Chicago Press, 1968), 274–76.

In its reliance on the opposition between "normative" and "deviant" structures, degeneration theory takes its place alongside other life sciences in the nineteenth century. As Michel Foucault has demonstrated, the life sciences depended largely on the primacy of the body as an organizing metaphor. Foucault has argued for the emergence in the late eighteenth century of the "medicalized" body: the body as mapped by practitioners of the newly ascendant life sciences. Where disease had once been defined in mechanical terms as a punitive attack on the body from without, it later came to be seen as a process inherent within the living organism. Disease diverted the organism from its "normal" state, meaning that the study of disease required first that the normative healthy body be identified. The binary opposition of health and sickness corresponded to an opposition of the normal and the pathological, and it was this fundamental dichotomy that came to structure thought in all the human sciences. "The prestige of the sciences of life," Foucault argues, derived in part from "the comprehensive, transferable character of biological concepts" and in part from "the fact that these concepts were arranged in a space whose profound structure responded to the healthy/ morbid opposition. When one spoke of the life of groups and societies, of the life of the race, or even of the 'psychological life,' one did not think first of the internal structure of *the organized being*, but of the *medical bipolarity of the normal and the pathological*. Consciousness lives because it can be altered, maimed, diverted from its course, paralyzed; societies live because there are sick, declining societies and healthy, expanding ones; the race is a living being that one can see degenerating; and civilizations, whose deaths have so often been remarked on, are also, therefore, living beings." See Foucault, *The Birth of the Clinic: An Archaeology of Medical Perception*, trans. A. M. Sheridan Smith (New York: Vintage, 1975), 34–35. Also apposite are Foucault's discussion of degeneration in *The History of Sexuality, Vol. 1*, trans. Robert Hurley (New York: Vintage, 1980), 116–20, and Georges Canguilhem, *The Normal and the Pathological* (New York: Zone, 1991).

9. Arthur Waugh, "Reticence in Literature," *The Yellow Book* 1 (1894): 217.

10. Buchanan, "Fleshly School," 340.

11. Nye, *Crime, Madness, and Politics*, 119.

12. Pick, *Faces of Degeneration*, 8.

13. On the uses of degeneration theory across a wide variety of late-Victorian disciplines, see the essays collected in Sander Gilman and J. E. Chamberlin, eds., *Degeneration: The Dark Side of Progress* (New York: Columbia University Press, 1985).

14. Antonio Gramsci, "Notes for an Introduction and an Approach to the Study of Philosophy of the History of Culture," in *An Antonio Gramsci Reader: Selected Writings 1916–1935*, ed. David Forgacs (New York: Schocken, 1984), 343. Further page references to this essay are given parenthetically in the text.

15. *Report of the Interdepartmental Committee on Physical Deterioration* (London, 1904), esp. iii, 13–14, 34–38; Michel Foucault, *Language, Counter-memory, Practice: Selected Essays and Interviews*, ed. Donald F. Bouchard (Ithaca, N.Y.: Cornell University Press, 1977), 154. In his otherwise useful *Idols of Perversity: Fantasies of Feminine Evil in Fin-de-Siècle Culture* (Oxford: Oxford University Press, 1988), Bram Dijkstra makes the unhelpful assertion that degeneration theory contributed solely to the "idealization of . . . white males and the concomitant assumption that somehow all others were degenerate" (160).

16. Arthur Symons, "The Decadent Movement in Literature" (1893), in *Aesthetes and Decadents of the 1890s: An Anthology of British Poetry and Prose*, ed. Karl Beckson, rev. ed. (Chicago: Academy Chicago Publishers, 1982), 135–36.

17. Eugene S. Talbot, *Degeneracy: Its Causes, Signs, and Results* (London: Walter Scott, 1898), 161–362.

18. Henry Maudsley, *Life in Mind and Conduct: Studies of the Organic in Human Nature* (London: Macmillan, 1902), 54.

19. J. Simms, *Physiognomy Illustrated* (1872), quoted in Pick, *Faces of Degeneration*, 52.

20. Bram Stoker, *Dracula* (1897; reprint, Harmondsworth: Penguin, 1979), 28–29.

21. Ibid., 406. Harker's descriptions also emphasize the Count's aristocratic features and bearing: aquiline nose, thin mouth and lips, domed forehead, and haughty demeanor. Even his hands initially strike Harker as "white and fine" (28). As we will see, associating degenerate traits with both the upper and the lower classes is one mark of degeneration theory's status as a middle-class discourse.

22. Robert Reid Rentoul, *Race Culture; or, Race Suicide (A Plea for the Unborn)* (London: Walter Scott, 1906), ix.

23. Under the rubric of "cerebral stigmata," for instance, Talbot gathered a diverse collection of phenomena, which he subdivided into categories like sensory degeneracy (deaf-mutism, color blindness, olfactory abnormalities), intellectual degeneracy (paranoia, insanity, hysteria, epilepsy, idiocy, "one-sided genius"), and ethical degeneracy (crime, prostitution, sexual perversion, drunkenness, pauperism). Under the same umbrella, W. Duncan McKim listed such "vexing conditions" as "the morbid fear of pins or broken glass . . . the dread of very large or small places, of crowded assemblies, of the dark, of being buried alive; . . . the impulse to count, to buy for the sake of buying, to hoard, to steal, to burn, to kill, to take one's own life." See Talbot, *Degeneracy*, 37, and W. Duncan McKim, *Heredity and Human Progress* (New York: G. P. Putnam's Sons, 1900), 47.

24. Quoted in Talbot, *Degeneracy*, 23.

25. Alexander Welsh, *Strong Representations: Narrative and Circumstantial Evidence in England* (Baltimore, Md.: Johns Hopkins University Press, 1992), esp. 1–42, 152–84.

26. See Talbot, *Degeneracy*, esp. 33–37.

27. Henry Maudsley, *Body and Will: Being an Essay Concerning Will in its Metaphysical, Physiological, and Pathological Aspects* (New York: D. Appleton, 1884), 32.

28. Walter Bagehot, *Physics and Politics; or, Thoughts on the Application of the Principles of "Natural Selection" and "Inheritance" to Political Society* (New York: D. Appleton, 1873), 2. Further page references to this work are given parenthetically in the text.

29. Ernest Renan, "What is a Nation?" (1882), in *Nation and Narration*, ed. Homi K. Bhabha (London: Routledge, 1990), 19.

30. Indeed, we can usefully compare Bagehot's definition with Shelley's discussion of imitation in the preface to *Prometheus Unbound* (1819) for the contrast it affords: "It is impossible that any one who inhabits the same age with such writers as those who stand in the foremost ranks of our own, can conscientiously assure himself, that his language and tone of thought may not have been modified by the study of the productions of those extraordinary intellects. It is true, that, not the spirit of their genius, but the forms in which it has manifested itself, are due, less to the peculiarities of their own minds, than to the peculiarity of the moral and intellectual condition of the minds among which they have been produced. Thus a number of writers possess the form, whilst they want the spirit of those whom, it is alleged, they imitate; because the former is the endowment of the age in which they live, and the latter must be the uncommunicated lightning of their

own mind." It is precisely the distinction between form and spirit that Bagehot erases, claiming instead that the spirit of any individual utterance is in fact determined by the form or style in which it finds expression. For the Shelley quotation, see *Shelley's Poetry and Prose*, ed. Donald H. Reiman and Sharon B. Powers (New York: Norton, 1977), 134.

31. Christopher Herbert, *Culture and Anomie: Ethnographic Imagination in the Nineteenth Century* (Chicago: University of Chicago Press, 1991), 141. As is apparent, my discussion of Bagehot is indebted to Herbert's suggestive reading of *Physics and Politics*. See esp. 128–49.

32. Edwin Ray Lankester, *Degeneration: A Chapter in Darwinism* (London: Macmillan, 1880), 59–60.

33. Maudsley, *Body and Will*, 321.

34. Ibid., 327.

35. Janet E. Hogarth, "Literary Degenerates," *Forthnightly Review*, n.s., 57 (1895): 586–92.

36. Max Nordau, *Degeneration* (1892; reprint, Lincoln: University of Nebraska Press, 1993), 17. Further page references to this work are given parenthetically in the text.

37. George Bernard Shaw, *The Sanity of Art: An Exposure of the Current Nonsense About Artists Being Degenerate* (1896; reprint, London: New Age Press, 1908), 17.

38. On this subject Nordau agrees with his contemporary Gustave Le Bon. In his study of crowds, Le Bon argued that groups of people "think" only through the "words and images" of others. Incapable of independent reasoning, they allow themselves to be formed by the strong rhetoric of their leaders. More often than not, however, the power of persuasion is an attribute of degenerate individuals, those "morbidly nervous, excitable, half-deranged persons who are bordering on madness." See Le Bon, *The Crowd: A Study of the Popular Mind* (London: T. Fisher Unwin, 1896), 34, 136.

39. "The Case of Wagner," in *Basic Writings of Nietzsche*, ed. Walter Kaufmann (New York: Modern Library, 1968), 626–27. The following quotations can be found on 613.

40. On the rise of aggressive interpretation in this period, see Allon White, *The Uses of Obscurity* (London: Routledge, 1981). On the professionalization of literary studies, see Gerald Graff, *Professing Literature: An Institutional History* (Chicago: University of Chicago Press, 1987), and Chris Baldick, *The Social Mission of English Criticism* (Oxford: Oxford University Press, 1983). Frank Kermode examines how the practice of hermeneutics is structured by professional protocols in "Institutional Control of Interpretation," in *The Art of Telling: Essays on Fiction* (Cambridge: Harvard University Press, 1983), 168–84.

41. See W. J. Reader, *Professional Men: The Rise of the Professional Classes in Nineteenth-Century England* (New York: Basic Books, 1966); Magali Sarfatti Larson, *The Rise of Professionalism* (Berkeley: University of California Press, 1977); and Andrew Abbott, *The System of Professions* (Chicago: University of Chicago Press, 1988).

## Mizruchi: Neighbors, Strangers, Corpses

1. W. E. B. Du Bois, *The Souls of Black Folk*, ed. John Hope Franklin (New York: Avon Books, 1965), 352–53. Subsequent references to this edition will be included parenthetically in the text.

2. See Samuel Preston and Michael Haines, *The Fatal Years: Child Mortality in Late-Nineteenth-Century America* (Princeton: Princeton University Press, 1991), who point out that the key variable in child mortality statistics was rural versus urban life, and cite Du Bois (*The Philadelphia Negro*) in support of their claim for the negative effects of Black "progress" (from farm to city) in the early modern period. Blacks in urban areas, they contend, "were subjected to many of the same mortality hazards as foreign immigrants to cities. But . . . were essentially beyond the pale of the social programs and settlement houses that were designed to ease the transition for immigrants to a new land" (94–95). They attribute the high rates of child mortality among Blacks to their isolation within populated areas: "Race was a caste-like status in 1900, and the degraded social and economic circumstances of blacks, who had virtually no chance of entering the mainstream of American life, is undoubtedly reflected in their exceptionally high mortality" (210). In general, "people furthest from the reach of the modern state—and furthest from one another—enjoyed the best health conditions." The modern state at this point in its history knew how to bring people together to their detriment, but had yet to achieve "the technical and social triumphs" that would reduce the risks of that association. Having neighbors in this period was costly.

3. Letter to Abiah Root, January 12, 1846, in *The Collected Letters of Emily Dickinson*, ed. Thomas H. Johnson (Cambridge, Mass.: Harvard University Press, 1958), 1:24.

4. Ibid., 24, 22.

5. Hopkins and Wells are quoted by Hazel Carby, "On the Threshold of Woman's Era: Lynching, Empire, and Sexuality in Black Feminist Theory," in *Race, Writing, and Difference*, ed. Henry Louis Gates (Chicago: University of Chicago Press, 1985), 310, 308.

6. See Martin S. Pernick, *A Calculus of Suffering: Pain, Professionalism, and Anesthesia in Nineteenth-Century America* (New York: Columbia University Press, 1985).

7. See, for example, the reference in *Souls* to "a color-prejudice that classes Phyllis Wheatley and Sam Hose in the same despised class" (336) or his observation from *The Negro American Family* (New York: Arno and the *New York Times*, 1909), that "few modern groups show greater internal differentiation of social conditions than the Negro American, and the failure to realize this is the cause of much confusion."

8. Frederick Hoffman, *Race Traits and Tendencies of the American Negro* (New York: Macmillan, 1896), 246–49.

9. Frederick Hoffman, *A History of the Prudential Life Insurance Company* (Newark, N.J.: Prudential Press, 1900) and *Pauper Burials and the Internment of the Dead in Large Cities* (Newark, N.J.: Prudential Press, 1917).

10. Du Bois's review appeared in *Publications of the American Academy of Political Science* (January 1897).

11. W. I. Thomas, "The Psychology of Race Prejudice," *The American Journal of Sociology* 9 (March 1904): 599.

12. These are drawn from Victor Turner's work on color symbolism in Ndembu ritual, quoted in *Sacrifice*, ed. M. F. C. Bourdillon and Meyer Fortes (New York: Academic Press, 1980), 21–22.

13. Robert Hertz, *The Collective Representation of Death*, trans. Rodney and Claudia Needham (Aberdeen, U.K.: University Press of Aberdeen), 76, 85.

14. Thomas, "Psychology of Race Prejudice," 600–604.

15. Hertz, *Collective Representation of Death*; W. E. Roth "Burial Customs and Disposal of the Dead," *North Queensland Ethnography Bulletin*, no. 9 (July 1907): 363–403; Nathaniel Shaler, *The Individual: A Study of Life and Death* (New York: D. Appleton, 1900); Newbell Niles Puckett, *Folk Beliefs of the Southern Negro* (1926; Montclair, N.J.: Patterson Smith, 1968).

16. Quoted in James Farrell, *Inventing the American Way of Death* (Philadelphia: Temple University Press, 1980), 69.

17. Charles Ellwood, review of *The Color Line: A Brief On Behalf of the Unborn*, by William Benjamin Smith, *The American Journal of Sociology* 11 (November 1905): 574.

18. Shaler, *The Individual*, 219.

19. Max Scheler, *The Nature of Sympathy*, trans. Peter Heath, ed. Werner Stark (Hamden, Conn.: Archon Books, 1970), 12–13.

20. Ibid., 263. I draw upon the work of Scheler, the era's foremost theorist of sympathy, because of the importance of this category for Du Bois in this period. Scheler's treatment of sympathy and the emotions represents a German tradition of critical sociology that seems especially compatible with Du Bois's thinking. Like Du Bois, Scheler is alert to the mixed consequences of increased contact among human kinds, as revealed by this sample from his book on sympathy: "The growth of social relations among nations and infra-national groups, and the increased solidarity of their interests, have not accentuated the heteropathic responses, as such, for all their effect upon our capacities for understanding. But the enrichment of understanding due to the greater intimacy of human contact has provided these responses with far more varied material. They have become, in consequence, unusually *diversified*, though the diversity extends to the *negatively* valuable as well as to the *positive*. In the course of its history, civilization has given rise to quite new forms of cruelty, brutality, envy, malice, etc. which never previously existed. Closer contacts and increased solidarity of interests have brought new 'vices' as well as new 'virtues,' in their train" (134). Any reader of Scheler must be struck by the work's eclecticism: a blend of Catholicism, socialism, and a critical sociology that anticipated the Frankfurt School. Scheler's own term for it was "the philosophy of the open hand." He was fascinated with the topics of ethnicity, cultural difference, and intolerance, an undercurrent of all his

writings, but perhaps most directly evident in his response to the first world war, *Der Genius des Krieges und der deutsche Krieg* (1915). His dominant intellectual concern was the role of the emotions as social forces. In the 1922 preface to his book on sympathy, Scheler mentions his intent to write on all of the major emotions, including "The Nature of Shame," "The Nature of Apprehension and Fear," and "The Nature of the Sense of Honour." His relatively early death (in 1928, at 54) prevented all but the book on sympathy and the book *Ressentiment*, published in 1912. Significantly, another projected study, first mentioned in 1912, elaborated in 1916, but never completed or published, was titled (in its final permutation) *Vom Sinn des Todes*.

21. Quoted in Robert Park, *The Crowd and the Public* (1904), ed. Henry Elsner (Chicago: University of Chicago Press, 1972), 32–33.

22. F. H. Giddings, *The Principles of Sociology* (New York: Macmillan, 1896), xiii–xiv.

23. A more recent example of the border text is *The Bell Curve* (New York: Free Press, 1994), by Richard Herrnstein and Charles Murray. As these examples show, part of the border text's appeal is its politically controversial nature.

24. Nathaniel Shaler, *The Neighbor: The Natural History of Human Contacts* (Boston: Houghton, Mifflin, 1904), 30–32. By the time he taught Du Bois, Shaler's reputation as a writer on racial topics was well established. They published in many of the same journals (*The Atlantic Monthly* and *The Independent*, for example), sometimes in the same issue. When Du Bois proclaims in his article "Is Race Friction Between Blacks and Whites in the United States Growing and Inevitable?" *The American Journal of Sociology* 13 (March 1908): 834–38, that "the world is shrinking together, it is finding itself neighbor to itself in strange, almost magic degree" it is difficult not to hear an echo of his teacher's book. *The Neighbor* is listed in the bibliography of Du Bois's edited volume, *The Negro American Artisan*, Atlantic University Publications, no. 17 (Atlanta, Ga.: Atlanta University, 1912), 14. And see W. Robertson Smith, *Lectures on the Religion of the Semites* (1889; New York: Ktav Publishing House, 1969), 437 and passim. Smith emphasizes that belief in the "sacred purposes" of the sacrificial skin predominated "at the stage of religious development in which the god, his worshippers, and the victim were all members of one kindred" (435–36).

25. Orlando Patterson, *Slavery and Social Death* (Cambridge, Mass.: Harvard University Press, 1982), 46–47.

26. Shaler, *Neighbor*, 196–97; 327–30.

27. Ralph Ellison, review of *The White Dilemma* by Gunnar Myrdal, in *The Death of White Sociology*, ed. Joyce Ladner (New York: Vintage, 1973), 82–83.

28. W. E. B. Du Bois, *The Negro in Business*, Atlanta University Publications, no. 4 (Atlanta, Ga.: Atlanta University, 1899), 14.

29. See Douglas S. Massey, *American Apartheid* (Cambridge, Mass.: Harvard University Press, 1993).

30. Stanley Lieberson, *A Piece of the Pie: Blacks and White Immigrants Since*

*1880* (Berkeley: University of California Press, 1980), 365. In a 1911 retrospective on the Emancipation era for a British audience, Du Bois makes plain "the economic core" of the decline in Black status through the period, which he calls, "renewed slavery by force and use of the courts." Black disenfranchisement, the construction of labor laws to facilitate imprisonment for debt and for leaving an employer, the neglect of Black schools, were so many means of ensuring "a backward step in the organization of labor such as no modern nation would dare to take in the broad daylight of present economic thought." W. E. B. Du Bois, "The Economics of Negro Emancipation in the United States," *The Sociological Review* 4 (1911): 310.

31. My use of the term is derived from Patterson's *Slavery and Social Death*.

32. See Du Bois, *Souls*, 267, and *Dusk of Dawn*, in *Du Bois: Writings*, ed. Nathan Huggins (New York: Library of America, 1986), 678.

33. The sociologist Lester Ward, for example, anticipates a "composite photograph" of "the great united world-race" of the future, with non-Aryan features reduced to a feminized "softening influence," in "Social Differentiation and Integration," *The American Journal of Sociology* 8 (May 1903): 733. Ward's prediction seems eerily fulfilled ninety years later by a *Time* magazine special issue, "The New Face of America" (fall, 1993), which features a computer-generated composite of "the kind of offspring that might result from seven men and seven women of various ethnic and racial backgrounds." Presented, according to its editors, "in the spirit of fun and experiment," the image seems remarkably free of all but the most muted of non-Caucasion attributes.

34. I am indebted here to Eric Sundquist's interpretation of *Souls* in *To Wake the Nations* (Cambridge, Mass.: Harvard University Press, 1993), see especially 490–539. The Songs were published in the following forms, *Hampton and Its Students*, ed. M. F. Armstrong and Helen Ludlow, with songs arranged by Thomas Fenner (New York: Putnam, 1874), and J. B. T. Marsh, *The Story of the Jubilee Singers with Their Songs* (Boston: Houghton Mifflin, 1872). See also Lawrence Levine, *Black Culture and Black Consciousness* (New York: Oxford University Press, 1977), 17–55, 159–70, and Houston Baker's fascinating account of *Souls* as a "singing book," in *Modernism and the Harlem Renaissance* (Chicago: University of Chicago Press, 1987), 58–68.

35. One of Du Bois's fullest contemporary prophecies of a worldwide culture of color was his response in the 1908 *AJS* debate on "Race Friction." There he describes the increasing prominence and self-awareness of the world's darker nations and rejects extinctionist and assimilationist arguments, asserting the inevitability of racial cohabitation across the globe. He replaces the vague problematic of the heart with the hard logic of bodies and numbers. Alternately imaged as "the darker two thirds" of the world, or "the mass of dark serfs and slaves," the world's colored populations will neither dwindle away, nor recede into decorative coloration in some world composite photograph of the future. Rather they will be prime contenders in the creation of a "new commerce" and "new humanity." For the full citation of this debate see note 24.

36. For those of my readers who remain unpersuaded by what may seem an unduly morbid characterization of attitudes toward Blacks at the turn of the century, let me offer the example of a postmodern drama set in this period, *The America Play*. I came upon it by chance after considerable research on this subject, and was struck by its conviction of the centrality of death in Black American life. The play tells the story of a Black gravedigger who resembles Abraham Lincoln and spends his life impersonating "the Great Man" in a variety of commercial ventures, from stage assassinations ("pay a penny . . . and shoot 'Mr. Lincoln'") to recitations of presidential addresses. The enormous ambition of Parks's design is evident from a brief summary of her themes: the collective struggle to master a national history of violence through the ritualization of violent acts (as in the portrayal of the Lincoln assassination caught in the perverse repetition compulsion of marketplace histrionics); the disappearance of the American past and its reinscription as a leisure industry ("theme park" and tawdry museum comprised of summer tourism's souvenirs); Moynihan's matriarchal Black family (of the absent father and mother who "gived intuh him on everything"); the cliché of Black culture's arrested development, its needing somehow to "catch up" to the dominant culture, with the revisionary hint that history might sometime soon be reconceived from the perspective of "the lesser knowns" with the "Great Men" playing "catch up" to them. But the heart of the play is its portrait of a Black American culture steeped in the rituals of death and mourning. When the Black mother hands her son his father's spade in the scene in act 2, titled "Spadework," the ironic doubling of tool and appellation (the handing of a spade to a "spade") confirms an indelible legacy. In the isolated, surrealist world of *The America Play*, gravedigging, mourning, and confidence keeping (secreting the final words of the dead) are the sole occupations. Perhaps most striking for my concerns is the portrayal of sympathy, as a stage effect, devoid of instinctive content. Sympathy, like any other human artifact, needs to be invented. The son recalls the day when his father first showed him "'the Weep,' 'the Sob' and 'the Moan.' How to stand just so with the hands and feet (to capitalize on what we in the business call 'the Mourning Moment')." Like any commodity, it can be bought and sold: "There's money init" the son is told. Parks's play, which premiered at the Yale Repetory Theatre on January 13, 1994, was published in *American Theatre*, March 1994, 25–39.

37. Orlando Patterson, "White Poor, Black Poor," *New York Times*, May 3, 1992, 17. Also relevant in this regard is the eloquent bestseller by Leon Bing, *Do Or Die* (New York: Harper Collins, 1991), an "insider account" of Los Angeles youth gangs composed mainly of African-American males. In the dead-end world of the Crips and the Bloods, one sacrifices another ("do") so as not to be sacrificed oneself ("die"). But of course this is a contradiction or even negation of sacrifice. What seems most revealing about the highly ritualized nature of gang life is the way it implicates and distorts sacrificial logic.

38. See Georg Simmel, "Exchange," in *Georg Simmel on Individuality and Social Forms*, ed. Donald Levine (Chicago: University of Chicago Press, 1971), 53–

54, and 44–50; Max Weber, "Science as Vocation," in *From Max Weber*, ed. H. H. Gerth and C. Wright Mills (New York: Oxford, 1946), 148, 153–56; Emile Durkheim, *Suicide*, trans. John Spaulding and George Simpson (New York: Free Press, 1961), 217–40, and *The Elementary Forms of the Religious Life*, trans. Joseph Ward Swain (New York: Free Press, 1965), 434–61.

39. See Smith, *Lectures*, 313 and passim, and Sigmund Freud, *Totem and Taboo: Some Points of Agreement Between the Mental Lives of Savages and Neurotics*, trans. James Strachey (New York: Norton, 1950), 135.

40. See, in *The Body in Pain* (New York: Oxford University Press, 1984), 238–39 and passim, Elaine Scarry's brilliant reading of the Passover mark's significance throughout the Hebrew Bible. She notes, for example, how it is "elaborated into an intricate blueprint of rescue" through God's instructions on the fine points of housebuilding in the story of Noah, and how it embodies an "explicit" "rhythm of substitution and sparing" in Malachi.

41. Scarry, *Body in Pain*, 360, cites the work of the art historian Kenneth Clark on "draped" and "undraped" portraits of Christ on the Cross.

42. Quoted by Peter Berger in *The Sacred Canopy* (New York: Anchor, 1969), 76–77.

43. David Levering Lewis, *W. E. B. Du Bois: The Biography of a Race* (New York: Holt, 1993), 228.

44. See Du Bois, "Race Friction," 837. For more on the gains of the Black middle-classes in this era, as expressed in efforts to "re-construct" or "re-present" the "American Negro," see Henry Louis Gates, "The Trope of the New Negro and the Reconstruction of the Image of the Black," *Representations* 24 (fall 1988): 129–55.

45. Orlando Patterson has noted in this regard that American lynchings occurring around the turn of the century sometimes even had cannibalistic overtones. From Patterson's commentary on the San Diego MLA Special Session, "The African-American Author as Sociologist," December 28, 1994.

46. James Elbert Cutler, *Lynch-Law: An Investigation into the History of Lynching in the United States* (New York: Longmans, Green, 1905), 3–4, 279, and passim.

47. Ibid., 111–12.

48. In *Violence and the Sacred* (Baltimore, Md.: Johns Hopkins University Press, 1977), 12–13, 95–98, Rene Girard goes on to note how the second ritual slaughter of the scapegoat often included the flagellation of its genitals, the sign that some sexual transgression, threatening "the violent abolition of distinctions" was being avenged.

49. Bourdillon and Fortes, *Sacrifice*, xvi.

## McWhirter: What's Awkward About *The Awkward Age*?

1. Henry James, *The Awkward Age* (Harmondsworth: Penguin, 1987); hereafter referred to as *AA*.

2. Preface to *The Awkward Age*, in Henry James, *The Art of the Novel: Critical Prefaces* (New York: Scribner's, 1934), 99; hereafter referred to as *AN*.

3. Stuart Culver, "Censorship and Intimacy: Awkwardness in *The Awkward Age*," *ELH* 48 (1981): 368–86.

4. Tzvetan Todorov, "The Verbal Age," trans. Patricia Martin Gibby, *Critical Inquiry* 4 (1977): 351–71.

5. Joan Wallach Scott, *Gender and the Politics of History* (New York: Columbia University Press, 1988), 49.

6. "Stanzas from the Grande Chartreuse," lines 85–86, in *Poetry and Criticism of Matthew Arnold*, ed. A. Dwight Culler (Boston: Houghton Mifflin, 1961), 187.

7. Citations are from the following unsigned reviews of *The Awkward Age*, as reprinted in *Henry James: The Critical Heritage*, ed. Roger Gard (London: Routledge & Kegan Paul, 1968), 282–98: *Bookman* 9 (July 1899): 472–73; *Spectator* 82 (May 1899): 647; *Literary World* 30 (July 1899): 227; *Saturday* 87 (May 1899): 598.

8. James's affinities with fin de siècle aestheticism are suggested as well by the novel's probable origin as a riposte to Wilde's *The Importance of Being Earnest*: see Paul V. Smith, "A Wilde Subtext for *The Awkward Age*," *Henry James Review* 9 (fall 1988): 199–208. According to Smith, James's first *Notebook* sketch for *The Awkward Age* is dated less than two weeks after the 1895 opening of *The Importance of Being Earnest*—the play, significantly, that was hurried into production to replace James's own *Guy Domville* (200). Focusing on structural and thematic similarities between Wilde's play and James's novel, Smith argues convincingly that *The Awkward Age* is best understood "as James's response to the complex, shadowing figure of Oscar Wilde" (207).

9. Jonathan Freedman, *Professions of Taste: Henry James, British Aestheticism, and Commodity Culture* (Stanford, Calif.: Stanford University Press, 1990), xviii, 128. Freedman's is the most comprehensive study to date of James's complex relationship with aestheticism.

10. From an unsigned review, *Literature* 4 (May 1899): 475–76; reprinted in Gard, *Henry James: The Critical Heritage*, 283–84.

11. Jacques Derrida, "Force and Signification," in *Writing and Difference*, trans. Alan Bass (Chicago: University of Chicago Press, 1978), 11.

12. Susan L. Mizruchi, "Reproducing Women in *The Awkward Age*," *Representations* 38 (1992): 101–30.

13. Henry James, *The Portrait of a Lady* (New York: Houghton Mifflin, 1963), 470.

14. See, for example, the reviews collected in Gard, *Henry James: The Critical Heritage*, 259–325 passim.

15. See James's letter to W. D. Howells of December 11, 1902, in *Henry James Letters*, ed. Leon Edel, vol. 4 (Cambridge, Mass.: Harvard University Press, 1984), 251. James "ruefully and blushingly" explains that *The Sacred Fount*, "like *The Spoils of Poynton*, *What Maisie Knew*, 'The Turn of the Screw,' and various others," had grown "by a rank force of its own into something of which the idea had, modestly, never been to be a book."

16. *The Letters of Henry James*, ed. Percy Lubbock (New York: Charles Scribner's Sons, 1920), 1:333.

17. Leon Edel, *Henry James: The Treacherous Years, 1895–1901* (New York: Avon, 1978), 261–64.

18. Ibid., 264.

19. Henry James, "The Future of the Novel," in *Henry James: Literary Criticism*, vol. 1, *Essays on Literature; American Writers; English Writers*, ed. Leon Edel and Mark Wilson (New York: Library of America, 1984), 106, 109.

20. Cornelia Pratt, "The Evolution of Henry James," *Critic* 34 (April 1899): 338–42; quoted in Richard Nicholas Foley, *Criticism in American Periodicals of the Works of Henry James from 1866 to 1916* (Washington, D.C.: Catholic University Press, 1944), 77.

21. James, "Future of the Novel," 108–9, 101.

22. Todorov, "Verbal Age," 368–69.

23. Joan W. Scott, "Experience," in *Feminists Theorize the Political*, ed. Judith Butler and Joan W. Scott (New York: Routledge, 1992), 24–25.

24. Ibid., 34.

25. Ibid., 36.

26. Henry James, *The Ambassadors*, ed. S. P. Rosenbaum (New York: Norton, 1964), 87.

### Felski: Fin de Siècle, Fin de Sexe

1. Jean Baudrillard, *The Transparency of Evil* (New York: Verso, 1993), 20–21.

2. Quoted in Will L. McLendon, "Rachilde: *Fin-de-Siècle* Perspectives on Perversity," in *Modernity and Revolution in Late Nineteenth-Century France*, ed. Barbara T. Cooper and Mary Donaldson-Evans (Newark: Delaware University Press, 1992).

3. Baudrillard, *Transparency of Evil*, 12.

4. Ibid., 22.

5. Ibid., 25.

6. Jean Baudrillard, *Cool Memories* (London: Verso, 1990), 149.

7. Donna Haraway, "A Manifesto for Cyborgs: Science, Technology and Socialist Feminism in the 1980s," in *Feminism/Postmodernism*, ed. Linda Nicholson (London: Routledge, 1990), 191.

8. Ibid., 204.

9. Sandy Stone, "The *Empire* Strikes Back: A Posttranssexual Manifesto," in *Body Guards: The Cultural Politics of Gender Ambiguity*, ed. Julia Epstein and Kristina Straub (New York: Routledge, 1991), 294. I am grateful to Andrew Parker for providing me with a copy of this text.

10. Arthur Kroker and Marilouise Kroker, *Body Invaders: Panic Sex in America* (New York: St Martin's Press, 1987) and *The Last Sex* (New York: St. Martin's Press, 1993).

11. Arthur Kroker and Marilouise Kroker, "Scenes from the Last Sex: Feminism and Outlaw Bodies," in *The Last Sex*, 18–19.

12. Gianni Vattimo, *The End of Modernity: Nihilism and Hermeneutics in a Postmodern Culture* (Baltimore, Md.: Johns Hopkins University Press, 1988).

13. See Gianni Vattimo, "The End of (Hi)story," in *Zeitgeist in Babel: The Postmodernist Controversy*, ed. Ingeborg Hoesterey (Indiana: Indiana University Press, 1991).

14. See my *The Gender of Modernity* (Cambridge, Mass.: Harvard University Press, 1995), chap. 6.

15. M. J. Devaney, "'Since at Least Plato' and Other Postmodernist Myths" (Ph.d. diss., University of Virginia, 1994).

16. Susan Bordo also makes this point. See "Feminism, Postmodernism and Gender-Scepticism," in Nicholson, *Feminism/Postmodernism*.

17. Gianni Vattimo, *The Transparent Society* (Baltimore, Md.: Johns Hopkins University Press, 1992), 3.

18. Judith Roof, "Lesbians and Lyotard," in *The Lesbian Postmodern*, ed. Laura Doan (New York: Columbia University Press, 1994), 59.

19. Arjun Appadurai, "Disjuncture and Difference in the Global Cultural Economy," in *The Phantom Public Sphere*, ed. Bruce Robbins (Minneapolis: University of Minnesota Press, 1993).

20. Bordo, "Feminism, Postmodernism and Gender-Scepticism," 144–45; Eve Kosofsky Sedgwick and Michael Moon, "Divinity: A Dossier, a Performance Piece, a Little Understood Emotion," in *Tendencies*, ed. Eve Sedgwick (Durham, N.C.: Duke University Press, 1993), 219–24.

## Mullaney: Mourning and Misogyny

1. *A journal of all that was accomplished by Monsieur de Maisse Ambassador in England from King Henri IV to Queen Elizabeth, Anno Domini 1597*, trans. and ed. G. B. Harrison and R. A. Jones (London: Nonesuch Press, 1931), 12.

2. Quoted from Christopher Haigh, *Elizabeth I* (London: Longman, 1988), 162.

3. Ibid., 166.

4. Ibid., 167.

5. On the history and culturally specific construction of emotion, see especially Norbert Elias, *The History of Manners* (1939), vol. 1 of *The Civilizing Process*, trans. Edmund Jephcott (New York: Urizen Books, 1978); Michelle Z. Rosaldo, "Toward an Anthropology of Self and Feeling," in *Culture Theory: Essays on Mind, Self, and Emotion*, ed. Richard Shweder and Robert Levine (New York: Cambridge University Press, 1984), 137–57; Catherine A. Lutz, *Unnatural Emotions: Everyday Sentiments on a Micronesian Atoll and Their Challenge to Western Theory* (Chicago: University of Chicago Press, 1988); and Carol Z. Stearns and Peter N. Stearns, eds., *Emotion and Social Change: Toward a New Psychohistory* (New York: Holmes & Meier, 1988). I have also benefited immensely from discussions with Michael

MacDonald on this topic, and from his own study of Protestant despair, titled "*The Fearefull Estate of Francis Spira*: Narrative, Identity, and Emotion in Early Modern England," *Journal of British Studies* 31 (1992): 32–61.

6. Clifford Geertz, "Thick Description: Toward an Interpretive Theory of Culture," in *The Interpretation of Cultures* (New York: Basic Books, 1973), 3–30, esp. 6–7.

7. See, for example, Renato Rosaldo, "Grief and a Headhunter's Rage: On the Cultural Force of Emotions," in *Text, Play, and Story: The Construction and Reconstruction of Self and Society*, ed. Edward M. Bruner (Washington, D.C.: American Ethnological Society, 1984), 178–95. I have borrowed the phrase "structures of feeling" from Raymond Williams, *Marxism and Literature* (Oxford: Oxford University Press, 1977), 128–35.

8. On the Tupinamba greeting, see Jean de Léry, *History of a Voyage . . .* , trans. Janet Whatley (Berkeley: University of California Press, 1989), 164.

9. For historical approaches to misogyny, see Katharine M. Rogers, *The Troublesome Helpmate: A History of Misogyny in Literature* (Seattle: University of Washington Press, 1966), and R. Howard Bloch, *Medieval Misogyny and the Invention of Western Romantic Love* (Chicago: University of Chicago Press, 1991). In a powerful recent essay, Valerie Wayne analyzes Renaissance misogynies as forms of "residual" ideology: oftentimes embodied in a single character who is criticized or denigrated by others, misogynistic discourse is superficially called into question at the same time it is kept alive and put to use by the dominant culture. See Valerie Wayne, "Historical Differences: Misogyny and *Othello*," in *The Matter of Difference: Materialist Feminist Criticism of Shakespeare*, ed. Valerie Wayne (Ithaca, N.Y.: Cornell University Press, 1991), 153–80.

10. Lawrence Stone, *The Family, Sex and Marriage in England, 1500–1800* (New York: Basic Books, 1977), 99. Although in other respects Stone's theory of the rise of "affective individualism" illuminates useful and suggestive ground, in the case of bereavement it only resembles a genuine history of emotion, amounting in fact to a progressive history of the present: if the past didn't feel or express itself as we do, then it must not have felt at all. For historians' critiques of Stone, see reviews by Keith Thomas, *TLS*, October 21, 1977, 1227; Christopher Hill, "Sex, Marriage, and the Family in England," *Economic History Review* 31 (1978): 450–63, esp. 462; and David S. Berkowitz, *Renaissance Quarterly* 32 (1979): 396–405. Michael MacDonald also addresses the shortcomings of Stone's view when he chronicles the prevalence of bereavement among Napier's patients in *Mystical Bedlam: Madness, Anxiety, and Healing in Seventeenth-Century England* (Cambridge: Cambridge University Press, 1981), 77–78, 103–4.

11. Juliana Schiesari examines melancholia, grief, and misogyny in *The Gendering of Melancholia: Feminism, Psychoanalysis, and the Symbolics of Loss in Renaissance Literature* (Ithaca, N.Y.: Cornell University Press, 1992). In her otherwise excellent study, however, she tends to treat melancholia and mourning as if they were relatively synonymous and interchangeable terms in the sixteenth century. In addition, she fails to note that grief, in terms of both feeling and expression,

was an emotion of some controversy in English Protestantism. As G. W. Pigman has shown in *Grief and English Renaissance Elegy* (Cambridge: Cambridge University Press, 1985), grief was one of the "natural" human emotions that radical Protestants sought to reform and even eradicate from properly Christian psyches. Philosophical and religious treatises stigmatized grief as un-Christian, a sign of sinful disregard for providence, to be met not with sympathy but with hostile and even angry "consolation"; unlike the continental material Schiesari surveys, such efforts at ideological proscription were not focused on women alone but on all Protestants, regardless of gender. As Pigman notes, such strictures against grief were at once short-lived and unsuccessful, but were vehement enough to suggest just the opposite of Stone's conclusion—a prevalence rather than an absence of such "un-Christian" feelings of bereavement.

12. On *Measure for Measure* as a displacement and regendering of Elizabethan monarchy, see Leonard Tennenhouse, "Representing Power: *Measure for Measure* in Its Time," *Genre* 15 (1982): 139–58; and more generally on the duke's manipulation of Isabella, see my own *The Place of the Stage: License, Play, and Power in Renaissance England* (Chicago: University of Chicago Press, 1988), 88–115. Figures of female autonomy and power are more radically apprehended in *Macbeth*, violently and systematically eradicated in the play's effort to imagine a male world fully independent of women. For impressive treatments of this aspect of the play, see Harry Berger Jr., "The Early Scenes of *Macbeth*: Preface to a New Interpretation," *English Literary History* 47 (1980): 1–31, and "Text Against Performance in Shakespeare: The Example of *Macbeth*," *Genre* 15 (1982): 49–80; and Janet Adelman, "'Born of Woman': Fantasies of Maternal Power in *Macbeth*," in *Cannibals, Witches, and Divorce: Estranging the Renaissance*, ed. Marjorie Garber (Baltimore, Md.: Johns Hopkins University Press, 1987), 90–121.

13. For example, in 1577 a tailor from Finchingfield named William Binkes declared, "What manner of religion we have in England I know not, for the preachers now do preach their own inventions and fantasies, and therefore I will not believe any of them"; quoted in F. G. Emmison, *Elizabethan Life: Disorder* (Colchester, U.K.: Essex County Council, 1970), 46.

14. Tessa Watt, *Cheap Print and Popular Piety, 1550–1640* (Cambridge: Cambridge University Press, 1991), 7–8.

15. For a more extended discussion, see my own *Place of the Stage*, 1–59.

16. Jean Howard, "Renaissance Antithreatricality and the Politics of Gender and Rank in *Much Ado About Nothing*," in *Shakespeare Reproduced: The Text in History and Ideology*, ed. Jean E. Howard and Marion F. O'Connor (London: Methuen, 1987), 163–87, esp. 164.

17. Of course, drama was *also* part of print culture; those plays published, whether with or without the participation of authors and the companies who claimed exclusive acting rights to them, enjoyed circulation beyond various venues of performance, and over time as well as space (surviving publications in all their variants providing our only direct access to the dramatic repertory of the times). The contemporaneous impact of the drama performed by London com-

panies beyond its immediate audience is difficult to assess, but cannot be automatically discounted. It is difficult to speak of the "national" character of any aspect of the production and circulation of knowledge in the period, and this is true of printed books as well. Plays and players traveled beyond the city both in terms of performing venues and circulation in printed form. Furthermore, audiences traveled as well, in the case of the higher social strata coming and going to and from the city with some regularity. Given the fluidity of the boundary between oral and print cultures, we should assume at least some secondhand dissemination of ideas and experiences, by oral description and narration, whether deriving from plays or printed works. Elizabethan and Jacobean drama also "traveled" beyond the boundaries of England. Foreign travelers frequently remarked upon the Elizabethan stage, providing sketches of stages and playhouses and descriptions of individual plays; English companies also traveled abroad, sometimes to establish a seasonal or permanent venue. In 1600, for example, traveling English players built a replica of the Fortune theater in Gdansk, where English companies performed English plays, apparently of recent London vintage, until 1650; see Jerzy Limon, *Gentlemen of a Company: English Players in Central and Eastern Europe, 1590–1660* (Cambridge: Cambridge University Press, 1985).

18. For an excellent speculation on the significance of this shift, see Louis Adrian Montrose, "The Purpose of Playing: Reflections on a Shakespearean Anthropology," *Helios*, n.s., 7 (1980): 51–74.

19. On this topic, see my *Place of the Stage*, esp. 88–115.

20. *The Spanish Tragedy* (1587), traditionally regarded as the play that initiated the subgenre on the Elizabethan stage, is almost entirely free of the misogynistic set pieces that become a generic requirement in the next decade; the passages added to the play in 1602, however, are typically gynophobic, as in Heironimo's remark that children merely "serve / To ballace these light creatures we call women." *The Spanish Tragedy*, ed. Charles T. Prouty (Arlington Heights, Ill.: Harlan Davidson, 1951), 4.4.8–9.

21. This and all subsequent citations of the play are from *Hamlet*, ed. Harold Jenkins (London: Methuen, 1982).

22. Although the play has been traditionally attributed to Cyril Tourneur, I am persuaded by recent arguments that Middleton is in fact the likely author. For a survey of the issue, see the introduction to Thomas Middleton, *The Revenger's Tragedy: A Facsimile of the 1607/8 Quarto*, ed. and intro. MacD. P. Jackson (Rutherford, N.J.: Fairleigh Dickinson University Press, 1983).

23. De Maisse, *A journal*, 82.

24. I agree with Lisa Jardine that, given the immediate context, "'gorge' here surely means 'throat' rather than 'bosom.'" See her essay "'Why should he call her whore?' Defamation and Desdemona's Case," in *Addressing Frank Kermode: Essays in Criticism and Interpretation*, ed. Margaret Trudeau-Clayton and Martin Warner (Champaign: University of Illinois Press, 1991), 124–53; for this emendation, 146 n. 13. Jardine's correction, it should be noted, is based not on de Maisse's text but on extracts reprinted in L. A. Prevost-Paradol, *Élisabeth et Henri IV*

*(1595–1598): Ambassade de Hurault de Maisse en Angleterre au sujet de la paix de Vervins* (Paris, 1855), 151 n. 1.

25. De Maisse, *A journal*, 25–26; quoted in Louis Adrian Montrose, "'Shaping Fantasies': Figurations of Gender and Power in Elizabethan Culture," in *Representing the English Renaissance*, ed. Stephen Greenblatt (Berkeley: University of California Press, 1988), 31–64, esp. 33–34. I am deeply indebted to this essay for initially drawing my attention to de Maisse.

26. Quoted in Prevost-Paradol, *Élisabeth*, 155 n. 2. Jardine, "Defamation," 147 n. 14, suggests that in this instance such "gestures of *revealing*" may expose a stomacher rather than flesh itself.

27. De Maisse, *A journal*, 36–37.

28. Montrose, "Shaping Fantasies," 34. Lisa Jardine, "Defamation," 130, suggests that the air of erotic provocation stems not from Elizabeth's behavior but from de Maisse's text alone: "The 'erotic provocation' belongs . . . to the text . . . not to the event (that is, to any of the Queen's many public appearances)." In a footnote, however, she shifts the blame to Harrison and Jones as translators: "In fact, it turns out to belong to the twentieth-century English translation . . . far more than to the *original* French" (147 n. 15; my emphasis). Jardine forgets here that she has not consulted the "original French" either, but this is a minor problem in relation to the other questions raised by her assertions. Having corrected one translation of *gorge* as "bosom" when the context clearly requires "throat" (see note 24), Jardine seems to imply that all references to an exposed bosom or to Elizabeth's repeated gestures with her clothing—opening an outer robe to reveal *whatever* lies beneath—are also called into question. Such details are, however, quite explicit in the Prevost-Paradol extracts. She also assigns a number of psychological attributes to de Maisse (when blaming erotic provocation on them rather than on Harrison and Rose) for which there is no textual support. Although she asserts that we should "take note of Hurault de Maisse's difficulty with the breach of decorum (*in his terms* [my emphasis]) of a woman of Elizabeth's age receiving him with *anything other* than a gown which entirely concealed her body" (147 n. 15), she cites no evidence of such a difficulty; the terms, as far as I can see, are hers rather than de Maisse's. Jardine says that de Maisse responds in "unseemly terms" (131) to this "breach"; I can find no "unseemly terms" in his account, and Jardine cites none. She says that a "preoccupation with visible flesh" (131) shapes de Maisse's description (contradicting, by the way, her assertion that this is largely the mistranslation of Harrison and Jones); but de Maisse is preoccupied with *all* details of Elizabeth's appearance and behavior in his audiences with her (hence the oftentimes confusing welter of detail about her clothing, even when, as in the fourth audience, she is wearing a high-necked gown revealing no flesh below her chin). Jardine asserts that the richness of Elizabeth's dress "reinforces [de Maisse's] anxiety about 'whoredom'" (130), for which she cites German and Italian associations of finery with prostitution—but nothing from de Maisse that supports such an association in the context of his diary or his attitude toward a monarch. I dwell upon these points because the claims and assumptions of

Jardine's essay can easily seem (as they did on my own first reading) to be more firmly grounded in a sound textual basis than is in fact the case. On careful review, I find both her representation of de Maisse and the use she puts it to—a critique of Louis Montrose's reading of the *Journal*—both problematic and curiously overdetermined.

29. Quoted from the editor's note to 5.1.187–88, *Hamlet*, ed. Harold Jenkins (London: Methuen, 1982): 554.

30. Marie Axton, *The Queen's Two Bodies: Drama and the Elizabethan Succession* (London: *The Royal Historical Society*, 1977), 12.

31. On the cultural dynamics of Elizabeth's reign, including her appropriation of Petrarchan conventions, see Louis Adrian Montrose, "'Eliza, Queene of shepheardes,' and the Pastoral of Power," *English Literary Renaissance* 10 (1980): 153–82; and "Gifts and Reasons: The Contexts of Peele's *Arraygnment of Paris*," *ELH* 47 (1980): 433–61.

32. Thomas Tuke, "A Treatise Against Painting," in *Blood and Knavery: A Collection of English Renaissance Pamphlets and Ballads of Crime and Sin*, ed. Joseph H. Marshburn and Alan R. Velie (Cranbury, N.J.: Associated University Presses, 1974), 176–93, esp. 188.

33. Laurie A. Finke, "Painting Women: Images of Femininity in Jacobean Tragedy," *Theatre Journal* 36 (1984): 357–70, esp. 364. For a related essay, see Shirley Nelson Garner, "'Let Her Paint an Inch Thick': Painted Ladies in Renaissance Drama and Society," *Renaissance Drama*, n.s., 20 (1989): 123–39; and for an admirable recent examination of the topic, see Frances E. Dolan, "Taking the Pencil out of God's Hand: Art, Nature, and the Face-Painting Debate in Early Modern England," *PMLA* 108 (1993): 224–39.

34. *Calendar of the Manuscripts of . . . The Marquis of Salisbury*, 18 vols. (London: HMSO, 1904), 10.172–73; quoted in Montrose, "Shaping Fantasies," 54. Waad refers to previous correspondence with Cecil concerning Edwardes, which does not appear in the *Calendar*, and which I have thus far been unable to locate.

35. Leonard Tennenhouse, *Power on Display: The Politics of Shakespeare's Genres* (London: Methuen, 1986), 85. For other recent assessments of the crisis of monarchical representation embodied in the play, see Annabel Patterson, *Shakespeare and the Popular Voice* (Oxford: Blackwell, 1989), 13–31, 93–119; and Robert Weimann, "Mimesis in *Hamlet*," in *Shakespeare and the Question of Theory*, ed. Patricia Parker and Geoffrey Hartman (London: Methuen, 1985), 275–91.

36. On the significance of stage position, see Robert Weimann, *Shakespeare and the Popular Tradition in the Theater: Studies in the Social Dimension of Dramatic Form and Function*, ed. R. Schwartz (Baltimore, Md.: Johns Hopkins University Press, 1978), 73–84, and 224–36.

37. Curiously, Francis Barker takes Hamlet at his word and regards his claim to have "that within which passes show" as an early or premature gesture toward a "deep" subjectivity of the kind that will be produced in the bourgeois individual of a later age; see Barker's comments on this scene in *The Tremulous Private Body: Essays on Subjection* (London: Methuen, 1984), 35–37.

38. Peter Erickson, *Rewriting Shakespeare, Rewriting Ourselves* (Berkeley: University of California Press, 1991), 83 and 86. For a related emphasis on the centrality of Gertrude's age and its Elizabethan topicality, see Janet Adelman, *Suffocating Mothers: Fantasies of Maternal Origin in Shakespeare's Plays, "Hamlet" to "The Tempest"* (New York: Routledge, 1992), 11–37. Jacqueline Rose offers a useful critique of psychoanalytic approaches in "Hamlet—the *Mona Lisa* of Literature," *Critical Quarterly* 28 (1986): 35–49.

39. Barbara J. Todd, "The Remarrying Widow: A Stereotype Reconsidered," in *Women in English Society, 1500–1800*, ed. Mary Prior (London: Methuen, 1985), 55. Todd's excellent study also provides a context for Shakespeare's will, specifically the disposition of his "second-best bed" to his widow, as well as for the Player Queen's remarks on remarriage. In his *Advice to a Son*, Ralegh felt called upon to stipulate that "if [thy wife] love again let her not enjoy her second love in the same bed wherein she loved thee" (cited in Todd, 73). Hamlet Jr.'s emphasis on Gertrude's "incestuous sheets" and Hamlet Sr.'s remarks on the "royal bed of Denmark" suggest that the untimeliness of the king's death was an outrage because it prevented him from setting his estate as well as his soul in order, by drawing up a properly patriarchal will—one that would have deprived Gertrude of the "royal," and presumably best, bed.

40. For a suggestive discussion of the gap between the object and means of theatrical representation, see Robert Weimann, "Bifold Authority in Shakespeare's Theatre," *Shakespeare Quarterly* 39 (1988): 401–17.

41. For recent critical assessments of English transvestite companies in relation to Renaissance constructions of sexuality, see in particular Stephen Orgel, "Nobody's Perfect: Or Why Did the English Stage Take Boys for Girls," *South Atlantic Quarterly* 88 (1989): 7–29; Laura Levine, "Men in Women's Clothing: Anti-theatricality and Effeminization from 1579 to 1642," *Criticism* 28 (1986): 121–43; Jean E. Howard, "Crossdressing, the Theatre, and Gender Struggle in Early Modern England," *SQ* 39 (1988): 418–40; Stephen Greenblatt, *Shakespearean Negotiations: The Circulation of Social Energy in Renaissance England* (Berkeley: University of California Press, 1988), 66–93; and Mary Beth Rose, "Women in Men's Clothing: Apparel and Social Stability in *The Roaring Girl*," *English Literary Renaissance* 14 (1984): 367–91.

42. For Freud's essay, "Mourning and Melancholia," see *The Standard Edition of the Complete Psychological Works of Sigmund Freud*, trans. and ed. James Strachey, 19 vols. (London: Hogarth Press, 1957), 14:243–58; for their revision of Freud's discussion of incorporation and introjection, see Nicolas Abraham and Maria Torok, "Introjection—Incorporation: Mourning *or* Melancholia," in *Psychoanalysis in France*, ed. Serge Lebovici and Daniel Widlöcher (New York: International Universities Press, 1980), 3–16, esp. 13–14, and *The Wolf Man's Magic Word: A Cryptonomy*, trans. Nicholas Rand (Minneapolis: University of Minnesota Press, 1986).

43. Jacques Derrida, "*Fors*: The Anglish Words of Nicolas Abraham and Maria Torok," trans. Barbara Johnson, foreword to Abraham and Torok, *The Wolf Man's Magic Word*, xi–xlvii, esp. xvi–xvii.

44. Pigman, *Grief and English Renaissance Elegy*, 2.

45. Quoted in Pigman, 1.

46. Arthur Kirsch, for example, attempts to register the emotional under-currents of Hamlet's plight in act 1, scene 2, by invoking a universal, trans-historical common sense: "What a person who is grieving needs, of course, is not the consolation of words, even words which are true, but sympathy." "Hamlet's Grief," *ELH* 48 (1982): 17–36, esp. 20. Neither sympathy nor even the "consolation of words" was the prescribed attitude toward grief in the period; Kirsch's "of course" lodges his comment in a world quite removed from that of Hamlet.

47. Michael MacDonald's study of the incidence of unresolved bereavement among Napier's patients would seem to support such speculation; see *Mystical Bedlam*, esp. 103–4, 158–60.

48. Modern psychology recognizes "anticipatory mourning" in various con-texts, but in the literature I have surveyed, the phrase seems not to include the aggressive desire—the wish, rather than the sorrowful anticipation, that some-one will die—that marks Hamlet's attitude toward Gertrude's sexuality. See Barbara O. Dane, "Anticipatory Mourning of Middle-aged Parents of Adult Chil-dren with AIDS," *Families in Society* 72 (1991): 108–15, and G. Nachmani, "The Difficult Patient or the Difficult Dyad: On Mourning the Death of a Parent Who Has Not Died," *Contemporary Psychoanalysis* 28 (1992): 524–51.

49. David Hunt, *Parents and Children in History: The Psychology of Family Life in Early Modern France* (New York: Basic Books, 1970), 183. On the skirted gowns worn by children of both sexes and the "breeching" age, see Phyllis Cunnington and Anne Buck, *Children's Costume in England: From the Fourteenth to the End of the Nineteenth Century* (New York: Barnes & Noble, 1965), 38, 52, 54, and 71; and Philippe Ariès, *Centuries of Childhood*, trans. Robert Baldick (London: Jonathan Cape, 1962), 57–58. Ariès asks of this practice a slightly misleading question: "Why, in order to distinguish the boy from the man, was he made to look like the girl who was not distinguished from the woman?" (58). First of all, the girl was distinguished from the woman, her costume shifting to adult style at around the same age; what is more, we do not know enough to assume that boys in skirts "looked like . . . girls[s]" to early modern eyes. Despite what registers as extreme effeminacy to us (see, for example, the portraits of Charles I's sons in Cunnington and Buck), we presume too much when we assume we know how the costume was gendered—female, male, androgynous, or neuter. How the practice relates to Renaissance single-sex theories also remains to be answered but may be a rele-vant issue. On the significance of children's clothing, I am also indebted to dis-cussions with Amanda Bailey and the extensive research she has conducted for the dissertation she is writing, "London Is Burning: Sartorial Signification On and Off the Early Modern Stage."

50. Quoted from *The Riverside Shakespeare*, G. Blakemore Evans, ed. (Boston: Houghton Mifflin, 1974).

51. Hamlet's anxiety over sexuality is global rather than specific; as Valerie Traub notes, "for Hamlet . . . *all* sex is unnatural"; see her illuminating essay on

Shakespearean translations of sexually vital women into dead or static objects, "Jewels, Statues, and Corpses: Containment of Female Erotic Power in Shakespeare's Plays," *Shakespeare Studies* 20 (1988): 215–38, esp. 218.

52. Judith Butler, *Gender Trouble: Feminism and the Subversion of Identity* (New York: Routledge, 1990), 63.

53. For the nineteenth-century invention of homosexuality, see especially David Halperin, *One Hundred Years of Homosexuality: And Other Essays on Greek Love* (New York: Routledge, 1990). For a recent and subtle revision of Halperin relevant to Renaissance constructions of sexuality, see Jonathan Goldberg, *Sodometries: Renaissance Texts, Modern Sensibilities* (Stanford, Calif.: Stanford University Press, 1992).

54. Adelman, *Suffocating Mothers*, esp. 130–46.

55. Illongot males, for example, process loss and rage by headhunting, participating in a psychic ritual that apparently succeeds (at least for Illongot *males*) in purging both grief and rage; see Rosaldo, "Grief and a Headhunter's Rage," 178–95. On the cultural specificity of even so apparently universal an emotion as anger, see Robert C. Solomon, "Getting Angry: The Jamesian Theory of Emotion in Anthropology," in *Culture Theory: Essays on Mind, Self, and Emotion*, ed. Richard Shweder and Robert Levine (Cambridge: Cambridge University Press, 1984), 238–54.

56. See Adelman, *Suffocating Mothers*.

57. This and subsequent quotations of Middleton's play follow the Regents Renaissance Drama edition (attributed to Cyril Tourneur), ed. Lawrence J. Ross (Lincoln: University of Nebraska Press, 1966).

58. Cited in Montrose, "Shaping Fantasies," 47.

59. Montrose, "Shaping Fantasies," 48.

60. See C. H. Herford, Evelyn Simpson, and Percy Simpson, eds., *Ben Jonson*, 11 vols. (Oxford: Clarendon Press, 1925–52), 1:142.

61. Peter Stallybrass, "Reading the Body: *The Revenger's Tragedy* and the Jacobean Theater of Consumption," *RenD*, n.s., 18 (1987): 121–48, esp. 132.

62. Gail Paster, "Leaky Vessels: The Incontinent Women of City Comedy," *RenD*, n.s., 18 (1987): 43–65.

## Foster: "The Sex Appeal of the Inorganic"

1. Jean Baudrillard, "The Year 2000 Has Already Happened," in *Body Invaders: Panic Sex in America*, ed. Arthur Kroker and Marilouise Kroker (New York: St. Martin's Press, 1987), 36.

2. Karl Marx and Frederick Engels, *The German Ideology* (New York: International Publishers, 1985), 133. Kruger takes the phrase "the sex appeal of the inorganic" from Walter Benjamin, *Charles Baudelaire: A Lyric Poet in the Era of High Capitalism*, trans. Harry Zohn (New York: Verso, 1983), 166. Benjamin writes that "fetishism . . . succumbs to the sex-appeal of the inorganic." Analyzing the fashion industry, he suggests that the expansion of the commodity structure into the

cultural sphere results in a crossing of commodity fetishism with sexual fetishism, in one of the first attempts to systematically link Marxism and psychoanalysis.

3. Fredric Jameson, *Marxism and Form: Twentieth-Century Dialectical Theories of Literature* (Princeton, N.J.: Princeton University Press, 1971), 104–5.

4. Fredric Jameson, *Postmodernism, or, The Cultural Logic of Late Capitalism* (Durham, N.C.: Duke University Press, 1991), 36.

5. Jameson, *Marxism and Form*, 105.

6. Gilles Deleuze and Felix Guattari, *A Thousand Plateaus: Capitalism and Schizophrenia*, trans. Brian Massumi (Minneapolis: University of Minnesota Press, 1987), 158.

7. These particular photos of Sherman's were included in the Post Human art exhibit that toured Europe from September 1992 to May 1993. For examples of Sherman's work, see Jeffrey Deitch, ed., *Post Human* (New York: Distributed Art Publisher, 1992), 132–33.

8. Bill Nichols, "The Work of Culture in the Age of Cybernetic Systems," *Screen* 29 (winter 1986): 33.

9. John L. Pollock, *How to Build a Person: A Prolegomenon* (Cambridge, Mass.: MIT Press, 1989), ix.

10. N. Katherine Hayles, "The Seductions of Cyberspace," in *Rethinking Technology*, ed. Verena Andermatt Conley (Minneapolis: University of Minnesota Press, 1993), 182.

11. I am arguing that popular culture offers a way to answer the question Mark Poster's book on new communication and computer technologies suggests it is still "too early" to ask—that is, what "linkages" exist "between the forms of domination and potentials for freedom that the theory of the mode of information reveals, on the one hand, and the advances of feminism, minority discourse and ecological critiques, on the other." Mark Poster, *The Mode of Information: Poststructuralism and Social Context* (Chicago: University of Chicago Press, 1990), 19.

12. John Walker, "Through the Looking-Glass," in *The Art of Human-Computer Interface*, ed. Brenda Laurel (Menlo Park, Calif.: Addison-Wesley, 1990).

13. Arthur Kroker and Marilouise Kroker, "Theses on the Disappearing Body in the Hyper-Modern Condition," in *Body Invaders: Panic Sex in America*, ed. Arthur Kroker and Marilouise Kroker (New York: St. Martin's Press, 1987), 31.

14. Howard Rheingold, *Virtual Reality* (New York: Summit Books, 1991), 376.

15. Randal Walser, "Spacemakers and the Art of the Cyberspace Playhouse," *Mondo 2000*, no. 2 (summer 1990): 60.

16. For two academic uses of this term, see N. Katherine Hayles, "The Life Cycle of Cyborgs: Writing the Posthuman," in *A Question of Identity: Women, Science, and Literature*, ed. Marina Benjamin (New Brunswick, N.J.: Rutgers University Press, 1993), and Jean-François Lyotard, especially the introduction to his book *The Inhuman: Reflections on Time*, trans. Geoffrey Bennington and Rachel Bowlby (Stanford, Calif.: Stanford University Press, 1991), 2, which defines inhu-

manity both ethically, as the inhumane, and philosophically, as a critique of humanism.

17. John Varley, *The Ophiuchi Hotline* (New York: Dial Press, 1977), 159.

18. See Veronica Hollinger, "Cybernetic Deconstructions: Cyberpunk and Postmodernism," *Mosaic* 23 (spring 1990): 29–44. Scott Bukatman develops this reading of what he calls the "virtual subject" in postmodern science fiction in his *Terminal Identity: The Virtual Subject in Postmodern Science Fiction* (Durham, N.C.: Duke University Press, 1993). In *The Possessed Individual*, Arthur Kroker argues that the central, though unspoken, term of French poststructuralist theory is "virtuality," and that all these writers should be understood as theorizing technology (2). Derrida's recent work on Marx supports this claim, with Derrida at one point quoting the English term "cyberspace" (*Spectres des marx* [Paris: Editions Galilee, 1993], 23) and elsewhere defining the convergence of the actual and the artificial by coining the terms "artifactuality" and "actuvirtuality" ("The Deconstruction of Actuality: An Interview with Jacques Derrida," *Radical Philosophy*, no. 68 [autumn 1994]: 28). See also Avital Ronell's recent comments on virtual reality and ideas of community (299, 304) and the chapter "Xerox and Infinity" in Baudrillard's *The Transparency of Evil: Essays on Extreme Phenomena*, trans. James Benedict (New York: Verso, 1992), 51–59.

19. Deitch, *Post Human*.

20. Hans Moravec, *Mind Children: The Future of Robot and Human Intelligence* (Cambridge, Mass.: Harvard University Press, 1988).

21. Quoted in Andrew Ross, *Strange Weather: Culture, Science, and Technology in the Age of Limits* (New York: Verso, 1991), 164, in a discussion of various critiques of humanism, including not only artificial intelligence but also deep ecology. Manuel DeLanda's work represents the most elaborate attempt to date to combine these two critiques around a concept of "inorganic life." In "Inorganic Life and Predatory Machines," in *Culture Lab*, ed. Brian Boigon (New York: Princeton Architectural Press, 1993), 37, he argues that "we need to create the conditions for a partnership or symbiosis with computers. We must determine how to let abstract machines incarnate at the interface between carbon-based and silicon-based creatures to create a new set of emergent properties—one that defines the union of humans and computers as a new species."

22. Hayles makes a distinction similar to the one I make here between these two narratives, when she distinguishes "*the body* as a cultural construct" from "the experiences of *embodiment* that individual people within a culture feel and articulate" (my emphasis). N. Katherine Hayles, "The Materiality of Informatics," *Configurations* 1 (winter 1993): 148. The classic statement of this distinction in feminist theory would be Adrienne Rich's argument for talking about "my body" rather than "the body." Adrienne Rich, "Notes Toward a Politics of Location," in *Blood, Bread, and Poetry: Selected Prose 1979–1985* (New York: Norton, 1986), 215. In a more recent essay, Hayles reads the history of cybernetics in order to demonstrate that the narrative of disembodiment associated with virtual reality technologies is grounded in an obsolete understanding of information as "a pattern

distinct from the physical markers that embody it" and "removed from the material substrate in which it is instantiated"; the result is to reinstitute a "very old and traditional distinction between form and matter," the same distinction that Descartes redefined as a mind/body dualism. N. Katherine Hayles, "Boundary Disputes: Homeostasis, Reflexivity, and the Foundations of Cybernetics," *Configurations* 2 (fall 1994): 464.

23. "When Man Is on the Menu," in *Incorporations*, ed. Jonathan Crary and Stanford Kwinter (New York: Zone Books, 1992), 42. See Stephanie Smith's essay on morphing and metamorphosis as central tropes in postmodern culture, "Morphing, Materialism, and the Marketing of *Xenogenesis*," *Genders* no. 18 (winter 1993): 67–86, for a critique of this belief in the liberatory effects of shape-changing. Elsewhere, Haraway argues for reconfiguring "what counts as knowledge in the interests of reconstituting the generative forces of embodiment," a project she refers to as "*materialized refiguration*." She goes on to argue that both the new technoculture and "feminist, antiracist, multicultural science studies" teach that "what counts as human is not, and should not be, self-evident." Donna Haraway, "A Game of Cat's Cradle: Science Studies, Feminist Theory, Cultural Studies," *Configurations* 2 (winter 1994); 62, 64.

24. Otter, "Against Man, the Challenger," *Dropout* (summer 1992): 22–24.

25. Melissa Scott, *Trouble and Her Friends* (New York: Tor, 1994), 128–29.

26. Although he does not explicitly define them as narratives, the curator of the Post Human art exhibit defines two similar attitudes toward the body when he speculates that "our current post-modern era can be characterized as a transitional period of the disintegration of the self. Perhaps the coming 'post-human' period will be characterized by the reconstruction of self," in Deitch, *Post Human*, 33. Lyotard's "Can Thought Go On Without a Body?" offers a more philosophical consideration of the relation of technology to the possibility of separating mind and body. This essay takes the form of a dialogue between "he" and "she." "He" ends by arguing that "it's appropriate to take the body as model in the manufacture and programming of artificial intelligence if it's intended that artificial intelligence not be limited to the ability to reason logically," while "she" argues that "your thinking machines will have to be nourished not just on radiation but on irremediable gender difference" and therefore on desire. Jean-François Lyotard, "Can Thought Go On Without a Body?" *Discourse* 11 (fall–winter 1988–89): 81, 86. See also Lyotard, *The Inhuman*, 16, 22.

27. Allucquere Roseanne Stone, "Split Subjects, Not Atoms; or, How I Fell in Love with My Prosthesis," *Configurations* 2 (winter 1994): 109.

28. In *Volatile Bodies: Toward a Corporeal Feminism* (Bloomington: Indiana University Press, 1994), 5–13, Elizabeth Grosz offers an extended reading of this Cartesian tradition in contemporary philosophy as she attempts to define a feminist alternative to it, one that does not depend upon some version of the mind-body dualism. See also Stone's comment, in "Split Subjects," 182 n. 9, that "the physical/virtual distinction is *not* a mind/body distinction." Instead, she argues

that the virtual is "a different way of conceptualizing a *relationship* to the human (or, for that matter, the transhuman or posthuman) body."

29. Rheingold, *Virtual Reality*, 345–53. Phillip Robinson and Nancy Tamosaitis's book *The Joy of Cybersex: An Underground Guide to Electronic Erotica* (New York: Brady Publishing, 1993) contains an overview of current erotic applications of computer technology, including a general introduction ("going online," "hunting for virtual sex"), a section on CD-ROM pornography, and a section on computer bulletin boards and chat services offering erotic interaction or the downloading of texts and graphics. The final section of the book, "CyberSex Visions," offers over fifty pages of speculation on future developments of these technologies, especially virtual reality, suggesting how current applications of computers to sexual uses are already informed by science fiction.

30. Bruce Sterling, ed., *Mirrorshades* (New York: Ace Books, 1988), xiii.

31. William Gibson, *Neuromancer* (New York: Ace Books, 1984), 5, 51, 6.

32. Thomas Foster, "Meat Puppets or Robopaths? Cyberpunk and the Question of Embodiment," *Genders*, no. 18 (winter 1993): 22–27.

33. In "The Pleasure of the Interface," *Screen* 32 (Autumn 1991), 308–9, 322, Claudia Springer also analyzes the same pages from this comic book, though she emphasizes the narrative of disembodiment, suggesting that the fact that the characters can alter their bodies in cyberspace only reinforces the devaluation of the body as an illusion, in opposition to the truth of the mind or consciousness.

34. Moravec, *Mind Children*, 122, 115, 122.

35. Steve Lohr, "Who Will Control the Digital Flow?" *New York Times*, October 17, 1993, section 4, 3.

36. Nicholas Negroponte, "Bit by Bit on Wall Street: Lucky Strikes Again," *Wired* 2 (May 1994): 144.

37. Lohr, "Digital Flow," 3.

38. Sherry Turkle, *The Second Self: Computers and the Human Spirit* (New York: Simon & Schuster, 1984), 309.

39. Deleuze and Guattari, *Thousand Plateaus*, 158.

40. The *Max Headroom* television show is the best popular example of this critique of the presumed need for a unitary agent of thought or consciousness, predicated as the show was on the ability of Max's computer-generated personality to appear in more than one place at once; for a feminist analysis of this aspect of the program, see Lynne Joyrich, "Critical and Textual Hypermasculinity," in *Logics of Television*, ed. Patricia Mellencamp (Bloomington: Indiana University Press, 1990), 163–65. A short story by one of the few women associated with the cyberpunk movement, Pat Cadigan's "Pretty Boy Crossover," in *Patterns* (Kansas City, Mo.: Ursus Imprints, 1989), and Phillip C. Jennings's sequence of stories *The Bug Life Chronicles* (New York: Baen Books, 1989) are two of the best representations of this desire to download consciousness into a computer in print fiction. In "Thinking of Oneself as a Computer," *Leonardo* 24 (1991): 586–89, Sally Pryor offers a critique of this desire, which emphasizes disembodiment,

rather than possibilities for refigured embodiment, with explicit reference to Cartesian traditions. See Rosi Braidotti, "Toward a New Nomadism: Feminist Deleuzian Tracks; or Metaphysics and Metabolism," in *Gilles Deleuze and the Theater of Philosophy*, ed. Constantin V. Boundas and Dorothea Olkowski (New York: Routledge, 1994), and Grosz, *Volatile Bodies*, for two different arguments about the possible value of Deleuze and Guattari's redefinition of embodiment for feminist critics.

41. David Tomas, "Old Rituals for New Space: *Rites de Passage* and William Gibson's Cultural Model of Cyberspace," in *Cyberspace: First Steps*, ed. Michael Benedikt (Cambridge, Mass.: MIT Press, 1991), 33, 94.

42. Bukatman, *Terminal Identity*, 328. In "Sex Machine, Machine Sex: Mechano-Eroticism and Robo-Copulation," *Mondo 2000*, no. 5 (spring 1991): 42–43, Mark Dery makes a point similar to Bukatman's, contrasting contemporary popular representations of desire and technology to McLuhan and quoting this same passage.

43. Stone, "Split Subjects," 109, 107. In science fiction, Candas Jane Dorsey's story "(Learning About) Machine Sex," in *Machine Sex and Other Stories* (Victoria, B.C.: Porcepic Books, 1988), offers a similar feminist critique of men's attitudes toward interactive computer technologies and indirectly critiques the genre of cyberpunk fiction.

44. Haraway, "When Man," 42. See also Donna Haraway, "The Promises of Monsters: A Regenerative Politics for Inappropriate/d Others," in *Cultural Studies*, ed. Lawrence Grossberg, Cary Nelson, and Paula Treichler (New York: Routledge, 1992), 301.

45. Donna Haraway, *Simians, Cyborgs, and Women: The Reinvention of Nature* (New York: Routledge, 1991), 181.

46. Mary Anne Doane, "Technophilia: Technology, Representation, and the Feminine," in *Body/Politics: Women and the Discourse of Science*, eds. Mary Jacobus, Evelyn Fox Keller, and Sally Shuttleworth (New York: Routledge, 1990), 163.

47. Andreas Huyssen, *After the Great Divide: Modernism, Mass Culture, Postmodernism* (Bloomington: Indiana University Press, 1986, 70), 164.

48. "Foreword," in Hajime Sorayama, *Hajime Sorayama* (Berlin: Benedikt Taschen Verlag, 1991), 9.

49. It is interesting to note that contemporary representations of masculinized robots and cyborgs fail to undo the gender narratives that Huyssen argues are reproduced in the figure of mechanical women. Films like *Robocop 2* and the Japanese cult favorite *Tetsuo: The Iron Man* represent women's desire for men who have been transformed into cybernetic organisms, and in both cases the women are placed in the traditional position of reassuring the men of their continued sexual desirability, as a means of reassuring them of their continued humanity. In *Terminator 2*, this ideological formation is displaced, as the cyborg becomes not lover but an ideal father and by extension an ideal husband.

50. Slavoj Žižek, *Enjoy Your Symptom! Jacques Lacan in Hollywood and Out* (New York: Routledge, 1992), 122–23.

51. Gilles Deleuze, *Masochism: An Interpretation of Coldness and Cruelty*, trans. Jean McNeil (New York: George Braziller, 1971), 28–29.

52. Ross, *Strange Weather*, 153.

53. Slavoj Žižek, *The Sublime Object of Ideology* (London: Verso, 1989), 118.

54. Kaja Silverman, *Male Subjectivity at the Margins* (New York: Routledge, 1992), 46, 50–51.

55. Anne McClintock, "Maid to Order: Commercial Fetishism and Gender Power," *Social Text* 11 (winter 1993): 108.

56. Richard Calder, *Dead Girls* (London: HarperCollins, 1992, 157, 161) and "Mosquito," *Interzone*, no. 32 (November–December 1989): 7. Subsequent references noted parenthetically in the text.

57. Calder seems to take the term "gynoid" from a British feminist science fiction writer, Gwyneth Jones, the author of *Divine Endurance* (New York: Tor Books, 1984). Sorayama acknowledges both these writers in a prefatory note to his most recent collection, *The Gynoids* (Tokyo: Treville, 1992).

58. In "A Manifesto for Gynoids: Reading Richard Calder," *Science Fiction Eye*, no. 9 (November 1991): 82–85, Takahashi Tatsumi discusses Calder's work in precisely this way.

59. Judith Butler, "Imitation and Gender Insubordination," in *Inside/Out: Lesbian Theories, Gay Theories*, ed. Diana Fuss (New York: Routledge, 1991), 22.

60. Ibid., 23.

61. Pat Cadigan's short story "Pretty Boy Crossover" and Laura Mixon's novel *Glass Houses* (New York: Tor Books, 1992) both represent the role of technology in relation to subcultural practices of subversive gender performance. Mixon's novel focuses on a lesbian character who operates a salvage robot using telepresence technology to occupy the robot's body, which she always refers to in the masculine.

62. Andrew Hodges, *Alan Turing, the Enigma* (New York: Simon & Schuster, 1983).

63. Alan Turing, "Computing Machinery and Intelligence," reprinted in *The Mind's I*, ed. Douglas Hofstadter and D. Dennet (New York: Penguin, 1982), 54. In "Automating Gender: Postmodern Feminism in the Age of the Intelligent Machine," *Feminist Studies* 17 (fall 1991): 441–45, Judith Halberstam offers a reading of these same biographical facts as illustrative of the relation between technology and gender, though without explicitly connecting Turing's representation of gender imitation to contemporary queer theory. See H. M. Collins, *Artificial Experts: Social Knowledge and Intelligent Machines* (Cambridge, Mass.: MIT Press, 1990), chap. 13, for an excellent discussion of the relevance of Turing's essay to contemporary artificial intelligence research. Collins points out in a footnote (247 n. 17) that the imitation game raises problems of gender socialization. Kathleen Biddick discusses Turing's personal history in relation to contemporary work on computer-simulated artificial life, and its challenge to definitions of the "human" in "Stranded Histories: Feminist Allegories of Artificial Life," *Research in Philosophy and Technology* 13 (1993): 174–75.

64. See Stone, "Split Subjects," 180–81, for a discussion of this aspect of virtual reality.

65. Oscar Wilde, *The Artist as Critic: Critical Writings of Oscar Wilde*, ed. Richard Ellmann (Chicago: University of Chicago Press, 1969), 393.

66. Turkle, *Second Self*, 309.

67. Wayne Koestenbaum, "Wilde's Hard Labor and the Birth of Gay Reading," in *Engendering Men: The Question of Male Feminist Criticism*, ed. Joseph A. Boone and Michael Cadden (New York: Routledge, 1990), 182–83.

In this index an "f" after a number indicates a separate reference on the next page, and an "ff" indicates separate references on the next two pages. A continuous discussion over two or more pages is indicated by a span of page numbers, e.g., "57–59." *Passim* is used for a cluster of references in close but not consecutive sequence.

Library of Congress Cataloging-in-Publication Data

Centuries' ends, narrative means / edited by Robert D. Newman.
    p.    cm.
Includes bibliographical references and index.
ISBN 0-8047-2649-3 (cl.)
ISBN 0-8047-2650-7 (pbk.)
1. Literature, Modern—19th century—History and criticism.
2. Literature, Modern—20th century—History and criticism.
I. Newman, Robert D.
PN761.C46    1996
809'.04—dc20
95-35923    CIP

Original printing 1996

Last figure below indicates year of this printing:

05  04  03  02  01  00  99  98  97  96